A CULTURAL HISTORY OF FAIRY TALES

VOLUME 4

A Cultural History of Fairy Tales
General Editor: Anne E. Duggan

Volume 1
A Cultural History of Fairy Tales in Antiquity
Edited by Debbie Felton

Volume 2
A Cultural History of Fairy Tales in the Middle Ages
Edited by Susan Aronstein

Volume 3
A Cultural History of Fairy Tales in the Age of the Marvelous
Edited by Suzanne Magnanini

Volume 4
A Cultural History of Fairy Tales in the Long Eighteenth Century
Edited by Anne E. Duggan

Volume 5
A Cultural History of Fairy Tales in the Long Nineteenth Century
Edited by Naomi J. Wood

Volume 6
A Cultural History of Fairy Tales in the Modern Age
Edited by Andrew Teverson

A CULTURAL HISTORY OF FAIRY TALES

IN THE LONG EIGHTEENTH CENTURY

VOLUME 4

Edited by Anne E. Duggan

BLOOMSBURY ACADEMIC
LONDON • NEW YORK • OXFORD • NEW DELHI • SYDNEY

BLOOMSBURY ACADEMIC
Bloomsbury Publishing Plc, 50 Bedford Square, London, WC1B 3DP, UK
Bloomsbury Publishing Inc, 1359 Broadway, New York, NY 10018, USA
Bloomsbury Publishing Ireland, 29 Earlsfort Terrace, Dublin 2, D02 AY28, Ireland

BLOOMSBURY, BLOOMSBURY ACADEMIC and the Diana logo
are trademarks of Bloomsbury Publishing Plc

First published in Great Britain 2021
Paperback edition published 2025

Copyright © Anne E. Duggan, 2021

Anne E. Duggan and Contributors have asserted their right under the Copyright,
Designs and Patents Act, 1988, to be identified as Author of this work.

Series design by Raven Design
Cover image: "Beauty with the Golden Hair" by Marie-Catherine
Le Jumel de Barneville, Baroness d'Aulnoy

All rights reserved. No part of this publication may be: i) reproduced or transmitted in
any form, electronic or mechanical, including photocopying, recording or by means of
any information storage or retrieval system without prior permission in writing from the
publishers; or ii) used or reproduced in any way for the training, development or operation
of artificial intelligence (AI) technologies, including generative AI technologies. The rights
holders expressly reserve this publication from the text and data mining exception as per
Article 4(3) of the Digital Single Market Directive (EU) 2019/790.

Bloomsbury Publishing Plc does not have any control over, or responsibility for,
any third-party websites referred to or in this book. All internet addresses given
in this book were correct at the time of going to press. The author and publisher
regret any inconvenience caused if addresses have changed or sites have
ceased to exist, but can accept no responsibility for any such changes.

A catalogue record for this book is available from the British Library.

A catalog record for this book is available from the Library of Congress.

ISBN: HB: 978-1-3500-9522-9
       PB: 978-1-3505-9413-5
       ePDF: 978-1-3502-8753-2
       eBook: 978-1-3502-8754-9
       set: 978-1-3505-9409-8

Series: A Cultural History of Fairy Tales

Typeset by Integra Software Services Pvt. Ltd.
Printed and bound in Great Britain

For product safety related questions contact productsafety@bloomsbury.com.

To find out more about our authors and books visit www.bloomsbury.com
and sign up for our newsletters.

CONTENTS

LIST OF ILLUSTRATIONS	vii
LIST OF TABLES	x
SERIES PREFACE	xi

Introduction: The Emergence of the Classic Fairy-Tale Tradition   1
Anne E. Duggan

1   Forms of the Marvelous: The Eighteenth-Century *merveilleux*   15
    Tatiana Korneeva

2   Adaptation: From Italy and France to Folk Traditions   37
    Charlotte Trinquet du Lys

3   Gender and Sexuality: From the *conteuses* to the English Governess   61
    Aileen Douglas

4   Humans and Non-Humans: Ambiguities of Agency and Personhood in Fairy Tales, 1650–1800   83
    Lewis C. Seifert

5   Monsters and the Monstrous: Of Ogre Pyramids, Ruby-Eyed Dragons, and Gnomes with Crooked Spines   103
    Kathryn A. Hoffmann

6   Space: Spatial References and Narrative Strategies in Eighteenth-Century Tales in East and West   129
    Richard van Leeuwen

7	Socialization: Tales of Wonder as Slight Channels *Rania Huntington*	149
8	Power: Gender, Class, and Politics in *Ancien Régime* Fairy and Oriental Tales *Anne E. Duggan*	171
NOTES		193
REFERENCES		208
NOTES ON CONTRIBUTORS		227
INDEX		229

ILLUSTRATIONS

0.1 Illustration of the tale "Nadir and Nadine" from
Christoph Martin Wieland's *Dschinnistan* (1786)   11

1.1 An engraving "Tableau magique de Zémire et Azor"
by François-Robert Voyez le jeune, after Jacques Louis Touzé   19

1.2 "Ah! Laissez-moi la pleurer," trio from *Zémire et Azor*
(act 3, scene 6)   20

1.3 An offstage instrumental prelude to the trio "Ah! Laissez-moi la pleurer" introduces the "magic picture" music (*Zémire et Azor*, act 3, scene 6)   21

2.1 Illustration of Charles Perrault's "The Fairies" from *Contes du temps passé de ma Mère L'oye* (London: T. Boosey, 1796)   53

2.2 An illustration from Walter Crane's version of *The Hind in the Wood* (London: Routledge, 1875)   55

2.3 Rosette at sea with her little dog Frétillon, from Andrew Lang's *The Red Fairy Book* (London: Longmans, Green, and Co., 1895)   57

3.1 Belle-Belle preparing to join the king's army; illustration by John Gilbert, from *The Fairy Tales of Countess D'Aulnoy* (London: Routlege, 1855)   64

3.2 Florine with King Charmant metamorphosed into the Blue Bird, illustrated by J. C. Demerville, from *Les Contes choisis* (Paris: 1847)   68

3.3 Sleeping Beauty's sumptuous surroundings, illustrated by Edmund Dulac, from *The Sleeping Beauty and Other Fairy Tales* (New York: Hodder and Stoughton, 1910)   75

4.1	Walter Crane's depiction of the wolf in very human terms, from "Little Red Riding Hood," in *Walter Crane's Toy Books* (London: George Routledge and Sons, 1875)	90
4.2	Pastoral setting of "Le Mouton" in a French edition of d'Aulnoy's tales, *Les Contes choisis* (Paris: 1847)	93
4.3	The two dead sisters before Prince Marcassin in a woodcut, from d'Aulnoy, *Le nouveau gentilhomme bourgeois ou Les fées à la mode*, vol. 3 (Amsterdam: Michel Charles le Cene, 1725)	98
5.1	"Monster Park," Sacred Grove (Sacro Bosco), Bomarzo, Italy. Architect Pirro Ligorio for Prince Pier Franceso Orsini	111
5.2	An engraving of d'Aulnoy's dragon-like Green Serpent, from *Nouveaux contes des fées* (Amsterdam: Estienne Roger, 1708)	112
5.3	*Jeu de bague chinois*, Parc Monceau, with gentlemen on a serpent-necked dragon and the disappearing hands of Chinese figures, from Louis Carrogis Carmontelle's *Jardin de Monceau* (1779)	114
5.4	*Le bossu à la canne (Hunchback with a Cane)* by Jacques Callot (*c.* 1616–22)	116
5.5	*L'estropié au capuchon (Cripple in a Hood)* by Jacques Callot (*c.* 1616–22)	117
5.6	An early eighteenth-century Russian lubok or print of Baba Yaga riding a pig to fight the infernal crocodile with a pestle	119
6.1	The liminal site of the palace of the king of the Ebony Isles by Edmund Dulac, from *Stories from the Arabian Nights* (London: Hodder and Stoughton, 1911)	135
6.2	A nineteenth-century illustration of a story from *Strange Tales from a Chinese Studio* concerning a female ghost, dreamscapes, and resurrrection	139
7.1	Frontispiece from the 1725 edition of *Chinese Tales: Or, the Wonderful Adventures of the Mandarin Fum-Hoam* (London, 1725)	152
7.2	Illustration of a scene from "Three Lives" collected in *Strange Tales from a Chinese Studio* (1886 edition)	154

7.3 Bridal Procession in the Rat's Wedding, from *Aka-hon
Nezumi no yomeiri* (*Red Book: The Mouse's Wedding*)
(Tsuruya, c. 1735–45)   164

8.1 The "so-called" Duchess Grognon seducing Gracieuse's father
with her wealth, illustrated by Gustaf Tenggren, from *d'Aulnoy's
Fairy Tales* (Philadelphia: David McKay, 1923)   176

8.2 Scheherazade, the heroine of *The Thousand and One Nights*,
illustrated by Edmund Dulac in *Stories from the Arabian Nights*,
retold by Laurence Housman (New York: George H. Doran, 1907) 179

8.3 The punished fairies from d'Auneuil's *La Tyrannie des fées détruite*
(1710) toiling away to run the machine that feeds water into the
enchanted gardens   183

TABLES

0.1 Tales Attributed to or Gathered around the Figure of d'Aulnoy, aka Mother Bunch, aka Queen Mab   4

0.2 Perrault in English   5

0.3 Non-exhaustive Publishing History of French Oriental Tales in English   8

SERIES PREFACE

Taking a transnational approach, *A Cultural History of Fairy Tales* seeks to deepen our appreciation for and knowledge about a type of *text* (understood in the broadest sense of the term) that is often taken for granted due to its association with children's literature, old wives' tales, and oral peasant culture. Whether we think of the Brothers Grimm or films by Walt Disney Studios, fairy tales are often viewed as naïve and timeless stories with universal appeal, which suggests they are ahistorical, innocent narratives. This series brings together scholars from a diversity of disciplines to challenge many of these preconceptions about the fairy tale, shedding light on its very complex cultural history.

The chapters included in these six volumes foreground how the fairy tale was deployed in different historical periods and geographical locations for all kinds of cultural, social, and political ends that cross categories of class, age, gender, and ethnicity. "Fairy tale" here serves as a broad umbrella term for what more generally could be referred to as "wonder tale," which encompasses but is not limited to texts that feature fairies, witches, enchanters, djinn, and other beings endowed with magical or supernatural powers; anthropomorphized animals; metamorphosis (humans transformed into animals or other objects and vice versa); magical objects; and otherworlds and liminal spaces. "Fairy tale" also refers to texts that may not include any of these qualities but have been received as—that is, read or categorized as or are generally considered to be—a fairy tale.

By moving from antiquity to the present and transnationally, chapters crossing the six volumes foreground, for instance, how ancient animal fables present both continuities and discontinuities with the representation of animals in later wonder tales; how conceptions of fairies, djinn, and other magical characters change across historical periods and geographical locations;

and how the very notion of what is marvelous, natural, or supernatural is understood differently across space and time. Chapters showcase the range of different types of characters and themes one can find in wonder tales as well as the multiple forms and functions tales can take. Together these volumes paint a broad picture of the ways in which different national tale traditions interact with and mutually influence each other, giving us a transnational and transhistorical understanding of the fairy tale. Indeed, readers will discover the rich, complex, and often ideologically charged cultural history of texts that can seem so familiar to us, which helps us understand them in new and exciting ways.

All six volumes cover the same eight themes so that the reader can gain a sense of continuities and discontinuities between types of characters, narratives, and traditions over time. Readers will move from *forms* of the fairy tale and the ancillary genres that fed into it to the history of *adaptations*, revealing the ways in which tales are always already a blend of multiple local, regional, and national traditions. A genre often focusing on questions related to development and initiation into adulthood and sometimes (less than we might think) concluding with marriage, tales often feature the norms of *gender and sexuality* grounded in a particular culture. Through the prevalence of non-human characters and problematic human figures, the fairy tale allows for the exploration of the boundaries between *the human and the non-human*, as well as between what is considered normal and *monsters or the monstrous*. As a nonmimetic genre, generally speaking, the fairy tale also plays with the delimitations between real and imaginary *spaces*, opening up both utopic and dystopic possibilities. Tales have often been used in the processes of *socialization*, for both children and adults, men and women, articulating class, gender, and ethnic differences. As such, tales cannot be separated from questions of *power* and ideology.

This cultural history of the fairy tale is divided into the following historical periods:

> Volume 1: A Cultural History of Fairy Tales in Antiquity (500 BCE–800 CE)
>
> Volume 2: A Cultural History of Fairy Tales in the Middle Ages (800–1450)
>
> Volume 3: A Cultural History of Fairy Tales in the Age of the Marvelous (1450–1650)
>
> Volume 4: A Cultural History of Fairy Tales in the Long Eighteenth Century (1650–1800)
>
> Volume 5: A Cultural History of Fairy Tales in the Long Nineteenth Century (1800–1920)
>
> Volume 6: A Cultural History of Fairy Tales in the Modern Age (1920–2000+)

Readers will come away with a new and fresh understanding of the fairy tale, which indeed enhances our appreciation for a genre that has touched many of us since childhood. Far from being naïve, innocent, timeless texts, *A Cultural History of Fairy Tales* foregrounds the ways wonder tales are embedded in sophisticated social, cultural, political, and artistic practices across history, anchored in specific cultural contexts that shape their meaning as tales are adapted from one cultural and historical context to another.

Anne E. Duggan, *General Editor*

Introduction

The Emergence of the Classic Fairy-Tale Tradition

ANNE E. DUGGAN

When most people think about the fairy-tale tradition today, the main references that immediately come to mind are Walt Disney films and the trilogy of Charles Perrault, the Brothers Grimm, and Hans Christian Andersen. Even twentieth- and twenty-first-century revisionist fairy tales by writers from Angela Carter and Emma Donoghue to Bill Willingham or in film and television series such as *Once Upon a Time* tend to focus on a corpus of tales Tom Shippey identifies as "core" tales, which could also be understood as our contemporary fairy-tale canon. These include "Bluebeard," "Snow White," "Cinderella," "Little Red Riding Hood," "Sleeping Beauty," "Rapunzel," "Beauty and the Beast," "The Frog Prince," and I would also add, "The Little Mermaid," along with "Aladdin" and "Ali Baba" from *The Thousand and One Nights* (Shippey 2006: 261). With the exception of "Beauty and the Beast," the best-known version of which was penned by Jeanne-Marie Leprince de Beaumont, all of these tales were produced and edited by male writers. However, the fairy-tale canon changes over historical periods and geographical locations, and what constitutes the fairy-tale canon of the twentieth- or twenty-first-century United States or Britain is not the canon of seventeenth-century France, or eighteenth-century German states, or nineteenth-century England. Importantly, the cultural history of the fairy tale in the long eighteenth century gave birth to many of these classic tales that would be canonized by Disney, but their future canonical status was not so clear, in fact, until the twentieth century. At its inception, women writers in France were at the forefront of the emergence of the classic fairy tale, and they weren't writing their fairy tales for children.

Just as Italy dominated the Western European production of fairy tales in the "Age of the Marvelous" (1450–1650; see Volume 3, this series) and German states/Germany finds itself at the forefront of tale production during the long nineteenth century (1800–1920; see Volume 5, this series), so France was the leader during the long eighteenth century (1650–1800). From the 1690s through the period of the French Revolution, while the fairy tales of Perrault and Leprince de Beaumont were popular, those of Marie-Catherine d'Aulnoy, published in 1697–8, were at least as celebrated across France, Britain, Holland, and German states, if not more so. Antoine Galland then took up the baton with the production of his translation and adaptation of *The Thousand and One Nights* (1704–17), launching the trend of the "oriental tale," which took Western Europe by storm. The figure of the female storyteller Scheherazade created a line of continuity between the women fairy-tale writers of the 1690s and the oriental tale of the early eighteenth century, at the same time that this figure would also be challenged in many oriental fictions, including those of François Pétis de la Croix and Denis Diderot. In their reframings of certain tropes from *The Thousand and One Nights*, the female storyteller often finds herself disempowered.[1]

It is important to take into account the role women and Middle Eastern and Asian writers played within the cultural history of the fairy tale in Europe. Although classic fairy tales are often associated with European male writers and editors, it was French women writers who played fundamental roles in the shaping of the genre, within France and beyond. Galland's later grafting of a Syrian text in Arabic—the manuscript of *Alf layla wa-layla*, or *A Thousand Nights and a Night*—onto the European tale tradition opened the way for Middle Eastern and Asian authors and their texts to impact the European literary field in very significant ways. However, it is important to note that the manner in which early modern Europeans understood texts from Syria, Turkey, China, and Japan were at times different from the lens through which early modern Syrians, Turks, Chinese, and Japanese readers would have understood these same works, given culturally distinct ways of understanding the limits delineating the real and the marvelous.[2] At the same time, the objectives of these texts often intersected in their criticism of immoral or unethical behavior or unjust rulers, their praise of virtuous heroines and heroes, and their explorations of the limits and possibilities of the real.

Essentially, the French fairy- and oriental tale traditions were significantly influenced, on the one hand, by the literary fairy tales of the sixteenth- and early seventeenth-century Italian writers Giovanni Franceso Straparola and Giambattista Basile (many of d'Aulnoy, Perrault, and Henriette-Julie de Murat's tales were modeled on those by the Italians);[3] and on the other, by Arab, Turkish, Persian, and Chinese tales (among other Eastern traditions), which often entered into the French literary sphere through translations of manuscripts collected through diplomatic and commercial exchanges. In turn, French writers produced a significant corpus of tales, emblematized by the forty-one volume *Cabinet des fées* (1785–9), that were widely read, translated, and adapted in Western Europe, most notably in England, Holland, and German-speaking states. The long eighteenth century is truly the age of the French wonder tale.

In what follows, I would like to first lay out the extent to which tales produced in France—sometimes drawing from Middle Eastern and Asian traditions—made their mark in England and Germany, in particular. Although the impact of the early modern French fairy and oriental tale certainly goes beyond England and Germany, to date research on reception in, for instance, Italy, Spain, or Russia is limited, and with respect to non-European traditions, one might argue that the direction tales were moving was from Asia and the Middle East (and even the Americas) toward Europe. I will then turn to the "function" of tales in the long eighteenth century, asking: what can fairy tales do, and for whom? As we will see, the cultural history of the fairy tale in the long eighteenth century takes us to unfamiliar canons and unfamiliar functions, from the early modern canonical status of d'Aulnoy and anti-monarchical tales to the beginnings of children's literature.

THE IMPACT OF THE FRENCH TRADITION

Because Perrault is better-known today, if not by name, then at least by his corpus of tales from "Cinderella" and "Little Red Riding Hood" to "Sleeping Beauty," one might be surprised by the fact that d'Aulnoy's tales dominated the English publishing market during most of the eighteenth century. Jennifer Schacker remarks: "D'Aulnoy's name had become well-known in eighteenth-century England, as her novels, her accounts of European travel and court scandal, and especially her intricate, highly self-aware, self-referential and influential fairy tales were translated and adapted for English audiences—resonating in the work of Ann Radcliffe, Maria Edgeworth, Anne Thackeray Ritchie, and many others" (2018: 164). Over the course of the century, her works—as well as select works by other writers, for d'Aulnoy's name came to generally embody the genre—appeared under her own name, sometimes rendered "Countess D'anois" or "Danois" as well as under the pseudonym of "Queen Mab" and "Mother Bunch." To give a sense of the degree to which d'Aulnoy's tales appealed to English readers in comparison to those by Perrault, Tables 0.1 and 0.2 provide a non-exhaustive publishing history.[4] Significantly, as Christine Jones observes, "three translations (with several reprints) of Madame d'Aulnoy's fairy tales were published before Charles Perrault's *Histoires et contes du temps passé* (1695) were translated in 1729" (2008: 240). While the publication rate of d'Aulnoy's tales remains fairly stable in English throughout the eighteenth

TABLE 0.1: Tales Attributed to or Gathered around the Figure of d'Aulnoy, aka Mother Bunch, aka Queen Mab.

Year	Title
1691	*The Story of Adolphus, Prince of Russia; and the Princess of Happiness.* London.
1699	*Tales of the Fairies.* Includes "Gracieuse et Percinet," "La Belle aux cheveux d'or," "L'Oiseau bleu," and "Le Prince Lutin."
1707	*The Diverting Works of the Countess D'Anois* (4 vols). Vol. 4, *Tales of the Fairies in Three Parts Compleat* (nine tales of vols 1 and 2 of *Contes des fées* and eleven tales from *Les Illustres fées* by Jean de Mailly).
1715	*The Diverting Works of the Countess D'Anois* (4 vols). Vol. 4, *Tales of the Fairies in Three Parts Compleat* (2nd edition). London.
1716	*The History of the Tales of the Fairies* (seven of nine tales from vols 1 and 2 of *Contes des fées*). London: B. Harris.
1721	*A Collection of Novels and Tales of the Fairies* (four tales by Henriette-Julie de Murat). London: W. Taylor and W. Chetwood.
1728	*A Collection of Novels and Tales of the Fairies* (republished). Also includes Louise d'Auneuil's *La Tiranie des fées détruite*.
1733	*Mother Bunch's Fairy Tales* (four tales by d'Auneuil). London: Newbery.
1737	*A Collection of Novels and Tales of the Fairies* (republished; 3rd edition).
1749	*A Collection of Novels and Tales of the Fairies* (republished; 4th edition).
1749	*The History of the Tales of the Fairies.* London.
1752	*The Court of Queen Mab: Containing a select collection of only the best, most instructive, and entertaining tales of the fairies* (1st edition; six tales by d'Aulnoy). London: Parnell/Cooper.
1758	*The History of the Tales of the Fairies.* London: Printed for C. Hitch and L. Hawes.
1766	*A Collection of Novels and Tales of the Fairies* (republished; 5th edition).
1770	*Queen Mab: Containing a select collection of only the best, most instructive, and entertaining tales of the fairies.* London: Parnell/Dodsley.
1776	*Mother Bunch's Fairy Tales; published for the amusement of all those little masters and misses.* London: Newbery.
1781	*The History of the Tales of the Fairies.* London: Printed for J. Bew.
1782	*Queen Mab: Containing a select collection of only the best, most instructive, and entertaining tales of the fairies* (republished; 3rd edition). London: Parnell/Dodsley.
1784	*Mother Bunch's Fairy Tales* (republished). London: Newbery.
1785	*Mother Bunch's Fairy Tales; published for the amusement of all those little masters and misses.* London: Newbery.
1785	*The History of the Tales of the Fairies.* London: T. Sabine.

1788	*The Mirror or Fairy World Displayed: A collection of Fairy Tales compiled for the amusement of Younger minds.* London: W. Lane.
1788	*The Palace of Enchantment, or entertaining and instructive fairy-tales.* Includes "Belle Belle [Fortunio]," "Princess Rosetta," "White Mouse," "The Golden Bough," and others. London: W. Lane.
1790	*Mother Bunch's Fairy Tales; published for the amusement of all those little masters and misses* (republished). London: Newbery.
1794	*The Palace of Enchantment, or entertaining and instructive fairy-tales* (republished). London: W. Lane.
1794	*Fairy Tales; selected from the best authors* (2 vols) (eleven tales by d'Aulnoy; three by Murat, one by Mailly, and four by others). London: [W. Lane].
1795	*Mother Bunch's Fairy Tales* (republished). London: Newbery.
1795	*The Enchanter; or Wonderful Story Teller.* London: W. Lane.
1799	*Queen Mab: Containing a select collection of only the best, most instructive, and entertaining tales of the fairies* (republished; 5th edition). London: Parnell/Dodsley.
1795	*Mother Bunch's Fairy Tales* (republished). London: Newbery.
1800?	*The History of the Tales of the Fairies.* London: T. Sabine and Son.

TABLE 0.2: Perrault in English.

Year	Title
1729	*Histories or Tales of Past Times.* Robert Samber. Also includes Marie-Jeanne L'Héritier's "Discreet Princess."
1741	*Histories: or tales of passed times. With Morals.* Englished by R. S. Gent (3rd edition). London. Printed for R. Montagu.
1755?	*Histories: or tales of passed times. With Morals.* Englished by R. S. Gent (3rd edition). London. Printed for M. Smith.
1761	*A Pretty Book for children; or an easy guide to the English tongue.* Includes LRRH, "Cinderilla," and a version of "The Fairies." Printed for J. Jewbery, J. Hodges, R. Baldwin, and B. Collins.
1763	*Mother Goose's Tales.* Salisbury: B. Collins; London: Mr Bristow.
1764	*Tales of Passed Times by Mother Goose with Morals.* Englished by R. S. Gent (6th edition). London: J. Melvil.
1765	*Mother Goose's Tales, in French and English, with Morals.* Englished by R. S. Gent (6th edition). London: sold by J. Priddon at the Feathers in Fleetstreet.
1767	"Puss in Boots" included after story of Dick Whittington and his cat in *The Fairing.* London: John Newbery.
1767	*Histories or Tales of Past Times. Told by Mother Goose.* London.

1769	*Histories or Tales of Past Times, Told by Mother Goose. With Morals.* Englished by G. M. Gent. (5th edition), corrected. Salisbury: printed and sold by B. Collins; London: Newbery and Carnan.
c. 1780	*Tales of Past Times, by Old Mother Goose with morals.* London: W. Osborne and T. Griffin.
1781	"Puss in Boots" included after story of Dick Whittington and his cat in *The Fairing.* London: John Newbery.
1783	"Puss in Boots" included after story of Dick Whittington and his cat in *The Fairing.* Dublin.
1785	*Histories of passed times, or the tales of Mother Goose. A new edition, to which are added two novels viz. The discreet princess, and the Widow and her two daughters.* Brussels: B. Le Francq.
1791	*Histories or tales of past times, told by mother goose. With Morals.* Englished by G. M. Gent (includes "Discreet Princess") (10th edition). Salisbury.
1796	*Histoires ou contes du temps passé/Tales of Passed Times by Mother Goose.* Englished by G. M. Gent (also includes "Discreet Princess") (7th edition). London: T. Boosey, Old Broad-Street, Royal-Exchange.
1800	*Tales of passed times: By Mother Goose. With Morals.* Includes "Discreet Princess." Edinburgh: John Moir.

century, Perrault's tales clearly pick up momentum starting in the 1760s, which Ruth Bottigheimer attributes to the earlier appearance, in 1737 and 1741, of his tales in "England's dual-language textbook market" geared toward boarding schools, truly entering the English mainstrein by 1767 (2002b: 7, 13).

To give a sense of the incredible appeal of d'Aulnoy's tales, novels, and travel literature, Melvin Palmer has shown that, from 1700 to about 1740, d'Aulnoy was the most published French author in England (1975: 238). The popularity of her works did not dwindle by the end of the century. M. O. Grenby observes that "between 1788 and the end of the century" publisher William Lane of Minerva Press

> raided d'Aulnoy's oeuvre to bring out at least six collections of fairy tales … Assuming a low estimate that the average print run was one thousand, Lane would have published twelve thousand copies of fairy tales in just twelve years. That several of his collections featured the same tales only accentuates Lane's confidence that the old French fairy tales would be popular and profitable.
>
> (Grenby 2006: 4–5)

D'Aulnoy's works continued to be popular in England throughout the nineteenth century, evident in the numerous adaptations of her tales to, on the one hand, the emerging market of children's literature and, on the other, the British stage, taking the form of holiday pantomimes.[5]

Just as d'Aulnoy and the other 1690s tale-tellers made a splash in English, so did *The Arabian Nights* and the oriental tales that came in its wake. Peter Caracciolo remarks:

> Antoine Galland's *Mille et une nuits* (1704–17) was the first, though partial, translation of the *Nights* [in French]. This, in turn, was translated into English in the first decade of the eighteenth century, and, as early as 1715, this Grub Street version of Galland's translation had reached its "Third Edition." It was to be many times reprinted during the rest of the century.
>
> (1988: 2)[6]

In the 1720s various tales from *The Nights* were serialized, and "by 1793 the English Galland had reached its eighteenth 'edition'" (Caracciolo 1988: 6).

François Pétis de la Croix's *Histoire de la sultane de Perse et les visirs, contes turcs* (Story of the Sultana of Persia and the Vizirs; Turkish Tales, 1707), and his *Les Mille et un jours, contes persans* (Thousand and One Days, Persian Tales, 1710–12) were also well received by the British reading public. Regarding the *Story of the Sultana*, Duncan Macdonald observes, "This book was translated almost immediately into English and published by Jacob Tonson in 1708" (1932: 412). In 1714, soon after the release of *Thousand and One Days*, Ambrose Philips produced an English translation also published by Tonson, and it hit its sixth edition by 1750 (Macdonald 1932: 417). Robert Samber, the first English translator of Perrault's tales, also translated Thomas-Simon Gueullette's *Chinese Tales or the Wonderful Adventures of the Mandarine Fun-Hoam* (1725), wishing "to capitalize on the vogue for oriental tales in the wake of the *Arabian Nights*, first published in English in 1706" (Lathey 2016: 85). Table 0.3 provides a non-exhaustive picture of the popularity of French oriental tales in English.

Although Germany has come to be known as the land of fairy tales, thanks to the popularity of the tale collections edited by Jacob and Wilhelm Grimm, much of the history of the genre in Germany owes a great debt to the French fairy- and oriental tale traditions of the long eighteenth century. French tales made their way to German-speaking states via several pathways. First, when Louis XIV revoked in 1685 the Edict of Nantes, which had legalized the practice of Protestantism in France, this provoked an exodus of French Protestants (known as Huguenots) to England, the Netherlands, and German states. As Jack Zipes has argued, "many of the tales that the Grimms recorded were of French origin because the Hassenpflugs [Grimm informants] were of Huguenot ancestry and spoke French at home" (2002: 29).[7] Thus some French tales made their way into German oral tradition due to the forced migration of Huguenots. Second, many educated German speakers would have known French and read these bestselling texts in their original language (see Zipes 2006: 78). Third, there was an increasing number of German translations of French tales, especially in the second half of the eighteenth century.

TABLE 0.3: Non-exhaustive Publishing History of French Oriental Tales in English.

Year	Title
1706	*Arabian Nights Entertainments*. London: A. Bell.
1708	*Turkish Tales; Consisting of several Extraordinary Adventures with the History of the Sultaness of Persia and the Visiers*. London: Jacob Tonson.
1712	*Arabian Nights Entertainments*. London.
1713	*Arabian Nights Entertainments*. London.
1714	*The Persian and the Turkish Tales compleat* (2 vols). Translated by William King. London: W. Mears at the Lamb, and J. Browne at the Black Swan.
1714–15	*Persian Tales* (3 vols). Translated by Ambrose Philips.
1715	*Arabian Nights Entertainments*. London.
1716	*A Thousand and One Quarters of Hours; Being Tartarian*. London: Jacob Tonson at Shakespear's Head.
1717	*Arabian Nights Entertainments*. London.
1718	*The Persian and the Turkish Tales compleat* (2nd edition). London: Mears, Lamb, and Brown.
1718	*Arabian Nights Entertainments*. London.
1721–22	*Arabian Nights Entertainments: Consisting of one thousand and one stories told by the Sultaness of the Indies* (10 vols). London: Printed for W. Taylor, W. Chetwood, and S. Chapman.
1725	*Arabian Nights Entertainments* (6th edition). London: J. Osborne and T. Longman.
1725	*Chinese Tales or the Wonderful Adventures of the Mandarine Fum-Hoam* by Thomas-Simon Gueullette. Translated by John McCay.
1726	*Arabian Nights Entertainments*. London.
1727	*Chinese Tales or the Wonderful Adventures of the Mandarine Fum-Hoam* by Thomas-Simon Gueullette. Translated by Robert Samber.
1728	*Arabian Nights Entertainments*. Dublin.
1729	*The Persian and the Turkish Tales compleat* (3rd edition). London: Mears, Clay, and Brown.
1736	*Arabian Nights Entertainments, told by the Sultaness of the Indies*. London.
1736	*Mogul Tales, or, The Dreams of Men Awake* by Thomas-Simon Gueulette. London: J. Applebee.
1743	*Mogul Tales, or, The Dreams of Men Awake* by Thomas-Simon Gueulette (2nd edition). London.
1753	*Arabian Nights Entertainments*. London: T. & T. Longman.
1759	*Tartarian Tales, or a Thousand and One Quarters of Hours*. London: Thomas Floyd.

1772 *Arabian nights entertainments: consisting of one thousand and one stories, told by the Sultaness of the Indies, to divert the Sultan from the execution of a bloody vow. Containing a better account of the customs, manners, and religion of the Eastern nations, viz. Tartars, Persians, and Indians, than is to be met with in any author hitherto published* (10th edition). London.

1776 *Arabian nights entertainments: consisting of one thousand and one stories, told by the Sultaness of the Indies, to divert the Sultan from the execution of a bloody vow* ... (4 vols) (10th edition). Dublin: W. Whitestone.

1777 *Arabian Nights Entertainments.* London.

1777 *Arabian Nights Entertainments.* Manchester.

1778 *Arabian Nights Entertainments* (10th edition). London: T. Longman.

1780 *Arabian nights entertainments: consisting of one thousand and one stories, told by the Sultaness of the Indies, to divert the Sultan from the execution of a bloody vow* ... (13th edition). Edinburgh and London.

1783 *Arabian Nights Entertainments.* Edinburgh.

1785 *Arabian Nights Entertainments* (10th edition). London: Harrison and co.

1789 *Arabian Nights Entertainments.* London: T. Longman.

1792 *Arabian nights entertainments: consisting of one thousand and one stories, told by the Sultaness of the Indies, to divert the Sultan from the execution of a bloody vow ....* London: C. D. Piguenit.

1792 *Arabian tales; or, a continuation of the Arabian Nights entertainments. Consisting of stories, related by the Sultana of the Indies,* ... (3 vols). Newly translated from the original Arabic into French, by Dom Chaves and M. Cazotte. Edinburgh: Belle and Bradfute et al. London: G. G. J. and J. Robinson.

1792 *Arabian tales; or, a continuation of the Arabian Nights entertainments. Consisting of stories, related by the Sultana of the Indies,* ... (3 vols). Newly translated from the original Arabic into French, by Dom Chaves and M. Cazotte. Montrose, Scotland: D. Buchanan.

1794 *Arabian tales; or, a continuation of the Arabian Nights entertainments. Consisting of stories, related by the Sultana of the Indies,* ... (3 vols). Newly translated from the original Arabic into French, by Dom Chaves and M. Cazotte.

1797 *The Oriental Moralist, or The Beauties of the Arabian Nights entertainments.* Boston: Printed by Samuel Bragg, Jr. for Wm. T. Clap.

1798 *Arabian Nights Entertainments.* Montrose, Scotland: D. Buchanan.

From the 1760s onward, several German translations and adaptations of French fairy and oriental tales appeared. Friedrich Immanuel Bierling published the *Cabinet der Feen* (*Cabinet of Fairies*, 1761–5), which "provided the German reading public with key French fairy-tale texts and sparked imitations of different kinds" (Zipes 2006: 79). In 1780, an anonymous collection of fairy tales aimed at children, *Feenmärchen für Kinder*, was published in Berlin and were in fact tales by d'Aulnoy (Grätz 1988: 19). This was followed by Friedrich Justin Bertuch's *Blaue Bibliothek aller Nationen* (1790–7), modeled on "the French *Bibliothèque bleue* and included tales from Mme d'Aulnoy and later French fairy-tale authors, as well as Oriental tales, and most consequentially for nineteenth-century Germany, the juvenalized *Contes du temps passé* (1697) by Charles Perrault" (Bottigheimer 2000: 268). It should be noted that the French *Bibliothèque bleue*, which refers to the blue-covered series of cheaply printed chapbooks centered in Troyes, France, published all kinds of texts, from alphabets and religious works to political satires. However, within the category of tales published, d'Aulnoy's works clearly dominated the eighteenth-century market.[8] This prominent position within the *Bibliothèque bleue* arguably led to the German publication of *Feen-Märchen der Frau Gräfin von Aulnoy* (1790–6; 4 vols), which included fairy tales by d'Aulnoy drawn from volumes 3, 4, 9, and 10 of the German *Blaue Bibliothek aller Nationen* (Grätz 1988: 19).

As Zipes has argued, "German translations of numerous French fairy tales helped German writers to form their versions in their own language to establish the 'German' literary genre in German-speaking principalities" (2006: 78). For instance, with the publication of Charles Joseph Mayer's monumental collection of French tales, the *Cabinet des fées* (1785–9; 41 vols), Christoph Martin Wieland translated and adapted several of the tales into German, which appeared in his *Dschinnistan* (*Jinnistan*, 1786–90) (Figure 0.1).

Jeannine Blackwell and Shawn Jarvis have shown how women writers such as Benedikte Naubert were influenced by d'Aulnoy in particular and French tales in general.[9] Jarvis notes that "Benedikte Naubert knew, and reponded to, tales from the French tradition (she makes overt references in *Velleda*, for example, to Madame d'Aulnoy)" (1992: 197). Her *Neu Volksmärchen der Deutschen* (*New German Folktales*, 4 vols) drew from "English, French, and pseudo-oriental sources" (Jarvis 2016: 407). For his part, Ludwig Tieck based several of his fairy-tale plays on tales by Perrault, including *Der gestiefelte Kater* (*Puss in Boots*, 1797), *Der Blaubart* (*Bluebeard*, 1797), and *Rotkäppchen* (*Little Red Riding Hood*, 1800).[10] Writers from Britain and German states, among other countries, drew heavily from the very popular French wonder tale tradition, reinventing their own versions of the tales as well as becoming inspired to explore their own traditions of the marvelous.

FIGURE 0.1: Illustration of the tale "Nadir and Nadine" from Christoph Martin Wieland's *Dschinnistan* (1786).

WHAT CAN FAIRY TALES DO?

Many people today immediately make the connection between "fairy tales" and "children's literature" and consider the genre as being primarily pedagogical. However, for much of the long eighteenth century, children's literature was, so to say, in its infancy, truly launched around the 1750s with the publication of Sarah Fielding's *The Governess: or Little Female Academy* (1749) and Jeanne-Marie Leprince de Beaumont's of the *Magasin des enfants* (1757), translated into English as *The Young Misses Magazine* (1761), which contained the classic tale, "Beauty and the Beast."[11] So, if the eighteenth-century tale was not aimed primarily at educating children, what was its function in the period?

As this volume makes clear, its functions were multiple and shifting across the long eighteenth century. Initially, the fairy tale attained popularity within French salon and court society in the 1690s. Writers such as d'Aulnoy, Perrault, Murat, Jeanne-Marie L'Héritier, and Charlotte-Rose Caumont de la Force, among others, reshaped material from the Italian fairy-tale writers Straparola and Basile. They often blended Italian storylines with tropes borrowed from the novel and novella as well as from oral culture, then infused the tales with references to French worldly culture to create aristocratic tales. Whereas writers such as d'Aulnoy, Murat, and La Force, who issued from the traditional nobility, used the genre in part to reimagine a world in which nobles were more autonomous and not subjected to the absolutist rule of Louis XIV, Perrault—a member of the upper bourgeoisie—opens up the possibilities for a commoner to become king. Women writers, or the *conteuses* as they have come to be known, systematically deployed the genre to empower female characters, presenting us with wise, intelligent, just, and powerful heroines who rule kingdoms and use their magical powers to help others. With respect to gender dynamics, their tales are often at odds with those penned by Perrault, who tends to depict his heroines in much more passive and disempowering ways.[12]

With the rise of the oriental tale, several French *philosophes*, including Diderot, Voltaire, and Montesquieu, drew from the genre to criticize the arbitrary power of the French monarchy. By projecting contemporary issues onto the space of the oriental Other, writers could allegorically tackle questions of political despotism and social injustice in veiled ways. The oriental tale also introduced into the cultural sphere notions of cultural relativism. Even if some of these representations remained problematic, the incorporation of Islam, Buddhism, and other religions into the tales could serve to relativize most notably French Catholicism, suggesting there are many other systems of belief in the world. By the end of the century, Jacques Cazotte's *Le Diable amoureux* (*The Devil in Love*, 1772), William Beckford's *Vathek* (1786), and Jean Potocki's *Manuscrit trouvé à Saragosse* (*Manuscript Found in Saragossa*, 1794) pushed this line of questioning accepted norms to explore the limits of the real and the supernatural, madness and reason, in ways that anticipate the nineteenth-century fantastic tale in the tradition of E. T. A. Hoffmann and Théophile Gautier.

Even as we consider the political functions of the tale in the long eighteenth century, they also clearly had social functions for both adults and children. Tales by the *conteuses*, attached to salon culture, communicated norms of acceptable behavior, including appropriate language, that would allow one to function effectively in elite Parisian society. A writer like Perrault contested some of the more progressive definitions of women's roles in the period and through his tales suggests that the spaces women should occupy to remain virtuous are domestic spaces such as the home or hospital and not the public spaces of opera or theater, and their function should be to serve husband, family, and general caretaking rather than engage in more worldly occupations.[13]

With the work of Fielding and Leprince de Beaumont, the social function of the fairy tale shifted to focus on the education of children, especially young girls. This is clear in the ways they redeploy the use of the frame narrative. Drawing from the model set by Giovanni Boccaccio in his *Decameron* (1353), authors such as Straparola and d'Aulnoy used the frame narrative to allow a group of elite adults to comment on and negotiate the meaning of the interpolated tales the different characters recount. In the case of Fielding and Leprince de Beaumont, a governess—Mrs. Teachum and Mademoiselle Goodness—moderates the telling of tales and the commentary about them for their young female charges, focusing on the moral lessons of the tales communicated in an explicitly pedagogical and moralistic manner. While *conteuses* such as d'Aulnoy, Murat, L'Héritier, and La Force put forth many heroines who exercise a broad range of agency and qualities, Fielding and Leprince de Beaumont present more limited and domestic spheres of action. Their works paved the way for later pedagogical writers of fairy tales such as Félicité de Genlis and the comtesse de Ségur. Importantly, these writers for the most part produced original fairy tales for children, but the works of Perrault and d'Aulnoy were also being adapted to the growing market for tales aimed at children. As Bottigheimer has documented, Perrault's tales were used in school primers for boys, suggesting that his tales were reshaped early on for the child reader in England. D'Aulnoy's aristocratic tales were being reframed for children through additions to titles such as *Selected for the Entertainment of Young People* or *For the Amusement of All Those Little Masters and Misses Who, by Duty to Their Parents, and Obedience to Their Superiors, Aim at Becoming Great Lords and Ladies* (Grenby 2006: 10). Even as these texts take the child as the ideal reader, questions of class, gender, and race remain pertinent in the shape different tales take.[14]

The fairy and oriental tale also were used to explore the limits of the human and of the real by, on the one hand, staging encounters between humans and non-human agents (non-human animals, "things," monsters), and on the other hand, situating tales within different types of spaces (realistic, dreamlike, liminal, supernatural).[15] The seventeenth century saw the emergence of René Descartes's notion of the animal as soulless automaton, which continues to inform contemporary conceptions of the non-human animal, allowing for their instrumentalization for the supposed benefit of humans. However, many fairy tales in the period implicitly challenge such notions by granting animals forms of agency that foreground their ability to reason and love. Even the fact that fairies, princesses, princes, and other types of characters are momentarily transformed into animals suggests that we should take heed when needlessly wishing to pursue their destruction. In the early modern period, disabled individuals were often put on display at courts and fairgrounds, while travel accounts reported other sorts of "curiosities" across the world, shaping concepts of the monstrous that fed into fairy tales. Increased exposure to non-European spaces through travel opened up conceptions of what is real and possible. Early modern tales drew from both baroque tropes of dreamlike, liminal spaces as well as from travel accounts of what Europeans imagined to be "exotic" lands to reimagine spatial as well as temporal limits.

The fairy and oriental tales were also appreciated for their aesthetic value and value as "spectacle." Early modern tales drew from and fed into opera and theater. For instance, d'Aulnoy's flying chariots bear more affinities with flying contraptions found in Jean-Baptiste Lully and Philippe Quinault's operas than anything that can be found in the fairy tales of Straparola and Basile.[16] Fairy and oriental tales inspired generations of playwrights in France, the German states, Italy, and Russia, and it is perhaps the value of fairy and oriental tales as "spectacle" that facilitates their adaptation to such visual genres. Genies who magically emerge out of bottles, a mysterious princess whose beauty astonishes those around her, princes who adorn themselves for their one true love, brilliant palaces, and caverns filled with glowing treasures all speak to the visually appealing appearances and surfaces that are part and parcel of the wonder tale in the long eighteenth century.

The cultural history of the fairy tale in the long eighteenth century challenges contemporary notions of canon, foregrounding different configurations and networks in which tales by d'Aulnoy as well as oriental tales dominated the Western European fairy-tale market. This is a period in which those tales that seem so dominant and familiar to us today, for instance "Cinderella" and "Sleeping Beauty," constituted in fact just another tale among an open sea of stories. This is also the period in which we witness the emergence of children's literature. However, the fairy and oriental tales remained largely designed for adult readers until the late eighteenth century, when, after Fielding and Leprince de Beaumont began specifically producing tales for young people, tales by Perrault, d'Aulnoy, and others underwent rebranding for this rising young readership. Fairy and oriental tales draw from and feed into different types of theatrical venues, and they provided imaginary spaces that allowed for the exploration and expansion of the limits of gender, political structures, religion, cultural norms, and last but not least, what it means to be human.

CHAPTER ONE

Forms of the Marvelous

The Eighteenth-Century merveilleux

TATIANA KORNEEVA

Over the course of the eighteenth century there is hardly another genre that provoked as many controversies, polemics, and aesthetic debates as the fairy tale did. No other form has undergone such an unprecedented transformation from being derided as a low, childish, and second-rate fiction to become the "most advanced literary venue of the period" (Sermain 2005: 8). Moreover, it may be argued that no other genre absorbed and appropriated motifs and themes from oral storytelling tradition, combining them with elements from other genres, and in its turn has been adapted to a plethora of literary, dramatic, and art forms (Mainil 2001: 71). In fact, after its emergence and creative explosion between 1690 and 1705 through the works of Marie-Catherine d'Aulnoy, Charles Perrault, and other French women writers such as Marie-Jeanne L'Héritier and Henriette-Julie de Murat, known as *conteuses* or *salonnières*, the *contes de fées* (French literary fairy tales) brought about the literary revolution and diversification of forms. Fairy tales were transposed into an infinite number of mediums, communicated different ideologies, and embraced all types of genres. Following the foundational period of the rise of the *contes de fées*, Antoine Galland's translations-cum-adaptations published in French as *Les Mille et une nuits* (The Arabian Nights) between 1704 and 1716 launched the second fairy-tale wave (1705–30) and thereafter inspired the penchant for exotic-erotic fantasy appearing in other genres written throughout the rest of the century.[1] The third and final phase of the fairy-tale vogue was characterized by the diversity and quantity of tales that appeared between 1730 and 1789. Writers and dramatists adapted fairy tales to theater, opera, and novel, and penned didactic, moral, philosophical, and libertine tales. While the didactic ones put emphasis on the moral edification already present in both the galant and oriental tales that dominated the beginning of the century, philosophical, satirical, and licentious tales reflected the intellectual and critical spirit of the age. Enlightenment thinkers found the fairy-tale patterns particularly apt to address the issues of injustice and arbitrary absolutist power; to debate and problematize the boundaries of class, gender, and sexuality; or to make a personal statement on women's role in the public sphere.

This chapter traces how writers, dramatists, and critics transformed the fairy tale into one of the most successful and cosmopolitan forms that became a common point of reference and convergence of many other literary genres. It surveys the forms the marvelous took and explores the literary, dramaturgical, sociopolitical innovations and developments that the genre introduced when it was adapted into other media and forms. Although the fairy tale enjoyed enduring popularity that acquired transnational dimensions, my focus here is on France, Italy, and Russia, centers whose primacy for the fairy-tale tradition was well established. The examples discussed herein are drawn from the well-known works of the leading exponents of the fairy-tale genre that have been chosen for the resonance they produced throughout the eighteenth century.

THE FRENCH *FÉERIE*

Eighteenth-century drama was characterized by an extensive evocation of magic and the supernatural, but the audience's infatuation with the marvelous onstage was not an entirely new phenomenon. The origin of the literary fairy tales conceived by French women writers can be traced back to early Italian operas, court ballets, and *divertissements* with their plots derived from mythology, pastorals, and epic romance.[2] Further, the French Baroque operas of Jean-Baptiste Lully and Jean-Philippe Rameau as well as the *tragédie lyrique* (musical tragedy) were filled with the most fantastic presentations of unreality. Another theatrical genre that widely exploited the use of magic, albeit in a different context, was the popular tradition of the Italian *commedia dell'arte* that was performed in Paris by Italian traveling troupes starting from the sixteenth century. Its scenarios favored incantation episodes, oracle scenes, and appearances of ghosts. Sorcerers figured among the improvised comedy's stock characters, along with astrologers, fairies, oracles, and spirits of the underworld. As David Buch details, unlike the sumptuous and lavish productions for the court that suggested a close parallel between the aristocratic and princely patrons and the divine powers, the marvelous in the *commedia dell'arte* served as an outlet for subversive social commentary. A touch of a magic wand reversed the fate of commoners or impoverished princes and could enable the powerless hero to correct the corruption of the powerful. The marvelous in popular theater thus imparted social change, and the benevolent fairy or genie was often a divine agent of justice, an embodiment of the spirit of reason (Buch 2008: xiv, 18).

Despite the marvelous being part of the legitimate and long-standing theatrical tradition, many objections had been raised over the course of the century. During the classicist-modernist controversy concerning the issues of verisimilitude, French writers of tragedy, such as Jean Racine,[3] and theorists from the camp of the ancients, notably Nicolas Boileau, derided and condemned the marvelous as unnatural, absurd, and vulgar. As the century progressed, magic and the *merveilleux* were deemed inappropriate for onstage representation by French philosophers and critics, for instance Denis Diderot and Jean-Jacques Rousseau, who dismissed fantastic spectacles as disruptive of the illusion created by theater (cf. Hobson 1982: 144). Even in Italy, theater reformers, such as Carlo Goldoni, who were looking for a model that would revitalize Italian theater within French dramatic practice,[4] succeeded in banishing the marvelous in one genre: the *dramma per musica* (musical drama). Regardless of the reforms desired by the Encyclopedists, the marvelous and the supernatural elements continued to appear in dramatic and operatic genres and had a sustained appeal to a broad and diverse audience. Composers set newly revised librettos of Philippe Quinault, Christoph Willibald Gluck's revamped marvelous operas triumphed in Paris, and large-scale operatic settings of fairy tales became popular (Buch 2008: xii–xiii). Not only did the fairy plays progressively come to rival serious and highbrow dramatic genres, but also they soon became a pan-European phenomenon. The supernatural flourished in all of Europe's theater venues with French *féeries* (fairy operas with ballet), Italian *fiabe teatrali* (theatrical fables), Russian opera-*skazkas* (operatic fairy tales), English pantomime extravaganzas, and German *Märchenopern* (fairy-tale singspiels).[5]

A quick look at the eighteenth-century theater repertoires and box office records shows the abundance of plays on magical subjects on every French stage: the Académie Royale de Musique made the *merveilleux* its specialty; the Comédie-Italienne, where *commedia dell'arte* had for long held sway, never dropped fairy plays from its repertoire. This theatrical venue was particularly favorable to the marvelous on its stage, both in terms of the use of the spectacular machines and plots involving fairy-tale characters, magic objects, and situations strongly derivative of the *commedia dell'arte* scenarios. The Parisian Fair theaters that also inherited the tradition of improvised comedy adapted numerous oriental tales to their stages, indulging the public's taste for the *féeries*.[6] But one dramatic genre in particular was filled with the most fantastic representation of unreality and devoted to the marvelous exclusively: the opera. As Louis-Sébastien Mercier argued, "un opéra doit être un conte de fée. Je trouverai assez ailleurs des pièces raisonnées et touchantes, qui parleront à la raison et à l'âme. Ici, je veux voir un monde étrange et de fantaisie" ("an opera needs to be a fairy tale. I can find enough rational and touching plays that speak to the reason and soul. Here I want a strange world and fantasy"; [1783] 1994: 446).

Attempting to provide a more nuanced taxonomy of the marvelous that flourished in French musical theater, two types of dramatic tales may be delineated. The first category comprises faithful adaptations of fairy tales from the collections by Perrault, d'Aulnoy, and Jeanne-Marie Leprince de Beaumont that exploited the success of the published tales. Perrault provided canvas for more than thirty dramatic plays,[7] and the story of "La Barbe-bleue" ("Bluebeard") was the most often adapted tale. This fact reveals the eighteenth-century taste for the most somber and gruesome tales from his collection in contrast to the following century, which would privilege more galant subject matters, such as "Cendrillon" ("Cinderella"). Perrault's tales that allowed a political reflection on the figures of power due to their focus on tensions between the small and powerless and the great and powerful, such as "Le Petit poucet" ("Little Thumbling") and "Le Chat botté" ("Puss in Boots"), occupied the second place in the dramatic settings of the fairy tales.

The variety of forms into which the theatrical *merveilleux* was cast in the second half of the eighteenth century ranged from comedy to *opéra-comique* and pantomime, from vaudeville and ballet to morality play. A case in point is dramatic adaptations of Leprince de Beaumont's tale "La Belle et la Bête" ("Beauty and the Beast"), which were transposed to the stage three times. In 1742 Pierre-Claude Nivelle de La Chaussée's three-act verse comedy *Amour pour Amour* (Love for Love) premiered at the Comédie-Française. It was a play about sentiment and sway of passions. A beast, which in this opera is named Azor, has been given a fearsome appearance by a fairy until he has inspired love: the difficulty is that he is forbidden to declare any emotions of love himself. Given that Azor does not have any particular virtues, this adaptation has little strength, but another version, *Zémire et Azor* (Zemire and Azor, 1771), an *opéra-comique* by Jean-François Marmontel (1723–99) set to music by André Grétry, became a worldwide success (Figure 1.1). The librettist borrowed the moral substance from Leprince de Beaumont's tale, the characters' names of his heroes and the oriental setting from de La Chaussée, but the conception of the unusual four-act "comédie-ballet mixing song and dance" with set changes and magical transformations came from Charles-Simon Favart's highly successful fairy opéra-comique *La fée Urgèle* (The Fairy Urgèle, 1765).

The plot mixed a variety of genres: fairy-tale form was combined with the *drame larmoyant* (tearful drama) with tears and sympathy, scenes of family reunion, and the sensibility of the disfigured prince. In this rendition,

FORMS OF THE MARVELOUS 19

FIGURE 1.1: An engraving "Tableau magique de Zémire et Azor" by François-Robert Voyez le jeune, after Jacques Louis Touzé. Public domain.

Azor, whom Marmontel made intelligent and a true "homme des lumières" (enlightened man), enchants Zémire visually, musically, and emotionally. The magic, however, plays a crucial role here, reaching the culmination point in the "tableau magique" (magic picture) (Marmontel, *Zémire et Azor*, Act 3, scene 6), one of the most celebrated scenes in the entire eighteenth-century *opéra-comique* (Marmontel 2002: 140–2). By means of a magic frame, Azor allows Zémire to see her family one last time, warning her that the picture will vanish if she comes near it. At first the picture is silent, but then Azor adds the voices of Zémire's father and sisters, who lament her captivity in the trio "Ah! Laissez-moi la pleurer" (Ah, let me lament her) (Figures 1.2 and 1.3).

To reproduce the dreamlike quality of the conjured image, Marmontel called for the trio to sound muted, and Grétry responded by having a wind sextet accompany the vocal lines from behind the stage. The voices and the image together produce an overwhelming effect on Zémire, and she throws herself at the tableau as if to reach her family but, as Azor predicted, the tableau instantly disappears.

The term tableau employed, together with the pictorial manner in which the play was staged, reveal Grétry's familiarity with Denis Diderot's reflections on the use of tableaux as means of intensifying the emotional and imaginative involvement of the audience. Diderot was the first to realize that drama was a genre capable of pairing the verbal description of actions with the direct presentation of visual images. For the French Encyclopedist, figurative painting represented an art that was closer to nature and more able to engage the spectator than was contemporary theatrical practice. To counter the artificial nature of theater, he offered a rather sophisticated theory of verisimilitude and theatrical illusion, developing the notion of the tableau, visually satisfying, essentially silent and seemingly accidental grouping of figures on stage, which

FIGURE 1.2: "Ah! Laissez-moi la pleurer," trio from *Zémire et Azor* (act 3, scene 6). Transcription to modern format by author. Public domain.

FIGURE 1.3: An offstage instrumental prelude to the trio "Ah! Laissez-moi la pleurer" introduces the "magic picture" music (*Zémire et Azor*, act 3, scene 6). Transcription to modern format by author. Public domain.

had the function to produce a realistic effect as well as a necessary illusion of reality whenever the narrative was unable to do so. The magic tableau in Marmontel and Grétry's adaptation thus represents a point of junction between the marvelous and the growing demand for realism, characteristic of the rationalization of the fairy tale in the second half of the century.

The third adaptation of Leprince de Beaumont's tale belongs to the pen of the moralistic writer and novelist Stéphanie Félicité de Genlis (1746–1830) and reveals how in the latter half of the century the *conte* serves as a vehicle for ideas on morality. Genlis's comedy *Beauty and the Monster* was included in the collection of plays for children, *Théâtre à l'usage des jeunes personnes* (1779, published in English in 1780 with the title *The Theatre of Education* that stressed the emphasis on education). Designed as a "moral treatise put into action," the play was destined for private theatricals. The dramatic settings of "Beauty and the Beast" are thus a sound example of both the variety of genres that were ready to welcome the fairy tale's marvelous and the evolution in the public's taste for the *féerie* that shifted, over the course of the century, from baroque spectacles for adults to moral tales for children.

The second category of dramatic reworkings of the fairy tales is constituted by the plays where the source tales appear either in the form of the fleeting references, quotations, or insertion of magic objects and archetypal characters of fairies or speaking animals, as it happens, for instance, in the *Arlequin roi des ogres ou Les Bottes de sept lieues* (Harlequin King of the Ogres, or the Seven-league Boots, 1720) by Alain-René Lesage, Louis Fuzelier, and d'Orneval, which mixes the *commedia dell'arte* buffoonery and fairy-tale motifs. Another French playwright who manifested a constant interest in this form of marvelous throughout his entire career was Pierre de Marivaux (1688–1763). In 1720 premièred Marivaux's *Arlequin poli par l'amour* (Harlequin Polished by Love), the play that deals with the topic of the dullard's deformities invisible to the eyes of his lover, already explored in Perrault's "Riquet à la houpe" ("Riquet of the Tuft").[8] Marivaux's plays, however, resembled even more closely, both in terms of plot and moral lesson, Catherine Durand's *conte* "Le Prodige d'Amour" ("The Miracle of Love"), published in *Les petits soupers de l'année 1699* (*The Little Suppers of 1699*). As Durand's protagonist Brutalis, Marivaux's Harlequin is handsome but egregiously stupid. The fairy, who falls in love with his body when she finds him asleep, abducts Harlequin to her fairy land, hoping to arouse his desires and awaken his intelligence. While Harlequin's stupidity prevents him from responding to the fairy's passion, it is his love for an innocent shepherdess (Brillante in Durand and Silvia in Marivaux) that bestows wit and intelligence on the hero. The machinations of the fairy are thus foiled, and the ensuing interest of the play lies in the effect of love on the hero's character—the central theme for Marivaux's theatrical production. The play hence bridged the transition from the galant tale to the moral one, as the subtext is a social critique of courtly manners, corrupt aristocracy, and the valorizing of love in the lower classes. Marivaux also responds to the shifting conception of the *merveilleux*: the *conte oriental*, characterized by broader philosophic concerns, found its counterpart in his social comedy *L'Ile de la raison* (The Island of Reason, [1727] 1993) set in a utopic island away from the corruption of civilization and governed by laws based on simple morality. The overtly moralizing tone of Marivaux's *Félicie* ([1757] 1994), which deals with the education of a young girl experiencing passionate love but stopped by a fairy before her passion could get out of hand, approached the *conte moral*.

The fairy-tale vogue in musical theater lasted until the end of the century. The dramatic renditions of the tales manifested a general trend to distance themselves from their originals through the rationalization of and avoiding almost all elements of the marvelous. An *opéra-comique* by Michel-Jean Sedaine and Grétry, *Raoul Barbe-bleue* (Raoul Blue-beard, 1789), can serve as an example. The play does not employ any stage machinery that facilitated the spectacular illusions, and the *merveilleux* is reduced to the color of the eponymous character's beard and the enchanted key to the closet with the corpses of his murdered wives, which has never been closed with the key.[9] In line with the ongoing process of civilization, the dramatic tales of the Enlightenment progressively suppressed violence and cruelty inherent in both popular tales and those by Perrault and d'Aulnoy. In response to the English-inspired rise of sensibility and the diffusion of the dramatic theories about the importance of emotionally engaging the spectator in the onstage fiction there is also a tendency to increase the sentimental dimension of the tales.

Another characteristic of dramatic adaptations is the reinforcement of the moral aspect of the story, which in some renditions is accompanied by subversion of the source fairy tale, in others by updating of the conservative ideology of the tales from the first wave. Ultimately, taking a distance from the source tales brings about modernity from the dramaturgical point of view as the playwrights find in the onstage manifestation of the marvelous a model to revitalize dramatic practice.

THE MARVELOUS IN ITALIAN THEATER

In Italy, the capacity of the fairy-tale genre to introduce the dramaturgical innovations was fully grasped by the Venetian playwright Carlo Gozzi (1720–1806), who transposed the narrative structure of the folk and literary fairy tales to the Italian stage.[10] Gozzi's ten meta-theatrical fairy plays had their origin in the mid-eighteenth-century debates on the reform of the Italian comic theater, the debates that were one of the most significant moments not only in theatrical life but also in Venetian culture in general. To the realistic comedies of his rival dramatists, Carlo Goldoni and Pietro Chiari, Gozzi responded with his new genre of the fairy drama, which contained an impressive number of transformation scenes, special effects, and *commedia dell'arte* stock characters. Calling his first play, *L'Amore delle tre melarance* (The Love of the Three Oranges, 1761), a "childish fable" entirely without serious parts, Gozzi also referred to it as "the tale that grandmothers tell to their grandchildren, adapted to theatrical performance" (Gozzi 2006: 402). These statements imply that the comedy was nothing more than the staging of an old folktale; but the description of its avid and passionate public reception suggests that *L'amore*'s admirers were not just victims of a collective hallucination caused by the fairy play's overwhelming visual representations of marvelous and magical metamorphoses. Although originating from the playwright supporting a *commedia dell'arte* comeback at the expense of his antagonists' realistic character comedies, the significance of Gozzi's fairy-tale comedies went far beyond the playwright's polemical intentions.[11]

To understand what is fundamentally at stake in Gozzi's project of engaging with the fairy-tale tradition, we must explore the motif of the melancholic sovereign that catalyzes the entire action of the comedy. Prince Tartaglia, the protagonist of the play—and an allegory of the Venetian public that audience members themselves would have recognized—suffers from hypochondriac melancholy. This illness was brought upon him by two "melancholic poets" (Gozzi 2004: 14), whom the author intended (and his audience understood) to be Goldoni and Chiari. At war with each other and disguised, respectively, as the magician Celio and the evil fairy Morgana, these two allegorical characters practice magic with political aims. Morgana promotes the cause of Tartaglia's antagonists who want to kill the prince and take his kingdom for themselves. Celio intends to defeat the plotters' plans by sending Truffaldino (who represents *commedia dell'arte*) to the court to heal the prince's malady by making him laugh. During feasts and spectacles set up to amuse Tartaglia, fountains of oil and wine are erected in front of the palace with the idea that seeing passers-by slipping and bumping into each other would cheer up the prince—and indeed this occurs: Tartaglia cannot control his laughter when he sees Morgana slip on the oil, recalling a similar scene in Giambattista Basile's *Tale of Tales* concerning Princess Zoza.[12] Celio and Truffaldino's plan is thus successful, but their victory is short-lived. Infuriated by Tartaglia's laughter, Morgana casts a spell that makes the prince fall in love with three magic oranges allegorically representing the three theatrical genres of comedy, tragedy, and improvised comedy. The quest for these oranges and their eventual acquisition ends with the cured prince's marriage to a maiden hidden inside one of the enchanted oranges—a figure who represents *commedia dell'arte*. In the overtly allegorical dimension of the play, therefore, the melancholy prince represents the Venetian audience, which is increasingly bored with Goldoni and Chiari's plays that consciously suppressed improvised comedy and the marvelous in theater. I argue that the prince's quest for the enchanted oranges allegorizes not only Gozzi's resuscitation of the fairy-tale tradition to revitalize Italian comic theater but also Tartaglia's evolution as a spectator from passive observer to critically productive audience member.

The significance of Tartaglia's humoral disease is explained by Gozzi himself in his "reflexive analysis":[13] the prince's melancholy can be read as a physical manifestation of the emotional frustration of the character himself—and, by extension, of the play's audience—with the forms of theater promoted by Gozzi's rival playwrights. When Gozzi represented the Venetian audience's disappointment with the dramatic works of Goldoni and Chiari through the allegory of Tartaglia's melancholy, he was advocating for a form of theater that enhances the spectator's sensory pleasure and satisfies a very human need to be diverted from melancholy. From Gozzi's standpoint, Goldoni and Chiari's realistic plays fail to create a dramatic illusion that would emotionally engage spectators. If Goldoni's plays were an onstage facsimile of real life, Gozzi believed instead that theater should provide a type of illusion that allows theatergoers to avoid seeing reality as it is. For Gozzi, therefore, it was important that playwrights represent their characters and their adventures on stage as overtly fictitious, and that the action take place in a world of pure fantasy. The setting of an imaginary realm populated by princes and kings was not an expression of Gozzi's reactionary and aristocratic ideology. Rather, it is indicative of his perceived need to create an unambiguous dissimilarity between the action onstage and the world from which that action draws its inspiration. Gozzi thus advocated a theater that can provide its audience with more than just a perfect facsimile of the mundane world. As follows from his synthetic description of what his theatrical tales present—namely "una forte passione, un seriofaceto, una chiara allegoria, una critica ragionata, la morale" (a strong passion, a serious facetiousness, a clear allegory, a reasoned critique, morality)[14]—he argued for a dramatic form that offers the true and the fantastical in a combination that both pleases spectators (through its dramatic marvels) and shows them something true to nature (through its realism).

Gozzi's conception of dramatic illusion grounded on the efficacy of the allegorical fairy-tale formula, elucidate why the playwright was convinced that "la passione del mirabile ... sarà sempre la regina di tutte le umane passioni" ("the passion of the wondrous ... will always be the queen of all human passions"; Gozzi 1772: 131). The next logical step at this point will be to ask why the Venetian audience's emotional response to art is translated, in *L'amore*, into the sovereignty of a prince? Gozzi maintained that "il Pubblico ha somma ragione di allettarsi di ciò che lo alletta, e di non voler cadere negli effetti ipocondriaci" ("the Public has the supreme right to be fascinated by what fascinates it and to wish not to be affected by hypochondria"; Gozzi 2013: 190). He was thus convinced that the audience relies upon the emotional appeal of theater in making its judgments, and empowered the public with an ability to decide for itself: "senza distinzioni di teste, il Pubblico intero ha una ragione comperata, di trovar cosa che lo intrattenga, e lo diverta" ("without any distinction, the whole Public has bought the full right to expect entertainment and amusement"; Gozzi 1804: 10). On careful reflection, therefore, the "nuovi generi di mirabile, e di forte passione" ("new, marvelous, and strongly passionate genres"; Gozzi 2013: 531) are, for Gozzi, genres that first and foremost allow for the creation of a new relationship between dramatic performance and the subjectivity of the spectator—a relationship in which audience responsiveness to art becomes of primary importance. Gozzi's allegorical equation of audience and prince, a figure for absolutist political authority in *L'amore*, means that the audience's response in *L'amore* came to exercise an aesthetic and cultural authority previously reserved only for a monarch. The fairy-tale form, therefore, not only opened up new perspectives on dramaturgy but also was a means by which Gozzi made his audiences understand their increasing power as art critics of theatrical production and their role as participants in a public sphere.

PRINCELY TALES FOR ROYAL HEIRS

As the theatrical adaptations of fairy tales enjoyed continued success, they contributed to the broad dissemination of fantastic material and helped to define a national character for several European regions. In Russia, there was an ever-increasing interest in Russian folk and historical past throughout the whole reign of Catherine II (1762–96). Tales were collected, written, translated, read, and sung, and the empress herself several times set aside politics and the affairs of state to write fairy tales meant as moral instruction for her grandsons—the future tsars Alexander I and Nikolai I. Between 1786 and 1789, she completed and produced four fairy-tale opera libretti and pioneered the creation of the genre of opera-*skazka* (comic operatic fairy tale), independent from foreign musical models. Several common threads run through Catherine's four operatic tales. The title hero in each is a teenage prince who grows in wisdom over the course of the spectacle by facing trials and overcoming temptations. Along with bravery, the plots test the princes' moral virtues, humility, generosity, filial piety, and devolution to their future cause. All the operas in various ways instilled the traditional imperial virtues of loyalty, tolerance, and firm rulership.

Catherine II's comic operas represent an interesting case of fairy-tale adaptations to another medium both because of the variety of forms the marvelous was cast into and the use the empress made of the genre. Although Catherine's four operas share a basic outline, each represents a distinct genre of operatic *skazka*. Her first opera, *Fevei* (1786), is a moral tale and in its turn an adaptation from the empress's own prose tale. The second, *Novogorodskii bogatyr' Boeslaevich* (Boeslaevich, Knight of Novgorod, 1786), is the first-known operatic adaptation of *bylina* or Russian heroic epic in verse, whereas the third *skazka*, *Khrabroi i smeloi vitiaz' Akhrideich' ili Ivan Tsarevich* (The Brave and Bold Knight Akhrideich or Crown Prince Ivan, 1787), is a wonder tale. The fourth play, also an adaptation of Catherine's prose tale, *Gorebogatyr' Kosometovich* (Woeful Knight Kosometovich, 1789) is a political satire on the Russo–Swedish War and, in particular, the king Gustav III, who is depicted as being brave in words but ridiculous in actions.

All Catherine's fairy operas use magic to transform mundane reality, but the marvelous in these plays disguise her other purposes. In her role as a monarch and a grandmother, the empress used the fairy tales to familiarize her grandsons with the concept of empire. At the same time the spectacular productions served to provide a wider audience of Saint Petersburg aristocracy and foreign diplomats with a historical argument for imperial expansion, thus advancing her political agenda: to legitimize Russia's standing as a European nation and emphasize Russia's cultural uniqueness. The tsarina thus chose to concentrate her literary ambitions on the specific genre because, combined with the operatic form, the fairy tale became a powerful political medium. As Lurana O'Malley compellingly argues, "the empress's literary endeavors were more than a distraction; the issues they addressed were central to her political and social philosophy" (2006: xiii).

Catherine's first *skazka* is a particularly good example.[15] The play features Fevei, the son of the Siberian tsar, in search of adventure. It begins with the prince's dream in which a beautiful maiden appears to him as a ballerina on stage. He wakes up fantasizing about his lover and craving to see foreign lands, worrying his royal parents. Although Fevei does not venture very far and remains obedient to his father and mother, his hymn to travel may be seen as a glorification of empire itself. The foreign realm is represented in the play by the visit of the Kalmyk ambassadors who come to ask favors of the tsar. The oriental flavor of their dance and song that repeat a folk motif means to invoke the exotic customs of the Kalmyks and reflects Catherine's overall project to assert Russia's uniqueness through pride in the variegated cultures under her control. The scene with the tsar accepting gifts of the ambassadors and promising peace in return reinforces the concept of imperial power. Over the course of the opera, Fevei exhibits bravery but remains obedient to his father and mother, accepting an arranged marriage with a princess from afar, only to realize as he removes the bridal veil that she is the subject of his dream. By complying with his parents' wishes Fevei thus exemplifies Catherine's idea of the ideal monarch.

Catherine's opera-*skazkas* thus exhibit her agenda to improve the monarchy by training better monarchs and simultaneously to promote the image of the empress as enlightened philosopher and pedagogue (Naroditskaya 2011: 87). Furthermore, in this period so crucial in the development of the ideologies of nation, citizenship, and patriotism, these opera-tales became a manifestation of Russian national culture and collective identities. Remaining in the theatrical repertoire throughout at least the first quarter of the nineteenth century, Catherine's opera-*skazkas* encouraged the publication of similar works and, like Genlis's collection of fairy plays, can be considered an early example of children's theater.

GENDER ROLES AND AN ENLIGHTENED EDUCATION

The mid-century was characterized by the turn to didactic and pedagogical tale, and Jeanne-Marie Leprince de Beaumont (1711–80), famous throughout Europe for her educational writings, may have done more to promote the fairy tale as a genre for all ages and classes than did any other writer. Unlike the seventeenth-century *conteuses* writing for a sophisticated audience who would appreciate the innuendo and ambiguity, Leprince de Beaumont's didactic tales served the purpose of instructing young ladies in manners and morals. In the foreword to her *Magasin des enfants, ou Dialogues d'une sage gouvernante avec ses élèves de la première distinction* (The Young Misses' Magazine, Containing Dialogues Between a Governess and Several Young Ladies of Quality, Her Scholars, 1756), Leprince de Beaumont stressed the urgent motivation for her educational journal, invoking the scarcity of books suitable for children, especially girls. Wanting to make learning a more attractive process, she resorted to fairy-tale narratives as they offered her a perfect camouflage for combining instruction with delight. The tales' action still takes place in fairy kingdoms, but the plots hinge on conduct rather than on adventurous circumstances, and the heroes and heroines allegorize the extremes of character and behavior. Indeed, the numerous tales interpolated in the *Magasin* are only a pretext for the sententious discourse elaborated in the morally weighted dialogues between governess and pupils referred to in the title. Thanks to her fourteen years as a governess in England, Leprince de Beaumont was aware that fairy tales could provide an excellent means to make young women understand "the disadvantages of arranged marriages" and "the misfortunes that can happen from the lack of indulgence for the whims of a husband" ([1756] 2008: 969). It is therefore this concern that induced Leprince de Beaumont to adapt for her *Magasin* the version of "Beauty and the Beast" by Gabrielle-Susanne de Villeneuve that deals with the issues of courtship, marriageability, and sexuality.[16]

Writing for a female audience, Leprince de Beaumont was especially concerned with instructing the pupils about which qualities make women of lower social standing desirable to men of high social position; it is no coincidence that the main plotline focuses on the story of the couple's courtship, an initially unhappy forced union between incompatible mates, followed by a happy resolution through the kiss that transforms the monster into the handsome husband. Given that the tale was designed to acquaint young women with specific notions of gender roles, it allowed Leprince de Beaumont to elucidate how male and female desirability was constructed in the eighteenth century and to problematize the previous paradigms of gender roles.

The story notably presents Beauty as a daughter who loves her father more than her other siblings do and is therefore willing to accept her role as an object in a transaction that allows her father to escape the economic ruin, on the one hand, and the monster to obtain a desired bride, on the other. Leprince de Beaumont thus shows that women's desirability stems from their willingness to give up any attempt to follow their personal desires for a suitor and acknowledge male authority.

Another quality that, according to Leprince de Beaumont, a woman has to possess to get a prospective husband is willingness to be a patient and dutiful daughter and wife. In fact, the merchant emphasizes that Beauty's merit consists not so much in her beauty but rather in patience, the supreme feminine virtue: "He admired the virtues of this young girl—especially her patience" (Zipes 2009: 234). Leprince de Beaumont was thus proposing an educational curriculum capable of producing a woman endowed with psychological depth rather than being merely a physically attractive surface, a woman who would excel in qualities that differentiate her in terms other than her family's wealth and title. By displaying tireless concern for the well-being of others, Leprince de Beaumont's protagonist embodies moral rather than material values or idle sensuality.

So far, all this seems very straightforward and points to the fact that Leprince de Beaumont preached conventional morality. However, already by describing a sex/gender system where women are passive objects of exchange and circulation between men, Leprince de Beaumont effectively even if discreetly denounces the practice of arranged marriages and reveals the uneasiness she felt concerning the oppressed status of her female contemporaries. Clearly, Leprince de Beaumont had no illusions about women's lot in society and could not overtly question a social order in which fathers and husbands possessed wide-ranging powers over women. However, as Jack Zipes and Lewis Seifert have demonstrated, the fairy-tale genre has an enormous subversive potential, and precisely by virtue of its marginality with respect to real life, it confirms itself as being in a privileged position to comment on social practices and gender dynamics.[17] Perfectly aware of the disquieting duplicity of the *conte de fées*, Leprince de Beaumont uses this genre in a way that allows her to take a feminist stance while remaining within the boundaries of the dominant male discourse. Her fairy tale has thus provided the *conteuse* with a means of highlighting the constructedness of desire and sexuality and made it possible for them to indicate a liberating option for their young female readership. By representing the marriage transaction as an economic or moral necessity rather than an emotional imperative, Leprince de Beaumont sustains the illusion of the heroine's autonomy and charts a path for girls to achieve success and self-definition without passing through the obligatory marriage plot.

Leprince de Beaumont's "Beauty and the Beast" is thus remarkably modern in its capacity to explore the performativity of gender identity and can therefore be read not only as a vindication of the rights of women but also as an attempt to renew social and gender relations. Moreover, by writing for children, Leprince de Beaumont opened up an important segment of the population to the literary fairy tale, which, up until the appearance of her works, was essentially an "adults only" genre. That she retained the fairy-tale and folkloric elements to promote exemplary moral behavior helped to establish the literary fairy tale as an accepted pedagogical tool as well as a cultural institution in France. By providing a juvenile audience with reading material suitable to their level of comprehension and adapted to their immediate interests, Leprince de Beaumont's *Magasin* constituted the premises of the emergence of children's literature and adolescent fiction in the nineteenth century.

THE QUEST FOR TRUTH: ORIENTAL AND PHILOSOPHICAL TALES

By the mid-century writers also found in the now well-established but ever-scandalous genre of the oriental tale a space of freedom where their sharp critical sense, polemical tendencies, self-irony, and libertine agendas could address and redress all sorts of issues (see Sermain 2005). The authors perceived the erotic potential of the oriental tale that drew attention to sensual pleasure, exposed the mysteries of the seraglio, and fed the imagination with voluptuous thoughts that would be taboo in a conventional setting. In this sense, the oriental tale that gradually supplanted the *conte de fées* during the course of the century was an avatar of the libertine tale embellished with exotic motifs and settings. Claude-Prosper Joliot de Crébillon (or Crébillon fils, 1707–77), Denis Diderot (1713–84), and Voltaire (1694–1778) spiced up some of their philosophical stories and novels with erotic oriental tableaux. Crébillon's *Le Sopha* (*The Sofa*, 1740), Diderot's *Les Bijoux indiscrets* (*The Indiscreet Jewels*, 1748), and Voltaire's *Le Crocheteur borgne* (*The One-Eyed Porter*, 1774) are among the works that underscore the imagined erotic aspect of Middle Eastern culture and include erotic descriptions in their tales to provide subversive commentary about French society and voice dissent. The sensuality suggested in the oriental tales seemed to appeal to these political and social observers as well as to their readers; its seductive and sometimes humorous quality made it an acceptable and safe medium for satire. Oriental motifs found their way into other literary genres as well, and Montesquieu's (1689–1755) *Lettres persanes* (*Persian Letters*, 1721) is an example *par excellence* of social critique. Jean-Jacques Rousseau (1712–78) wrote a fairy tale, "La Reine fantastique" ("Queen Fantastic," 1754), that ridiculed the monarchy, bourgeois marriage, and women.

All of these kinds of tales were somewhat small essays in philosophical fiction, for beyond an occasional emphasis on the exotic and the marvelous, it is social, religious, and philosophical problems that come to the fore. It is, however, under the pen of Voltaire, unquestionably the master of social and political satire, that the philosophical tale achieved a unique form. This uniqueness may be defined as an episodic narrative structured by frequent changes of scenes resulting from travel, and controlled by a central theme; the problem of evil in *Candide* (*Candide, or Optimism*, 1759); providence in *Zadig* (*Zadig, or Destiny*, 1747); the limits of human knowledge in *Micromégas* (*Micromegas*, 1752); and the link between nature and civilization, as well as the question of toleration in the reign of Louis XIV in *L'Ingénu* (*The Ingenu*, 1767). The educative process that takes place in the *conte philosophique* is one where the Voltairean hero becomes something he was not at the start of his journey, while the main aim of the tale consists in showing how he reaches greater wisdom. The protagonist learns to assess himself and trace the concatenation of his thoughts, and his awareness of this chain of becoming helps him to free his mind of prejudices. Despite the evident ideological content of Voltaire's tales, the reader is drawn into identifying with characters and situations. His fictional universe—created through the grotesque, the absurd, the marvelous, the sentimental—aims at constructing a paradoxical image of civilization and human life, which constantly challenges us to make sense of the fiction.

The form of the fairy tale that encapsulated a general moral truth disintegrates in Voltaire's hands to become a grotesque caricature profoundly at odds with reality, and such a masterpiece as *Candide* is a rich example. The basic facts of the story are well known: Candide is a disciple of Doctor Panglos, who is himself a disciple of Leibnitz and his philosophical optimism. From the outset, however, the protagonist endures a long series of misfortunes that make it impossible for him to continue to believe that ours is "the best of all possible worlds"; each turn of the story further undermines Pangloss's arguments. Through this story Voltaire impresses upon the reader that cosmic optimism is unwarranted and foolish. In the final pages the title character learns to ward off boredom, depravity, and poverty and to find relative contentment through the cultivation of his garden. It thus seems that Voltaire advocates replacing Pangloss's optimism with meliorism, or the claim that the world can be made better. Yet a better world is only a possible and not a necessary outcome. Even this possibility seems to be more an individual affair, and Voltaire gives little indication that a perfect society is within human reach. From his garden Candide can watch boats carting people into exile and others carrying stuffed heads to be presented to the sultan (Voltaire [1759] 2000: 76–7). In the end, *Candide*'s meliorism seems to consist as much in an escape from the world's troubles as in a solution to them.

Unlike the seventeenth-century tales by Perrault, to quote but one example, the characters' formative experience consists not in the avoidance of vice but rather in a hesitant progress toward self-knowledge gained with difficulty (Iotti 2009: 114). The philosophical *contes* are hence designed less to communicate a set of moral truths than to encourage independence of mind. Voltaire uses the veil of fable only on condition that it conceals "some subtle truths." As the title character of *L'Ingenu* remarks: "Ah! s'il nous faut des fables, que ces fables soient du moins l'emblème de la vérité! J'aime les fables des philosophes, je ris de celles des enfants, et je hais celles des imposteurs" ("Ah! if we need fables, at least let these fables be the emblem of truth! I love the fables of the philosophes, I laugh at those of children, and I hate those of impostors").[18]

As Gianni Iotti claims, Voltaire endlessly deforms myths and ancient tales, he tells new stories, ironically using the expression of the past—this reuse of earlier languages is perhaps his most typical stylistic trait. "Voltaire, an admirer of traditional literary forms, appropriates them inappropriately, undermining them with excessive concision" (Iotti 2009: 120–1). But if fairy tales were identified in this period with the supposed ignorance of our great-great-great-grandmothers, the ironical borrowing by the *philosophes* of such models as the oriental and fantastic tales contributed, paradoxically, to the survival of those literary forms (119). Moreover, by presenting these central issues (such as the nature of providence, the problem of evil, the pursuit of happiness) via a medium usually associated with low forms of entertainment, Voltaire makes us see them in a new light.

MORAL TALES, OR FAIRY TALE CONTESTED

In the last quarter of the century authors thus came to see in fairy tales the potential for social commentary on contemporary society, and the *conte moral*, also labeled sentimental tale, became a form of popular expression of enlightened ideas about injustice, female subordination, poverty, and the relationship between citizens and the state. Under the impulse of Marmontel, who brought together into the collection entitled *Contes moraux* (*Moral Tales*, 1755–65) about forty tales previously published on the pages of the influential journal *Mercure de France*, the fairy tale was officially transformed into a moral one. Marmontel's moral tale assimilated the narrative structure of the fairy tale as well as its chronological imprecision, presence of miracles and the hero's trials and tests. They were largely driven by plot and characterized by "obvious patterns of polar opposites so that the reader can be directed more easily towards the points of view the author wishes to put forward" (Astbury 2000: 12). Marmontel's tales were hybrid as they drew on the vogue for *contes de fées* ("Les Quatre Flacons," Four Phials), oriental tales ("Soliman II," Soliman the Second), and libertine tales ("Alcibiade"). Marmontel's *Contes moraux* are to be considered not just as tales with a moral purpose but also as tales that endorse Enlightenment social mores. His tales are *contes de fées* without *fées*, fairy tales without fairies, and precisely due to the disappearance of the fairies, it is virtue that comes to perform the miracles.

Marmontel's "Le Mari Sylphe" ("The Sylph-Husband," 1761) is an emblematic case of the transformation that the fairy *merveilleux* undergoes when transposed into the frame of the *conte moral*. After having left the convent to marry her arranged husband the marquis de Volange, Elisa rejects his advances, finding only in imaginative literature "something to engage, to move, to melt her. The fable of the sylphs was in vogue." In short, Elisa believed in sylphs and "was thoroughly persuaded that, next to a lover, the most dangerous being in nature was a husband" (Marmontel 1821: 365). To heal his wife of such irrational chimeras, the desperate husband, with the help of her confidant, impersonates a sylph every night until Elisa falls in love with the realized "pictures of imagination." In this way she passes from erroneous illusions to practical happiness in real life. Elisa's enchantment with sylphs represents an illusion of vision, a projection of erotic desire, a mistake of inexperience, and an obstacle to virtuous behavior that only the reason of the husband can cure. As Nicolas Veysman (2007) maintains, it is an anti-fairy tale, in which the *féerique* turns against itself to constitute the subject matter of the ironic spectacle in which the reader is invited to smile at the naïve astonishment of the heroine when she discovers that the genies and fairies are not supernatural phenomenon but a state of mind conjured by a skilled illusionist. In Marmontel's ironically constructed but moralizing plots, the irrational is conjured up only to be denied, and the enchantment, characteristic of *contes de fées*, becomes a conventional metaphor.

NOVEL AND SUBVERSION OF THE FAIRY TALE

If marvelous and didacticism could happily coexist within one work, the same was also true for the relationship between fairy tale and the libertine novel. In fact, in the Marquis de Sade's (1740–1814) hands, the fairy tale experienced yet another transformation, which mirrored the social, cultural, and political upheavals of a society in the years leading up to the French Revolution. In Sade's *Justine, ou les Malheurs de la vertu* (Justine, or The Misfortunes of Virtue, 1791) fairy tale becomes a major structuring device that allows one to make observations about the mores, institutions, and philosophies identified with the tumultuous final years of the Enlightenment.

In Sade's violent pornographic novel named after its main character, the virtuous and virginal Justine is reduced to poverty following the death of her father. Despite her attempts to be good and retain her virginity, she suffers repeated rape, brutal torture, humiliation, and degradation, forever escaping from one abuser only to fall into the hand of another. Over the course of the novel, it never occurs to Justine that she can easily break out from the endless cycle of capture, imprisonment, and being framed for crimes of which she is innocent by adopting the characteristics of her torturers: ruthlessness and *libertinage*. Her inability to follow the amoral rules and her acquiescence to the sexual barbarity inflicted upon her ultimately reveal the traditional submissive role of women. Although Sade entertains his readers with passages filled with fantasy and descriptions of extreme libertine pleasures, his novel shows structural affinities with Perrault's *contes* and moral tales rather than with the oriental and libertine ones. Indeed, Sade seems to take the very storyline of innocent, weak virtue attacked by unscrupulous villainy from Perrault. The threats (explicitly sexual in nature) to the helpless victims, always young women, actualized in Sade, are already present in Perrault's *contes*: murder ("Bluebeard," "Sleeping Beauty"), cannibalism ("Little Tom Thumb"), incest ("Donkey Skin," "Griselda"), and rape ("Little Red Riding Hood"). But Sade is also playing on the tradition of sentimental tales when he sets the worst atrocities in the innocent countryside, isolated castles, or remote locations supposedly far from the corruption of the city.

In the same way that *Justine*'s narrative structure resembles that of Perrault's and moral tales, so the character descriptions also draw extensively on the fairy-tale models laid out previously. As a number of critics have noted, Perrault's influence is evident especially in Sade's depiction of women that is similar to the portrayal of Perrault's fairy-tale heroines.[19] Justine may not live "happily ever after" with her Prince Charming, but in other respects she closely typifies the Perraldian heroine, whose very survival depends upon her conforming to the tacit expectations set forth by a patriarchal society.

For Perrault women are victims and long-suffering martyrs; for Sade, too, women are particularly interesting when they are in distress. In *Justine*, the heroine has turned into a victim and her qualities serve only to make her sufferings more piquant. The works of both authors are concerned with sexual initiation: in Perrault's tales, the heroine must be uncorrupted to be worthy of the honors and the marriage that awaits her; in Sade's oeuvre she must be uncorrupted to produce greater scandal when she is either corrupted or destroyed despite her innocence.

The lesson implied by Sade is the antithesis of that implied by Perrault's tales and their *moralités*. In Perrault, the ogres are outwitted, virtue is rewarded, and passive characters, such as Cinderella, are saved too. In Sade's world, the reverse happens: physically and spiritually beautiful women can expect only rape, torture, and murder. No one comes to save the victim at the last moment, and marriage does not lead to living happily ever after. Justine's persistent adherence to virtue goes unrewarded, which implies that the dichotomy of good and bad, right and wrong was too simplistic for Sade, and the belief in reward for those who have suffered went against his atheism. By reversing conventions, Sade aims to cloud the moral issues almost always presented in black and white in the moral tale. Since for Sade sex is an expression of society being built on force, he uses the fairy-tale format as a means of entertainment disguising social criticism. In fact, the British feminist novelist and short-story writer Angela Carter sees Sade as a political writer and a "moral pornographer" who puts pornography into the service of women, or at least creates an ideology not inimical to women ([1978] 1993: 19). In this regard, Sade's purpose was no different that of the female fairy-tale writers of the first and second vogues and anticipates the fairy-tale revisions of Carter.

Sade, however, did not believe in many of the ideas behind the *conte de fées* and sentimental tales of the *ancien régime*, but rather than openly denounce them, he chose to undermine them from within. By publishing his *Justine*, along with his other libertine tales, such as the collection *Les Crimes de l'amour* (The Crimes of Love, 1800), Sade reworked and reversed the fairy-tale tradition established in the years leading up to the French Revolution.[20]

ONE-HUNDRED YEAR VOGUE: A CONCLUSION

Seen through the examples in this chapter, necessarily inexhaustive, it would be possible to conclude that the proliferation of the forms of marvelous in the eighteenth century was intimately related to the tastes and contradictions of the Enlightenment, the period that was dominated by mistrust of the irrational and by abandonment of the world of illusions, but also known for its interest in the obscure side of perception and a hyper-skeptical frame of mind. The Enlightenment's retellings and adaptations of fairy tales were thus an interweaving of reason and unreason, irony and enchantment, which have long haunted European literature. On the one hand, these retellings were characterized by a general trend to reduce the marvelous dimension in favor of the intrigue that privileged sentimental, philosophical, and moral issues, the realism in terms of plot, as well as the move toward greater political and social commentary.[21] On the other hand, the marvelous, fantastic, and phantasmagoric elements in eighteenth-century literary and dramatic works manifested themselves as a narrative strategy, as an *escamotage*, a constant concealment of a thought that is impossible or difficult to tell otherwise in a society based on a rigid control of behavioral codes. The many forms that fairy tales took in this century show that it was a genre that expressed, exacerbated, and elaborated upon the series of crises, in literature, theater, politics, religion, and history that characterized the Enlightenment. These adaptations, rewritings, reappropriations of marvelous material themselves can be considered as an experiment with the limits of what can be thought, written, narrated, or performed on stage.

The historical trajectory of the marvelous through the eighteenth century could be defined as a parabola: from being scorned and dismissed as a minor and insignificant genre to having become a form of a transnational success that allowed authors to introduce innovations and developments both in literature and theater venues, then ending up being reversed and undermined at the hands of *philosophes*, moralists, and libertine writers. Paradoxically, however, it is these grotesque, parodic, and satiric reworkings of the wonder and fairy tales contributed to the legitimation and popularity of the marvelous. Ultimately, therefore, the extraordinary variety of the forms the marvelous took in the eighteenth century and the multifaced transformations it underwent allow us to define the eighteenth century as the golden age of the marvelous.

CHAPTER TWO

Adaptation

From Italy and France to Folk Traditions

CHARLOTTE TRINQUET DU LYS

The French term for fairy tale, *conte de fées*, was born from a typo, inserted in the title page of the first collection of tales by Madame de Murat (Henriette-Julie de Castelnau, Countess of Murat), dedicated in 1698 to Marie-Anne de Bourbon, Princess Dowager of Conti.[1] It is, however, Madame d'Aulnoy (Marie-Catherine Desjardins, Countess of Aulnoy) who first coined the expression *contes des fées* (tales of the fairies), and the term fairy tales was yet to be established as the name of the genre. Some other expressions used by the women tellers at the time were: *conte tiré des fées* (tales coming from the fairies), as well as *Nouvelles* (novellas), *Histoires* (stories), and so on. Murat's first volume is one of eighteen collections of similar stories written between 1690 and 1705, with a total of seventy-five tales, by eleven literary personalities issuing from elite circles of French high society. Although the literary fairy-tale genre became solidified in France in the 1690s, preparing the way for the later trends of the oriental, philosophical, and licentious tales, its development is due in large part to the adaptation of Italian tales written by Giovanni Francesco Straparola and Giambattista Basile. About half of the French corpus can be linked to theirs, whether it is the adaptation of one fairy tale from one or both Italian authors, or an adaptation of several tales to make a new one. Indeed, the fairy tale in the long eighteenth century is indebted to adaptations of Italian tales in the 1690s and later of Arabic, Turkish, and Persian tales, launched by Antoine Galland's translation and adaptation of *The Thousand and One Nights* from 1704 to 1717.

To account for the history of adaptation in the long eighteenth century, this chapter is divided into three distinct sections. First, I provide an overview of the history of tale adaptations in France in the long eighteenth century. Second, I explore the history of the specific adaptation of the genre from the Italian to the French texts, from the 1550s to the 1690s, tracing possible pathways that made these adaptations possible. Finally, I illustrate the way in which these adaptations have created the modern landscape of literary and folk fairy tales through a case study of the adaptation of tale type "The Kind and Unkind Girls" (ATU 480) and that of "The White Bride and the Black Bride" (ATU 403).[2] Importantly, in the eighteenth and nineteenth centuries in Britain and the German states, French tales will serve as the point of departure for further developments in the adaptation of the fairy-tale genre.

OVERVIEW OF THE HISTORY OF ADAPTATION: A FRENCH PERSPECTIVE

The year 1690 marks the date of the first publication of a French fairy tale, inserted in a short novel by d'Aulnoy: *History of Hypolite, Count of Duglas*, "L'Ile de la Félicité" ("The Island of Felicity"), narrated by the title character Hypolite. According to the embedded narrator, this is "un conte approchant ceux des fées" ("a tale approaching those of the Fairies") that recounts the adventures of the mythological Prince Adolf of Russia, who finds himself on the island of fairy princess Felicity. Then, between 1691 and 1696, d'Aulnoy, Charles Perrault, Marie-Jeanne L'Héritier de Villandon, and Catherine Bernard published a total of eight stories that correspond in structure, subject, and style to this emerging literary genre. The years 1697 and 1698 are the years containing the largest fairy-tale publications, totaling fifty tales, four-fifths of the entire publication of the last decade of the seventeenth century. These fairy tales were penned by Perrault, d'Aulnoy, Charlotte Rose de Caumont de La Force, Murat, Louis de Mailly, François Nodot, and Jean de Préchac. After 1699, the vogue had already begun to fade. Murat, Catherine Durand, Nodot, and Eustache Le Noble published eight more tales by 1700, and L'Héritier published her last tale, "Ricdin-Ricdon" (an early version of "Rumpelstiltskin"), in 1705. In the first fifteen years of the 1700s, Louise de Bossigny, Countess d'Auneuil, Durand, and François de Salignac de La Mothe-Fénelon produced another twenty stories in the same style but were soon surpassed by the translation and adaptation of an Arabic manuscript, *Les Mille et une nuits* (*The Thousand and One Nights*, 1704–17) by Antoine Galland, which launched the eighteenth-century vogue of the oriental tale.

The model for the first vogue narratives had already existed since the 1550s in Italian baroque court literature. To create their corpus, the French storytellers certainly had knowledge of the collections of Giovanni Francesco Straparola

(1480–1557) and Giambattista Basile (1566–1632) and were inspired by their stories to the point that some of their adaptations—often taken by editors and critics as the "original" version or as an adaptation from oral tradition—closely resemble their Italian models who themselves were influenced by earlier narrative traditions, as we will see in the next two sections.

The women writing fairy tales after 1715 are more numerous than their 1690s counterparts, but their publications are few and far between, seldom reprinted, and have been forgotten because many were not reproduced in the forty-one volume *Le Cabinet des fées* (1785–9), edited by Charles-Joseph Mayer, which included the majority of the tales published since 1690 and served as a fairy-tale canon in the period. During the period 1715–75, Louise Cavalier Levesque, Madeleine-Angélique de Gomez, Elisabeth Dreuillet, Françoise Le Marchand, Catherine de Lintot, Julie de Guenani, Marquise de Lassay, and Marianne Agnès Falques all wrote sixteen fairy tales that adapted the fairy-tale structure of the first vogue and are serious in content. Marguerite de Lussan's *Les veillées de Thessalie* (The Nights of Thessalie, 1731–41), a volume framed and comprised of eight evenings, was more successful and reprinted six times in the eighteenth century; it constitutes volumes twenty-six and twenty-seven of the *Le Cabinet des fées* and thus represents the only canonized work among this group of writers. Based on mythological motifs, the pastoral novel,[3] and fairy tales, the stories focus on love and magic, and are all first-person narration. Lussan's work was so appreciated by her contemporaries that Jacques Autreau adapted the *Veillées* into a play in 1734 for the Théâtre-Français, entitled *La magie de l'amour* (The Magic of Love).

Gabrielle-Suzanne de Villeneuve, who wrote two collections of fairy tales, *La jeune Américaine ou les contes marins* (The Young American Girl and the Tales Told at Sea, 1740) and *Les Belles solitaires* (The Beautiful Solitaires, 1745), received more recognition than her fellow women writers of the post-1715 generation. Even though Jeanne-Marie Leprince de Beaumont never mentioned the source for her now canonical version of "Beauty and the Beast," it was with Villeneuve's "La Belle et la Bête" ("Beauty and the Beast") in mind that she wrote her own adaptation of the story, which she included in her *Magasin des enfans* (The Children's Magazine, 1756). However, while Villeneuve's stories still draw on the style of seventeenth-century aristocratic fairy tales with subplots or intercalated stories, and had an intended audience of adults, Leprince de Beaumont's collection of fourteen moralistic fairy tales are adapted for children and adolescents, and promote, with a plot reduced to an almost archetypal simplicity, the proper behavior of young girls in eighteenth-century French and British high societies. Significantly, the *Magasin des enfans* represents one of the earliest texts in the history of fairy tales written expressly for children. Leprince de Beaumont's fairy tales are among the few penned by a woman remembered by posterity.[4]

It would not be a reach to say that women storytellers in the eighteenth century suffered from the immense success of Antoine Galland's *Les Mille et une nuits* (*The Thousand and One Nights*), which led to the shift in popularity from the fairy tale to the oriental tale, and from a predominantly female authorship to a male one. Adapted from a fifteenth-century Syrian manuscript he never provided but that was probably known by some contemporaries, Galland introduced the *Nights* to European readers as a compilation of stories. He grouped stories already known in European literature (adapted by Giovanni Boccaccio, Geoffrey Chaucer, Giovanni Sercambi, and others) with the stories told by Scheherazade, and the stories of "Sindbâd the Sailor," which were part of a different manuscript. Finally, he adapted the short stories told by Hanna Diyab into significantly longer tales, much in the style of the women fairy-tale writers of the 1690s before him. His own recension, though closer to the original text than some later adaptations, has been criticized by contemporary French scholars and acclaimed by French Arabists (Grotzfeld 2004: 226), because of his combination of stories coming from different sources and his textual rendering for the French eighteenth-century audience.

With the success of Galland's adaptation of Arabic tales, François Pétis de la Croix translated from an incomplete Turkish manuscript the fictional tales of the *Histoire de la sultane de Perse et des vizirs* (*The Story of the Sultana of Persia and the Viziers*, 1707) and several Arabic religious, administrative, and legal texts, to ostensibly render his adaptation more authentic. Three years later Pétis began translating and adapting, probably from another Turkish manuscript, *Les Mille et un jours* (*The Thousand and One Days*, 1710–12), adjusting the original title, which is closer to *Relief After Hardship,* to capitalize from the familiarity of the French public with *The Thousand and One Nights*.

The success of Galland and Pétis de la Croix's adaptations transformed the French literary field, launching the fashion of the oriental tale and inspiring countless authors in the 1700s. While Galland and Petis's texts remain close to original to some extent, the tales in Abbé Jean-Paul Bignon's *Aventures d'Abdalla* (*The Adventures of Abdalla*, 1712–14), for instance, are completely invented by the author, with a variable degree of authenticity: he goes from dressing Western tales with an oriental flavor to creating original adventures that resemble the more authentic tales of Galland and Pétis. Nonetheless, Bignon shows his great knowledge of oriental cultures in his ability to adapt their elements into his corpus. From 1715 onward, authors chose one of these two models proposed by Bignon for their production, until the first vogue and the oriental tale were adapted by the writers of satirico-parodic tales in the 1730s and licentious tales in the mid-1730s, following the success of Antoine Hamilton's "Le Bélier" ("The Ram," 1730; see Hamilton et al. 2008) and Claude Proper Jolyot de Crébillon's *L'Ecumoire, ou Tanzaï et Néadarné* (*The Skimmer: Or the History of Tanzai and Neadarne*, 1734). Authors such as Jacques Cazotte with his *Mille et une fadaises: Contes à dormir debout* (A Thousand and one Twaddles, Tales for Sleeping Standing, 1742), a series of soporific tales told by an abbot, adapt Hamilton's parodic techniques who deconstructed the genre by reversing the roles of the protagonists from Galland's frame story and adding paratexts in the margins to disorganize its narrative coherence (Perrin 2008: 10–13). The licentious tale, a subcategory of the parodic tale, exemplified by "Tanzaï et Néadarné," reverses the so-called naivety and morality of the first vogue of fairy tales into transparently veiled erotic scenes of human desire. Crébillon is one of the key authors in literary fairy tales of the 1700s, not only because of his popularity as a writer but also for the fact that he is at the origin of the crossroads between the traditional and the Orientalizing tales, which constitute the essential ingredients for the creation of the licentious tale (Crébillon 2009: 12). His role in the fairy-tale genre was recognized immediately by his peers and although he follows the road opened by Hamilton, according to Regime Jomand-Baudry he brought libertinage to the genre, contaminated his tales with all possible literary genres in vogue at the time, and integrated within his tales a dialogue with his contemporaries about the genre itself, societal advances, and philosophical thoughts (14, 17–18, 24). One of his most renowned tales, *Le Sofa, conte moral (The Sofa, a Moral Tale,* 1742) was immediately translated by Eliza Haywood and William Hatchett (*The Sofa,* 1743), even though it was banned in France for its immorality and the characters' resemblance to famous contemporaries, including Louis XV. The vogue of licentious tales, although extremely popular and widely read, was never reprinted in the *Le Cabinet des fées* because of the tales' depravity and was mostly adapted into fantastic and decadent tales in the following century in France by authors such Theophile Gautier and Prosper Mérimée but also abroad, with E. T. A. Hoffmann's work drawing from tales by Hamilton and Cazotte. Additionally, tales such as Leprince de Beaumont's "Beauty and the Beast" gave space for didactic tellers to develop their publications of moralistic fairy tales aimed at children, as they did proliferate in the nineteenth century all over Europe. Writers, for instance Sarah Fielding (England) and Benedikte Naubert (Germany), adapted aspects of d'Aulnoy's tales, and the Grimms adapted for their own public many of the first vogue of fairy tales, including Perrault's "Little Red Riding Hood," "Cinderella," "Sleeping Beauty," "The Fairies," and La Force's "Persinette" ("Rapunzel").

ADAPTATION OF THE ITALIAN TALE AND CREATION OF THE FRENCH LITERARY TALE: 1550s–1690s

With this broad overview of tale adaptations in the long eighteenth century in France, we will turn to closely examining the particular example of French adaptations of Italian tales. The influence of Italy in France, from the

Renaissance to the middle of the seventeenth century, was so great that it profoundly altered French high culture, offering new perspectives in the arts, sciences, architecture, literature, music, theater, and court etiquette, among other cultural practices. If the influence of Italy declined during the second half of the century, Italian novelists such as Torquato Tasso, Ariosto, and Boccaccio were far from forgotten. Italian cities still maintained considerable intellectual interest compared to other cities in Europe thanks to their many courts and academies. In the case of fairy tales, the two Italian authors who influenced the French storytellers, Straparola and Basile, shared similar social backgrounds and wrote for similar audiences, which might explain why they appealed to our French fairy-tale writers. Of the seventy-five stories published between 1690 and 1700 in France, thirty-eight of them—half of the corpus—have been considered by scholars to be of folk origin. In fact, of the thirty-eight French tales corresponding to a folkloric tale-type (that is, corresponding to a category within the ATU classification system), thirty of them drew from Straparola or Basile or both and were sometimes purely adapted, and sometimes combined with other tale types and material by the authors of the French corpus.

Marga Cottino-Jones traces Straparola's sources for his *Piacevoli Notti* (*Facetious Nights*, Venice, 1550–53) to medieval texts such as Sercambi's *Novellino* (*Little Novella*, 1390–1402), and Girolamo Morlini's Latin *Fabulae* and *Novellae* (*Fables* and *Novellas*, [1520] 1855), whose first edition (in Naples) seems to have been published in 1520 (Cottino-Jones 2000: 173). Very quickly *Facetious Nights*, a collection of seventy-five novellas including fifteen fairy tales, became known in France through a Lyonnais publisher, Guillaume Rouille (or Rovillé), who had been apprenticed to the Venetian printer Giolito. Ian Louueau (or Jean Louveau) freely translated the first part of the book under the title *Les facetieuses Nuictz du Sieur Iean François Straparole* (*The Facetious Nights of Lord Giovanni Francesco Straparola*), printed in Lyon in 1560. This version includes the twenty-five stories of the first five nights. The edition was reproduced in 1572 by Benoist Rigaud, another Lyonnais printer, this time as a pocket-size volume. In 1573, the two parts were combined in France by Pierre de Larivey, who translated the second part (nights six to thirteen), corrected the translation of Louveau, and added some sonnets and songs. This edition was reprinted twelve times until 1615, and not sixteen times as Murat claims in her *Histoires sublimes et allegoriques* (*Sublime and Allegorical Stories*), published in 1698. After 1615, there is no longer any trace of reprints, which corresponds to the fact that the volume had been censored and put on the index by the Inquisition for obscenity (decree of September 16, 1605).[5]

The 1570s French edition of *Facetious Nights* begins with Larivey's dedication to François Rogier, King Charles IX's adviser, treasurer, secretary, and controller of wars. As the storytellers would repeat in the following century, it was with the intent to entertain the scholarly minds at court that the author published them: "pour sa naïve recreation, j'avoye ja, dès l'an passé faict traduire d'italien en françois ... Ce petit present donc trouvera, s'il vous plaist, faveur en vostre presence, asseuré que vostre esprit y prendra fruict de quelque recreation aggreable" ("for its naïve recreation, I already had it translated last year from Italian to French ... this little present will find, therefore, if you please, favor in your presence, sure that your intellect will be appeased in this fun entertainment," Straparola [1573] 1857: 1–3; my translation). These ideas of entertainment and diversion will serve as the framework of the 1690s fairy-tale publications.

The frame story of Straparola's *Facetious Nights* fits perfectly with the sixteenth and seventeenth centuries' novelistic tradition of both France and Italy, all of which was modeled on Boccacio's *Decameron* (1353) in which real and fictive characters relate stories to each other. Other collections of novellas in this tradition include Marguerite de Navarre's *Heptaméron* (1558) and Jean de Segrais and Anne Marie Louise de Montpensier's *Nouvelles Françaises* (*French Novellas*, [1656] 1990), and in the 1690s, collections of fairy tales by d'Aulnoy and others. Raymonde Robert observes that the frame stories of the *Decameron* and *Heptaméron* depict a small group of people in danger telling stories to maintain their morale (1982: 330). However, the group's situation is slightly different from Straparola's *Facetious Nights* collection, which is closer to that of the later *Nouvelles Françaises*. In both cases, it is for the sake of entertainment and not for distracting from danger that the stories are recited. The danger faced by the characters from the frame narrative of the *Decameron* and *Heptaméron* is replaced by a situation of exile in the *Facetious Nights* and *Nouvelles Françaises*. Because of this exile, entertainment is necessitated by the care of the hostesses to recreate a new court that is as pleasant as the one they left. The French storytellers adapt this tradition for their frame narratives, since many of the women tellers, for instance Murat and La Force, were effectively writing in exile after being sent away from court by Louis XIV for various reasons. In *Le Gage touché, histoires galantes et comiques* (*The Wager Paid, Galant and Comic Stories*, 1700), Eustache Le Noble also adapts Straparola's way of introducing the tellers: they will be chosen by a draw.

Over the course of the thirteen nights of *Facetious Nights*, a small community of intellectual women and their hostess, Lucrèce, tell some seventy-five *favole* (novellas), fifteen of which are fairy tales. Ruth Bottigheimer divides these stories into three categories of *märchen*, or tales: non-magical folk tales; restoration tales that incorporate elements of magic; and rise tales (or elevation tales), in which magic is indispensable to narrative resolution (2002a: 2). The most typical case of a restoration tale found in the collection of Straparola is that of "Peau d'Âne" ("Donkey Skin," night 1, fable 4), where a princess loses her noble status at the beginning of the story to recover it at the end, which also occurs in Perrault's adaptation of the tale in 1694. For the elevation tales, the most emblematic example is that of the protagonist of the tale type "The Cat as Helper," for which two versions were written—Straparola's "Constantine" (11-1) and Basile's "Caglusio" (day 2, fable 4)—before Perrault's well-known adaptation of their versions, "Le Chat Botté" ("Puss in Boots"), appeared. According to Bottigheimer, Straparola invented the basic plot of the elevation tales; their structure groups all the indispensable elements to make it a rags-to-riches narrative: poverty, tasks, tests, trials, magic, royal marriages, and finally wealth. Examples of restoration tales already existed in medieval romances, but Straparola simplified their structure to create a new model of fairy tale. Most women writers of the 1690s adapted the model of the restoration tale or transformed the elevation tales into restoration ones. For instance, La Force, Murat, and d'Aulnoy never use a character that is not noble at birth and change systematically all of the non-noble characters from the *Facetious Nights* into either magical characters or kings, queens, and their offspring. Perrault mostly adapts the elevation tales as they are in Straparola, without changing the social class of the protagonists. He also adapts two restoration tales, "Donkey Skin" from Straparola and "Sleeping Beauty" from Basile.

Almost all the tales found in *Facetious Nights* were adapted by the storytellers of the late seventeenth century, except for two tales of elevation (Straparola 5-2 and 10-3), as observed Bottigheimer (2005: 25). "The Doll That Bites" (Straparola 5-2), concerning a doll that defecates silver and gold when in the hands of its rightful owners but defecates plain old excrement in the hands of its kidnappers, can be found in nineteenth-century French folklore adaptations, especially in Provence, the West Indies, and Haiti. However, French folklorist Paul Delarue notes that a mention of the tale is made in the correspondence of the Princess Palatine, sister-in-law of Louis XIV, under the title of "Kacka mamma" (Delarue and Tenèze [1953] 1997: 480), proving that this tale was circulating in the courtly milieu of the end of the seventeenth century, if not in writing, at least orally.

It should be noted that many motifs used by Straparola are found later in the 1690s tales and in nineteenth-century folklore. For example, some tales found in the *Facetious Nights* use certain marks of recognition for their characters, the most notorious being the stars on the forehead of Clarette's and Lancelot's children (4-3), adapted by d'Aulnoy in her "Princesse Belle-Etoile et le Prince Chéri" ("Princess Beautiful Star and Prince Chéri"). Other specific motifs used by Straparola are redeployed by French tale-tellers, such as the gift of gems that fall from the heroine's hair when combed (3-3 and 4-3), which both Perrault and L'Héritier adapt in their respective tales, "Les Fées" ("The Fairies") and "Les enchantements de l'éloquence ou les effets de la douceur" ("The Enchantements of Eloquence or the Effects of Gentleness"). As for apples, which play an important role in the plot (2-1, 3-4, 4-3), we find its most notorious adaptation in the Grimms' "Snow White."

While it is recognized that Straparola's tales indeed served as inspiration for the 1690s storytellers, the case of Basile's influence has been less documented and even put into question. Contrary to Straparola, Basile was never mentioned as a source by the 1690s tellers. Fortunately, we now know a lot about him, thanks to the work carried out by Benedetto Croce at the end of the nineteenth century, and more recently by Nancy Canepa, Suzanne Magnanini, and other contemporary scholars (see Canepa 1999, 2003; Maganini 2007a). *Lo cunto de li cunti* (*The Tale of Tales*) is a posthumous work published by Basile's sister from 1634 to 1636, the first part of which (day 1) is dedicated to Basile's last patron. It is composed of forty-nine tales framed by a fiftieth, recited over the course of five days, at the rate of ten stories a day, nine for the last day. Unlike Straparola's *Facetious Nights*, which contains only fifteen fairy tales among novellas and other types of texts, each of Basile's stories has a didactic proverb, and most of them are set within a marvelous world, which places Basile in the history of literature as the first author to have produced a full-fledged collection of fairy tales. In contrast to the *Facetious Nights*, very early translated into French, *The Tale of Tales* remained in vernacular Neapolitan until 1742. Between 1636 and 1697, it was reprinted six or seven times. The edition of 1674 is the most interesting because it was printed by a Frenchman, Antoine Bulifon, recently established in Naples, who, according to Croce, saw that the book was in constant demand (see Basile 1932: lxi). This edition became standard, and the reprints of Rome in 1679 and Naples in 1697, as well as the seven that followed in the eighteenth and nineteenth centuries, were based on it (Basile 1932: 186–7). In 1683, in Naples, the *Pentamerone* was, in the words of Liodardo Nicodemo, "[a] most gallant and most pleasant of books, which is in the hands of everyone" (quoted in Basile 1932: lxii).[6]

During the thirty years of his career, Bulifon forged an important network of relations with literary newspapers, other French and Italian printers in Naples and in other European cities, notably in Parma, Leipzig, Amsterdam, Lyon, and Troyes. Along with the Kingdom of Sicily, Naples was under Spanish rule, which brought it closer than any other Italian city to the great royal courts of Europe. The Neapolitan academies grouped the noble intellectuals of both countries, favoring the passage of ideas and cultural developments between Italy and Spain. It should be noted that d'Aulnoy's mother served as a spy at the Court of Spain in the 1660s and 1670s and that d'Aulnoy visited her around 1678–9, at which time Basile's collection was reprinted twice. Magnanini demonstrates that in November 1683, a copy of Nicodemo's *Addizioni copiose* (*Copious Additions*), mentioning *The Tale of Tales*, was sent to the Parisian Benedictine monk Jean Mabillon, via his friend and Bulifon's correspondent in Florence, Antonio Magliabechi. The latter owned *The Tale of Tales* since 1682, which he obtained from Bulifon. Mabillon, who lived in the monastery of Saint-Germain-des-Prés, specialized in the study of medieval texts. Financed by Louis XIV's minister Jean-Baptiste Colbert, his official mission in Italy was to buy books and manuscripts for the French royal library in Turin, Milan, Rome, Venice, Florence, and Naples, including 432 from Bulifon himself. Indeed, on October 20, 1685, Mabillon was received in Naples by the French bookseller and also met Nicodemo via Magliabechi (Magnanini 2007b: 86). If we do not have the list of the books brought back to France by Mabillon, Magnanini sees a very strong possibility that Bulifon advised him about *The Tale of Tales*, since it was so popular in Naples (87).

The stories of *The Tale of Tales* were only adapted by Perrault, L'Héritier, and d'Aulnoy, who wrote in Paris, except for the exceptional case of La Force's "Persinette," which was written in exile. Magnanini identifies several ways through which *The Tale of Tales* could have arrived into the French tellers' hands. It could have traveled from the royal library to that of the French Academy of which Perrault was a member, since many books were given by the king to the library of the Academy. It could also have passed from the abbey of Saint-Germain-des-Prés during one of the meetings with men of letters that Mabillon gathered around him, like Bossuet, whom Perrault frequented at the French Academy. Bossuet would have even visited Bulifon's bookshop in 1697. Finally, Bulifon himself could have brought it when he came to France to promote his catalog (2007b: 87–8).

Basile's *The Tale of Tales* provides two elements that are not present in Straparola's tales and that are important to the constitution of the French fairy-tale tradition. First, the tales all end with a rhyming proverb, which anticipates the moral of the story found at the conclusion of the French tales.[7] In 1696, L'Héritier, in her dedication to the tale "The Enchantements of Eloquence," explains that the reason these sorts of tales are written is to prove a maxim or a morality (1696: 302). All seventeenth-century fairy tales end with a morality, which takes the form of a rhymed poem or proverb.

The second element not found in Straparola is the association of the stories with tales of nurses. In Basile, a fictional motley of old women recount tales at the request of Prince Tadeo to satisfy the cravings of his false wife.[8] Canepa shows that Basile's female storytellers repeatedly refer to their stories as tales their grandmothers told them (see Canepa 2003: 38; Basile 1932: night 1, tale 9; night 2, tale 1). Perrault links the source of his tales to the folk nurses reciting orally to children, exemplified in the frontispiece of the 1695 edition of his tales. L'Héritier adapts this tradition by referring to the tales told to her as a child by literary personalities, transforming the context of popular oral telling into the one of literary salons, where literary texts were recited before an intellectual and elite audience. For instance, in the preface preceding her tale "The Enchantements of Eloquence," dedicated to the duchess of Epernon, a literary figure herself, L'Héritier states: "Une dame, très instruite des antiquitez Grecques & Romaines, & encore plus savante dans les antiquitez Gauloises, m'a fait ce conte quand j'étais enfant" ("A lady, very knowledgeable about Greek and Roman antiquities, and even more learned about the French ones, told me this tale when I was a child," 1696: 180). In doing so, she not only transfers the tale telling from the Italian urban streets to literary salons, but also from popular tellers and audiences to sophisticated and literary salon and court aficionados. Adapting herself to this same tradition, Murat will speak about old fairies, referring to popular tellers, favoring the modern fairies, referring to her fellow women tellers.

The stories in *The Tale of Tales* often start with the scene of the gifts bestowed by the fairies, and almost always end with one or more weddings, structurally anticipating the 1690s tales. They are the length of those of Perrault and present the characters in a black-and-white way that resembles those penned by the French storyteller. The general style of *The Tale of Tales* is very similar to that of d'Aulnoy and especially Perrault, if we remove all the vernacular Italian vocabulary that would have shocked French decorum, which at the time prohibited vulgarities and obscenities. As an example, when Perrault adapts Basile's version of "Sleeping Beauty," entitled "Sole, Luna e Talia" ("Sun, Moon, and Talia"), in which the hero copulates with the sleeping, unconscious princess, Perrault removes this rape scene and replaces it with a quick "wedding," which, without challenging norms of decorum, acknowledges for his audience that they are permitted to have sex (and notably the princess is awake). Over the course of two years Sleeping Beauty has two children, similar to Basile's tale.[9] Basile often repeats adjectives, diminutives, and uses words coming from a lower social register, which gives the tale a popular, childish, or comical effect or tone. Even though d'Aulnoy's fairy tales are longer and the plots are more developed, she often imitates the childish or popular tone and some of the plays on words used by Basile, while avoiding all vulgarities and using a higher social register. For example, one finds expressions such as *corona topesca* (mousy crown, "La pietra del gallo" day 6, tale 1) that, untranslatable in French because of the adjectivization of the substantive "rat," does not fail to remind us of d'Aulnoy's *Miolarde Majesté* (Meowing Majesty) of "La chatte blanche" ("The White Cat"). Both Perrault and d'Aulnoy often repeat their adjectives as Basile did before them, giving their text the naivety that often confused the critics about the intended audience of the tales, and made them conclude that they wrote for children. Like Basile, who wrote for an audience of highly educated literary men, the Parisian tellers intended to amuse their sophisticated adult audience.

There are also important differences that mark the evolution of style between the Italian and French stories. For instance, in Straparola and Basile, we find religious references not found in the French texts. They often include imagery that opposes Christians and Turks, so that, for example, ogres do not eat *fresh flesh* as in Perrault's tales, but rather *Christian meat*. With Basile, stories are always presented as having happened to someone real, and the realms and itineraries of travelers are often given according to a geographical reality, which puts his stories in the tradition of the novella, a genre grounded in the real. In the French tales, on the other hand, geography belongs to the fantastic realm, and the kingdoms are, if not completely fictitious, allegorized. French tellers had to compose their tales under the heavy censorship that Louis XIV had in place, and even if the tales are evocative of the period in which they were created, they remain under the veil of the marvelous. However, they don't lack criticism of the period, and in that sense, they reproduce what Basile was doing himself in his tales. They all were acute critics of the time in which they were writing, and satirized the political power under which they were living. These differences, more than the similarities, probably contributed the most to the innovations the French writers made of the Italian tales to create what today we would recognize as a fairy tale. Indeed, even though the universe of the French tales is sometimes evocative of Louis XIV's Court, the geography is set in a universe that revolves around the tales and defines them as their own microcosm, allowing their authors, and especially Perrault, to render them generic. The *once-upon-a-time* kingdom of the French tales becomes a collective formula that can be taken up by any culture at any time, since, reduced to its basic structure, as was done with the adaptation of the literary tales in chapbooks in France, it is not grounded in a specific cultural, historical, or geographical context.

At least eighteen tales found in the French corpus of the 1690s can be traced back to Basile's *The Tales of Tales*. Except for La Force's "Persinette," an adaptation of Basile's "Petrosinella" (a Rapunzel-like tale), all were adapted by three storytellers: Charles Perrault, his niece L'Héritier, and d'Aulnoy. In the case of L'Héritier, it is quite easy to trace the source of her tales, since she wrote so little. "The Enchantments of Eloquence" comes from "Le doie pizzelle" ("The Two Cakes," day 4, tale 7); "L'adroite princesse, ou les aventures de Finette" ("The Adroit Princess, or the Adventures of Finette") is based on "Sapia Liccarda" ("Wise Liccarda," 3-4). "Ricdin-Ricdon," a version of "Rumpelstiltskin," owes its beginning (before falling into an allegory probably related to literary quarrels) to "Le sette cotennuzze" ("The Seven Doves," 4-4). In the case of her maiden warrior tale "Marmoisan," it is inspired by Straparola's "Costanzo-Costanza" (11-1) but draws on elements from Basile's tales to stretch her story, such as "La Serva d'Aglie" ("The Garlic Patch," 3-6) for which L'Héritier adapts the scene of the heroine's missed recognition.

Perrault and d'Aulnoy's rewriting strategies are often more complex. In their adaptations of Straparola and Basile, they tend to blend aspects of both authors' tales. Tracing Basile's influence on Perrault's corpus is not difficult, since he wrote only nine fairy tales, six of which can be traced directly back to the Italian tellers, and the most interesting example is the adaptation of "Le Chat botté" ("Puss in Boots"), which is a mixture of both "Cagliuso" (Basile 2-4) and Straparola's "Constantino" (9-1) (Trinquet 2012: 177). Perrault's "Sleeping Beauty," a direct adaptation of Basile's "Sun, Moon and Talia," reflects his bowdlerization of certain motifs to accommodate his audience. For instance, Perrault replaces the queen's attempt to feed her adulterous husband his children by another woman (the sleeping beauty character) with the invented figure of the ogress queen, mother of the prince, who desires human flesh and wishes to eat the children herself. We will turn to another adaptation of Basile's tale by Perrault in the third part of this chapter ("The Fairies").[10]

D'Aulnoy's adaptation of the Italian's fairy tales could be the subject of a separate study, and in her case, we must look at her tales scholars have considered to be folkloric as well as those they consider to be of her own invention to understand the extent of her debt to Basile, on the one hand, and the debt of folk tellers to d'Aulnoy, on the other.[11] She is the teller who complicates everything as she adapts tales from the Italians, while incorporating elements of her contemporaries' tales and of her own creation, to produce a unique and prolific repertoire. For instance, the case of her tale "Belle Belle ou le Chevalier Fortuné" ("Belle Belle or the Knight Fortuné") is significative. She follows the structure of "Marmoisan," L'Héritier's adaptation of Straparola's tale "Costanzo-Costanza" (4-1), which concerns a daughter who must disguise herself as a man to fight in the name of her father. However, she complicates the plot by incorporating elements adapted from Basile's "La Polece" ("The Flea," 1-5) and "Lo Gnorante" ("The Ignorant," 3-8), both of which are tales about "Extraordinary Companions" (ATU 513), who serve as the hero's—or in this case, the heroine's—helpers. It would be strange if she did not have a copy of *The Tale of Tales* in hand when composing her tales, because many of the motifs in her stories thought to have popular traces or to be of her own invention are found in the Italian collection.

Establishing Basile as a source of many 1690s French fairy tales, themselves relayed by European authors into the literature and folklore of their own countries, can change the perspective through which we understand the history of European fairy-tale adaptation, and the birth of folkloric fairy tales. By studying the adaptation of Italian fairy tales by French authors, one can ascertain that most of the literary fairy tales considered folkloric were not adapted from French folklore, as previously thought. In France, scholars such as Delarue and Marc Soriano have assumed, based on the corpus of French folktales established in the nineteenth century, that the plots of literary fairy tales from the 1690s were adapted from tales of the peasant class of the time. However, scholarship by specialists of orality in early modern France such as Geneviève Bollème demonstrates that novels of chivalry, relayed by the literary fairy tales of the seventeenth and eighteenth centuries, and popularized in the widely disseminated Troyes's chapbook series *La Bibliothèque bleue* (*The Blue Library*), reached an exemplary popularity in France and in all of Europe during the Romantic period, as evidenced as well by the enormous success of *Le Cabinet des fées* (1785–9). L'Héritier argues that fairy tales are French in origins and fed into Italian literature in the Middle Ages to then be relayed back into French 1690s tales to them by Italian tellers (L'Héritier de Villandon 1705). Straparola and Basile are the link that was required to understand the evolution of the fairy-tale genre in Europe, from the Middle Ages to the nineteenth century, and especially during the long eighteenth century.

CREATION OF THE MODERN LANDSCAPE OF LITERARY AND FOLK FAIRY TALES: THE EXAMPLE OF "THE KIND AND UNKIND GIRLS" AND "THE WHITE BRIDE AND THE BLACK BRIDE"

In what follows I will focus on what I have referred to elsewhere as the "folklorization" of literary tales to explore the impact of the adaptation of Italian fairy tales by French fairy-tale writers in the long eighteenth century that in turn were adapted as folktales.[12] Tales about kind and unkind girls and false brides are particularly interesting with respect to this process of folklorization. These two types of tales share a similar structure with Basile's "The Two Cakes" (4-7), in which a kind girl is rewarded with pearls emerging from her hair when combed and roses and jasmine flowers from her mouth, and the unkind girl is punished with a foaming mouth that emits toads, then the unkind girl tries to take the place of the kind girl beside the king; and "Le tre Fate" ("The Three Fairies," 3-10), in which the kind girl is similarly rewarded by fairies and is eventually united with a prince after her unkind stepsister momentarily usurps her place as the prince's bride. From these two tales, we find twelve literary tales in four languages, and about eighty folkloric versions in French. However, it is only when the French storytellers of the 1690s adapted Basile's tales that we find the separation of the two episodes (kindness rewarded and unkindness punished; the false bride overcome) into two distinct tale types. The international cataloguing into ATU 480 ("The Kind and Unkind Girls") and ATU 403 ("The White Bride and the Black Bride," also known as "The False Bride") is therefore based on an arbitrary classification that takes place due to the modifications French tellers made to their Italian sources. To remedy the defects of the traditional classifications and following Claude Brémond (1973), I will break down the structure of Basile's narratives into a certain number of sequences. From this breakdown, it will be easy to comprehend how the French storytellers adapted Basile's tales to generate new ones that eventually were categorized by scholars as different tale types. "The Three Fairies" and "The Two Cakes" are based on the same subject: kind and unkind girls and the false bride; the structure is similar with a repetition of sequences from one tale to the other, and there are only a few motifs that change, as is often the case with Basile's tales.

We can split the structure of the two tales into five narrative sequences:

(1) *Introduction*: Presentation of the characters and their situation; the heroine is sent out of the house with a task.

(2) *Part 1* (ATU 480): Encounter with the supernatural being: task; task accomplished; reward according to the accomplishment of the task.

(3) *Transition*: Meeting with the future spouse: promise of marriage or marriage.

(4) *Part 2* (ATU 403): Heroine's journey (with or without her husband); substitution of heroine with anti-heroine; refusal or acceptance of the fiancé-husband; help from the supernatural animal; recognition; marriage; punishment of the wicked.

(5) *Conclusion*: Morality in the form of a proverb.

THE SEPARATION OF TALES INTO TWO STANDARD TALES

Before Basile and "The Two Cakes," Straparola had already written the tale of "Biancabella" (3-3), which includes the episode in which the unkind sister becomes the false bride (ATU 403-A), and some of its narrative sequences and motifs have infiltrated Basile's tales and the French folklore. Although "Biancabella" is recognized as being part of the tale type "The Maiden Without Hands" (ATU 706), there are many more sequences and motifs comparable to "The False Bride." In Straparola's tale, the eponymous heroine was born with her twin sister, a fairy snake called Samaritana, tied around her neck. This motif allows the complete elimination of the episode concerning the fairy who tests the girls. Instead, the fairy-sister offers a gift to the heroine in return for her obedience: producing pearls and rings when she is combed, and flowers when she washes her hands. Biancabella is married to King Ferrandino of Naples, but he soon goes to war against the king of Tunis. He leaves his wife in the care of his stepmother, who had two daughters from a previous marriage. During the king's absence, the stepmother sends Biancabella to be killed in the forest by some servants and puts her daughter in the king's bed. When he returns, he is told that his wife is sick, which justifies the lice falling from her hair and her dirty hands. Meanwhile, the servants spare Biancabella in the forest, cut off her hands (in the tradition of "The Maiden Without Hands") and tear out her eyes, and bring them back to the stepmother as proof of her death. Biancabella is then rescued by a poor man, who is very happy with her prodigies, as well as by her sister who saves her from bleeding to death by applying herbs on her wounds. The three characters settle in an alabaster and porphyry palace that Samaritana builds against the king's palace, with a laurel bark struck three times on the ground. From there, they invite the king and the stepmother for dinner, followed by storytelling. Biancabella's actual story is told by one of the young female storytellers who asks in the end how the wicked woman should be punished. The cunning stepmother proposes a furnace to burn the culprit. The king recognizes Biancabella thanks to her gold chain around her neck, and the stepmother and her daughter end up in the furnace.[13]

Published in his collection *Les Fées illustres* (*The Illustrious Fairies*, 1698), the Chevalier de Mailly adapts Straparola's tale to produce his "Blanche-Belle," a shorter, more romantic and more tasteless version than the original. Blanche-Belle is not sent to be killed in the forest but rather is sent to the castle of the stepmother's fairy friend, where she is very well taken care of by black men and dwarf slaves. The recognition scene is due to a sylph, the presupposed father of Blanche-Belle, who carries her in the air to her husband who had taken refuge from the fake Blanche-Belle.

At the end of the seventeenth century in France, we find for the first time Basile's two tales separated into the two parts: the beginning of both tales correspond to the tale-type "The Kind and Unkind Girls" (ATU 480) and the second part corresponds to the false bride tale-type, "The White Bride and the Black Bride" (ATU 403). The fairies' gift to the kind girl, the first part of "The Kind and Unkind Girls," was adapted by Perrault in "Les Fées" ("The Fairies"; see Figure 2.1) and by L'Héritier in "The Enchantments of Eloquence."

The second part concerning the false bride was adapted by d'Aulnoy in "La princesse Rosette" ("The Princess Rosette," form A of ATU 403), in which the nursemaid's daughter tries to take Rosette's place beside the king of the peacocks; "La biche au bois" ("The Doe in the Woods," elements of form A and B of ATU 403), in which one of the princess's maids of honor tries to substitute herself to marry Prince Guerrier; and Chevalier de Mailly's "Blanche-Belle" (form B of ATU 403).

Perrault and L'Héritier seem to have adapted the first part of the tale of "The Two Cakes" to write respectively "The Fairies" and "The Enchantments of Eloquence." Later, the Brothers Grimm take up the structure of "The Three Fairies" and stop at the transition (the meeting of the future spouse), as the French did before them, in their tale "Frau Holle" ("Mother Holle"). It is impossible to say whether one of the two French storytellers was inspired by the other: Perrault had already composed the tale in 1695 since it is part of his 1695 manuscript, and L'Héritier published "The Enchantments of Eloquence" that same year. The two tales are nevertheless formed from an identical structure and repeat the same patterns, with some differences. First, L'Héritier makes a long digression on the subject of novels, which allows her to base the morality on a different theme than that of Basile and Perrault: here, verbal eloquence is important, which places the story in the context of salon conversation, a typical intellectual pastime of the tellers and their audience. Then she inserts the romantic encounter of the prince and the heroine at the fountain, before the fairy has gifted her with the spitting of precious stones—L'Héritier does not like

FIGURE 2.1: Illustration of Charles Perrault's "The Fairies" from *Contes du temps passé de ma Mère L'oye* (London: T. Boosey, 1796). Public domain.

love at first sight or arranged marriages—while Perrault follows the motif of monetary interest as with the Basilian king. If there are differences with Basile's tales, they are generally symmetrical in French tales. In Basile, it is usually an old woman who makes predictions. It is therefore an old woman who comes to the fountain in "The Two Cakes." In France, it is almost always the fairies who hold the threads of the plot, therefore a fairy is expected to appear: Perrault's motif of the fairy as an old hag taken from popular culture becomes that of a young fairy disguised as a peasant woman in L'Héritier's tales, following as always the literary tradition of her time. The motif of food (the cake) in Basile takes the form in France of a drink. The donations received by the heroines are simplified by the French storytellers: instead of precious gems falling out of her hair when combed, and roses and jasmine when she breathes (the motif of the foot is totally removed), L'Héritier's heroine receives precious gems that come out of her mouth "every time she makes a finite sense when speaking"

(1696: 260) by the fairy Eloquentia nativa, while Perrault's is granted flowers and precious gems by the fairy when she speaks, due to her kindness.

The final difference is that the tale stops at the transition, when the tale is about to shift to the meeting of the future spouse. In both Perrault and L'Héritier's tales, the prince carries the heroine away from her mean family and marries her. The ending of L'Héritier's tale is formulated as in Basile by a proverb while Perrault concludes his tale with two moralities in verse. Both French storytellers, however, focus on the positive element of the tale whereas Basile emphasizes the negative: the French reward the good characters, whereas Basile's focus is on punishing the antagonistic characters:

> e Puccia, cacciata da chillo regno, iette sempre pezzenno, e pe n'avere semmenato 'no poccorillo de pizza appe sempre carestia de pane: essenno volontà de lo cielo Che chi non ha pietà, pietà non trova.
>
> (and Puccia, banished from the kingdom, wandered begging, and for not having given a small piece of cake, she still remains without bread: therefore, the heavens decide that one who does not have pity, pity does not find.)
> (Basile [1634–6] 1976: 337; my translation)

> Le bonheur de cette personne dura autant que sa vie, qui fut longue; et sa destinée et celle d'Alix prouvèrent ce que j'ai avancé d'abord, que souvent: Doux et courtois langage/Vaut mieux que riche apanage.
>
> (The happiness of this person lasted as long as her life, which was long; and her destiny and that of Alix proved what I advanced first, that often: Sweet and courteous language is better than rich inheritance.)
> (L'Héritier 1696: 265; my translation)

THE FALSE BRIDE, SECOND PART OF THE BASILIAN TALES

For the second part of Basile's two tales, the adaptations are more complicated. D'Aulnoy adapts the second part of "The Two Cakes" to write "The Princess Rosette," which gives the form A of the tale type "The False Bride" (ATU 403) in France. In form A, the future bride's brother(s) brings her portrait to a king who then decides to marry her, but she is substituted by her ugly stepsister on the way to his kingdom. Form B of the French ATU 403, which incorporates the motif of the heroine being gifted with precious stones, corresponds to the second part of Basile's tale "The Three Fairies," and is formed by a combination of both Mailly's "Blanche-Belle" and Straparola's "Biancabella." D'Aulnoy's "The Doe in the Woods," published a year after "The Princess Rosette," is a amalgamation of several motifs belonging to different tales and adds the metamorphosis of the heroine into a white doe as she is substituted with her governess' daughter while on her way to her future husband (Figure 2.2).

The structure follows fairly closely that of "The False Bride" to be classified by Delarue as belonging to the two forms A and B of the tale-type 403. The Grimms' "Die weisse und die schwarze Brau" ("The White Bride and the Black Bride"), which gives its name to the international tale-type, is a combination of "The Two Cakes" and "The Princess Rosette," but incorporates the motif of the heroine's metamorphosis (she is transformed into a white duck during her substitution with her half-sister on their way to the king's castle), and thus corresponds to the French forms A and B, exemplified by d'Aulnoy's "The Doe in the Woods." Thus, not only are the tale-types divided from the separation of Basile's tales in the 1690s, but the separation of the tale-type 403 into forms A and B in France comes from the two literary models of the French storytellers, Mailly and d'Aulnoy. If one looks at the motifs and the sequences as they appear in folkloric

FIGURE 2.2: An illustration from Walter Crane's version of *The Hind in the Wood* (London: Routledge, 1875). Public domain.

versions, one finds a combination of all the literary versions mentioned above, showing that the literary fairy tales were adapted by the authors of chapbooks and *Bibliothèque bleue* in France before they were collected in the nineteenth-century French countryside.

In the Gascon version of ATU 403-A, which Delarue considers the archetypal version in France, one finds what I call motif leftovers: having played a fundamental role in the narratives of Straparola, Basile, and d'Aulnoy, the motifs' original meaning is lost and replaced by a simple episode that does not advance the plot. For instance, in Straparola's tale "Biancabella," the heroine's mother-in-law wants to murder her during her husband's absence (in this version, the marriage takes place before the substitution of the false bride). To do this, the stepmother asks her servants to lead Biancabella in the forest and kill her; but they just tear out her eyes and cut her hands off and bring them back as proof of her death, which is an indispensable element of the plot.

This rather violent episode is not reproduced in Mailly's version, who instead locks his heroine in a fairy's castle. In the Gascon version, which follows at this time the structure of "The Two Cakes" and "The Princess Rosette," the heroine is taken by her entire family to her future husband, and during the journey by car, the stepmother asks her to give her eyes to her daughter. The stepmother then throws the blind heroine into a swamp and replaces her with her own daughter.[14] We forget the reason for her blindness in the narrative sequence where the heroine is recovered by an old man, the motif coming from both the versions of Straparola ("Biancabella") and d'Aulnoy ("The Princess Rosette"). We find it again in the following sequence, during which the girl makes golden cattails and sends the old man's wife to exchange them for her eyes at the church door. The old woman exchanges them with the heroine's eyes that the king's wife (the substituted sister) had kept in her pocket. Once both eyes are put back in place, the pattern is excluded from the plot. While in Straparola's version, the motif is essential to unfolding the plot, in the folk version it is superimposed on the plot without playing a role in it. This variant of the motif adds nothing to the plot and does not advance recognition but proves that the folkloric tales were adapted from several literary versions from the sixteenth to the nineteenth century, probably via the eighteenth century's chapbooks.

In the following sequence of the French folk archetype, the girl goes out to sea, of her own free will, and we do not really know why she had a little dog—we had never heard of it before—and "washing her hands over the sea, made a golden chain" (Delarue [1953] 1997: 48). Here we are in the presence of three combined motifs that come from "The Princess Rosette" and "The Two Cakes." In both literary versions, the heroines are thrown into the sea during their trip to their future husband by the false bride or her mother.

In Basile's tale, the heroine is recovered by a siren who holds her captive by a golden chain. She often comes to shore to feed her brother's geese, who play the role of the supernatural helpers in this tale. They talk to her, and as she responds, the king's servant's curiosity is awakened, leading to her recognition as the true bride. D'Aulnoy replaces the geese with "[Rosette's] little dog, called *Frétillon*, who was green like a parrot, who had only one ear and who danced to delight" (Delarue [1953] 1997: 189), in other words, another supernatural animal whose characteristics are more aristocratic than peasant (Figure 2.3).

Nevertheless, he plays the same role in the structure of the story, helping, through his actions, others to recognize the princess: he steals the king's meal in his kitchen for three days, which starves the latter; the king's confidant, in turn, follows the dog to the old man's house where the heroine had taken refuge, and recognizes her. In both case we thus find the motif of food that leads to the recognition. In the Gascon version, the golden chain has no other purpose than to close the dialogue between the heroine and the dog, a dialogue that will intrigue the king and bring the plot to the point of recognition:

FIGURE 2.3: Rosette at sea with her little dog Frétillon, from Andrew Lang's *The Red Fairy Book* (London: Longmans, Green, and Co., 1895). Public domain.

> "Petite chienne, la mienne mie ?"—"Plaît-il, madame la maîtresse ?"—"Où sont mes neuf frères ?"—"Pendus aux plus hautes fenêtres du Louvre du roi."—"Ma belle-sœur ?"—"Endormie dans les bras du roi."—"Ma belle tante?"—"Dans la salle du roi qui goûte."—"Tire, tire ma chaîne, / Que la mer m'emmène. Le roi entendit cela. Il envoya ses troupes briser cette chaîne; elles ne purent la briser. Et toujours la fille disait …"
>
> ("Little dog of mine?"—"What, Mistress?"—"Where are my nine brothers?"—"Hanging from the highest windows of the King's Louvre."—"My stepsister?"—"Asleep in the arms of the king."—"My beautiful aunt?"—"In the king's room having a snack."—"Pull, pull my chain, / Let the sea take me. The king heard that. He sent his troops to break this chain; they could not break it. And always the girl said …")
>
> (Delarue [1953] 1997: 49; my translation)

We recall that in "The Two Cakes" the king failed to cut the chain the first time, and returned the next day, on the advice of the heroine, with a saw. Contrary to all expectations, the folktale's heroine marries the king without her chain being broken, and the motif that concluded her dialogue with the dog is completely forgotten. The importance that the chain took in the plot of Basile's version—since, by retaining the heroine captive, it slowed down the denouement and introduced the materialistic reason for marrying the heroine, as with Perrault—is reduced in the Gascon version to nothing, and the motif is rendered useless. As previously seen, d'Aulnoy replaces Basile's geese with the dog in "The Princess Rosette"—a motif that she invented—to bring about the recognition scene.

When Italian and French tales do not provide a motif for the French folk tellers, German versions do. The dialogue between the dog and the heroine that we have just quoted from the Gascon tale is adapted from the Grimms' "The White Bride and the Black Bride" and also functions as a recognition scene. In this version, the heroine, thrown into the river by the stepmother during her trip to meet her future husband, metamorphoses into a duck when she gets in contact with water. Having swum into the kitchen, she asks the kitchen boy:

> "Was macht mein Bruder Reginer ?" Der Küchenjunge antwortete: "Liegt tief bei Ottern und Schlangen." Fragte sie: "Was macht die schwarze Hex im Haus ?" Der Küchenjunge antwortete: "Die sitzt warm ins Königs Arm." Sagte die Ente: "Daß Gott erbarm!" und schwamm den Gossenstein hinaus.
>
> ("What does my brother Reginer do?" The waiter replied, "Sitting in a hole with snakes and otters." She asked, "What is the black witch [the sister-in-law] doing in the house?" The waiter replied, "She is beloved in the arms of the king." The duck said, "May god have mercy!" And she returned by the sewer.)
>
> (Grimm and Grimm [1812–58] 2015: 257–8; my translation)

Note that the motif of the heroine metamorphosed into a cane ("The Three Little Gnomes in the Forest" and "The White Bride and the Black Bride") is a reminder of the motif found in Basile with the brother who guards the ducks. The final recognition in both tales, the female duck being decapitated by the king, takes again the motif of the end of the enchantment, where the animal metamorphizes into the human form of the heroine. The same motif can be found in d'Aulnoy's "La Chatte Blanche" ("The White Cat"). In her "Doe in the Woods," the heroine also recovers her human form after her lover wounds her during a hunt. Of the ten French folk versions of the tale-type "The White Bride and the Black Bride" (ATU 403-B), six involve the motif of metamorphosis, including two hounds and four birds (a duck, a goose, a dove, and a bird). The Grimms' two tales also use, to grant recognition, the motif of the animal that enters the kitchen and goes to speak to a servant who reports the story to the king, which comes from "The Princess Rosette." Finally, it seems that it was d'Aulnoy who invented the aristocratic motif of the heroine's portrait with which the future husband falls in love ("The Doe in the Woods" and "The Princess Rosette"), which is then repeated in the Grimms' "The White Bride and the Black Bride." If we look at each variant of the motifs that constitute the twenty-three French folk versions of "The False Bride" collected from French folklore and compiled by Delarue, we find that they adapt all of the nine literary versions written by the Italian, French, and German storytellers. For the few not found in the literary versions, there is nothing original enough to not be derived and adapted from an element already existing in the literary versions. For example, in some versions prevalent in the south of France, the heroines follow a trail that descends toward a river. The motif is based on the same principle as that of "The Three Fairies," where the heroine follows her basket that has fallen into a ravine. The heroine makes a downward progression toward her rite of passage manifested in the fairies' castle by her crossing the door's threshold under which she receives the star on her forehead and the gifts. This progression toward the rite of passage is also found, among other things, in the Grimms' "Frau Holle," where the heroine falls into the well in which she is washing her thread, then goes back covered with gold, a pattern reminiscent of the gold embroidered dress in Basile's "The Three Fairies."

What, however, is most important for the study of the fairy-tale adaptation in the long eighteenth century is to realize that the French stories of the late seventeenth century are the link between the Italian tales and the folkloric ones of the nineteenth century, sometimes via the Grimms' versions themselves. As it is no secret that the Grimms rewrote many of their versions from the French and Italian literary corpi, via their French Huguenot informants for the French corpus and the printed versions for the Italian corpus, and that their influence in France and in the colonies was considerable, it is not surprising to find in the nineteenth- and twentieth-century European folktales all these mixed elements of European literary tales, reprinted in simpler version in about fifty million copies of chapbooks published each year in France by the 1850s. As this analysis has shown, the responsibility for the separation of the tale types "The False Bride" and "The Kind and Unkind Girls" lies with the French storytellers as they adapted Basile's tales for their own audiences. If the "archetypal" version of Gascony already existed in the French 1690s, which is not only impossible to prove but also very illogical, it seems that the storytellers did not need it to write their literary versions. As Marc Fumaroli concludes regarding Perrault's "Les Fées": "If Claude Bernard did not find a soul under his scalpel, we found under ours no trace of the 'popular art,' dear to the romantics and Marc Soriano" (1982: 186). On the other hand, to deny the interest of folk storytellers for literary texts is to diminish their potential ability to rewrite something other than their own traditions, as well as to reinterpret and adapt texts that do not come from their repertory, which goes against all the scholarship of orality.

CONCLUSION

Studying the adaptation of fairy tales in early modern Europe allows us to understand the complexity and the richness of the fairy-tale genre. Despite the very popular fairy tales of d'Aulnoy, reprinted in France and translated in English and German throughout the eighteenth and nineteenth centuries, many of the other women's early modern tales were forgotten and relegated to prohibited readings, and we might have never found their existence if it was not for the folklorists who gave a snapshot of the genre's adaptation and dissemination during the Romantic period. It piqued scholarly interests in the early 1900s and started one of the most extensive quests for original texts within their own sociohistorical contexts. It, however, took another century to determine the origins of the French early modern vogue and reestablish the Italian writers as its source. The method of distribution, either—or both—textual and oral, is at the center of scholarly interest regarding early modern and contemporary societies. Without the European writers, we might not have had a classic fairy-tale genre; however, without the transformation of the genre in the eighteenth century and the popularity of the *Arabian Nights*, as well as compilations such as Meyer's *Cabinet of the Fairies*, the millions of rewritings of the best fairy tales into chapbooks, and especially the European folk tellers who adapted and expanded the tradition, the immense popularity of the genre might have become no more than a literary curiosity catalogued in one of the numerous volumes of Marquis de Paulmy and Comte de Tressan's *Bibliothèque universelle des romans* (*Universal Library of Novels*, 224 volumes, 1775–89).

CHAPTER THREE

Gender and Sexuality

From the conteuses *to the English Governess*

AILEEN DOUGLAS

In 1690 the aristocratic salonnière Marie-Catherine le Jumel de Barneville d'Aulnoy published in Paris a highly successful novel, *Histoire d'Hypolite, Comte de Duglas* (The History of Hypolitus, Earl of Douglas). Within it was a short narrative, "L'Ile de la Félicité" ("The Island of Felicity"), the first in a wave of literary fairy tales published in France over the next twenty-five years. Adolphe, a Russian prince, spends three hundred happy years with his fairy lover, Princess Felicity, until his masculine desire to gain military fame and renown causes him to depart the Island of Felicity. Given a magnificent horse on which to make his return journey, Adolphe is warned by Felicity that come what may he must not put his foot on the ground. Once on earth, however, Adolphe is duped by Time, disguised as an old man needing help, and fatally does what he has been warned against. The plot of "The Island of Felicity" enacts a generic feature of fairy tales; that is, being in and out of time. Literary fairy tales may appear timeless but they are written in particular societies and at particular historical moments. Initiating the literary fairy tale as genre, d'Aulnoy also demonstrates the form's capacity to question and revise gendered notions of virtue and power current in her society.[1]

Late seventeenth-century French fairy tales emerged from the literary salon, in which the telling of elaborate tales formed part of conversation and sociability.

With the publication of d'Aulnoy's *Les Contes des fées* (*Tales of the Fairies*, 1697) the term *contes des fées* or *contes de fées* became current in France; subsequently English translations will render it "fairy tale," thus ushering the concept into the English literary field. Of the term, considered in the broad evolution of culture, Jack Zipes has said it is "a declaration of difference and resistance ... projecting moral and ethical conflicts in alternative worlds" (2012: 24). By 1715, 112 such narratives had appeared, nearly two-thirds of them published by women.[2] Of these, d'Aulnoy's tales—her initial volume and a further collection *Contes nouveaux ou les fées à la mode* (New Tales or the Fairies in Fashion, 1698)—and Charles Perrault's *Histoires ou contes du temps passé. Avec des Moralités* (Stories or Tales of Time Past. With Morals, 1697) would prove the most enduring, powerfully shaping readers' understandings of the fairy tale throughout the eighteenth century in France, England, as well as Germany.

This chapter first discusses gender and sexuality as thematic and structural aspects of the works of d'Aulnoy and other *conteuses*, with a focus on constructions of masculinity and femininity in the context of louis-quatorzième patriarchy. It then explores the workings of gender in the fairy tales of Perrault, also a frequenter of salons, a member of the Académie Française, and leading voice of the Moderns in the *Querelle des Anciens et des Modernes* (Quarrel of the Ancients and the Moderns). In its final section the chapter moves forward to England, at mid-century, where fairy tales such as those by the English writer Sarah Fielding, and the French émigrée Jeanne-Marie Leprince de Beaumont, emerged in commercial print culture. Thus this chapter looks at gender and sexuality as the fairy tale shifts across national lines and from a genre with an adult readership to one explicitly designed for children and adolescents and especially girls. In the process, the elaborate tales of the *conteuses* are simplified, while the partial displacement of the term "fairy tale" by "moral tale" suggests an increased awareness of how the tales might shape young girls according to gendered social norms. Throughout, the fairy tale holds conservative and subversive elements in tension. While the almost ubiquitous trope of "happy ever after" marriages supports patriarchal ideology, an emphasis on female rationality promotes female autonomy, while the deployment of metamorphosis unsettles ideas of gender.

MADAME D'AULNOY AND THE *CONTEUSES*

D'Aulnoy and her fellow *conteuses* "identified the fairy tale as a genre with something to say about gender and sexuality," allowing them to experiment with "constructions and reconstructions of the male and female" (Haase 2004: vi–vii). Certain elements and themes recur in their tales, including the problems of patriarchy; marvelous transformations, which can have implications for gender; and an emphasis on female agency and creativity as women figure prominently as heroines and tellers as well as authors of tales. In the final decades of Louis XIV's absolutist rule, the fairy-tale form allowed the *conteuses* a space sometimes to confirm but more often to unravel the rhetoric of patriarchal authority increasingly emphasized in the domestic and state spheres. In the imagined space of the fairy tale, heroes and heroines are transformed into bees, birds, serpents, and monkeys. The effect of these metamorphoses is to denaturalize the human body, estranging the reader from familiar notions of sexual difference and the social codes based upon that difference. The use of transformation in the fairy tale enabled women writers to challenge gender and sexual norms in the patriarchal society of Louis XIV.

Historians of late seventeenth-century France have delineated how the absolutism of Louis XIV drew on a language of "divine paternalism" that represented the king as the father of his people (Fox 1960: 136). At the same time, a "Family-State compact" engendered "a state model of political power wedded to male authority" (Hanley 1989: 27). It is in the context of seventeenth-century representations of the *pater familias* that the remarkable recurrence of weak kings in the fairy tales is to be understood (Jasmin 2002: 351). Amongst contemporary tale writers it is d'Aulnoy who "goes the furthest in exploring the darkest sides of paternal authority" (Seifert 1996: 165). Her tales commonly represent paternal figures as lacking or inadequate, where they are not corrupt and dangerous. The conspicuous failure of fathers to govern their households responsibly, and their selfish pursuit of their own desires, makes their children, especially their daughters, vulnerable.

In "Gracieuse et Percinet," for instance, the young princess Gracieuse is directly imperiled by her father's actions. Dazzled by the wealth of the monstrous Duchess Grognon, and the streams of coins, pearls, and diamonds that flow from the barrels in her cellar, the widowed king, "qui aimait uniquement l'argent" (who loved only money), makes an unsavory bargain (d'Aulnoy [1697] 1997: 34).[3] In return for the key to the cellar he agrees immediately to marry Grognon, who relentlessly persecutes her stepdaughter. In "L'Oiseau bleu" ("The Blue Bird") another widowed king is easily seduced into an unwise second marriage, the narrator observing, "Il suffit très souvent de connaître le faible des gens pour entrer dans leur cœur & pour en faire tout ce que l'on veut" ("Very often, you just have to know someone's weak spot to get under their skin and have them do as you wish"; d'Aulnoy [1697] 1997: 74).

The king in "La Belle aux cheveux d'or" ("Beauty with the Golden Hair") is both infantile and tyrannical. He cries like a child when Beauty rejects his proposal of marriage and arbitrarily imprisons his emissary, Avenant: "pour sa récompense d'avoir si bien servi le roi, on l'enferma dans la tour avec les fers aux pieds & aux mains" ("in return for his loyal service to the king, he was shut up in the tower with his hands and feet fettered"; d'Aulnoy [1697] 1997: 70). In these fairy tales, weak kings and fathers are often undermined by malign female agency: men cannot exercise power and evil women usurp it. In this way, the stories comment not only on male insufficiency but also on a system of gender roles in which women too are complicit.

The removal of the father's protection precipitates the suffering of Gracieuse and of Florine in "L'Oiseau Bleu," but it also challenges the heroines to take care of themselves. The more sympathetic father in "Belle-Belle, ou le Chevalier Fortuné," contrasts with the earlier examples, but here too paternal incapacity initiates the heroine's adventures. The kingdom is at war and all noblemen are required to join the king's army, or send a son instead. Old, and without a son, Belle-Belle's father is unable to meet the king's demands. Assuming a male disguise, and substituting herself for her father, Belle-Belle goes off to join the king's army (Figure 3.1).

FIGURE 3.1: Belle-Belle preparing to join the king's army; illustration by John Gilbert, from *The Fairy Tales of Countess D'Aulnoy* (London: Routlege, 1855), p. 474. Public domain.

Belle-Belle not only passes as male but also succeeds dramatically as the Chevalier Fortuné—slaying a dragon and serving as the king's emissary—thereby showing gender roles to be constructed rather than natural. Bidding Belle-Belle farewell as she departs on her first mission, the king acknowledges her aptitude as a male quester: "allez où la gloire vous appelle. Je sais que vous avez tant d'adresse dans toutes les choses que vous faites & particularièrement aux armes" ("follow the call of glory. I know how much skill you have in everything you do and especially in arms"; d'Aulnoy [1698] 1998: 243). Belle-Belle's cross-dressing is even more notable as a challenge to gender roles in the context of a story where the king has been defeated in battle, his kingdom has been despoiled, and he relies on courtiers such as Belle-Belle to reestablish order.

As Adrienne E. Zuerner has convincingly shown, this tale may be considered "oppositional discourse" for the way in which it exposes what the "official myth" of royal absolutism occluded: "the fallibility and vulnerability of the monarch" (1997: 207). That Marie-Jeanne L'Héritier and Henriette-Julie de Murat also penned maiden warrior tales speaks to the popularity of such a theme that challenged the paternalism and patriarchy of the regime of Louis XIV. Sharing the same device as d'Aulnoy's "Belle-Belle"— a heroine who cross-dresses and undertakes military duty for the sake of her father—L'Héritier's "Marmoisan, Or the Innocent Deception," also plays with fixed notions of gender. The heroine Marmoisan fights bravely on the battlefield but risks exposing her sex through her concern for tidiness and cleanliness. Ultimately, in the figure of Marmoison, L'Héritier proposes an androgynous idea of heroism that combines "the best qualities of the two sexes united in one person" (Seifert and Stanton 2010: 81).

In patriarchal societies female chastity is fundamental to lines of inheritance and the transmission of property. That chastity is the fundamental and absolutely necessary quality of early modern elite women is nicely encapsulated by L'Héritier's tale, "L'Adroite princesse ou les aventures de Finette" ("The Discreet Princess or the Adventures of Finette").[4] A king about to go on crusade, and worried about the welfare of his three daughters in his absence, has a fairy construct three glass distaffs that will shatter if the possessor's honor is infringed. He also installs his three daughters comfortably in a tower with instructions that on no account must anyone be admitted. The malicious prince Rich-Craft tricks his way into the tower and seduces two of the sisters on successive nights. Each of their distaffs shatters. Subsequently, these two sisters, who are gullible but not malicious or licentious, are shamed when they give birth to Rich-Craft's children. When Rich-Craft attempts to seduce the third sister, Finette, she defends herself with an enormous hammer, and subsequently uses intelligence and quicksightedness to best him. The king returns, punishes the sisters who find a premature death due to their own dispositions, and Finette eventually succeeds in a loving marriage, ironically, with the brother of Rich-Craft, Handsome-to-See.

L'Héritier endows Finette with qualities typically associated with masculinity, notably an interest in, and capacity for, public affairs. Earlier in the tale she alerts her father to a deceptive clause in a treaty he is about to sign and dictates a substitute to him. In a sly commentary on the separation of women from the public world, L'Héritier has the king give his minister permission to supply Finette with dispatches on current affairs (placed in the basket along with food) to peruse while she is in the tower. "Finette" treats the question of chastity and the perceived vulnerability of young women in the absence of male guardians but, like d'Aulnoy's heroines, Finette is able to fend for herself, and moreover, like Belle-Belle and Marmoisan, proves to be essential to defending the kingdom.

A good deal of the delight afforded to the reader of the tales of d'Aulnoy, L'Héritier, and the other *conteuses* comes from shape shifting and transformation. As well as providing readerly pleasure, such metamorphoses also enable what Patricia Hannon has called "the circulation of experimental identities" (1998: 16). As a trope, metamorphosis is inherently double. It immediately forces awareness of what a body has been, and what it now is. Materially, metamorphosis shows how different physicalities constrict and liberate; symbolically it can challenge sophisticated power structures that rhetorically incorporate the body. Often, the effect of metamorphosis in fairy tales is to put body and mind at odds. Estrangement from conventional understandings of how mind and body relate has obvious implications for gender, especially in a society where women are particularly associated with the physical life of the body, and men with the principles of rationality.

A simple yet subversive example occurs in "L'Oiseau Bleu." Having fallen in love with Florine, King Charmant refuses to marry her stepsister Truitonne, and as punishment is turned into a blue bird for seven years. Even though Charmant needs to be put in a cage to be protected from predatory cats, he still thinks he may be able to continue to govern in his avian state. In this, he is quickly disabused by his enchanter friend: "Oh! s'écria son ami, la chose est différente! Tel qui veut obéir à un homme, ne veut pas obéir à un perroquet: tel vous craint étant roi, étant environeé de grandeur & de faste, qui vous arrachera toutes les plumes, vous voyant un petit oiseau" ("Oh, cried his friend, things are different now. Those who would obey a man will not obey a parrot: those who feared you as a king, surrounded by grandeur and pomp will be the ones who'll pull out all your feathers, now that you are a little bird"; d'Aulnoy [1698] 1998: 99). Charmant's experience causes him to reflect on age-old commonplaces regarding appearance and reality, on how deceptive a brilliant exterior can be. Even more searchingly, metamorphosis raises fundamental questions concerning essence and identity.

Perhaps the most reflective and engaging working out of such themes is d'Aulnoy's "Babiole." A queen gives birth to a much-longed for and beautiful baby girl. Owing to the machinations of the fairy Fanfreluche the baby turns into a little monkey. The queen determines to destroy the creature but by chance Babiole is saved. Taken to the court of a neighboring kingdom, Babiole becomes a pet and is especially cherished by the prince, who happens to be her cousin. Years pass and one day the court is astonished when Babiole begins to speak with "une petite voix douce & claire, si distincte que l'on n'en perdait pas un mot! Quelle merveille! Babiole parlante, Babiole raisonnante!" ("a sweet, clear, little voice, so distinct that not a word was lost. What a marvel! Babiole can speak, Babiole can reason"; d'Aulnoy [1698] 1998: 447). At court, Babiole is given a fine education and continues to enjoy conversation with her cousin the prince.

Unhappily, the king of the monkeys, Magot, hearing of Babiole's gifts, sends an emissary requesting her hand in marriage. The proposal forces Babiole to declare her own love to the prince who, astounded, laughs at her, makes a joke of their lack of compatibility, and urges her to marry Magot. He then further offends her by desiring her to send him her first-born monkey baby. Fleeing a forced marriage, Babiole eventually finds herself back where she was born. Here, unaware that she is speaking to her own mother, Babiole laments that misfortune has made her an ape, but one with understanding: "Car enfin, que puis-je ressentir, lorsque je me vois dans mon miroir, petite, laide & noire, ayant des pattes couvertes de poils, avec une queue & des dents toujours prêtes à mordre, & que d'ailleurs je ne manque point d'esprit, que j'ai du gout, de la délicatesse & des sentiments" ("How am I supposed to feel when I see myself in a mirror, small, ugly, and black, with paws covered with hair, with a tail, and teeth always ready to bite, and at the same time know that I have intelligence, taste, sensibility, and feeling?"; d'Aulnoy 1998: 459). Babiole's predicament is matched by that of Princess Laideronnette in "Serpentin Vert" ("Green Serpent"). Made hideous by a malevolent fairy soon after her birth, Laideronnette too has wit, intelligence, and feeling but her cursed looks make her hide herself away in retirement. The plights of Babiole and Laideronnette, constricted by bodies that cause them to be misunderstood and underestimated, represent an exaggerated version of what women can experience in societies where understandings of the sexed body dominate ideas of female personhood and the social roles women are permitted to play.[5]

Metamorphosis unsettles the cultural meanings of human physicality, and it also opens up treatment of sexuality, both in terms of desire and repugnance. It introduces a polymorphous quality to the tales, which in turn permits sexual expression that might otherwise be censored (Jasmin 2002: 342). Charmant's transformation into a blue bird allows him to spend whole nights with his imprisoned lover Florine (Figure 3.2). For two years of her captivity Florine is perfectly contented because "Elle avait la satisfaction de parler toute la nuit à ce qu'elle aimait" ("she had the pleasure of talking all night long with the one she loved"; d'Aulnoy [1697] 1997: 91).

FIGURE 3.2: Florine with King Charmant metamorphosed into the Blue Bird, illustrated by J. C. Demerville, from *Les Contes choisis* (Paris: 1847), between pp. 68–9. Public domain.

D'Aulnoy's "L'Oranger et l'abeille" ("The Bee and the Orange Tree") recounts the travails of Princess Aimée and her cousin and lover Prince Aimé. In the verse moral concluding the story, the narrator reflects on how, even when alone together in the wilderness fleeing ogres, Aimée ensures that propriety is observed:

Avec un tendre amant, seule au milieu des bois,
Aimée eut en tout temps une extrême sagesse;
Toujours de la raison elle écouta la voix.
Et sut de son amant conserver la tendresse.

(With a tender lover, alone in the midst of the woods,
Aimée had at all times great wisdom
Always she listened to the voice of reason,
And knew how to keep her lover's fondness.)

(d'Aulnoy [1697] 1997: 276)

The verse ends by exhorting Beauties to be proud and severe with their lovers. Yet, this moral concludes a tale in which the metamorphosis of Aimée into a bee, and Aimé into an orange tree, has allowed for the fulfillment of the lovers' desires: "elle s'enferma dans une des plus grosses fleurs comme dans un palais, & la véritable tendresse, qui trouve des ressources partout, ne laissait pas d'avoir les siennes dans cette union" ("she enclosed herself in one of the largest flowers as in a palace, and true love, which finds sustenance everywhere, found it in this union"; d'Aulnoy [1697] 1997: 270). Escaping the constraints of human physicality can often allow for the satisfaction of physical desire.

If metamorphosis can facilitate desire, it can also allow for the opposite: the expression of repugnance. The disgust and fear fairy-tale heroines can experience when confronted with the metamorphosed hero, such as that, for example, felt by Laideronette in relation to the green serpent, permits coded expression of resistance to undesired or forced marriage. Two versions of the fairy tale "Riquet à la houppe" ("Riquet with the Tuft") by Catherine Bernard and Perrault show varied treatments of this theme. In Bernard's tale, Mama, the stupid but beautiful daughter of a Spanish nobleman, is offered intelligence by the hideously ugly Riquet, King of the Gnomes, but only on condition that she marry him after a year has passed. Reluctantly, when the year is up, Mama marries Riquet and moves to his underworld palace. When Riquet discovers that his wife has been unfaithful with her handsome lover, Arada, his revenge leads him to transform his rival so that husband and lover appear identical. The cynical conclusion is that: "In the long run lovers become husbands anyway" (Zipes 1991a: 100).

In Perrault's story, too, the young heroine accepts intelligence on the condition that she marry the ugly Riquet. In this happier case, however, fairies have given the bride the power to render a man handsome should she truly wish it. This she does: "Quelques-uns assurent que ce ne furent point les charmes de la Fée qui opérèrent, mais que l'amour fit cette Métamorphose" ("Some say it was not only the magic of the Fairy at work, but that love effected this metamorphosis"; Perrault 1999: 109). In restoring enchanted husbands to their original selves, fairy tales may appear to cancel out and contain the heroine's feelings of repulsion and fear, but such feelings have nonetheless been expressed. In Perrault's worldly version, "love" is seen as a self-deluding power that enables women to deal with marital prospects otherwise too unpalatable to confront. This approach to the story anticipates Jeanne-Marie Leprince de Beaumont's "Beauty and the Beast," in which the heroine's overcoming of repugnance is seen as a moral imperative.

The creative and transformative power fairies wield within the tales appealed to the *conteuses* as a way of describing their own literary powers. Henriette-Julie de Murat dedicated her *Histoires sublimes et allégoriques* (Sublime and Allegorical Tales) to the "fées modernes" (modern fairies) and a prefatory epistle to the work addressed her fellow writers as such. In a celebration of their shared art, Murat combined a playful faux historicism, snobbery, and an assertive account of what was distinctive about her literary peers. According to Murat, fairies in the past had been far from glamorous. Mainly preoccupied with low domestic tasks such as sweeping the house and putting children to bed, they did however have the power occasionally to transform themselves into cats, monkeys, and bogey-men to frighten the young and the feeble-minded. Of these women, the only traces now remaining were what she called—in a jibe at the way Perrault referred to the supposedly popular origins of his own rather different and recently published stories— "Contes de ma Mere l'oye" ("Tales of Mother Goose"). The modern fairies, Murat's glittering contemporaries, present a striking contrast: "Vous ne vous occupez que de grandes choses, dont les moindres sont de donner de l'esprit à ceux & celles qui n'en ont point, de la beauté aux laides, de l'éloquence aux ignorans, des richesses aux pauvres, & de l'éclat aux choses les plus obscures" ("You only occupy yourselves with important things, of which the least are to give intelligence to those who have none, beauty to the ugly, eloquence to the ignorant, wealth to the poor, and brilliance to the most obscure things"; Murat 1699). Moreover, the modern fairies dress better and "n'habitez que dans la Cour des Rois, ou dans des Palais enchantez" ("only live in the courts of kings or in enchanted Palaces"; Murat 1699). Disdaining both routine domestic tasks and women's supposed connection with the superstitious tales of popular culture, elements brought together in the figure of Perrault's "Mother Goose," Murat emphasizes the high social status of the modern fairies, their truly transformative powers, and their possession of enchanted palaces they have themselves created.

As has been well documented by scholars such as Raymonde Robert, the *conteuses* drew plentifully on folklore motifs (1982: 127–9). Highly literary and intertextual, the tales reconfigure a wide range of sources, including mythology, the classics, and contemporary literature. In addition to prefaces and dedications such as Murat's that emphasize the artistry of the *contes*, the tales themselves can be highly self-referential. A striking example here is d'Aulnoy's White Cat who, in the tale of that name, lives in a castle beautifully adorned by a mural depicting various fairy tales: "Les murs étaient d'une porcelaine transparente, mêlée de plusieurs couleurs qui repésentaient l'histoire de toutes les fées depuis la création du monde jusqu'alors: les fameuses aventures de Peau d'Âne, de Finette, de l'Oranger, de Gracieuse, de la Belle au bois dormant, de Sepentin vert & de cent autres n'y étaient pas oubliées" ("The walls were of transparent porcelain, washed with various colors that represented the history of all the fairies since the creation of the world: the famous adventures of Donkey Skin, Finette, Orange Tree, Gracieuse, Sleeping Beauty, the Green Serpent, not forgetting a hundred others"; d'Aulnoy [1698] 1998: 165–6).[6]

Through these self-referential moments, women writers of fairy tales such as d'Aulnoy and Murat asserted their own creativity, comparing the transformative power of writing to that of their fairy characters, thus claiming public space in the world of print. While the conventional endings of the majority of the tales "may satisfy the imperatives of gender and state ideology ... the existence of unconventional roles for upper class women is not erased or ultimately foreclosed" (Seifert and Stanton 2010: 33). Disguising, cross-dressing, and metamorphosing the bodies of fairy-tale heroes and heroines destabilizes social norms that depend on recognizably sexed bodies, and unsettles the ideology of patriarchy fundamental to late seventeenth-century French society. The women authors who carried out such magical transformations capitalized on the possibilities the fairy tale afforded to explore and very often subvert different forms of gender and sexuality.

CHARLES PERRAULT, *STORIES OR TALES OF TIME PAST. WITH MORALS* (1697)

Charles Perrault was acquainted with some of the *conteuses* and their works—L'Héritier, author of "The Discreet Princess," was a relative—and, in his tales, Perrault drew on some of the same sources and tropes as did his female contemporaries.[7] Unlike the tales of the *conteuses*, however, which tended to be long and elaborate, Perrault's stories offered extremely condensed treatments of his subject matters. This striking difference has led Elizabeth Wanning Harries to propose two models for the fairy tale as genre, one "complex" and the other "compact" (2001: 16). D'Aulnoy named her 1697 collection *Tales of the Fairies*, and, as we have seen, it is with her title that the very term "fairy tale" originates; Perrault in presenting his *Tales* chose to privilege "time past." D'Aulnoy's fairy realms offered readers images of marvelous worlds inspired in part by the glittering example of Versailles and ornate opera settings;[8] Perrault, on the other hand, purportedly offered readers access to a historically earlier version of a humbler everyday world. These fundamental aesthetic differences involve gender in several ways.

Perrault's *Tales* consisted of eight stories, four of which—"Le Petit Chaperon rouge" ("Little Red Riding Hood"); "La Barbe-bleue" ("Blue Beard"); "Le Chat botté" ("Puss in Boots"); and "Le Petit poucet" ("Tom Thumb")—contained no fairies at all. In none of the stories are there any descriptions of fairy palaces, lands, or realms. This deliberate exclusion on Perrault's part relates to his sense of his work's purpose. Dedicating the *Tales* to Élisabeth-Charlotte d'Orléans, the niece of Louis XIV, Perrault stated: "Il est vraie que ces Contes donnent une image de ce qui se passe dans les moindres Familles ... mais à qui convient-il mieux de connaître comment vivent les Peuples, qu'aux Personnes que le Ciel destine à les conduire?" ("It is true these stories give an image of what goes on in the most humble families ... but who is better suited to know how the people live, than those Heaven has destined to lead them?"; Perrault 1967: 89).

In the dedication Perrault seems to belittle the tales he is publishing, saying they are devoid of reason, the kind told in the homes of the poor to young children by those unable to give any other instruction, but he also asserts the value of the tales in providing morals to suit readers with different abilities. The frontispiece of the volume depicts a woman spinning and telling stories to three children, while the wall behind them bears the words that give the work its subtitle, "Contes de ma Mere L'oye" ("Tales of Mother Goose"). The image apparently celebrates the cozy storytelling scene and the centrality of the female figure to it. If one believes the dedication, however, this is essentially a scene of ignorance and superstition. In the tension between the frontispiece and the dedication we see how Perrault both appropriates, and distances himself from, the power traditionally associated with the female storyteller in the home. He associates his *Tales* with the domestic sphere in a way his female contemporaries, constructing enchanted palaces, refused to do.

As mediator of the stories to a range of readers, the narrator of the *Tales* performs a dual function: mediating the stories upwards toward a governing elite, he reveals the workings of popular culture, thereby making the lower orders more amenable to control; mediating the stories downwards, he provides morals that will encourage readers to exert self-discipline. The disciplinary purpose of the publication is clear in the title and in the dedication, but the inclusion of morals that seem at times ill suited to what has just been read confuse the issue. Zipes has given a powerful account of literary fairy tales as part of a civilizing process that aimed to "reinforce the regulation of sexuality in modern Europe" and has observed that, while this process was volatile and multifaceted, "Perrault fixed the ground rules" (Zipes 1993: xi, 7). Maria Tatar, meanwhile, has discussed Perrault's *Tales* as part of "pedagogy of fear" designed to discipline children (Tatar 1992: 22–50). Considered as part of a civilizing process, or in terms of pedagogy, Perrault's *Tales* are notably gendered, and often in problematic ways.

Several of Perrault's tales allow for upward social mobility but permit this to happen through trickery and morally dubious stratagems. In "Puss in Boots," a destitute miller's son is made wealthy thanks to the machinations of his only "possession": his wily cat. Moreover, the "Moral" of the tale pushes aside the advantages "De jouir d'un riche heritage / Venant à nous de père en fils" ("Of enjoying a rich inheritance / Passed on from father to son") in favor of the chance to acquire wealth through skill and industry (Perrault 1999: 87). In Tom Thumb, the youngest son triumphs, and does so considerably against the odds. Born no bigger than a thumb (hence his name), Tom Thumb remains a tiny, delicate child. His parents think he is an idiot because he hardly ever speaks. Even so, Tom Thumb manages to foil his parents' plans to abandon all seven children in the woods; to save himself and his brothers from a cannibalistic ogre; and to gain the ogre's wealth through a trick. Weaklings are often scorned and pilloried, the "Moral" of the tale goes, but "Quelquefois cependant c'est ce petit marmot / Qui fera le bonheur de toute la famille" ("All the same, it's sometimes this little chap / Who brings happiness to the entire family"; Perrault 1999: 123). In a patriarchal, patrilineal system, it is only the eldest male child who benefits from the transmission of wealth. What these stories suggest to younger sons is that it is possible to make a go of it in such a system, despite their apparent exclusion, and that trickery and cunning are perfectly permissible in this context. As such, Perrault challenges constructions of masculinity, notably the privileged position of the eldest son, maintained regardless of merit.

In contrast, the success of Perrault's heroines (though not all succeed) is achieved through stereotypically feminine virtues of kindness and beauty that allow them to be assimilated into the patriarchal order through marriage. In "Les Fées" ("The Fairies"), the nameless heroine kindly gives an old woman a drink of cool water. The old woman, a fairy in disguise, rewards the girl by having diamonds fall from her mouth every time she speaks: "douce paroles" ("kind words") are more valuable than diamonds or sovereigns (Perrault 1999: 92). As good as she is beautiful, Cinderella forgives her cruel sisters, installs them in the palace with her, and finds them good husbands: beauty is a treasure, the "Moral" of the tale goes, but "bonne grâce / Est sans prix, et vaut mieux encore" ("kindness / Is without price and worth still more"; Perrault 1999: 101). The virtues of selflessness and consideration of others that Perrault's most fortunate heroines possess are compatible with gendered, restricted, and subordinate social roles.

If Perrault's fortunate heroines are virtuous, not all virtuous heroines are fortunate, as is seen in "the most widespread and notorious fairy tale in the Western world" (Zipes 1993: xi). Red Riding Hood is sent by her mother to visit her sick grandmother. Going through the woods, she meets a wolf and tells him where she is going. The wolf beats the girl to her destination and devours the grandmother. Red Riding Hood meets the same fate. Shocking in its brevity, "Little Red Riding Hood" does not accord with the qualities for which Perrault explicitly valued fairy tales: "Virtue is rewarded everywhere, and vice is always punished" (Perrault 1967: 5).[9] The little girl is a much-loved child, "sa mère en était folle, et sa mère grand plus folle encore" ("her mother was mad about her, and her grandmother even more so"; Perrault 1999: 70). This blameless little girl does exactly what she is told. Indeed, her fatal misfortune occurs in carrying out of a generally praiseworthy task especially associated with women: visiting the sick with provisions. Arguably, the child's misfortune is related to the absence of male guardians who would have better prepared the "pauvre enfant" (poor child), for the possible dangers of her walk in the woods. The "Moral" claims that what the tale shows is that young people "Surtout de jeunes filles/Belles, bien faites, et gentilles, / Font très mal d'écouter toute sorte de gens" ("Especially pretty young girls, well behaved and kind / Do very badly when they listen to just anybody"; Perrault 1999: 72). As the "Moral" continues, the tale is revealed to be an allegory warning against male sexual aggression, against predators of a different sort, who appear charming but are encroaching and dangerous, "Suivent les jeunes Demoiselles / Jusque dans les maisons" ("Following young ladies / Even into their very homes"; Perrault 1999: 73). The events of "Red Riding Hood" are bewildering if considered in terms of rewarding the good and punishing the bad, but the "Moral" makes the perversity of Perrault's version of the tale clear. It is precisely because Red Riding Hood is pretty, sweet, and well behaved, cocooned in all female households, and unaware that any contact with men can be dangerous, that she becomes prey. Wolves of all kinds will be wolves. Lupine nature, aggressive male sexuality, is a given, which must be accepted and negotiated.[10]

Grandmother's cottage, where Red Riding Hood meets her unhappy fate, and the woodcutter's dwellings that feature in other tales, are the kinds of humble homes in which Perrault, in his dedication, envisaged his tales being told. Like Red Riding Hood, Sleeping Beauty is another heroine who suffers domestic misadventure, albeit in a far grander setting (Figure 3.3).

"La Belle au bois dormant" ("Sleeping Beauty in the Woods") contains two parts. The first part, ending when the Prince's kiss awakens the enchanted Sleeping Beauty, is well known. In the second part, drawing on Giambattista Basile's "Sole, Luna e Talia" ("Sun, Moon, and Talia," 1634), the Prince and Sleeping Beauty marry and have two children but, until he inherits the kingdom on the death of his father, the Prince keeps the marriage secret because he is afraid of his mother, an ogress. Acting as regent in her son's absence, the ogress determines to eat first one grandchild, then the other, and finally the queen, Sleeping Beauty. She is tricked by the steward, who brings all three intended victims to safety and presents the ogress with dishes of game in their stead.

Perrault's "Sleeping Beauty in the Woods" counterpoises two opposed images of women. There is the immobile Sleeping Beauty, whose story "captures, with a single stroke, the notion of woman on display, to be looked at as erotic spectacle" (Tatar 2014: 143). Then, there is the ogress, with her criminal appetites. In the absence of male control, she gives way to these with the matter of fact declaration that: "Je veux manger demain à mon diner la petite Aurore" ("Tomorrow, I want to eat little Aurore for dinner"; Perrault 1999: 66). In a touch of black comedy, and a parody of good housekeeping, she further instructs the steward that her granddaughter is to come with "Sauce-Robert" (an onion and mustard sauce). Either entirely powerless or out of control, the women in the story "are unsuitable for positions of power. Incapable of governing themselves, they most certainly cannot govern others" (Duggan 2008: 223).

FIGURE 3.3: Sleeping Beauty's sumptuous surroundings, illustrated by Edmund Dulac, from *The Sleeping Beauty and Other Fairy Tales* (New York: Hodder and Stoughton, 1910). Public domain.

Sleeping Beauty and the ogre, ethereal beauty and grotesque monstrosity, create powerful representations in binary opposition. This opposition is mitigated slightly by more naturalistic descriptions of the body that occur across the story. As the Prince approaches the enchanted castle, he sees men and animals who all appear dead, but he knows from the red faces and noses of some that they have simply fallen asleep drinking. The ogress's intended cannibal acts also generate an awareness of the body that goes beyond the visual. Aurore is only four, so the steward substitutes a tender young lamb for her; a kid substitutes for Jour, her brother. Saving Sleeping Beauty, however, poses difficulty: "La jeune Reine avait vingt ans passés, sans compter les cent ans qu'elle avait dormi: sa peau était un peu dure, quoique belle et blanche; et le moyen de trouver dans la Ménagerie une bête aussi dure que cela?" ("The young Queen was twenty, not counting the hundred years she has slept: her skin was a little tough, however lovely and white; and how to find in the menagerie a beast as tough as that?"; Perrault 1999: 67). The steward's predicament is a momentary reminder that even the loveliest body is still texture and material. The representation of Sleeping Beauty as pure "erotic spectacle" is also complicated by the insinuations, in the scene of her awakening, that she has physical desires of her own: "Alors comme la fin de l'enchantement était venue, la Princesse s'éveilla; et le regardant avec des yeux plus tendres qu'une première vue ne semblait le permettre: 'Est-ce vous, mon Prince?' lui dit-elle, 'vous vous êtes bien fait attendre'" ("Then as the end of the enchantment had come, the Princess woke up; and looked at him with eyes more tender than a first view would seem to permit: 'Is it you, my Prince?' she said to him, 'you took your time'"; Perrault 1999: 64). Sleeping Beauty's explicit and immediate admiration of the Prince flouts propriety (as the narrator reminds us). That she recognizes the Prince owing to the "songes agréables" (sweet dreams) that the good fairy has procured for her during her long sleep, gives Sleeping Beauty an erotic point of view and experience. The awakening scene, as well as the Prince's matrilineal heritage (he is half-ogre) are among textual elements that contribute to Lewis C. Seifert's bravura reading, in which he argues that while "Sleeping Beauty in the woods" appears to be about "the inevitable triumph of heterosexuality," it turns out to invite "a more skeptical if not perverse view of the ostensible love plot" (2015: 22).

Tales such as "Sleeping Beauty" and "Cinderella" are among the most famous love plots in Western literature, but even in "Sleeping Beauty" there is a reminder that money and wealth alone motivate many marriages. Of the Prince's own mother, the ogress, we are told that "le Roi ne l'avait épousée qu'à cause de ses grands biens" ("the King only married her because of her great wealth"; Perrault 1999: 66). "La Barbe-bleue" ("Bluebeard"), Perrault's darkest tale, begins with an inventory of Bluebeard's wealth and possessions. Only then is it revealed that his blue beard makes him so ugly that women fly before him, and that mystery as to what became of his various wives causes disquiet. To facilitate his courtship of a neighbor's daughter, Bluebeard hosts a splendid entertainment in the country: "enfin tout alla si bien, que la Cadette commença à trouver que le Maître du logis n'avait plus la barbe si bleue, et que c'était un fort honnête homme" ("in the end everything went so well, that the younger daughter began to find that the Master of the house no longer had such a blue beard, and that he was a very respectable man"; Perrault 1999: 66). Wealth and splendor allow Bluebeard's wife, who is never named, to overlook his peculiarities. In her husband's absence, trusted with the keys to every room in the house, she enters the single room forbidden to her. Here, she finds Bluebeard's former wives hanging from the walls and the floor clotted in blood. She drops the key in shock and it becomes stained with blood that she cannot remove. When Bluebeard returns, he knows from the stained key what his wife has done. Only the arrival of the wife's brothers saves her from the fate of her predecessors.

"Bluebeard" is a story that "deviates from fairy-tale norms by turning the groom into an agent of villainy" (Tatar 2004: 19) but the first "Moral" to the tale implicitly finds the wife culpable, invoking misogynistic stereotypes of female curiosity. To act on curiosity often causes regrets: "C'est, n'en déplaise au sexe, un plaisir bien léger" ("It is, no disrespect Ladies, a trivial pleasure"; Perrault 1999: 80). Gendering curiosity, particularly curiosity acted upon in spite of prohibition, places the wife in a long tradition of reprehensible women, including Eve and Pandora. Not only does this "Moral" seem to exonerate the male murderer to find fault with his would-be victim, but even the least perceptive of Perrault's readers could see that this "Moral" runs completely counter to what the story itself enacts, because it is the wife's compulsion to disobey her husband and see what is in the forbidden room that saves and ultimately rewards her. Transgressing Bluebeard's commands, she avoids the fate in store for her, inherits all Bluebeard's wealth, generously provides for her family; and marries again. This assertive heroine understands marriage as a matter of calculation and enterprise (Hannon 1998: 61–2). That the heart of the story lies in the upturning of gender hierarchies, rather than stereotypical female faults, is sourly suggested in the second "Moral." Competent readers, it says, will recognize this is a tale from the past because such terrible husbands no longer exist; the modern husband has relinquished power: "Près de sa femme on le voit filer doux; / Et de quelque couleur que sa barbe puisse être, / On a peine à juger qui des deux est le maître" ("You see him going along mildly near his wife; / And whatever color his beard might be / It is hard to say which of them is the master"; Perrault 1999: 81). The moral insinuates that in contemporary French society overweening women have overturned the power of their husbands and thereby the natural order.

That Perrault's tales are set in the past, but moralized for a range of contemporary readers, bifurcates the volume's relationship to time and progress with uneven, gendered, and confusing implications. Male adventurers such as Puss in Boots and Tom Thumb flourished "once upon a time" and in the late seventeenth-century France in which their tales were read. The elemental battle between wolf and prey is presented as an allegory for female vulnerability to male sexuality in the supposedly civilized modern city. The reader is told the murderous excesses of Bluebeard belong in the past, but only because it is clear that modern husbands are henpecked. Kindness and graciousness will gain a chaste young woman a husband, but marriage, the subject of several cynical narrative asides, seems not to be such a glittering prize. Without the "Morals" (eventually the *Tales* would be published without them) Perrault's representations of gender become more coherent: depictions of active non-elite males who can insinuate themselves into patriarchal power structures and of women subsumed into marriage but ubiquitously prey to male violence.

THE FAIRY TALE IN ENGLAND

Perrault envisaged that both adults and children would read his tales. In 1729, Robert Samber, the first translator of the work into English, retorted to criticism that the tales were "low and childish" by saying it should be remembered that they were "designed for Children" even though their excellence both as to "Narration and Moral" made them delightful for adults as well (Perrault 1729). Although fairy tales were popular reading material in England, few original English tales were produced, and the market was dominated by translations. Here, d'Aulnoy was the dominant figure. Her tales were quickly translated into English and had appeared in four separate collections by 1728 (Palmer and Palmer 1974: 227–8). Regular reprints of her works ensured that, "if there was one writer associated with fairy tales in England at the end of the eighteenth century, it was d'Aulnoy" (Jones 2008: 254). Early English translations contained paratextual elements that drew attention to the works' origins in a world of elite sociability, to their literary self-consciousness, and to a projected adult female readership (Douglas 2015: 182–3). Over time, however, the image presented of d'Aulnoy in translations changed, as did the projected readers of her works. By the end of the century, d'Aulnoy's fairy tales increasingly appeared in abridged form, and the writer "had been transformed from an adult wit into a children's author" (Jones 2008: 242).

Unlike d'Aulnoy, those women producing fairy tales in England, notably Sarah Fielding and Jeanne-Marie Leprince de Beaumont, were middle-class writers who earned a living from writing and teaching. Their tales, explicitly written for children, featured mainly young female protagonists, and were part of a growing bourgeois and commercial book market. When she published *The Governess: or Little Female Academy* in 1749, Fielding was already a successful author, though, as she chose to publish her books either anonymously or pseudonymously, she was not known as such. *The Governess* was innovative on two main grounds: it was the first full-length work in English explicitly written for a younger audience, and it was also the first work to be set in a girls' boarding school. Fielding's work has been seen as disseminating "highly conservative mores and prescriptive codes" (Zipes 2012: xi), and of socializing girls in the virtues of self-effacement and humility (Fish Wilmer 1995: 310).

The Governess is unquestionably didactic, but that it simply teaches submission is arguable. The novel begins with a scene of discord as the girls, aged between seven and fourteen, fight over a bowl of apples, but under the guidance of the oldest girl, Jenny, and through a process of storytelling and conversation in the garden, the girls come to accept that "endeavouring to please and love each other" leads to happiness (Fielding 1968: 118).

Two of the tales the girls share are fairy tales. Commenting on the first of these, which involves two giants, Mrs. Teachum expresses reservations: "Giants, Magic, Fairies, and all Sorts of supernatural Assistances in a Story, are only introduced to amuse and divert ... by no means let the Notion of Giants or Magic dwell upon your Minds" (Fielding 1968: 166). The second tale, "The Princess Hebe," draws upon motifs and characters familiar from the tales of d'Aulnoy: a dispossessed princess; an ineffectual male ruler; rivalry between benign and malign fairies. When Hebe's father dies, his brother, controlled by his evil wife, forces the young girl and her mother to flee. They find refuge with the good fairy Sybella in the woods of Ardella. Like Hebe and her mother, Sybella has suffered adversity, in her case brought about by the mistakes of her misguided father. He has, however, given Sybella two gifts: the traditional magic wand and (an Enlightenment addition) "Strength and Constancy of Mind" (234). When Hebe is given the opportunity to regain the throne she demurs, citing a preference for a "private life." Her mother, however, objects that Hebe should not "refuse the Power that would give her such Opportunities of doing Good, and making others happy; since, by that Refusal, the Power might fall into Hands that would make an ill Use of it" (274). The emphasis in Fielding's text on the control of the passions does not lead inevitably to female submissiveness. Hebe does not marry, and contrasting her moral autonomy with the passive virtue of Perrault's Cinderella and Sleeping Beauty, Linda Bree remarks: "There is not a handsome prince in sight ... an educated woman has become capable of ruling a whole kingdom alone" (1996: 68).

The amenability of the fairy-tale form to radical, feminist ideas is apparent in a later eighteenth-century tale by the Irish writer Elizabeth Sheridan (Douglas 2015). Like Fielding's Hebe, Sheridan's Emeline is a dispossessed princess who undergoes various adventures and trials. When, again like Hebe, Emeline hesitates to ascend the throne, a fairy overcomes her reservations. Significantly, the fairy instructs the future queen in the contract between ruler and ruled, and the legitimacy of rebellion: "the compact being mutual, a failure on your side, frees the subject from allegiance" (Sheridan 1783: 96). Sheridan subtitled her work "a moral tale." Morality and social convention can often go together, but in neither Sheridan nor Fielding are the terms simply equivalent. In their tales rational heroines exercise their moral natures in powerful ways that exceed the conventional social roles allowed to women.

In 1756, Jeanne-Marie Leprince de Beaumont, a French governess living in London, published *Magasin des Enfans ou Dialogues entre une sage Gouvernante et plusieurs de ses Élèves* (The Children's Magazine or Dialogues between a Wise Governess and Several of her Students). As the title suggests, Leprince de Beaumont followed Fielding's design of feminocentric conversation but deviated from the earlier writer in having her governess, Mrs. Affable, supervise the conversations and tell all the tales. The disciplinary ideals informing Leprince de Beaumont's work are indicated on the title page, which advertises that each child will speak according to her "Genius, Temper and Inclination" but also that "Their several Faults are pointed out, and the easy Way to mend them, as well as to think, and speak, and act properly" (Leprince de Beaumont 1767).

The title page of Leprince de Beaumont's work significantly promises "Contes moraux" ("Moral Tales"), and in a long preface (subsequently dropped from the English translation) she questions the suitability of fairy tales for children. With the *conteuses* clearly in mind, Leprince de Beaumont states that the style in these works is difficult and that they are dangerous for children in whom they inspire "idées dangereuses & fausses" ("dangerous and false ideas"). The little morality they have is "noyé sous un merveilleux ridicule" ("drowned in ridiculous wonder"). Perrault's tales, in contrast, provide clear morals with which the teacher can work. Leprince de Beaumont's explication reveals the historical specificity of certain ideas of the "moral":

> Je trouve moyen de faire comprendre aux enfans, lors qui'ils lisent *la Barbe Bleue,* les inconvéniens d'un mariage fait par intérêt; les dangers de la curiosité, les malheurs qui peuvent arriver du peu de complaisance, qu'on a pour les caprices d'un époux; l'inutilité du mensonge, pour éviter le châtiment.
>
> (I find a way to make children understand, when they read *Bluebeard*, the disadvantages of a marriage of self-interest; the dangers of curiosity, the misfortunes that can come from too little accommodation of the caprices of a spouse; the fruitlessness of lying to avoid punishment.)
>
> (Leprince de Beaumont 1756: iv–v; my translation)

Despite her reservations, Leprince de Beaumont did draw on the work of the *conteuses* for several of the fairy tales included in the *Magazine*. The source for the most famous of these tales, "Beauty and the Beast," was a much longer and more ornate version by Gabrielle-Suzanne de Villeneuve.[11]

In Leprince de Beaumont's version of the tale, a wealthy merchant loses all his money and is forced to move with his six children to the country. One day, he hears that one of his ships has come in and goes to salvage what he can of his fortune. His two older daughters ask that he return with all sorts of finery; his youngest, Beauty, asks only for a rose. Returning home, the merchant is benighted in a storm but finds refuge in a grand but seemingly empty house where he is magically provided with good food, and a warm bed. Leaving the next day, he sees a rose bush and, remembering his promise to Beauty, plucks a flower. Suddenly appearing, the Beast declares the merchant must die for his trespass unless one of his daughters voluntarily takes his place. This Beauty agrees to do. She grows fond of the Beast but always rejects his proposals of marriage. When Beauty fails to return from a visit to her family, the Beast believes she has abandoned him and resolves to die. Beauty, seeing the Beast in a dream, returns and finds him near death. Realizing that she does love him, she agrees to be his wife. Immediately, a handsome prince stands before her, his enchantment ended by her voluntary gift of love.

Like Belle-Belle, Beauty sacrifices herself for her father, in the first case by going to war, in the second case by entering a marriage. Unlike d'Aulnoy's green serpent or blue bird, who can delight their lovers with intelligent conversation, Leprince de Beaumont's beast cannot offer this, having also been condemned to simplicity of mind. All he can offer Beauty—apart from considerable luxury—is kindness. Leprince de Beaumont's tale feminizes the beast by giving him a quality particularly praised in fairy-tale heroines, thereby reassuring reluctant brides that marriage, however it appears, need not be fearful. Beauty's sacrifice has "a civilizing function," transforming the Beast into a prince and thereby "regenerating a whole society of men and women" (Korneeva 2014: 245). Significantly, though, it is not the perfect happiness of Beauty and her husband that elicits the first response from Mrs. Affable's auditors, but the ghastly fate of Beauty's unpleasant sisters, transformed into living statues. When some pupils doubt they could marry Beast, the teacher makes clear the moral imperative of women as objects of exchange in patriarchal marriages: "those who do well are always rewarded: if Beauty had refused to die instead of her father, or if she had been ungrateful to poor Beast, she would not have been a great queen afterwards" (Leprince de Beaumont 1767: 68–9). "Beauty and the Beast" soon proved popular as a stand-alone story, excerpted from the *Magazine* and designated, following Leprince de Beaumont's own usage, as a "moral tale."[12] The moral, as pointed out by Mrs. Affable, is that young girls must be prepared to overcome their own feelings and accede to arranged marriages, even unpalatable ones.

In England, in the second half of the eighteenth century, the fairy tale underwent several notable shifts. It shed its elite accoutrements and was produced by bourgeois writers for young middle-class readers. It was perhaps as a tribute to the commercial spirit of her adopted country that Leprince de Beaumont's Beauty—unlike her predecessor in Villeneuve—is not revealed to be a princess, but remains a merchant's daughter. If the cultural significance of the term "fairy tale" is its announcement of "difference and resistance" and "alternative worlds" (Zipes 2012: 12) then its displacement by the term "moral tale" in the later eighteenth century may also indicate an intention to abandon alternatives, to inculcate gender and social norms, and to mold young readers to the *status quo*. As we have seen, however, moral tales by Fielding and Sheridan employ fairies whose teachings challenge gender expectations and allow young heroines to achieve autonomy.[13]

CONCLUSION

In the period 1690 to 1800, the literary fairy tale was a form particularly associated with women writers. Often embedded in longer works, especially novels, the publication of fairy tales permitted the expression of a female voice outside the domestic sphere and facilitated a distinctive female presence in the public space of print culture. Late seventeenth-century tales by elite French women were elaborate, intertextual, and self-referential, and they often foregrounded the figure of woman as author. In the different context of mid-eighteenth-century England, middle-class women writers working in a commercial print culture grasped the pedagogic usefulness of the fairy tale and produced simpler tales as suited a younger audience.

The prominence within literary fairy tales of marriage, equated with a "happy ever after" resolution for the hero and heroine, would seem to suggest the ideological compatibility of the form with patriarchy. The system of rewards and punishments at work in the tales also clearly regulates female sexuality and agency in line with patriarchal needs: female chastity is rewarded and any deviation castigated; female appetite, and especially a desire for power, is seen as grotesque and is also subject to punishment. Powerful as these conservative elements are, fairy tales also diverge strongly and distinctively from patriarchal ideological imperatives, evident in particular in the fairy tales by writers such as d'Aulnoy, Murat, and L'Héritier. The threat of forced or undesired marriage is potent throughout the tales and often precipitates the heroine's quest. Repeated representations of the father figure as weak and undeserving of authority undermine power structures and open up the possibility for female rule. The *Tales* of Perrault suggest that patriarchal structures are not completely rigid and can be subverted, at least by enterprising males. The works of d'Aulnoy and other *conteuses* present active and lively heroines, while the creation of an alternative fairy realm and the use of metamorphosis unsettles gender norms and renders ideas of male and female fluid, unpredictable, and inventive. In mid-eighteenth-century "moral tales," fairy instructors guide heroines to autonomy and the exercise of power. Uneasily holding conservative and subversive elements in tension, the fairy tale always has the potential to disrupt.

CHAPTER FOUR

Humans and Non-Humans

Ambiguities of Agency and Personhood in Fairy Tales, 1650–1800

LEWIS C. SEIFERT

Of all the many reasons fairy tales have an urgent contemporary relevance, the treatment they reserve for humans and their relation to their surrounding natural world is surely among the most pressing. Of course, it goes without saying that other genres and other art forms also draw our attention to how humans think about and interact with their environment and the non-human beings and objects that inhabit it. But there are many reasons why the framing of this question by fairy tales deserves particular scrutiny. Most obviously, perhaps, by virtue of their archetypal status in cultures across the globe, fairy tales—and in particular the fairy tales of the period 1650 to 1800, which include some of the best known of all fairy tales in the Western European tradition—present some of the most memorable scenes of the human encounter with the natural world. Fairy tales often propose seemingly simple scenarios of this encounter, while pointing to profound and complex consequences.

Take the example of Charles Perrault's "Le Petit Chaperon Rouge" ("Little Red Riding Hood," 1697). In addition to a much-glossed sexual dynamic, Little Red Riding Hood's encounter with the wolf in the woods shows the high stakes of human contact with the non-human. Little Red Riding Hood falls into a trap set by a crafty wolf intent on satisfying his hunger. But why she falls into this trap in the first place is of particular significance for Perrault's narrator, whose wry comment about the heroine being unaware of the danger of speaking with wolves highlights the epistemological dynamic at work in this encounter: to be human is to know and to be wary of the non-human. To be human is as much a matter of *knowing about* as it is of *acting on* the natural world and the living beings within it. This example allows us to formulate a starting hypothesis, namely that fairy tales have at their core the objective of defining what it is to be human and that definition necessarily involves working through a relationship with the natural world and the beings that inhabit it. Fairy tales do not provide a singular or straightforward answer to what it is that constitutes this relationship—what boundaries do or do not exist between the human and natural world. There is cultural and historical variance, but there is also variance within cultures and historical periods, even within the work of individual tellers and writers. But what fairy tales *do* provide is a paradoxical means of understanding the place of the human in the natural world. For, by suspending "natural" laws—by placing its characters in a *super*natural environment—they make listeners and readers acutely aware of the dependence humans have on their environment.

We should take this paradox seriously because the supernatural environment of fairy tales does important cultural work in framing and also, in some instances, of thinking beyond the dominant paradigms of understanding the relationship between the human and the non-human. And so we might ask: what sort of cultural work does the supernatural context of the fairy tale do for defining or even contesting the relation of humans to their environment? This question is all the more urgent at a moment in time when the consequences of the Anthropocene, the period of geologic time during which humans have effected disruptive (and destructive) change to the earth's climate, are becoming ever more apparent (Ellis 2018). Pollution, rising sea levels, mass extinctions of species, and increased frequency of destructive storms are but some of the more visible outcomes of human transformation of the natural world. In the face of such dramatic events, some might dismiss turning to fairy tales as a means of understanding and confronting the role of humans in environmental change. If solutions to ecological disaster necessarily require scientific expertise and engagement, they also make it imperative to come to terms with the discursive representations that ground human exploitation of natural resources. The stories humans tell themselves about their relation to the natural order are neither trivial nor irrelevant; they are, rather, crucial for understanding the assumptions underlying humans' response to and interaction with their natural surroundings. In literary terms, this is as true for the fairy tale as it is for more elite literary forms such as pastoral (a literary portrayal of idealized country life), the novel, or poetry. One might even argue that the fairy tale, because of its broad popular status, condenses and communicates a culture's most central ideological suppositions in ways more broadly influential than other more elite texts and forms. So, there remains much to be gleaned from a consideration of fairy tales as a vector through which the human encounter with the natural world is portrayed and mediated.

The cultural work of fairy tales in defining and contesting the prevailing relation of humans to their natural environment is by no means a feature reserved for more contemporary times. In fact, the period covered by the present volume (1650–1800) was a decisive one for what has come to be understood as the modern consensus around what distinguishes nature from culture and non-human from human.[1] Early modern scientists and philosophers are credited with erecting the rigid boundaries between nature and culture and between humans and non-humans that Western cultures accept as givens. The "new science" of the European sixteenth and seventeenth centuries and its discoveries in astronomy, physics, and biology were premised on a clear distinction between human observer and natural phenomena. In the work of Nicolaus Copernicus, Francis Bacon, Galileo Galilei, and René Descartes, to name but a few, humans were accorded a status outside of the physical order they endeavored to describe and explain, while nature became an "ontologically autonomous domain, a field of inquiry and scientific experimentation, an object to exploit and improve" (Descola 2005: 133). To be sure, Christianity had emphasized the notion that humans are superior to nature (128), but early modern European scientific and philosophical inquiry gave this opposition a new and influential formulation. Hereafter, the dividing lines between nature and culture and between non-human and human were seemingly unassailable, a matter of fact. And yet, as the anthropologist Philippe Descola reminds us, modern Western cultures are very much an anomaly in the ways they have isolated humans from the natural world: "More common is the tendency to treat elements of the environment as persons endowed with cognitive, moral and social qualities analogous to those of humans, making possible the communication and interaction between classes of beings at first glance very different from one another" (70). By making both humans and nature autonomous categories, early modern European thought turned away ever more decisively from the continuous and relational perspectives of most other world cultures.

Of course, it was in the early modern period—and at the same time as its scientific and philosophical interrogations of the human and the natural world—that European fairy tales flourished and came into their own as a distinct literary genre. To recognize this congruence leads to the question of what relation there might be between the two—between the scientific and philosophical distinction between the human and the natural worlds, on the one hand, and the rise of the fairy tale as a European literary genre, on the other. The question I have in mind here is less a causal one—did the emergence of the "new science" contribute to the rise of the fairy tale?—and more a relational one: what connections are there between early modern fairy tales and the contemporaneous distinction between humans and nature? Without denying that a causal connection is entirely possible, it is more feasible and more productive in the long run to consider whether and how fairy tales enact the radical oppositions between nature and culture and between human and non-human found in European scientific and philosophical discourses of the period. How do fairy tales represent the dichotomy between humans and nature that modern Western cultures have taken for granted? Do they confirm it? Or, instead, do they resist it? Do fairy tales give human beings, alone, the status of persons? Or do they extend personhood to other beings as well? There are no simple or straightforward answers to these questions, either for the period that is the focus of this chapter or for any other period. And yet, I would assert that to pose these questions is to open up a field of inquiry into the relevance of fairy tales for thinking through the consequences of, as well as solutions to, the divide between humans and nature, not only in the past but also in our present.

THE AMBIGUITIES OF THE HUMAN

Humans are far and away the most common and the most prominent characters in early modern European fairy tales. Indeed, the presence of humans is nearly obligatory for the genre since stories with strictly animal characters are generally classified as a separate genre (animal fables), whether or not they contain magical elements.[2] Given this fact, it would hardly be an exaggeration to claim that fairy tales have as their central mission to explore and define what it means to be human. The range of situations human fairy-tale characters experience involve some of the most momentous of the human life cycle—the vagaries of birth, the challenges of childhood, the obstacles to love and marriage, parenthood, old age, and death. In addition, numerous fairy tales from this period involve plots with an almost exclusively human cast of characters. Considering this focus, one could be easily tempted to conclude that fairy tales are anthropocentric, both in the sense of giving central billing to humans but also in the sense of according humans a privileged ontological status. But to reach this conclusion would be to mask the complexities of fairy-tale characters. For, beyond those explicitly designated as human, there are others, particularly supernatural ones, whose exact species is less clear and who may or may not count as human. Complicating matters are the minimalist descriptions of fairy-tale characters overall. But even when they are indeed described, their powers as much as their features are the primary focus. Supernatural creatures are often modeled after humans, with hyperbolic or hypertrophic traits and powers.

Fairies are perhaps the most numerous of this group, especially in French fairy tales.

Contrary to their Victorian counterparts, they are of full-sized human form. And unlike many other supernatural characters, fairies inhabit both the human world and their own realm, and they can be either helpers or opponents (to use Vladimir Propp's terminology[3]). But neither role necessarily differentiates them from humans. Instead, the rare descriptions present them as liminal figures, with either superlatively or monstrously human traits. The Fairy Amazone (a helper) in Marie-Catherine d'Aulnoy's "Princesse Carpillon" has an otherworldly appearance as an "amazon" (defined at the time as a "Woman of courage, male and warrior-like"[4]) but is nonetheless a "lady" (*dame*):

> Right then there came out a chariot of diamonds, pulled by swans, in which was one of the most beautiful ladies in the world. She had a helmet on her head of pure gold, covered with white feathers. Its visor was raised, and her eyes shone like the sun. Her body, covered with an ornate breastplate, and her hand armed with a lance all of fire displayed sufficiently that she was an amazon.
>
> (d'Aulnoy 2004: 624)

And when the Fairy Carabosse (an opponent) appears in d'Aulnoy's "Princesse Printanière," she is repulsive, both because of her deformed and putatively hideous features and because of the beings that accompany her: "They see coming in a wheelbarrow pushed by two dreadful little dwarves an ugly woman whose feet were crooked, whose knees were under her chin, with a big hump, crossed eyes, and skin blacker than ink. She held in her arms an ugly little monkey that she was breastfeeding, and she spoke a jargon no one understood" (d'Aulnoy 2004: 263–4).

This description, which emphasizes Carabosse's physical deformity and racialized otherness ("skin blacker than ink"), renders her only marginally human by the company she keeps (dwarves and a monkey) and, not insignificantly, by her incomprehensible language ("a jargon no one understood"). Her black skin and her "jargon" may liken her to a provincial peasant,[5] in which case she would register as just barely human given the prejudices of the period's elites (Ronzeaud 1988). Elitism is certainly on display in the reaction of the Queen, who banishes Carabosse from her sight, saying: "Go away, big hag ... you are nothing but an ill-bred woman to come before me looking the way you are. If you stay any longer, I'll have you thrown out" (d'Aulnoy 2004: 264). If the Fairies Carabosse or Amazone are at least marginally human, they also illustrate that there is no monolithic species of humans in fairy tales—or in the prevailing biases of the early modern period more generally. Class and racial prejudices reflect a rigid hierarchy from which human or humanoid characters cannot escape.

Like fairies, supernatural characters that are unambiguously opponents/adversarial occupy a nebulous category of species that is both human and other. For the first appearance of the word "ogre" in his fairy tales (in "Donkey Skin"),

Perrault gives the following definition in a footnote: "Wild man who ate little children" (Perrault 2005: 147). The use of the word *sauvage* (wild) and the reference to cannibalism in this definition recall the period's thinking about indigenous peoples of the Americas. (Striking as well is the use of the past tense, which implies that "ogres" are a thing of the past and not simply a figment of the fairy-tale imagination.) Furthermore, with the implicit comparison, it is questionable whether ogres are fully human, just as the humanity of the "savages" of the New World was itself open to debate in the period (Melzer 2012).[6] Other ogres have no less of a tenuous relationship to the species of humans. In Perrault's "La Belle au bois dormant" ("Sleeping Beauty"), the mother of the Prince who marries the eponymous heroine is described as being "de race ogresse" ("of Ogre lineage"). Even if the meaning the French word "race" is closer to "lineage" than to "race" in contemporary English or French, the Queen Mother occupies an ambiguous position in relation to the fully human characters. If she *is* of a lineage—or a family—like any other human and if she has no outwardly visible distinguishing traits, she nonetheless stands apart for her rumored cannibalistic urges: "People whispered at Court that she had the inclinations of ogres, and that watching little children pass by she had all the difficulty in the world to keep from jumping on them" (Perrault 2005: 193). That this detail is expressed as a rumor indicates that she is not visibly different from other (human) members of her court. To be an ogre is to look and be like any other human, save for the nearly irrepressible urge to cannibalize children. The ogre in Perrault's "Le Petit Poucet" ("Little Thumbling") is similarly ambiguous: on the one hand, he is monstrously frightful but, on the other, he is worthy of tongue-in-cheek compassion when, noting his wife's fear at Little Thumbling's false claim about the ogre's life being in danger, the narrator asserts that "this ogre never failed to be an extremely good husband" (249). The narrator's irony serves to humanize, at least somewhat, the ogre. His cannibalistic urges notwithstanding, he was still capable of living up to at least one human virtue—that of being a good husband.

Ranging from admiration and astonishment (in cases of helper fairies) to fear and repulsion (in cases of opponent fairies, ogres, and genies, for instance), the reactions of human characters to the marginally human supernatural beings are deeply instructive. The encounter of humans with their marginally human or human-like supernatural others—be they fairies or ogres—evokes emotions that suggest the vulnerability and dependence of the fully human protagonists. Be it positive (such as the awe and astonishment displayed at the spectacle of the Amazon Fairy in "Princesse Carpillon") or negative (such as the repulsion evoked by the Fairy Carabosse or the brothers' fear of the ogre in "Little Thumbling"), the reaction to the supernatural helper or opponent thus underscores the connection between humans and the ambiguously human beings they encounter. Humans do not and cannot exist in isolation from one another, nor can they exist in isolation from those marginally human supernatural beings who bring either aid or danger, comfort or fear. This state of absolute dependence and of total vulnerability contrasts sharply with the presumption of autonomous distance given to human observers in early modern science and philosophy. Even if the human characters of early modern fairy tales are, far more often than not, victorious over the obstacles and threats they face, it is their connection, their relational embeddedness with other human and ambiguously human beings that is decisive. And to the extent that the victorious heroes and heroines of the early modern fairy tale embody exemplary humanity, they do so only with the mediation of their ambiguously human helpers and opponents.

NON-HUMAN ACTORS

If what qualifies as human in early modern fairy tales is ambiguous (especially for supernatural characters), the non-human is at first glance more straightforward. Everything that is not explicitly or ambiguously human—or of human form—is non-human. But what, in an affirmative sense, does it mean to be "non-human"? Critical use of this term refers to both living beings (animals, plants, insects, ecosystems) and inanimate objects (both natural and human-made) that are not of recognizable human form.[7] And so, as it is commonly used, the "non-human" covers a wide range of phenomena that do not necessarily share many common traits. Fairy tales are of course replete with non-human creatures and objects of all sorts, from the most realistic to the most fantastical. The most frequent are naturally occurring animals (mammals to fish, supernatural to real), fantastical animals (e.g., dragons), plants, naturally occurring inanimate objects (e.g., the stone door in "Ali-Baba"), inanimate human-made objects (e.g., the seven-league boots in Perrault's "Little Thumbling"), objects endowed with animate features (the enchanted horse in the eponymous tale of the *Mille et une nuits* [*The Thousand and One Nights*]).[8] Beyond the many differences among these non-human life forms and objects, the one trait they share—besides not having a human or humanlike body—is that of playing a decisive narrative role, most often in relation to human (or ambiguously human) characters. For instance, the forest in many fairy tales is the site where human protagonists encounter obstacles but also the means of overcoming them. And so, the forest is more than the physical backdrop for the events of the plot, but an actor in its own right, that is, an agent that acts *upon* and is acted *upon*. What is peculiar about the agency of non-humans in fairy tales, of course, is that it is endowed or contiguous with a supernatural dimension.

The agency given to these non-human actors in the fairy tale is not unlike the personhood attributed to lifeforms and natural objects by many non-Western cultures. If personhood is defined as a clear intentional agency (whether expressed or not), then the tendency of many non-Western cultures (as Descola has shown) to attribute what I am calling the agency of non-human actors in the fairy tale are, arguably, persons in this broad sense of the term. Beyond this, what personhood entails is variable, with some non-humans displaying cognition and language making them altogether similar to human characters (the wolf in "Little Red Riding Hood" comes to mind; see Figure 4.1).

But others may display an agency without clearly demonstrating either cognitive or linguistic intention (a magic wand that spins thread, embroiders cloth, styles hair, and dresses in Marie-Jeanne Lhéritier de Villandon's "Ricdin-Ricdon"). But if both humans and non-humans are "persons" in the sense just described, what then might we conclude about the relative status of each in the early modern fairy tale? Is human personhood superior to non-human personhood? Coequal with it? Or inferior to it? Do early modern fairy tales stage the encounter of human and non-human persons so as to privilege the human, or not?

FIGURE 4.1: Walter Crane's depiction of the wolf in very human terms, from "Little Red Riding Hood," in *Walter Crane's Toy Books* (London: George Routledge and Sons, 1875), p. 2. Public domain.

The short answer to all these questions would be "yes," since there are examples to be found to support the hypotheses behind each of them. Given the vast diversity of fairy tales produced between 1650 and 1800, this is not surprising, of course. Still, a more precise answer would be that, overall, this corpus works to reinforce an anthropocentric perspective, that is, to privilege the human over the non-human. This too is not surprising, all the more so because of the scientific and philosophical context of early modern Europe. Beyond this—and all the while keeping in mind the question of whether or not early modern fairy tales privilege the human—it is ultimately more productive to consider *how* the human and the non-human come into contact and *how* relations between the human and the non-human are negotiated. In the remainder of this chapter, I will turn to specific examples of the encounter between the human and the non-human in the early modern fairy tale: the relation between natural and social spaces, between humans and animals, and between humans and objects. The discussion that follows is in no way exhaustive or comprehensive, but instead aims to outline some of the central ways that early modern European fairy tales imagine the relations between the human and the non-human and to indicate paths for future study.

NATURAL AND SOCIAL SPACES

One of the most recognizable topoi of the fairy tale (of any period) is the departure from a domestic—and inherently human—space and the move into or through a natural space of some sort (a forest, for instance). In Marie-Jeanne Leprince de Beaumont's "La Belle et la Bête" ("Beauty and the Beast," 1757), a father ventures through a forest on his way home from a port city and is forced by a storm to seek refuge in a mysterious castle, where he is confronted by the Beast. In Perrault's "Sleeping Beauty," a prince, hunting in the countryside, spies the towers of a castle surrounded by a thick wood, which opens a path for him. As transitional moments leading up to dramatic events (the father's confrontation with the Beast; the Prince's discovery of the sleeping princess), it is easy to overlook the importance of this contact with natural space.[9] But it is in these moments—when human protagonists encounter the natural world—that the fairy tale gives form and definition to the human and the social as such. If the natural setting is inhospitable (as in the two examples above), then the return to or the establishment of a discrete domestic space is all the more clear, and the contrast between the natural and the social—the non-human and the human—all the more striking. This is often the case in the fairy tales of the early modern period, and of other periods as well.

But the interactions between human fairy-tale protagonists and their natural surroundings can also blur the distinction between the social and the natural. The French *conteuses*, for instance, recycle the pastoral representation of natural spaces made famous by Honoré d'Urfé's novel, *L'Astrée* (1607–27). The nature depicted in this novel is by no means realistic, but instead an idealized *locus amoenus* (a topos referring to a space of safety or comfort), a refuge from the constraints and dangers of court life where nature is thoroughly domesticated and becomes a backdrop for social interaction. Many early modern fairy tales (particularly those of several of the French *conteuses*) reflect this understanding of natural space, in which the domestication of nature is amplified by supernatural means. Reducing the spatial description to a minimum, Henriette-Julie de Murat gives the following description of the Island of Magnificence—which also gives its name to the title of the tale—where the Fairy Plaisir (Pleasure) had constructed her palace:

> In the age when fairies were esteemed, there was one of the most famous who held her court on an island surrounded by a league-wide lake, big and deep, which one could never cross without the consent of Queen Pleasure (that's what the fairy was called) and then only by supernatural means such as on the back of some monstrous fish, on a flying chariot, or something similar. This island was called the Island of Magnificence.
>
> (Murat 2006: 223)

Subjected to the control of the fairy and accessible only by supernatural means of transportation, the Island of Magnificence is a site of magical domestication. Compared to this succinct and vague description, the narrator continues with an enumeration of the building materials and contents of the fairy's palace, domesticating the island all the more (see 223–4). In another tale by Murat, "Jeune et belle" ("Young and Beautiful," 1698), a different fairy discovers a sleeping shepherd, Alidor, with whom she falls in love. Using her fairy powers she transforms his surroundings into an idyllic realm: his sheep are covered with "silk whiter than snow," his cabin is decorated with tapestries made from jasmine and orange flowers, the simple floor becomes porcelain (Murat 2006: 122–3). In contrast, d'Aulnoy often pokes fun at such hyperbolically idealized settings in "Le Mouton" ("The Ram," 1697). When Princess Merveilleuse wanders into the kingdom of the Ram, she is greeted with what at first seems to be a fairly typical pastoral retreat (Figure 4.2).

But quickly the marvelous becomes hyperbolic, and ridiculously so: through a vast plain filled with fragrant flowers runs a wide river of orange blossom water in turn bordered with fountains of "Spanish wine, rose and orange liqueur, spiced wine, and a thousand other sorts of liqueurs" (d'Aulnoy 2004: 414). On the branches of trees hang cooked delicacies of all sorts: quails and rabbits, turkeys, chickens, pheasants, ortolans (415). When it rained, crawfish bisques, broths, foies gras, sweetbreads, sausages, meat pies, pâtés, fruit preserves, gold coins, pearls, and diamonds fell from the sky (415). Rather than

FIGURE 4.2: Pastoral setting of "Le Mouton" in a French edition of d'Aulnoy's tales, *Les Contes choisis* (Paris: 1847), between pp. 76–7. Public domain.

delighting in these surroundings, Merveilleuse finds them frightful and, in tears, asks Mouton to return her home (416). Through her reaction to the quasi-monstrous pastoral nature, Merveilleuse indirectly advocates for a natural space unadulterated by human and literary convention. And so, along with a clear parody of the pastoral ideal, d'Aulnoy's tactic here opens a space for critiquing its domesticating logic, setting her apart from many of her fellow *conteuses*.[10]

HUMANS AND ANIMALS

Along with natural spaces, animals constitute a significant means of distinguishing the human from the non-human. Of course, few narrative forms are inhabited by as many non-human animals as fairy tales. Animals are quite simply everywhere in fairy tales, and early modern fairy tales are no exception. Beyond their ubiquity, fairy-tale animals come in a great variety of forms, from fictional to real, from anthropomorphic to zoomorphic, from humans in metamorphosis to authentic animals, among others. But in whatever form, fairy-tale animals necessarily bring attention to the line dividing the human from the non-human, whether to blur or erase that line or to put it into sharp relief.

Early modern fairy tales appeared at a crucial moment for the Western understanding of the animal, for it was in the seventeenth century that Descartes formulated his theory of the "animal machine," one of the most influential manifestations of the early modern scientific and philosophical drive to separate nature from culture and the human from the non-human. For Descartes and his followers, animals were devoid of the intelligence and feeling that characterized human beings and were notably lacking in language. While the theory of the "animal machine" was highly influential, it was also very controversial when first proposed since it refuted a strain of European thought that blurred the distinctions between humans and animals and endowed the latter with anthropomorphic traits.[11] For Descartes and his followers, though, animals were clearly inferior to human beings, which was not a new idea in itself (Christian thinking also subjected animals to an inferior status, for instance). What was different about this theory was the importance it placed on rationality as a distinctive trait of the human. In short, for Descartes, humans were thinking beings and animals were not. Whereas other philosophical traditions—even those that stressed human superiority—tended to blur the lines between humans and animals, Descartes sought to erect a firm barrier between the two.

It is against this backdrop and the controversy created by Descartes's "animal machine" that we should consider the many animals of early modern fairy tales. At first glance, fairy-tale animals give the lie to the Cartesian theory of the animal-machine. Often endowed with language and feelings, they do not act by instinct alone. Leaving aside for the moment the case of humans in animal form, other fairy-tale animals, especially those that are central characters, are regularly granted fully anthropomorphic traits. And many fairy-tale animals possess supernatural abilities besides. Such is the case of the horse Camarade in d'Aulnoy's "Belle-Belle, ou le chevalier Fortuné" ("Belle Belle or the Knight Fortunate," 1698). As the fairy who assists the eponymous heroine explains: "He only eats once every eight days, there's no need to go to the trouble to groom him, he knows the past, the present, and future … He will give you advice so good that sovereigns would be extremely pleased to have councilors who resembled him. You should look on him more as your friend than as your horse" (d'Aulnoy 2004: 801–2). With astoundingly minimal physical needs and superhuman knowledge and wisdom, Camarade would seem to be the very antithesis of the Cartesian animal-machine.

Beyond resisting the constraints of the Cartesian animal-machine, what do these fairy-tale animals have to tell us about animals? Are they simply humans in animal guise, little more than metaphors for the human? Such is the conclusion that Perrault suggests at the end of his version of "Little Red Riding Hood," for instance.[12] But things are not nearly so clear-cut for the myriad other animals that inhabit other early modern fairy tales, which underscore a difference between animals and humans, but also map out the ethics underlying the relations between animals and humans.

Many fairy-tale animals might best be understood as hybrid creatures that combine traits associated with both humans and animals. As such, they offer the possibility of revealing cultural understandings of what constitutes the human and the animal, both differentially and relationally. One particularly illuminating example is found in various early modern iterations of the Puss in Boots tale. First told by Giovan Francesco Straparola (night 11, fable 1), then retold by Giambattista Basile ("Cagliuso" [day 2, tale 4]) and Perrault ("Le Maître Chat ou le Chat botté" ["The Master Cat, or Puss in Boots"]), the story involves a poor peasant boy who, upon his father's death, inherits a cat that uses all the ruses of a trickster to assure the boy both wealth and marriage. But the three versions diverge in their description of the cat and its relation to the principal human protagonist.

In Straparola's tale, the cat is not described as such, so the incongruity of its mediation is not particularly obvious. Still, the cat is "enchanted" (Straparola 2015: 394) and also displays (human?) moral virtues (compassion for the boy Costantino and anger at his cruel brothers). As a character performing the role of adjuvant or helper, it is perhaps unsurprising that the cat (which is female) disappears with nary a mention at the very end so that the spotlight can shine solely on Costantino and his new bride, Elisetta. But in Basile's version, the cat remains the center of attention right through the end. After craftily manipulating things so that Cagliuso, her master, gains the king's favor and his daughter in marriage, the cat finds herself cast aside with ingratitude and then ends the tale with a word of warning: "'In short, the more you do, the less you should expect. Good words and wicked actions deceive only the wise and the mad'" (Basile 2007: 168). In the mouth of the cat, this lesson can be read as a call to be grateful, of course, but also to honor the bonds between humans and animals. Her selfless actions on Cagliuso's behalf underscore human dependence on and human responsibility toward animals. Basile's version operates from the presumption that animals are owed the gratitude and respect of humans, that there is, in sum, a bond connecting them.

Compared to Straparola's and Basile's tales, Perrault's "The Master Cat or Puss in Boots" features a decidedly more hybrid cat that on the one hand is very much of a cat (chasing after mice and other prey) and that on the other speaks and reasons as humans do, and without provoking the slightest bit of surprise in his (Perrault's cat is male) human interlocutors. The antics of Perrault's cat are even more of a central focus than those of his Italian predecessors, and yet Puss in Boots's relations with humans are fraught with more ambiguity as well. Puss in Boots is neither an "enchanted" being (as in Straparola's tale) nor an indignant victim (as in Basile's version), but instead a crafty cat who not only tricks a king into giving his daughter in marriage to his master but also outsmarts an ogre, killing him to appropriate his castle and riches. Above all, Perrault sets aside the presumption the master should show gratitude toward the cat, as in Basile's iteration. Instead, the tale ends with a wry comment about Puss in Boots becoming a "great Lord" and running after mice for pleasure alone. But Puss in Boots then disappears entirely from the final versed morals. The obvious point is cast aside, especially in the second moral,[13] such that the cat becomes the impossible intermediary, unavailable to readers living in a world where cats do not intervene on their behalf. Whatever connections exist between the miller's son and Puss in Boots—between humans and animals— are irrelevant and impossible, one might then conclude. It is as if Perrault amplifies the incongruity of Puss in Boots, the cat endowed with a rhetorical power and a cunning savvy beyond the abilities of the human protagonists, all the better to set him outside the bounds of any meaningful ethical relation with humans. Perrault's version of the story seems intent on denying or at least ignoring the interdependent relationship between human master and trickster cat that Straparola and especially Basile lay out. Like Descartes, Perrault erects a wall of difference between animal and human that forecloses the relational potential of the Puss in Boots tale and the ethical responsibility of humans toward animals.

HUMANS AS ANIMALS: METAMORPHOSIS AND THE HUMAN/ANIMAL DIVIDE

Of all the ways that fairy tales bring attention to the relations between humans and non-humans, the metamorphosis of humans into animals is certainly among the most frequent, if not the most prominent. Of course, metamorphosis is a well-established mythological and literary motif long before the appearance of the early modern fairy tale. Ovid's *Metamorphoses* (8 CE), with multiple instances of humans transformed into animals, is perhaps the most celebrated and influential example from antiquity. Thus, the metamorphoses of humans into animals (and usually back into human form) that are to be found in fairy tales are by no means unfamiliar to early modern readers. But the appearance of human → animal metamorphosis in fairy-tale plots at a time when new philosophical and scientific inquiries (such as those of Descartes) into the specificity of humans and animals opens the way for a new and different focus on the ontological dividing line between humans and animals in the fairy tale.

Whether in mythology or folklore, human → animal metamorphosis is most commonly the result of a curse or a punishment imposed by a supernatural being. In Leprince de Beaumont's "Beauty and the Beast," for instance, Beast's enchantment is caused by a wicked fairy. Framed in this way, metamorphosis is necessarily an undesirable state since it subjects humans to what is presented as a subordinate (animal) form. During their metamorphosis, humans very often retain their human consciousness but are "trapped" in animal bodies, thus they are forced to live an existence deemed to be inferior and tortured. After being changed into her eponymous animal form, Désirée, the heroine of d'Aulnoy's "La Biche au bois" ("The Doe in the Woods," 1698) reacts with shock and despair upon seeing her reflection in a fountain:

> "What!," she said, "Today I find myself reduced to suffering the strangest adventure that can befall an innocent princess such as I am under the reign of the fairies. How long will my metamorphosis last? Where should I withdraw to so that lions, bears, and wolves do not devour me? How will I be able to eat grass?" In the end she asked a thousand questions of herself and felt the cruelest distress possible.
>
> (d'Aulnoy 2004: 708)

The questions Désirée asks herself bespeak a sharp divide between her interior humanity and her exterior animality: her mind is disconnected from her body and is incapable of understanding her new existence as a doe. What she cannot grasp in this moment of non-recognition then provokes utter despair, and this in stark contrast to the humorous, even mocking stance of the narrator (as is typical of d'Aulnoy's tales). Making light of Désirée's condition, the narrator points out that "if something could console her, it was that she was as beautiful a doe as she had been a beautiful princess" (d'Aulnoy 2004: 708). Even while suggesting an equivalence across difference (a beautiful human translates into a beautiful animal), the result is at once a distancing of the (human) reader from the (hybrid human-animal) protagonist and an exploration of her psychological drama. And at no point is the hierarchy of human superiority and animal inferiority ever unsettled.

But in a few early modern fairy tales, human → animal metamorphosis opens a space for questioning this very hierarchy. In another tale by d'Aulnoy, "Le Prince Marcassin" ("Prince Wild Boar," 1698), the psychological anguish of the eponymous hero arises from never having experienced corporeal humanity while being raised at court by his royal (human) parents.[14] When he is rejected by two sisters forced, in succession, to marry him in spite of their repulsion for his animal likeness, he pushes the first to suicide and kills the second after discovering her plot to kill him (Figure 4.3).

Seized by guilt and deeming himself unsuited for human society, he flees court for the forest where, he says to himself:

FIGURE 4.3: The two dead sisters before Prince Marcassin in a woodcut, from d'Aulnoy, *Le nouveau gentilhomme bourgeois ou Les fées à la mode*, vol. 3 (Amsterdam: Michel Charles le Cene, 1725). Public domain.

> I'll go to the depths of the forests to lead a life that suits a good and honorable wild boar. No longer will I play the gallant man. I won't find any animals who reproach me for being uglier than they are. It will be easy for me to be their king, for I'm blessed with reason, which lets me find the means of mastering them. I'll live in more tranquility with them than I lived in a Court destined to obey me, and I won't have the misfortune of marrying a sow who stabs herself or who wants to strangle me.
>
> (d'Aulnoy 2004: 985)

In this rationale for seeking refuge in the forest, among animals, Marcassin adopts an admittedly ambiguous stance toward the human vs. animal hierarchy. Marcassin justifies his preference for the company of animals by reproducing an utterly human *libido dominandi*: unable to exercise his princely role among humans, he intends to put his (human) reason to work mastering the animals. But while reiterating the singularly human domination of the animal world, Marcassin inverts the human-animal hierarchy by referring to the two women who had rejected him as "laies" (sows), a derogatory appellation to say the least! A short while later, however, he displays a quite different attitude, the result of his time among animals: "I've learned, since I've been an inhabitant of these forests, that nothing in the world is to be freer than the heart. I see that all the animals are happy because they do not constrain themselves. I didn't know their maxims then; I know them at present, and I truly feel that I would prefer death to a forced marriage" (d'Aulnoy 2004: 987). Putting aside the preeminence of human reason—and, thus, mastery—Marcassin lauds the superiority of the animals' "maxims," suggesting that humans would have much to learn from their animal counterparts, especially in matters of the heart. When, at the conclusion of the tale, Marcassin sheds his boar skin to become a man who is "extraordinarily handsome and good looking" (993), he does so transformed by the time spent among his fellow animals. And so, while reestablishing a hierarchy in which human is superior to animal, it also marks an acknowledgment that humans and animals do not exist in separate realms, either cognitively or ethically.

HUMANS AND THE VITAL INANIMATE

As it is used in contemporary critical discourse, the category of the non-human includes not only animate lifeforms but also inanimate matter and objects. And fairy tales, of course, are replete with objects of all sorts, and especially magical objects. Theoretical work in "new materialisms" has emphasized the need to recognize the vitality of all things, both animate and inanimate, and, further, their capacity "not only to impede or block humans but also to act as quasi agents or forces with trajectories, propensities and tendencies of their own" (Bennett 2010: viii).[15] This theoretical perspective positions itself in opposition to the dominant Western treatment of nature as inert, fixed, and subordinate to human agency. In contrast it posits that animate and inanimate non-human forms are dynamic and possess an agency of their own, making them co-creators, with humans, of existence broadly conceived.

Fairy tales, of course, are particularly rich in potential for imagining the vitality of inanimate objects. As Marina Warner points out, in fairy tales "while magical life forces flow principally through natural phenomena—flora, fauna, bodies," the "vehicle of magical effects does not ... need to have possessed life in the first place: *inorganic* things are also animate and dynamic" (Warner 2014: 29; italics in the original). Amy Greenhough explains, further, that in fairy tales, "the natural laws of the world are 'held in suspension,' opening up spaces for reconsiderations of matter's agency" (2019: 459). For Greenhough it is especially contemporary revisions of fairy tales that, in her words, "remind us of social constructions of naturalness, but also of the wonders of nature, the vitality of matter, and the interconnectedness of existence" (460). But earlier iterations also confer agency to non-human objects while underscoring the limits of *human* agency and the interconnections between the human and the non-human.

Objects of all sorts abound in early modern fairy tales, and the most memorable are granted magical powers. Indeed, fairy-tale magic very often manifests itself through inanimate objects, even if the ultimate purpose is to help or hinder an animate being (human or non-human). The bloody key in Perrault's "La Barbe-bleue" ("Bluebeard," 1697), a tale otherwise devoid of magical effects, is complicit with the murderous husband, allowing him to detect his wife's transgression and causing her anguished torture. But despite this complicity, the origins of the key and its relation to Bluebeard are wrapped in mystery. It acts on its own precisely when Bluebeard is away from his castle. Still, in the end, the key's powers are incapable of preventing the violent end to Bluebeard's serial murders and the final triumph of the heroine.

If the bloody key can be understood as an extension of Bluebeard's own agency, other objects, as Warner notes, "cannot simply be possessed or controlled by their human users; they possess a life of their own and the power to influence the life of their human user" (2013: 197). The seven league boots in Perrault's "Little Thumbling," for instance, originally belong to the ogre who intends to kill and eat the eponymous hero and his brothers, only to be foiled when Little Thumbling tricks him into killing his own daughters. To pursue the brothers who have fled his house, the ogre puts on his boots, which allow him to travel seven leagues (approximately thirty-four kilometers) in a single stride. But when the ogre stops to rest and falls asleep, Little Thumbling pulls off the boots from the ogre's feet. When he then slips them on, they shrink to fit his feet, at which point the narrator explains: "since they were Fairy they had the gift of enlarging or shrinking depending on the legs of whoever put them on, such that they happened to be as snug on his feet and his legs as if they had been made for him" (Perrault 2005: 248). Even though they do the ogre's bidding, the boots are not bound to him and immediately adjust to their new owner, allowing Little Thumbling to acquire riches for himself and his family. The point, though, is that the boots are not simply the extension of their owner's agency but are something approaching free agents, and amoral ones at that. They have a utilitarian function for their human owners, but they do not, of their own volition, take sides in the Manichean struggle between the ogre and Little Thumbling.

The seven league boots in "Little Thumbling" also highlight the extent to which humans in fairy tales would be powerless without them. It is doubtful whether the hero, in spite of his cunning, would be able to bring about the happy ending without the aid of the magic boots. Even in a fairy tale such as this one, the hero cannot accomplish his predestined liquidation of lack (to cite a key function of Propp's model) solely by himself. For that to happen, his agency must be supplemented with the agency of the boots. Little Thumbling and his boots are coconspirators in the struggle to overcome the ogre and to forge a better life for himself and his family.

The capacity of fairy tales to delineate human dependence on inanimate forms is on spectacular display in Antoine Galland's *The Thousand and One Nights* (1704–10); the first European translation/adaptation also known as the *Arabian Nights*. It might even be argued that at least some of the immense appeal of the *Nights* in this period can be attributed to the range of magical objects—many unfamiliar to European folkloric and literary traditions—that appear in the tales. The "Story of Prince Ahmed and the Fairy Pari-Banou," a tale Galland adapted from his Syrian informant Hanna Diyab,[16] features a particularly striking abundance of magical objects and materials, each leading to the next and each revealing human dependence on non-human objects. They are crucial at the beginning of the tale, when a Sultan sends his three sons on separate quests to bring back "the most extraordinary and the most singularly unusual object" (Galland [1704–17] 2004: 3:268), the reward for which will be the hand of the princess Nourrounihar in marriage. Houssain, the eldest, finds a flying carpet; Ali, the middle brother, an ivory tube with televisual powers; and Ahmed, the youngest, a magical healing apple. Although the brothers are competing against each other, they end up combining the powers of their discoveries: when Ali uses his ivory tube to see Nourrounihar and discovers she is ill, Houssain proposes they fly back to their father's palace on his carpet so that Ahmed can heal her with the apple. The complementarity of these objects and the collaboration of the three brothers make it impossible for the sultan to give any one of them the princess. As he points out, each one of them was dependent on the other two to heal the princess. And this mutual interpersonal dependence is founded first of all on the complementarity of the three objects they find. No one of them could heal the princess, even with a magical object. Instead, they each were forced to acknowledge both their individual powerlessness and the combined efficacy of their three magical objects. These objects are also powerful in countering the sultan's plan to decide which one of his sons to wed with the princess. There is no one single "unusual object," as the sultan assumed, but instead three. The diversity and power of non-human objects confound human plans.

Inanimate objects continue to exert their power over humans as the sultan proposes a new quest for his sons: the one to shoot an arrow the farthest will have the princess. Ahmed's arrow leads him to the underground realm of the Fairy Pari-Banou, where the magnificence of her palace astounds him:

> He saw diamonds, rubies, emeralds, and all sorts of fine jewels, used with pearl, agate, jasper, porphyry, and all sorts of the most precious marble, without speaking of the furnishings that were of an inestimable luxury, everything displayed in a profusion so astonishing that, quite far from having seen anything similar, he confessed there couldn't be anything like it in the world.
>
> (Galland [1704–17] 2004: 3:291)

Recalling the detailed descriptions of palatial luxury by the seventeenth-century *conteuses*, this scene and Ahmed's reaction are the effect of Pari-Banou's powers, which are the central focus of this tale. For later, she reveals that it was she who had made it possible for the brothers to find the flying carpet, ivory tube, and magical apple. And when, at the end of the tale, the sultan demands that Ahmed find seemingly impossible things (a miniature pavilion, water from the fountain of the lions, and an ugly dwarf with a magical iron club), each time Pari-Banou comes to his aid. Her powers, then, are inextricably tied to the magical objects of the tale. They are not only an extension of her fairy agency, in a real sense they *are* her agency, making her into a cyborg-like character.[17] But more importantly, with the objects under her power, Pari-Banou contests the patriarchal norms enforced by the sultan: it is she who chooses Ahmed, usurping the sultan's role, and at the end of the tale, and under her control, it is her brother, the ugly dwarf Schaïbar, who kills the sultan with his iron club. So, it would be more precise to say that *both* Pari-Banou *and* the magical objects contest patriarchal norms, pushing the boundaries of conventional early modern female subjectivity.[18] More generally, the relationship between Pari-Banou and magical objects of the tale remind us that human and non-human agency are deeply interconnected and that human agency almost always requires the intervention of non-human agents to attain its objectives.

The fairy tale became a Western literary genre at a pivotal moment in the history of the human understanding of its relation to the natural and material worlds. Placing themselves apart from these worlds, Western philosophical and scientific subjects asserted a mastery over them that set the stage for and then accelerated the destructive effects of the Anthropocene. Early modern fairy tales both confirm and resist this effort to create a clear hierarchy privileging the human over the non-human. Contemporaries such as Perrault and d'Aulnoy penned fairy tales that reveal very different, even opposing visions of how humans might understand and engage with the world around them. But this ambivalence can be useful as we twenty-first-century humans consider our relation to all that we cast as non-human. On the one hand, it allows us to unpack the logic underlying human exploitation of nature. But on the other, it speaks to a long-standing aspiration for a deep and abiding connection with the non-human. Making that connection and addressing the consequences of the Anthropocene require far more than fairy tales, to be sure. But fairy tales can nonetheless focus our attention on the agency of non-human forms—both animate and inanimate—and thereby contribute to a broadened understanding of what it means to be human in and with the world.

CHAPTER FIVE

Monsters and the Monstrous

Of Ogre Pyramids, Ruby-Eyed Dragons, and Gnomes with Crooked Spines

KATHRYN A. HOFFMANN

To read monsters in fairy tales of the long eighteenth century is to encounter giants with eyes on stalks, griffins, sphinxes, winged serpents, ruby-eyed dragons, and a bee-like apparition the size of a whale, its abdomen covered in crystal tiles. There are male "monsters" of various sorts: a rhinoceros necromancer, a yellow dwarf, tree-men with root feet, and a fairy king hobbling about on his boneless legs with the help of diamond crutches. Among the females there are marmot, frog and raspberry fairies, and a grotto fairy with a multihued face. Fairies voyage astride ostriches, frogs, or a bomb-spewing three-headed, twelve-legged green horse. Some are furies with serpent hair. There are innumerable humans turned into cats, deer, monkeys, fish, sheep, exotic birds, furniture, and a porcelain tea set.[1]

Many fairy-tale monsters are beings of recognizable late seventeenth- and eighteenth-century civilities and sensibilities. Ogres, gnomes, and humans turned into creatures by the fairies often inhabit places of hyper-civilization. Some have palaces magnificent enough to vie with that of Versailles with orange groves, fountains, and menageries. They entertain visitors with optical games and fireworks and serve cups of chocolate on porphyry tables. Others reveal darker areas of the eighteenth-century imaginary at work: beliefs in the power of maternal imagination to deform; tastes for the "exotic" that will shape consumption and trade as well as feed fears of otherness; intolerance of corporeal difference and of the marks left on bodies by disease and the passage of time. Among the gentle and ludic things there are problematic "monsters" that are part of imaginaries that ran through colonialist projects and would, in the centuries to follow, feed racial ethnology, hygiene, criminology, and psychiatric institutions ... imaginaries that are themselves some of the "monsters" to come.

READING IN THE CITIES OF FATAPOLIS (FAIRYOPOLIS) AND BABIOLE (TRIFLE)[2]

Il vit des choses plus extravagantes les unes que les autres.

(He saw things, each more extravagant than the other.)
—La Force, "Tourbillon" (2005b: 366)

In a century of imagination that is impossibly broad, in texts that often resemble the palace in Charlotte Rose Caumont de La Force's "Tourbillon" (1698) where extravagance is followed by more extravagance, one needs to read somewhere, to choose a toehold even in an amorphous genre, and even with the knowledge that the toehold may, in proper fairy-tale fashion, turn into a toad and walk away.[3]

Because the vast bulk of eighteenth-century fairy tales were written in France from the 1690s on, this chapter will concentrate on French examples, with a few from Italy, Germany, England, and Russia. Generally, the long century will be considered as extending from the 1690s to the turn of the nineteenth century. During this period, a particular kind of ludic monstrous explodes, producing innumerable works of imaginative literature of various and often intermingled genres: fairy tales, devil tales, fantastic tales, fables, dreams, real, imaginary, and extraordinary voyages, satirical fantasies, cabalistic fantasies, dissertations on angels and demons, imaginary libraries, romances, philosophical novels, dialogues among devils, and works of indeterminate genre called in French *badinages* or *oeuvres badines*.[4]

Many works of imaginative literature appeared under imaginary imprints, published from the fictional cities of Balivernopolois, Babiole, Bagatelle, Cocuxopolis, Fatapolis, Frivopolis, Risopolis, Pittorescopolis, and Pneumatopolis (Twaddlopolis, Knickknack, Trinket, Cuckoldopolis, Fairyopolis, Frivopolis, Laughopolis, Picturesqopolis, Pneumatopolis) as well as one named "Où l'on a pu" ("Where we managed to").[5] One needs, at least in part, to be willing to read fairy-tale monsters in places devoted to chatter, gossip, trifles, knickknacks, frivolity, laughter, the picturesque, and things that lend themselves to deviations or are full of air.

It is an imagination that weaves together Greek and Roman mythology, medieval literature, tales from witchcraft trials, medicine, philosophy, maps, and travelogues. It produces fascinating narrative slips across the disciplines. In the space of a century, women dismount from the dogs and the flying goats, sticks and brooms given to them in the overheated imaginaries of demonologists, to find themselves more decorative forms of transportation including chariots of gold, diamonds, and hearts, drawn by swans, winged salamanders, turkeys, tigers, and horses with emerald and ruby wings. Ogres leave the dark caves of myth and folklore to serve as picturesque decoration for garden walks. Sea monsters find their way off of Renaissance maps and into rivers and canals where they spout fireworks during festivals. Others sit placidly and ornamentally under genteel ladies off for sleigh rides. The monstrous slips into the decorative and the ludic. Many of the forms of the shifting imaginary take shape not only in literature but also in realms that can be only briefly evoked here, including theater sets, opera machines, ballet, festivals, garden architecture, the decorative arts, entertainment, and fairground displays.

That certain forms of materiality count, and are worthy of attention, in fictional places sometimes called Knickknack or Picturesqopolis should not be surprising. How they might count is another matter. What follows below, in ogres, dragons, fairies, and gnomes, are bits of Barthesian texts, in the broadest sense of anything that can be interpreted: written texts, visual texts, object-texts, body-texts, place-texts (such as gardens and palace rooms), and discipline-texts (including medicine and early ethnology), caught just briefly in moments of crossings, hookings, and unhookings. At those moments, the disciplines no longer make sense, or make sense differently, because what they once saw as their borders are either no longer there or they are there but broken, replaced by productive spaces filled with movement and criss-crossed by fascinating things that the disciplines can never contain. Michel Serres filled his theoretical spaces with Mercury flying about with messages and noisy *parasites* (both as parasites and white noise). Michel Butor tried to catch the spots of *textamorphose* (textamorphosis) where texts simultaneously suggest directions and invite wanderings.[6] Among the many things one might notice at the edges of things and in the spaces where fairy tales wander into the spaces of other disciplines, are the traces of fireworks offered by a beast with clinking scales and the wakes left by fairy-tale monsters that climb delicately out of a lake of mercury to perch on a crystal palace.[7] The flying fairies and their mounts pass by, in the space of the intertext, the flying dragons and gods, goddesses, and zephyrs of operas, machine plays, and festivals.[8] They exist in the wakes of real boats carrying ostriches and rhinoceroses, diamonds and rubies across the seas.

There are innumerable ephemeral moments in the spaces of the intertext, things to see in those spaces, and ways to approach them. The objects that make only brief appearances here—carousels, perfume bottles, garden sculptures, or sleighs—capture only a bit of the "thinginess" that ties fairy tales to broader historical realms of marvels.[9] In the moments where I try to catch a few of the fairy-tale monsters as they slip across the disciplines and reveal the overlap of imaginative practices, I am indebted to more scholars of the interdisciplinary than I can list.

THE BIG, THE UGLY, THE MUD-COVERED: MONSTERS IN SEARCH OF A DEFINITION

By the publication of Ambroise Paré's *Des Monstres et prodiges* (*On Monsters and Marvels*) ([1573] 1982) in the late sixteenth century, the categories of the monstrous and the marvelous had already become inseparable, each pulling the other automatically into view. In his treatise, Paré attributed monsters to divine wrath, an absence, excess, mingling, or corruption of seed, illnesses and accidents, the smallness of the womb, demons and devils, the indecent posture of woman, maternal imagination, and wicked malingerers. In the late seventeenth century, some of those categories were still visible while others had moved to the background.[10]

The definition of *monstre* ("monster") in Antoine Furetière's 1690 *Dictionnaire universel* was a "prodige qui est contre l'ordre de la nature, qu'on admire ou qui fait peur" ("prodigy that is against the order of nature and that one admires or that causes fear," 1690: vol. 2). Furetière's definition is itself a marvelous hodge-podge of ancient theories and contemporary medical notions. Furetière lists cyclopes, centaurs, and the Hydra as the monsters that *were*—and are thus no longer—mixing them with African animals, two-headed children, and animals with extra parts on display in fairs. Furetière added: "Monstre, se dit aussi de ce qui est extraordinairement laid. La petite verole a tellement defiguré ce visage, que c'est un vrai monstre. Cet avare a épousé un monstre, une femme laide à faire peur" ("Monster is also used for that which is extraordinarily ugly. Smallpox has so disfigured this face, that it is a true monster. That miser married a monster, a frightfully ugly woman," 1690: vol. 2).[11]

In Furetière's definition, the fright- and awe-inspiring monsters of old have already given way to things far more banal. His examples of a "monster" include pock-marked men and ugly women, a massive unsymmetrical building, a disorganized book, and people thrown into a quagmire who emerge covered in mud.[12] "Monster," he indicated, is also used to admiringly describe a extraordinarily large and expensive fish served at table: "On dit aussi, qu'on sert des monstres sur une table, pour dire, des brochets, des saumons, des carpes, des turbots d'une grosseur et d'un prix extraordinaire" ("It is also said that monsters are being served at table, meaning pike, salmon, carp or turbot of extraordinary size and costliness").

By the late eighteenth century and the *Encyclopédie*, little of the exuberance of sixteenth- and seventeenth-century definitions was seemingly left, if one looks only under the subject headings for "monster." There were only two entries with the heading "monster" in the *Encyclopédie,* one under botany for monstrous plants and the other for zoology. Yet the word "monster" still appeared 150 times in the *Encyclopédie,* in entries under law, fatherly love, geography, Aristotelianism, metaphysics, history, whaling, mythology, theology, morals, rhetoric, philosophy, ichthyology, grammar, literature, poetry, maternal imagination, sculpture, surgery, zoology, chemistry, pharmacy, gardening, music, and pyrotechnics, the last referring to pyrotechnic effects for marine monsters used in water entertainments.

Reading fairy-tale monsters among giant fish on banquet tables, ugly ladies, maternal imagination, and pyrotechnic effects in water entertainments involves loosening the concepts of monsters from some of the meanings of Paré's time, and letting other meanings and disciplines come to the fore.

OGRAMORPHOSIS: FROM CYCLOPES TO A RHINOCEROS[13]

In the morphological approach to folktales by Vladimir Propp, monsters are part of the group of adversaries; figures that temporarily block the hero's progress and thus the movement of the tale toward its end. Nothing in Propp's approach involves or even encourages spending time looking at monsters. However, in a period when writers constructed lengthy tales, in which they often devoted long pages to description of characters, places, and things that are marvelously beautiful or marvelously monstrous, reading involves tarrying in those descriptions. It requires considering the description of monsters—the description of anything in the tales for that matter—as significant, as an element to be studied, not as a digression from a narrative assumed to be moving from beginning to end.

Ogres are the descendants of the cyclopes, the giants, and sometimes the Kaberoi. They are remainders of Horkos (Oath) and the one-eyed Polyphemus, fragments of myths of the past. Usually of prodigious size (although at least one ogre in a tale by Giambattista Basile is a dwarf), often with tastes for human flesh, ogres do not merely fit within definitions of the monstrous.[14] They are the rare type of fairy-tale monster that merits a separate entry in seventeenth- and eighteenth-century dictionaries and the *Encyclopédie.*

Charles Perrault, in the dedication of "Peau d'Ane" ("Donkey Skin") referred to "contes d'ogre et de fée" ("tales of ogres and fairies").[15] The 1701 edition of the *Dictionnaire universel,* revised and expanded by Henri Basnage de Beauval, included a new entry for *ogre* defined as a "sorte de monstre, d'homme sauvage qui mangeoit les petits enfans, et qu'on feint avoir été du temps des Fées, dans les contes qu'on en fait" ("sort of monster, wild man who ate little children and that one makes believe was from the time of the fairies, in the tales told about them," Furetière 1701). The word *ogre* defined as "a man-eating giant," entered the *Oxford English Dictionary* in 1713, on the heels of a translation of the *Arabian Nights* from French to English (Hennard Dutheil de la Rochère 2013: 330n10). Ogres were added to the French Academy's dictionary in the fourth edition in 1762, and appeared in the *Encyclopédie* in an entry largely unchanged from the time of Perrault: "sorte de monstre, de géant, d'homme sauvage, qu'on a imaginé et introduit dans les contes où il mange les petits enfans: l'ogre est contemporain des fées" ("a sort of monster, giant, wild man that was imagined and introduced into fairy tales where he eats little children: the ogre is a contemporary of the fairies," Diderot and d'Alembert 2017: 11:429).[16]

Human-eating ogres and giants appear in tales in France since the Middle Ages as well as in Italy, Germany, and England. With the exception of Perrault—who generally spends little time on corporeal or scenic description in his tales and indicates only that the ogre children in "Le Petit poucet" have little grey eyes, hooked noses, and long pointed teeth—ogres are among the imaginatively described monsters in a number of tales. In Basile's earlier "Lo cunto dell'uerco" ("Tale of the Ogre") the ogre is a fancifully hairy, bow-legged dwarf with tusks hanging down to his toes:

> He was a little old midget; a bunch of dried twigs; his head was bigger than an Indian squash, his forehead all lumpy, his eyebrows joined; his eyes popped out of his head, his nose was dented by two horse's nostrils that looked like two sewer mains, his mouth was as big as a grape press, with two tusks that hung all the way down to the little bones of his feet; his chest was hairy, his arms like spinning reels, his legs vaulted like a cellar, and his feet as flat as a duck's. In short, he looked like a wicked spirit, an old demon, a filthy pauper, and the spitting image of an evil shade, and he would have made Roland tremble with fright, Skanderbeg quake with terror, and the most skilled wrestler grow pale.
>
> (Basile [1634–6] 2007: First entertainment of the first day, 44)

Ogres have a particular desciptive fancifulness in later French tales. The ogress in Marie-Catherine d'Aulnoy's "Finette Cendron" is a comically monstrous figure, fifteen feet tall and thirty feet around:

> Elle n'avait qu'un oeil au milieu du front, mais il était plus grand que cinq ou six autres, le nez plat, le teint noir et la bouche si horrible, qu'elle faisait peur; elle avait quinze pieds de haut et trente de tour.
>
> (She had only one eye in the middle of her forehead, but it was larger than five or six others, a flattened nose, dark skin, and such a horrible mouth that she was terrifying; she was fifteen feet tall and thirty around.)
>
> (d'Aulnoy 2004: 447)

Her ogre husband, his basket full of children that he devours fifteen at a time, is six times taller than she, with one great ugly eye.[17] The ogres in d'Aulnoy's "L'Oranger et l'abeille" ("The Orange Tree and the Bee") are donkey-eared and comically humped both front and back, or to be as playful as eighteenth-century texts themselves, both hunchbacked and hunchfronted:

> Jamais il n'y eut de plus hideuses figures, avec leur oeil louche placé au milieu du front, leur bouche grande comme un four, leur nez large et plat, leurs longues oreilles d'âne, leurs cheveux hérissés, et leur bosse devant et derrière.
>
> (Never have been seen more hideous figures, with their squinting eye in the middle of their forehead, their mouth as big as an oven, their wide and flat nose, their long donkey ears, their hair standing on end, and their humps both front and back.)
>
> (d'Aulnoy 2004: 336)[18]

The ogre Pendagrugeon in Marie-Madeleine de Lubert's "Blancherose" is not just any ogre. He is the fire-breathing emperor of the ogres, a being of whimsical hybridities, with the long neck of a dromedary and eyes on the ends of stalks:

> Elle crut mourir en apercevent Pendagrugeon. Il était haut comme environ un grand géant; sa tête, portée sur un long col de dromadaire, avait la vraie physionomie d'un sanglier, excepté qu'il lui sortait des deux côtes du front deux espèces de tuyaux, au bout desquels étaient ses deux yeux.
>
> (She thought she would die when she saw Pendagrugeon. He was more or less as tall as a big giant; his head was carried on the long neck of a dromedary, had the true physiognomy of a boar, except for the fact that two things like tubes came out of both sides of his forehead, on the end of which were his two eyes.)
>
> (Lubert [1737–55] 2005: 347)

He arrives surrounded by ten thousand frightful ogres, the fifty ugliest of which carry him on an ogre pyramid. In a narrative world that has little use for restraint, the ogre in Lubert's "Peau d'Ours" ("Bearskin"), ruler of a hundred million ogres, is sometimes hairy and at other times appears as a rhinoceros. He is highly susceptible to female beauty, exclaiming so loudly at the sight of the princess that the island trembles and he has to transport the princess, who has fainted, to the palace on his rhinoceros-back. He hunts bears for her supper.

Among the orgresses—who overlap with evil witches, fairies, and cannibal mothers-in-law—one of the most fanciful is the ogress Cancan "La Princesse Coque-d'oeuf et le Prince Bonbon" ("Princess Eggshell and Prince Bonbon") attributed to Lubert. Cancan has a nose so tiny that it can be seen only with a microscope and breasts so large she needs to carry them around in a wheelbarrow. Coiffed with stingray tails woven into her hair, wearing turnips for earrings, her teeth break from eating too many wafers and waffles, then she can eat mush only, much to the relief of the children (Lubert [1737–55] 2005: 419–20).

Ogres, giants, and other monster figures sometimes live a quite civilized existence. In the English tale of Jack Spriggins, the giant Gogmagog has "the richest apartments imaginable" (Merryman 1734: 46) with furniture and gardens as splendid as those of Versailles. The several thousand ladies and ten thousand knights in his palace are furnished "with every refreshing Liquor" (48) as they wait to be eaten. Riquet à la Houppe, king of the gnomes in the tale by Catherine Bernard, has an underground palace with magnificent apartments, where he offers a comedy and a ball. The "horrible monster" Green Serpent has a palace with pearl roofs, jewel-incrusted walls, bathtubs of gilded crystal, and a serving force of a hundred tiny pagodas of both banal (wood and earth) and rare materials (jewels, coral, crystal, or porcelain), who play instruments ("Le Serpentin Vert" ["Green Serpent"]; d'Aulnoy 2004: 579).[19]

Their social behavior is often civilized as well. The hairy ogre of Carl Gustf Tessin's *Faunillane ou l'Infante jaune* (1741) plays the lute and has a musical group. The clawed monster of *Les Mille et un jours*, almost the size of a giant, has the art of *badinage* (banter) and "riait, badinait comme les autres hommes" ("laughed, bantered like other men") while dining (Pétis de la Croix [1710] 2006: 751). In Lubert's "Etoilette," sensitive yellow centaurs entertain a girl for the price of a flower. The ogress mother-in-law in Perrault's "La Belle au bois dormant" ("Sleeping Beauty") likes her victims garnished in *sauce Robert*.[20] In Catherine de Lintot's "Tendrebrun et Constance" the fairy Vicieuse (Vicious) conjures up a monstrous winged toad that she feeds with cakes of sugar and almonds that would suit eighteenth-century tastes, except for the third ingredient: caterpillars.

Fairy-tale ogres appear in a world in which giants have already been pacified and put into the service of pleasure for centuries, serving particularly as decorative garden sculptures. Since the Renaissance, guests to Prince Pierre Francesco Orsini's villa outside of Rome have taken a stop from their garden walks among sculpted furies, dragons, sphinxes, and sirens, in a grotto formed in the shape of an ogre's gaping mouth (Figure 5.1).

Since 1580, Giambologna's giant/mountain Appennino has hunched picturesquely over a water feature at Villa Demidoff outside of Florence. In Versailles the bronze giant Enceladus is buried among rocks; a pleasurable, glittering stop on a garden walk and a place to reflect on the consquences of overreaching. Sculptural, spouting water, opening a mouth for a genteel stop for refreshment in a garden, or literary, pacified ogres bend themselves toward pleasure.

FIGURE 5.1: "Monster Park," Sacred Grove (Sacro Bosco), Bomarzo, Italy. Architect Pirro Ligorio for Prince Pier Franceso Orsini. Photograph by Brook Ellis.

AMUSING ONESELF WITH DRAGONS, GRIFFINS, TRITONS, AND TURKEYS

Furetière defined a dragon as a "serpent monstrueux qui est parvenu avec l'âge à une prodigieuse grandeur. Les anciens naturalistes se sont égayez à descrire ce monstre en diverses manières" ("monstrous serpent that over time has grown to a prodigious size. The ancient naturalists amused themselves describing this monster in various ways," 1690: vol. 1).

Fairy tellers too amused themselves with the description of dragons. The dragon in d'Aulnoy's "La Chatte blanche" ("The White Cat") with wings of a thousand bizarre colors, is restrained by chains of diamonds (2004: 780). In Lubert's "Tecserion," Mélidor is transformed into a dragon with ruby eyes, attached with diamond chains to the palace walls ([1737–55] 2005: 97). Another character in the tale wonders if the fairy keeps her dragon in her menagerie (99). D'Aulnoy's "Serpentin Vert" ("Green Serpent"), with his greenish wings, a body of a thousand colors, ivory claws, and eyes of fire (579) could hide himself easily among the many real Renaissance and early modern jewels made of baroque pearls and precious stones formed in the shape of winged dragons, sirens, tritons, and chimeras (Figure 5.2).[21]

FIGURE 5.2: An engraving of d'Aulnoy's dragon-like Green Serpent, from *Nouveaux contes des fées* (Amsterdam: Estienne Roger, 1708).

In the eighteenth century, these decorative dragons no longer produce the terrors of old. In Lubert's "Princesse Belle-Etoile," a dragon with twelve feet, three heads, six wings, and a body of bronze that has already devoured 500,000 people, runs away in terror at the sight of his own image multiplied in a mirror ([1737–55] 2005: 192–4).

Dragons and griffins are only some of a vast cohort of fantastic and sometimes comically improbable animals drawing fairy chariots or serving as mounts. Draught animals on the monstrous side include winged salamanders and bats with a raven coachman and a black beetle postilion for d'Aulnoy, a white viper with flaming eyes in Lintot's "Le Prince Sincer," and a thousand hissing serpents in Tessin's *Faunillane*.[22] The fairy of d'Aulnoy's "La Princesse Carpillon" travels in a diamond chariot pulled by swans, all contained in a globe of fire and surrounded by an azure haze (2004: 624). Other chariot animals range from the jewel-like golden steeds with wings of emeralds and rubies in Basile's "Golden Root," to the exotic birds and "megafauna" of menageries: turkeys in d'Aulnoy's "Le Nain jaune" ("The Yellow Dwarf"), and tigers in Lubert's "La Princesse Lionnette et le Prince Coquerico."[23] Draught animals sometimes include the improbably barnyard: green mice and a rose-colored baby rat, winged frogs, chickens, or snails.[24] Some, like the flying dolphins of d'Aulnoy's "Babiole," reflect still-uncertain notions of the natural world, while La Force's moles with rose-leaf wings in "Plus belle que fée" (2005a) are purely marvelous hybrids.

Some fairies change draught animals to suit their moods. The Desert Fairy in "Le Nain jaune" uses bats most days, but sometimes replaces them with swans (d'Aulnoy 2004: 555). In d'Aulnoy's "La Biche au bois" ("The Hind in the Wood"), the fairies change their draught animals with their moods and intents. On peaceful missions, they use white pigeons or small ravens. On days when they are angered, they change to flying dragons, fire-breathing garter snakes, lions, leopards, and panthers (690).

Among the many mounts for fairies, enchanters, the enchanted and their retinues are ostriches in d'Aulnoy's "Chatte Blanche," a bronze elephant in Lubert's "La Princesse Couleur de Rose et le Prince Celadon" ("The Rose-Colored Princess and the Celadon Prince"), and a fire-colored camel in her "Tecserion." In "Le Nain Jaune" the king rides off on the tail of a siren, while the Desert Fairy, coiffed with serpents *à la* Tisiphone, rides about on a winged griffin (d'Aulnoy 2004: 558, 553). In d'Aulnoy's "La Grenouille Bienfaisante" ("The Beneficent Frog") there are frogs and snails for the fairy's fifty ladies-in-waiting and a twelve-footed, three-headed, fire-, cannonball-, and bomb-spewing green horse the fairy conjures up for the prince. The fairy herself travels on a litter the size of two eggs or on a sparrow-hawk. In Lintot's "Tendrebun et Constance" the prince is carried off on a griffin, while the fairy Vicious uses a winged toad with a saddle embroidered with glow worms.

The creatures of myth, menageries, barnyards, and reveries are joined by new monsters of complicated parts and sometimes phantasmagoric hybridities. The lions in "Le Nain Jaune" have two heads, eight feet, four rows of teeth, and skin as hard as tortoisehell (d'Aulnoy 2004: 545). The creature in Charles de Fieux, chevalier de Mouhy's *Lamekis* is particularly imaginative:

> Qu'on se figure, si l'on peut, l'assemblage de tout ce que l'esprit humain peut concevoir, aidé de tout ce que la fiction pourroit suggérer .... Je vis perpendiculaiement au dessus de ma tête, une masse opaque et extraordinaire, ayant la forme d'une Abeille dont les aîles étoient étendues: la grandeur de son corps étoit de celle de la plus grosse Baleine, le dessus de son dos paroissoit écaillé, et chacune de ses écailles avoit le même mouvement que celui de la respiration; le nombre de ses pattes étoit prodigieux, elles se mouvoient perpétuellement, et le froissment qu'elles faisoient les unes contre les autres, ressembloit au clictis [cliquetis] des armes. Pour la tête de cet animal; elle est difficile à définir.

> (Imagine, if you can, the mixture of all that the human mind can imagine, aided by all that fiction might suggest .... I saw perpendicularly above my head, an extraordinary opaque mass, having the form of a bee with wings extended; it was as large as a big whale, its back seemed to be covered in

scales and each of the scales had the movement of respiration; it had a prodigious number of feet; they moved perpetually, and the sound made of their rubbing against each other resembled the clinking of arms. As for the head of this animal, it would be difficult to describe.)

(Mouhy 1737: 66–7)

In the wake of chariots drawn across the sky by dragons and turkeys, among the winged toads with glow-worm saddles, ostriches, and moles with rose-leaf wings the monsters of old and fear disappear, replaced with marvels. It is the very particular monstrosity of the long eighteenth century with a tendency to become aesthetic.[25]

By the eighteenth century, nearly all the creatures of myth have long been drafted into ludic and decorative service. Since the Renaissance, veritable legions of sculpted and gilded dragons, winged dolphins, seahorses, mermaids, tritons, sphinxes, and harpies have cavorted in gardens and fountains across Europe. New tastes for dragons mark the eighteenth century. They decorate fashionable Chinese export porcelain (MasterArt 2020). Eighty dragons perch picturesquely on the Kew Gardens Pagoda in London, built in 1762. In 1770 Frederick the

FIGURE 5.3: *Jeu de bague chinois,* Parc Monceau, with gentlemen on serpent-necked dragons and the disappearing hands of Chinese figures, from Louis Carrogis Carmontelle's *Jardin de Monceau* (Paris: Delafosse, Née & Masquelier, 1779). Public domain.

Great ordered his own Dragon house for the Sanssouci Park in Potsdam. The *jeu de bague chinois*—a merry-go-round today—created for the Duc de Chartres at Monceau (or Mousseau) in 1775 had male riders perched on fanciful dragons, one with a snake-like neck and head. The ladies floated through the air on cushions held in the outstretched hands of sculpted figures representing reclining Chinese men. One hand of the sculpted figures held a parasol, while the hand holding the cushion disappeared, suggestively, under the ladies' skirts (Figure 5.3).

In 1776, at the Petit Trianon in Versailles guests of Marie-Antoinette would ride about on a slightly modified version; the men astride a dragon or a chimera, the ladies with a more genteel seat on a peacock.[26] Winter entertainments included riding on sleighs in the shape of winged dragons, dolphins, and sirens driving twisted snakes.[27] Furniture sported dragon decorations or seemed capable of walking or slithering away on paws, claws, hooves, and serpent heads.[28] The monstrous slips into the marvelous, a seemingly non-dangerous monstrous-marvelous that is ludic, collectable, and available to be consumed in multiple ways.

DWARVES, ENCHANTERS, AND FURIES

> Si tu n'es point trop engagée, j'ai un nain qui serait bien ton fait.
>
> (If you aren't already too committed, I have a dwarf who would be just the thing for you.)
> —D'Aulnoy, "Babiole" (2004: 521)

Male antagonists appear in many forms, including sorcerers, enchanters, magicians, devils, beasts, a blue-bearded murderer, and other men with dangerous and secret places, things, names, or identities. "Hideous" ones include the seven-eyed sorcerer Dort-d'un-oeil of Lubert's "La Princesse Coque-d'oeuf et le Prince Bonbon." In the criss-crossing threads of myth, folklore, and real-world intolerances of physical difference that maintained fairground displays and the practice of keeping family and court dwarves, many of the male "monsters" are men of short stature. To that stature authors add a range of ludic peculiarities. D'Aulnoy's dwarf in "Le Nain Jaune" is as yellow as the oranges in his trees. In "La Chatte Blanche," King Migonnet's beard is full of canaries' nests and his ears stick out a foot above his head. His leg bones missing, he crawls on his eagle feet with the aid of crutches made of diamonds (d'Aulnoy 2004: 787–8). The son of the fairy Noirjabarbe in Louise Cavalier Levesque's "Le Prince des Aigues Marines" ("The Prince of the Aquamarines" [1722] 2007), is a picturesquely "monstrous" dwarf:

> Il était encore mille fois plus méchant que sa mère. C'était un monstre. Il était nain: une bosse par-devant, et une autre par-derrière, le rendaient encore plus difforme. Ses yeux étaient petits, enfoncés et bordés de rouge; son nez camus laissait voir jusqu'au fond de son cerveau: ses cheveux roux et

plats couvraient son front ridé, et plein de bosses et cicatrices; sa bouche large n'avait plus qu'un reste de dents pourries; ses lèvres pâles couvraient la moitié de son menton; ses jambes étaient torses, et son coeur était encore mille fois plus horrible que sa figure.

(He was a thousand times more evil than his mother. He was a monster. He was a dwarf: a hump in the front and another behind, made him even more deformed. His eyes were small, deep-set and red-rimmed; the back of his brain could be seen through his pug nose: red straight hair covered his wrinkled forehead, full of bumps and scars; his wide mouth had only a few rotten teeth; his pale lips covered half his chin; his legs were crooked, and his heart was a thousand times more horrible than his face.)

([1722] 2007: 293)

In Lintot's "Le Prince Sincer" a pointy-nosed dwarf, with red hair and beard, has a body "tout contrefait" (all deformed) and a single leg. He whirls about on his leg when the wind blows; a comical monster wind vane ([1735] 2007a: 612–13). The dwarves of fairy tales take shape within a broader imaginary of people of short stature developed over centuries in paintings of court dwarves, Jacques Callot's etchings of gobbi, and the sculptures of the Dwarf Garden of Mirabell Palace in Austria, to mention only a few (Figures 5.4 and 5.5). Within that imaginary, grotesque and comic elements were unfortunately the norm.

FIGURE 5.4: *Le bossu à la canne (Hunchback with a Cane)* by Jacques Callot (*c.* 1616–22). Public domain.

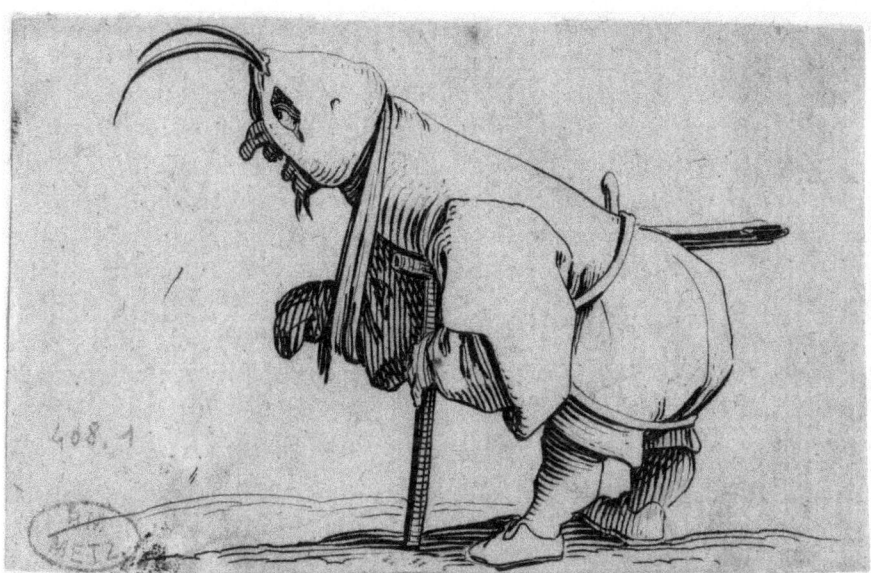

FIGURE 5.5: *L'estropié au capuchon (Cripple in a Hood)* by Jacques Callot (c. 1616–22). Public domain.

In the tales, good fairies are generally marvelous but not monstrous. The monstrous category, however, clearly applies to their evil or simply cranky sisters, especially the elderly ones.[29] The fairy Carabossse in d'Aulnoy's "Princesse Printanière" first appears as a tiny hunchbacked nursemaid, her knees under her chin, and suckling a monkey. Later she arrives in her own shape: "une petite magotine affreuse, dont l'habit était de peau de serpent, et sur sa tête un gros crapaud qui servait de fontange" ("a hideous little grotesque dressed in serpent-skin, and on her head a big toad served as a top knot," d'Aulnoy 2004: 282).[30] Some of the angry fairies are described as furies. The fairy Envieuse (Envious) in the Comte de Tessin's *Faunillane* rides about in a chariot of hearts pierced with arrows, drawn by a thousand serpents, and with an unusual option: an in-chariot fury hairdresser:

> Une femme qui avoit un air de colique, étoit dans cet horrible équipage, sa robe étoit noire, parsemée de flammes de brillans, les serpens qu'elle portoit en guise de cheveux étoient renoués d'un ruban feuille morte, et derrière elle, on voyoit une Furie qui boucloit son tignon couleuvré avec un fer chaud.

> (A bilious-looking woman was in this horrible carriage, her dress was black, strewn with sparkling brilliants, the serpents that she wore by way of hair were tied with an autumn-leaf colored ribbon, and behind her could be seen a Fury who was curling her serpentine headwear with a hot iron.)

> (1741: 12–13)

Witches and the witch trials get tongue-in-cheek references in number of fairy tales. On the porcelain walls of Chatte Blanche's palace can be read the history of all the most famous cats, along with "les sorciers devenus chats, le sabbat et toutes ses cérémonies" ("sorcerers who became cats, the sabbath and all its ceremonies," d'Aulnoy 2004: 758–9). A bit later, the prince momentarily reflects "toute cette chatonnerie tenait un peu du sabat et du sorcier" ("all this catliness had a whiff of the sabbath and witches," d'Aulnoy 2004: 762) before giving himself over to the pleasures of the cat's festival world.

Vasilii A. Levshin's ten volumes of *Russkie skazki* (*Russian Fairy Tales*), published between 1780 and 1783 were influenced by French and German models. In "The Tale of the Noble Zoleshanin, a Knight in the Service of Prince Vladimir," Baba Yaga has the traits of witch, ogress, and evil fairy:

> Suddenly a great whirlwind arose, the trees made way on both sides, and I saw Baba Yaga galloping in a mortar that she urged on like a horse, with an iron pestle. Her appearance was so frightening that I started trembling when I saw her. And how could one not be frightened? Imagine a very dark and thin woman seven arshins high,[31] with teeth one-and-a-half-arshins long, sticking out on both sides, like a wild boar, her hands adorned with bear claws .... The sky darkened from the great number of ravens, kits, and owls that flew in; they circled over Baba Yaga's courtyard, letting out a nasty cry which must cause one to feel horror even before the witch's arrival .... Her eyes were like red-hot coals, bloody foam flowed from her mouth, and her fangs made a dreadful noise when they scraped. "Oho" she roared, jumping from her mortar and throwing aside her pestle. "I could hardly wait for you, Zvenislav! I'll eat well now, you came to take away my precious booty, and you came at the right time: I'm very hungry."
>
> (Kostiukhin 1988: 387, 390; quoted in Johns 2004: 12–13)

Baba Yaga, in Levshin's tale, is the essence of evil, created by the devil from the steam of twelve nasty women cooked in a cauldron (Johns 2004: 13) (Figure 5.6).[32]

There are many reminiscences in fairy tales of stories once told under torture; tales of frogs and toads, transformations, women accused of doing things to babies, bewitching men, creating havoc with words, wands, and looks, and riding off into the skies.[33] In d'Aulnoy's "La Princesse Belle Etoile et le Prince Chéri," the fairy in proper witch-like fashion uses her wand to turn the food on the banquet table into fricasseed serpents. The demonologist Henri Boguet, in his *Discours exécrable des sorciers* (1602) had once truly suspected apples were the food weapon of witches looking to lead their victims to the devil. He told a story of a noisy apple that he believed had made noise for two hours on an Annecy bridge in 1585 (Boguet 1602; Hoffmann 2001: 465). In d'Aulnoy's fairy tale, it is a singing apple, protected by a dragon, that makes beautiful music

FIGURE 5.6: An early eighteenth-century Russian lubok or print of Baba Yaga riding a pig to fight the infernal crocodile with a pestle. Public domain.

and can tell a princess to wake (d'Aulnoy 2004: 927–30). While there were still some, including Pierre-François Muyart de Vouglans, writing on the presence of demons on Earth in 1780, beliefs in witches and demons were generally waning.[34] That left multiple elements of the witch tale imaginary available to be woven into fairy tales, losing the odors of death, fear, and burning embers.[35]

"JE VOUS FÉE ET REFÉE"—TEMPORARY AND SERIAL MONSTERS

The fairy in Lubert's "Blancherose" says to the ogre Pendragon: "Je te fée et refée" ("I fairy you and I fairy you again") so that he may turn himself into a fish, a wolf, or a bird ([1737–55] 2005: 354). The verb *féer*, "to fairy," had already entered the 1701 edition of Furetière's *Dictionnaire universel*, defined fancifully as a "vieux mot qui se disoit autrefois en parlant de certains enchantements qu'on attribuoit aux Fées. Il n'a d'usage que dans cette phrase prise des vieux contes de Fées: je vous fée et refée" ("old word that used to be used when speaking of certain enchantments that were attributed to fairies. It is used only in this phrase taken from old fairy tales: I fairy you and I fairy you again," Furetière 1701: vol. 2, s.v. *féer*).[36]

Many of the monsters of the fairy tales are temporary ones: princes and princesses turned into creatures of all sorts for a panoply of reasons including maternal pregnacy desires, fairies angered or spurned in a myriad of possible ways by a character or his/her parents, the rejection of a suitor chosen by a fairy, and fairy disputes.

The main characters, and at times their courts as well, turn into an astounding variety of animals and things. Animals include cats, deer, monkeys, beasts, a bluebird, a rooster, a whiting king and courtiers with fish heads, princes with snail helmets, a half whale, and a crayfish. In Lintot's "Le prince Sincer" a girl must teach snails to dance or be turned into one herself.[37] In some tales unfortunate princes and princesses are turned into objects. One princess becomes a doll in Lubert's "La Princesse Camion." Another in "La Princesse Couleur de rose et le Prince Céladon" is turned into a weeping and speaking book. In the anonymous "Le Prince Perinet ou l'origine des pagodes" (1730) the entire court is transformed into a porcelain tea service.[38] The prince-turned-into-a-teapot triumphs over his adversary by falling on his head. In Lubert's "Le Prince glacé" characters are turned into tables. The princess of Tessin's *Faunillane*, having slapped a giant, is left in pieces in a garden, her head bouncing about on the grass until she can be reassembled (1741: 11–19).

Like other monsters, transformed humans often remain civilized social beings. D'Aulnoy's White Cat goes hunting mounted on a monkey, offers fireworks, plays, and fashionable *collations* (light meals). The beast of Villeneuve's *La Belle et la Bête* is an enormous monster, with scales that clink as he walks ([1740] 2010: 43) and an elephant-like trunk. Yet his palace is a model of civility, its avenue bordered by four rows of orange trees. His guests find perfumed candles and chandeliers made not of crystal but of diamonds and rubies (51). They are served cups of chocolate at night (48) and fashionable light meals of cakes, dried fruit, and liqueurs on tables of porphyry. He has a library, gardens with fountains, and an aviary with exotic birds. He entertains Beauty with monkey theater and optical games, and the marriage is celebrated with three hours of fireworks (87).

Fairies transform other fairies. In Louise de Boissigny d'Auneuil's "La Princesse Léonice" one fairy turns another into a greyhound. In the rare case of a woman who has had more than enough of suitors, Velleda in the German writer Benedikte Naubert's "Der Riesentanz" (1795) transforms her lovers into green boulders in the shape of rams and flies off into the ethereal spaces.[39]

In the taste for excess, serial transformations become a feature of tales. In Jaques Cazotte's *Le Diable amoureux* (*The Devil in Love*, 1772), Béelzébut (Beelzebub) appears in the form of a camel head, a spaniel, an Italian singer, a male or female page that claims to be a sylph, before transforming again (perhaps) into the camel-headed Beelzebub. In Tessin's *Faunillane,* a mite undergoes a series of transformations:

> À peine ouvrait-elle les yeux à la lumière du jour, qu'on vit entrer dans la chambre où elle était un ciron, qui peu après devint une fourmi, puis une araignée, puis un hanneton, puis un ver à soie, puis un lézard, puis une grenouille, puis un crapaud, puis une vipère, puis une couleuvre, puis un serpent à sonnettes, puis un crocodile, et puis un dragon ailé, portant la Fée Envieuse sur le dos.
>
> (Hardly had she opened her eyes to the light of day, when could be seen entering the room where she was a mite, that shortly afterwards became an ant, then a spider, then a maybug, then a silkworm, then a lizard, then a frog, then a toad, then a viper, then a garter snake, then a rattlesnake, then a crocodile, then a winged dragon, carrying the fairy Envious on its back.)
>
> (20)[40]

The series of "puis" (then) marks the rhythms of the transformations, culminating in a dragon mount for an evil fairy.

BODIES: THE UNFORTUNATE "MONSTROUS" OF DIFFERENCE

There are other bodies marked as "monstrous" in the tales. To follow them is to enter the complex history of bodies, and the social perception and institutional treatment of bodies that were once seen as non-normal, that were termed bizarre, abnormal, frightening, or so profoundly "other" that they were unincorporable in notions of beauty, normality, and at the worst, believed impossible to include in the category of the human.

The Anatomical Monstrous

What could be called an "anatomical monstrous" was always part of definitions of the monstrous and techniques for understanding and/or isolating bodies. Like Paré, Aldrovandi, Furetière, and many before him, Johann Heinrich Samuel Formey, in his entry on zoological monsters for the *Encyclopédie,* tied the monstrous to notions of physical difference and deviation from what were perceived to be anatomical norms.

Les uns ont trop ou n'ont pas assez de certaines parties; tels sont les monstres à deux têtes, ceux qui sont sans bras, sans piés; d'autres pechent par la conformation extraordinaire, & bisarre par la grandeur disproportionnée, par le dérangement considérable d'une ou de plusieurs de leurs parties, & par la place singuliere que ce dérangement leur fait souvent occuper; d'autres enfin ou par l'union de quelques parties qui, suivant l'ordre de la nature & pour l'exécution de leurs fonctions, doivent toujours être séparés, ou par la désunion de quelques autres parties qui, suivant le même ordre & pour les mêmes raisons, ne doivent jamais cesser d'être unies.

(Some have too many parts or not enough; such as monsters with two heads, those that are armless or legless; others break the rules of conformation by being extraordinarily and bizarrely conformed, disproportionately large, or through the disarrangement of one or more of their parts, and by the unusual place they occupy because of this disarrangement; others finally by the union of several parts which, according to the order of nature and for the execution of their functions, must always be separate, or by the disunion of other parts which, according to the same order and for the same reasons, must never cease to remain united.)

(Diderot and d'Alembert 2007: 10:671)

Sometimes the unattractive characters reflect standards of beauty of the day, or the realities of hygiene. The prince finds Longue-Epine (Long Thorn) in d'Aulnoy's "La Biche au bois" too tall for his taste. Both Longue-Epine and the fairy Vicious in Lintot's "Tendrebrun et Constance" have blackened teeth, in the real world, the result of high sugar consumption and poor dental hygiene by the wealthier classes.

"Monstrous" fairy-tale figures of short stature or with crooked legs, twisted spines, scars, bumps, and lumps reflect the realities of dwarfism, the effects of rickets, scoliosis, age, and the sequels of maladies that could be seen in real people. In the eighteenth century people of unsually short stature continued to serve as entertainment at courts and the palaces of the nobility, that history still needing study in France. The "court dwarf" Nicolas Ferry, born in France, ended up in the eighteenth-century Polish court where he rode around the palace in his goat-drawn cart, and was once served in a cake.[41]

The fairy in Lubert's "La Princesse Lionette et le Prince Coquerico" has a horn in the middle of her forehead. By the time of Lubert's tale, published in 1743, a number of people with cutaneous horns—skin growths that resembled horns—had been on display. In the late sixteenth century there had been the Welsh Margaret Gryffith and the French François Trouvillou, the latter displayed in a hair suit with an accompanying story of supposed witchcraft. His portrait was included in Aldrovandi's *Monstrorum Historia* (1642). In the seventeenth century the English Mary Davis, the Scottish Elizabeth Lowe, and the Dutch Margaretha Mainers were on display. Prints and engravings in anatomical works continued to be produced throughout the eighteenth century for a curious public. Eighteenth-century travelers recorded seeing the actual horns of Mary Davis and Elizabeth Lowe in museums in London and Edinburgh.[42]

The harpsichord-playing, portraited monkey-princess Babiole in d'Aulnoy's tale resembles hypertrichotic women who were on display in the seventeenth century, including the famed Gonzales family at the courts of France and Parma, and other women who performed at fairs and on streets such as Barbara Urslerin, who played her harpsichord for the public several decades before d'Aulnoy's Babiole did. These were women and men sometimes suspected to have been the product of bestial copulations or wayward maternal imagination.[43] The number of transformations and misadventures in fairy tales that are the product of maternal desires for fairy fruit, fairy parsley, or for pregnancy itself appear along with a new wave of eighteenth-century treatises in the debate on maternal imagination. The tales and the treatises are part of a long history of setting female desire and imagination as dangerous.[44] Ageism, already in play at the time of the witch trials, remains in play in the tales. The most dangerous fairies are often the eldest, with years added for comic effect. The toad-riding fairy in Lintot's "Tendrebrun et Constance" is two thousand years old.

There are other gendered orders and hierarchies under construction. In Lubert's "Etoilette" a king described as "effeminé" (effeminate) gets a beating by a prince incensed at the fact the queen is off at war while the king is lounging in bed. All the "habitants effeminés" (effeminate inhabitants) of the island need to be taught war, along with architecture, sculpture, and arts (Lubert [1737–55] 2005: 381). The arts are in service of defining socially acceptable masculinity within the tale.

The Growth of an "Ethnological" Monstrous

In her dedication of *Contes du sérail*, Marianne-Agnès Pillement Falques wrote "La bizarrerie orientale a été quelquefois bien reçue dans ce pays" ("exotic oddities have sometimes been well received in this country") with typical understatement (*Contes/Madame Levesque* et al. 2007: 735). Fairy tales unquestionably reflected and served themselves to construct complex tastes for a non-European "exotic," with intrigues set in, characters from, and pastimes reflective of a dizzying number of real and fictionalized-real places set as sites of exotic otherness. D'Aulnoy's "Chatte Blanche" has ballets performed by cats and monkeys dressed as Chinese and Moors. D'Auneuil has settings and characters from Morocco, Grenada, the Canary Islands, Numidia, Mauritania,

Persia, and Turkey. La Présidente Dreuillet's "Le Phénix" ([1735] 2007) is set in Armenia (with a French flair—the realm has several "Vichy" thermal stations). In the century of *Les Mille et une nuits* (*The Thousand and One Nights*), *Les Mille et un jours* (*Thousand and One Days*), François Pétis de la Croix's *Histoire de la sultane de Perse et des vizirs*, Thomas-Simon Gueullette's *Les Mille et une heure: Contes Péruviens* (*Thousand and One Hours: Peruvian Tales*), and many more tales than can be listed here, characters and story lines cross ancient and contemporary worlds that include Egypt, ancient Persia, Turkey, India, Java, Sumatra, the Philippines, Tibet, Ceylon, China, Ethiopia, Crete, Portugal, and Peru, among others.[45]

Fairy tales set in "exotic" zones develop within broader notions of the exotic that take form in many ways, from the Brazilian village in Renaissance Rouen, through the colonial period and long after, and shape a monstrous that could be termed "ethnological," despite the fact that the word itself would not appear in a French text until 1834 or in a French dictionary until 1878.[46] Notions of difference tied to bodies, skin, hair, practices, and places marked by their distance from Europe are in construction and visible in the tales.

Furetière notes, in the *Dictionnaire universel* under the entry for *affreux* ("awful," "dreadful"): "Afrique a des monstres et des déserts affreux" ("Africa has dreadful monsters and deserts," 1690: vol. 1, s.v. *affreux*). Africa was the source of many of the real marvels of seventeenth-century collecting: ivory, ostrich eggs, coral, gold, topaz and heliotrope, birds and large mammals for menageries. Limited knowledge of the natural world, and an enduring taste for fantasy continued to fill Africa with a number of fictional marvels, among them giant flying dragons, hippopotami with claws, and unicorns.[47] Depictions of African women (who may be lumped together under the term "Ethiopian" in fairy tales) are particularly problematic. D'Aulnoy has the Black Princess (La Princesse Noire) of "La Biche au bois" describe her own beauty, with a narrative inflection that makes it abundantly clear that it is to be read with ironic inversion: "regardez la noirceur de mon teint, ce nez écrasé, ces grosses lèvres, n'est-ce pas ainsi qu'il faut pour être belle?" ("look at the blackness of my color, this squashed nose, these fat lips, this is what makes a woman beautiful, don't you agree?," 2004: 700). In Lubert's "Etoilette," a princess finds to her horror she has been transformed into a well-dressed Ethiopian, but the magnificence of her clothes "ne la consolait pas de la perte du plus beau teint du monde" ("did not console her for the loss of the most beautiful shade in the world" [1737–55] 2005: 385). She finds her dark color so "affreuse" (awful) that she tries to kill herself. Expectedly, she will be turned white again so she can marry the prince. Africa, source of slaves brought to South American mines, Caribbean plantations, and the homes of noble ladies, is source of a monstrous to be introduced only to be vanquished or erased.

"Le prince des Aigues-Marines" by Louise Cavalier, known as Dame Levesque, opens on the *île des sauvages* (island of savages), amid the cries of *barbares* (barbarians)[48] assembled to choose a king. They dance around the piles of their dead victims. These "monsters," as the narrator calls them, kill the arriving foreigners and drink their still-warm blood in honor of their gods. The description of their "barbarian" customs takes several pages, and includes a forest festival complete with a thousand savage beasts, vases of human blood, and a throne covered in a lion skin. The monstrous is rather a hybrid romp around the globe. They are vanquished by just one look at a cursed European prince who is taller than average and has the most beautiful long blond hair in the world, falling in large curls on his shoulders. By the end, the blond hero returns the cadavers of the savages (preserved by magic air) to life, they lose their ferocity, and the island is henceforth *policée*, that is to say, "civilized." There are emergent forms of fantasy that might be called (albeit with terms that would not yet make sense in 1744) ethnological horror fiction.

The palace of Serpentin Vert (Green Serpent) in d'Aulnoy's tale is filled with the tiny collectable porcelain figurines known as "pagodas." The fairy-tale ones are of materials ranging from diamonds, emeralds, coral, crystal, or porcelain to wood and earth. Some are beautiful, some gracious, some hideous, with "bouches à l'oreille, des yeux de travers, des nez écrasés" ("mouths on their ears, crooked eyes, squashed noses," d'Aulnoy 2004: 582). Some of them are able to stand still. Others—just like the real collectable porcelain figurines with nodding heads and articulated hands—cannot stop their heads or hands or feet from moving.[49] Nortandose, Prince of the Blue Island in "Le Prince Perinet ou l'origine des pagodes," is ludically dispatched at the end by being turned into a pagoda. Chinoiserie figurines sit historically among innumerable other images of non-European "exotics" made into torch and lamp supports, shaped into perfume bottles and figurines, appearing on porcelain tableware, as architectural details, decoration for sleighs and carriages, busts and fountain sculptures, woven into arabesques and *singerie* wall art.[50] Human "exotics" turned into decorative knickknacks vector meanings of the domination of the exotic through collection and use. There is an entire realm of early exoticism in the decorative arts as they intersect with fiction.

The fictional monsters both reflect and surely helped shape developing constructions of the "normal" and what became conceived of as ugly, unacceptable, or deviant for publics. In "monster" texts—fictional, medical, anatomical, or other—ageism, sexism, racism, notions of supposedly appropriate gendered behaviors, and fears of difference can be seen in construction. Fairy tales contain things other than Pierre Mabille's "universal realities."[51] There are fascinatingly complex realities rooted in centuries, places, institutions, and notions that extend throughout the social imaginary.

REHABILITATING THE MONSTROUS AND IMAGINATION

Reading the development of the monstrous marvelous more fully involves reframing, revaluing, and rehabilitating forms of imagination more generally. It involves undoing Voltaire's condemnation of fairy-tale imagination. He wrote in his entry on "imagination" for the *Encyclopédie*:

> Il faut un très-grand art dans toutes ces imaginations d'invention, et même dans les romans; ceux qui en manquent sont méprisés des esprits bien faits. Un jugement toûjours sain regne dans les fables d'Esope; elles seront toûjours les délices des nations. Il y a plus d'imagination dans les contes des fées; mais ces imaginations fantastiques, toûjours dépourvues d'ordre & de bon sens, ne peuvent être estimées; on les lit par foiblesse, et on les condamne par raison.

> (A very great art is required in all these imaginatons of invention, and even in novels; those who lack it are disdained by well-ordered minds. An always sound judgment reigns in Aesope's fables; they will always be the delight of nations. There is more imagination in fairy tales; but these fantastic imaginations, always lacking order and good sense, cannot be esteemed; one reads them out of weakness, and one condemns them out of reason.)
> (Diderot and d'Alembert 2017: 8:562)

Voltaire's condemnation was made within the context of Enlightenment projects that sought to push fairy tales, devil texts, and all the literature that arose in the realm of Fatapolis, to the margins of the literary canon, where many of the fairy tales would remain for centuries.

Many might beg to differ with Voltaire. The waves of seventeenth- and eighteenth-century fairy tales, the flood of nineteenth-century fantastic literature, science fiction, and innumerable forms of fantasy in novels, television shows, and films throughout the world today, speak to an enduring taste for fantasy and the peculiar force of "monsters" and of things that go beyond.

* * *

The eighteenth century offers hinge points in the history of monsters, where some of the monsters of old continue, transformed and evacuated of terrors, and new "monsters"—of medicine and fields that will grow into ethnology, hygiene, psychiatry, and criminology—along with social notions of beauty, can be seen starting to take shape.[52] Todorov suggested ways to break down the marvelous into hyperbolic, exotic, instrumental, and scientific forms. The monstrous marvelous is among the dozens of other types one might propose.

The spaces of monsters, marvels, and imagination are being explored today in their innumerable facets by scholars not just in literature but in the histories of medicine, religion, anthropology, architecture, garden design, popular culture, art and the decorative arts, cartography, and material culture. Among scholars with broad approaches to fairy tales and other forms of culture are many of the authors in this series whose work on tales, salons, gender, society, marvels, and medicine informs and, quite literally, brackets this chapter. Major scholarly works on monsters and fantasy with broad perspectives include Lorraine Daston and Katharine Park on monsters, Max Milner on the devil in French literature, Noémie Courtès on magicians and magic, Emanuelle Sempère on the marvelous. To read monsters in broader contexts, one needs Philippe Ariès on death, Umberto Eco on ugliness, Angelica Groom and Peter Sahlins on menageries, scholars of the witch trials, banquets, festivals, fairgrounds, merry-go-rounds, gardens, orientalism, and the nascent fields of teratology, anthropology, hygiene, psychiatry ... of as many fields as there have been in which one once imagined there were prodigious, frightening, or marvelous things. A comprehensive bibliography of the fairy-tale monstrous would take volumes.

Monsters have never been real beings or objects. Notions about otherness, difference, and the non-human arise in the spaces of the social imaginary where literature, art, philosophy, natural history, medicine, and law connect. They take their shape at borders where disciplines mix. An attention to the monstrous and the marvelous can help wrest *Le Cabinet des fées* in its forty-one volumes—itself once called a "monstrous" collection—out of eighteenth-century notions that sought to push fairy tales into the margins of the Enlightenment.[53] It involves letting disciplinary borders blur, in the very century where enlightenment projects set those boundaries as a social, philosophical, and pedagogical project. It deepens the context for dragon pagodas, chimera sleighs, and Chinese carousel figures. It lets some of the shadows of the Enlightenment become more visible. Reading monsters offers routes through complex orders of culture, where the imaginary cities of Badinopolis, Bagatelle, and Babiole are not just pleasant cities toward which to voyage but also instructive ones, reminders of the place of imagination not only in literature but in society in much broader ways.

ACKNOWLEDGMENT

Special thanks are given to my students at the University of Hawai'i and at the Istituto Lorenzo de' Medici in Italy who indulged my taste for fairy tales and material culture. Their own research on banquets, cookbooks, fashion, festivals, the decorative arts, gardening, jewels, machine plays, animals, menageries, art, travel, and trade fed my own knowledge and imagination. Every one of them is thanked.

CHAPTER SIX

Space

Spatial References and Narrative Strategies in Eighteenth-Century Tales in East and West

RICHARD VAN LEEUWEN

It is a commonplace to say that every text, whatever its genre, presupposes a certain relationship with a spatial environment. A text can only be understood if the reader is able to situate it in a context of space and time. References to space in texts can be either implicit—giving only indirect indications—or explicit—giving clear markers of a representation of space within the text. In both cases, the reader will use these indications to construct a coherent spatial vision in which the narrative is taking shape or, in the case of fiction, in which the characters act out their roles. The indications may thereby refer to a "real" environment outside the text (Paris or the Indian Ocean) or refer to an imaginary or undefined place (forest or island). An author may also prefer a combination of the two, referring to an imaginary street in Paris or an undefined island in the Mediterranean. In all these cases, spatial elements will help the reader to establish a relationship with the text and link the textual framework of space to their own experience and framework of space.[1]

The observations above imply that an author, for instance of a fictional text, has the freedom to use spatial references as part of his narrative strategies. We might say, even more emphatically, that spatial references are among the most significant instruments to manipulate the readers' relationship to the text and, concomitantly, to regulate the process of interpretation. The essence of this manipulative instrument lies in the nature of spatial markers as a form of referentiality: spatial elements are not only part of a representation of space within a story, allowing the characters their—fictional—habitat; they also always refer to a vision of space outside the story, which can be imagined by the reader and connected to claims of realism within the text. A reference to "Paris," for instance, or to a "bedroom" in a fictional text, will always be related by the reader to their experiences and fantasies, with their connotations, to the real counterparts of these fictional spaces. This association of real and fictional spaces, through strategies of referentiality, not only affects the reader's notion of the level of realism of the story as a whole but also their interpretation of the individual characters, their adventures and relationships, which, after all, are embedded in this spatial nexus.[2]

In this chapter we will explore references to space in a type of fictional literature that could be categorized as "stories of marvel" in the eighteenth century. This broad category would include generic types such as fairy tales and stories of magic, but also types in which elements of marvel and magic are incorporated as part of a larger narrative structure, such as fantastic tales, romances, novels containing supernatural elements, stories and novels containing suggestions of supernatural forces, etc. The rationale behind this broad approach is, first, that we do not want to confine ourselves to Western literatures only, but also include works from Asian and Muslim traditions, with their own generic types; second, that a narrow definition of the "fairy tale" as a type in Western literature would not do justice to the ways in which, especially in the eighteenth century, fairy tales evolved and were incorporated into new generic forms; and, third, that although the various generic types obviously differ in general purport and specific details, their common ground—both in Western and non-Western literatures—is that they explore the boundaries and relationship between supernatural, fictional, and experiential realities. Therefore, although forms and effects may differ, they have a common purpose. And, as we argued above, since spatial references are a powerful instrument to suggest the "realism" of the story and manipulate the sense of reality in the reader, it follows that they have a crucial role in all the stories in which the relationship between supernatural forces, fiction, and reality is investigated, and that it is interesting to compare strategies in possibly diverse textual forms and settings.

It should be observed here that it is not our intention to reveal a kind of Jungian archetypal connection between an obvious diversity of texts. It is evident that the interpretation of fictional texts of whatever type is different within differing cultural, temporal, and societal contexts. This is even more true for literature that speculates about the relationship between the "natural" and "supernatural" worlds, or between reality and fictionality, since the awareness of these relationships have differed according to time and place. Perceptions of these constructions in eighteenth-century Europe were obviously different from those of medieval Europeans or eighteenth-century Persians. However, these differences are mainly due to different interpretative contexts and would not by definition preclude common strategies of exploring the place of the "supernatural" in real experience. It is our hypothesis that it is useful to examine parallels in narrative strategies used for this exploration within different cultural contexts and generic forms and, moreover, that spatial references are suited for this kind of comparison because they are so universal as an instrument to establish the connection between the reader's experience of reality and the fictional text.

It can be argued that Western and non-Western literatures followed different trajectories, particularly in the eighteenth century, which witnessed a significant transformation of literary conventions such as the rise of the realist novel in Europe. It seems, at least superficially, that the eighteenth century marked a decisive break with previous literary forms and thus heralded the emergence of "modern" literature. Still, there are several ways in which the various traditions can be connected, and, here too, the element of space is significant. First, although European literature in the eighteenth century shows many new trends that separated "modern" literature from its medieval and early modern predecessors, even in the new genres several elements of earlier narrative strategies were preserved. Although the tradition of the romance of chivalry became obsolete after the sixteenth century, we can still find tropes of wandering knights, damsels in distress, and chivalric virtues until well into the nineteenth century. This is particularly true of the "magical" elements in romances, such as the journey of the hero to mysterious lands, or various kinds of medievalism in Gothic literature. Therefore, in the categories of literature that are under discussion here, which are often seen as a counter current against mainstream novelistic realism, the interest in the interaction between natural and supernatural realms within fictional literature seems to be continued, albeit in different generic forms and in a different epistemological context.[3]

Second, although perceptions of the nature of the relationship between the supernatural and the real may differ according to the cultural and religious environments, I would argue that the habit of using literature to explore this relationship is a common pursuit. In the Islamic tradition, there has always been a reflection upon the value of "fanciful" stories, comparable with the juxtaposition of "fables" and "histories" in medieval literary criticism. In Chinese intellectual debates, there have been periods in which invented stories were criticized in ways comparable to attitudes during the European Enlightenment, because they were prone to deceive the audience. To be sure, in all these periods of rational skepticism, the literature of the marvelous flourished, although its function and appreciation changed. Frivolous fancy was often reprehended, but the exploration of its effects, its relation to fictionality, and its significance for discovering the natural–supernatural divide remained. Fairy tales and their related genres were perhaps rejected as fantasies, but their narrative procedures and referential connotations were still indispensable.[4]

Third, it is in the eighteenth century in particular that Eastern and Western literary traditions became structurally connected. It was above all the first translation of *The Thousand and One Nights*—the French translation of Antoine Galland, which appeared between 1704 and 1717—that introduced Europe to a vast and rich collection of Arabic literary material, which was in its turn affected by the Indian, Persian, and Turkish traditions. This material not only served as a repository of new literary motifs to be used by European authors; it also provided examples of new narrative concepts and techniques that influenced experiments with new literary forms. Throughout the eighteenth century, *The Thousand and One Nights* became structurally incorporated into European literature, not only as an element of Orientalism but also as a model for narrative strategies and generic forms. Due to its hybrid and ambiguous form and concept, it had a highly innovative impact on literati who searched for new literary forms. After the emulations of Crébillon fils, Denis Diderot, Jacques Cazotte, William Beckford, and Christoph Martin Wieland, the influence of *The Thousand and One Nights*, and thereby of "oriental" literatures, remained endemic in the European literary tradition.[5]

The impact of *The Thousand and One Nights* in the eighteenth century is relevant to our discussion on two levels. First, due to its seemingly uncomplicated interaction between supernatural and natural elements, it gave a new impetus to the debate about supernatural phenomena in literature. On the one hand it supplemented medieval perceptions of multiple realities with a huge reservoir of new concepts and models, and on the other hand it showed how these models could be integrated into literature as a form of fictionally representing a complex reality. This appealed in particular to the inquisitive mind of Enlightenment Europe. Apart from the narrative and conceptual aspects of *The Thousand and One Nights*, the work, or at least its French rendering, also contributed to the incorporation of the "Orient" into the domain of referentiality in a new way. The Orient had already had a great significance in European early modern romances, as a realm of mystery, magic, and adventure. During the eighteenth century, the Orient gradually became part not only of the imagination but also of reality and of the epistemological debate about the relationship between reality and fiction (see Osterhammel 2013).

It would seem that partly as a result of "Oriental" interference, the Western literary tradition embarked upon a separate, "modern," trajectory, distinct from the Eastern traditions. This is to some extent true, since in the Arabic, Persian, and Urdu traditions older genres were preserved. Still, this traditional material served as containers for new additions and literary innovation, and the adoption of new themes combined with old tropes. Thus, in the eighteenth century, versions of ancient romances can differ markedly from their predecessors. In China, in the seventeenth and eighteenth centuries, traditional literary material—for instance fairy tales—were incorporated into newly conceived novels or collections of tales. The resemblances and differences between the Eastern and Western traditions are not our main interest here. What is more relevant is the domain where the different traditions converged and overlapped, that is, their concern with the interrelationship between the natural and the supernatural; the imaginary and the real; fiction and reality. And, within this concern, the use of spaces as elements of narrative strategies to visualize and explore the interfaces and boundaries between human reality and the realms of the divine, semi-divine, or magical forces.

After these introductory observations, we will now proceed to discuss some of the main narrative strategies connected to spatial representations and constructions. Needless to say, due to the enormous amount of material and its diversity, our discussion can only indicate some starting points for research rather than a survey of the field as a whole.

SPACE AND NARRATIVE STRATEGIES

As explained above, constructions of space in literary texts can be utilized by authors to produce various effects. The principle is that by marking off spatial domains, various kinds of boundaries are inserted into the story. These boundaries provide a kind of framework in the story, which reflects its narrative unfolding. Boundaries imply a regime of differences and segregations, contacts and communication, exclusion and inclusion, stagnancy and movement, and so on. In general, they impose a necessity of interaction between the diverse domains; they create imbalances that require action to restore the status quo; they provide incentives for a story to begin; they represent hierarchies connected to the roles of the protagonists. The effects created by these differences and manipulated by authors to endow their story with structure and meaning can be detected at three levels: first, on the level of narrative structure, spatial entities can be linked to specific persons, events, or episodes in the story, resulting in an overlap of narrative structural elements and spatial elements; second, on the level of symbolic structure, spatial domains can stand for specific qualities, values, and connotations, providing the story with interpretive coherence; and, third, on the level of referentiality, spatial markers govern the relationship of a text with the outside world, at least for the author and the reader.

The most evident examples of stories in which spatial constructions play a decisive role are the medieval romances, both in Western and in non-Western literatures. Both in romances of chivalry and of love we find heroes forced by circumstances or by inner urges to set out on a journey to fight enemies or to find their beloved, or both. They roam through landscapes that mirror their emotional and psychological condition; their mobility is opposed by forms of stagnancy and enclosure, of themselves, in prisons or forests, or of the coveted damsels, in fortified strongholds or palace harems. Usually their journeys are steered by supernatural forces, such as fate, or interventions by astrologers, magicians, demons, or talismans. They usually wander off into unfamiliar, enchanted spaces, in which they have to prove their courage, ingenuity, and moral integrity. In the end they return to their homes, accompanied by their bride, to secure the continuity of the dynasty and consummate true love. Of course, this basic pattern may be varied upon in many ways, or be carved up into several narrative components, but in most cases it shows the essential narrative function of opposing immobility and movement, enclosure and dynamism (see Campbell 1973; Hutchinson 1992; Van Leeuwen 2007).

In Eastern literatures, romances of this type go back to ancient models, but they were still very popular in the seventeenth and eighteenth centuries, in various versions, compositions, and languages. An example of a popular narrative of this kind is the story of "Qamar al-Zaman and Budur," which was introduced to the European audience in the translations of *The Thousand and One Nights*. In this story, Qamar al-Zaman, a young prince, refuses to marry any of the princesses proposed to him by his father, and he is subsequently incarcerated in a tower of the palace. This dungeon is a favorite abode of *jinn*s, or demons, who, fascinated by his beauty, allow him a glimpse of the equally attractive princess Budur, who lives in faraway China. Fate intervenes to liberate the prince and indicate the itinerary he has to follow to conquer his beloved. In this story, we see how two kinds of supernatural forces, fate and *jinn*s, conspire to guide the hero to his destiny, after he has gone to several spatial domains, overcome many obstacles, and withstood dangers and trials, which indicate the phases of his progress. In the end, he proves his suitability to ascend to the throne after his marriage to his beloved.[6] This pattern can also be perceived in the immensely popular romance of Hamza, an historical hero in the Islamic tradition, and, for instance, in the traditional story of Yue Fei, the historical Chinese hero, which was recorded in a romance-novel around 1700 by Qian Cai (see Cai 1995; Lakhnavi and Bilgrami 2007).

In European literature, too, the pattern of the medieval romances retained some importance. Although the chivalric order of society waned, romances such as the cycles of Amadis of Gaul and Oliva de Palmera were extremely popular in various languages in the premodern period. In the eighteenth century the fantastic stories of Claude-Henri de Fusée, abbé de Voisenon, Antoine Hamilton (*Fleur d'épine*, 1730), and Crébillon fils, often inspired by *The Thousand and One Nights*, adopted the old combination of itineraries of the hero and supernatural interventions (see Ballaster 2005; Dufrenoy 1946–75; Hamilton 1813; Martino 1906; and Voisenon 1746). In Germany, Christoph Martin Wieland parodied the genre in his *Oberon* (1780) and William Beckford emulated the journeys of *The Thousand and One Nights*-like characters in his peculiar pastiches. Furthermore, Beckford adapted some stories from the Wortley-Montague manuscript, which was in his possession at the time (now in the Bodleian Library), and collected them in *Suite de contes arabes* (1770s–80s). The story of "Histoire du Prince Ahmed" stages a young, lazy adolescent who is sent out into the world by his father and wanders through enchanted landscapes, full of palaces with young maidens, strange figures, deserts. He traverses the *Plaine des Ginns*, which is full of skeletons, with his friend Prince Ahmed, haunted by the curse of the children of Zouc Zouc. The prince tells the story of his love for Princess Neubahar. The story is a typical example of exotic Orientalism, with enchantments, sublime landscapes, strange encounters, sensuality, (homo)eroticism, travesty, seduction, and so on, systematically referring to the realms found in *The Thousand and One Nights* (see Beckford 1992, [1782] 1993; Wieland [1780] 1964) (Figure 6.1).

FIGURE 6.1: The liminal site of the palace of the king of the Ebony Isles by Edmund Dulac, from *Stories from the Arabian Nights* (London: Hodder and Stoughton, 1911). Public domain.

The most interesting example is perhaps the intriguing and complex novel *Manuscrit trouvé à Saragosse* (Manuscript Found in Saragossa) by the French-Polish author Jan Potocki. In this story, the Flemish prince Alphonse van Worden is called back to the Spanish Court in Madrid. On his way through the Sierra Morena he appears to be trapped in a mysterious enchantment, which prevents him from continuing his journey. Spectres of beautiful Moorish maidens, who try to seduce him to give up his faith, are alternated with horrific, violent scenes. In the end, the apparent supernatural phenomena turn out to be enacted by a Moorish shaykh who reveals to the hero that he is partly of Moorish descent and tries to persuade him to relinquish his faith and secure the dynastic continuation of his Moorish family. In this text, which was written at the end of the eighteenth century and was First published in 1814, several tendencies converge: the pattern of the medieval romance, the influence of oriental elements, the development of the "modern" novel, and the exploration of the relationship between supernatural forces, reality, and the imagination (see Potocki [1810] 2008).

It is part of the generic conventions of these romances and neo-romances that the hero for a period of time is entrapped in a kind of spatial limbo, a place where the regular laws of nature are suspended or absent, and which represents a labyrinth where the hero has to use his ingenuity and perseverance to find his way out. The stalemate in which Potocki's hero finds himself is a nice example of this state, which seems to be part of an initiatory process. The passage of time has stagnated; there seems to be no way out; there are no signs linking the environment with a familiar reality. In medieval and early modern romances, mountain ranges, deserts, and islands, but also intricate urban mazes, forests, and the Orient provide the settings for these intermittent episodes, which usually reveal the confused condition of the hero and allow fate and supernatural forces to intervene. These ambiguous spatial domains can conveniently be conceptualized as "Otherworlds," spaces that seem to be subject to their own systems of natural, social, and political laws and which are segregated from the human world by a clear or diffuse boundary (see Byrne 2016).

In the predicament of Potocki's hero, Alphonse van Worden, we can see a modern interpretation of the ancient idea of the Otherworld. The hero, and the reader, are led to believe that they have entered a space dominated by ineffable and magical forces, which in the end are revealed to be an ingenious deception. The hero's stay in this intermediate world tests his ability to navigate through a world full of mystery and dangers, and in the meantime initiates him into his past and in his true identity. In the romances in the Asian traditions, the ambiguity about the ontological status of the Otherworld is usually not made explicit; here the Otherworld is strange but still a quite acceptable representation of the ways in which parallel realms interact with the natural domain of humanity. An interesting example is the charming love romance of *Sayf al-Muluk and*

Princess Badi'at al-Jamal, which was popular in various languages and versions throughout the Muslim world and was published in French translation in 1745.[7] The story relates the peregrinations of prince Sayf al-Muluk in search of his beloved, instigated by a token from Solomon, the prophet, sewn in a garb presented to him as a gift. Traveling great distances over land and seas, Sayf enters the world of the *jinn*s, which exists as a kind of parallel reality next to the natural world, or, more precisely, as a layer within the natural world that at certain points in space intersects with it. This realm, which is also explored in many other fanciful stories, is the domain where the hidden forces of nature are located and where *jinn*s and other demonic beings reside under the authority of King Solomon (see Marzolph and Van Leeuwen 2004: 1: 362–4; see also Shackle 2007).

Otherworlds are also a common component of romances of chivalry. In the aforementioned epic narrative of Hamza, for example, the hero is at a certain point in the story abducted by a *jinn* queen who needs his support in her struggle against rival kings. Thus for some time Hamza continues his astonishing feats in the realm of the *jinn*, which is situated at the extremity of the earth, in the Qaf mountains, which mark the edge of the inhabitable world. Here he has to overcome giants with magical powers and the ability to shift their shapes at will, and he becomes trapped in powerful talismans that he has to neutralize. The purpose of this excursion is obvious: it enables Hamza to prove his superhuman prowess and ingenuity, strengthening his status and reputation in the human world where he continues to fight for justice and his beloved (see El-Zein 2017; Lakhnavi and Bilgrami 2007).

In romances, Otherworlds are not only inserted as a way of complicating the narrative procedure and include a new level of imagined reality; they also introduce spatial realms that shape the interpretive understanding of the story. They represent a counterworld that disrupts the universality of a moral order and problematize the reader's vision of reality. The hero, as a privileged, extraordinary specimen of mankind, succeeds in crossing a boundary, through his courage and perseverance, or because it was ordained by fate, and enters a world that is not governed by the regular laws of nature or society. They represent, above all, a world in which another form of authority reigns, with its own mechanisms of power and magical devices. The successful outcome of the hero's interaction with these forces not only buttresses his heroic status but also maps out a relationship between the supernatural domain and the human order, providing the latter with a counterimage and a sense of rationality. The relationship is not always unproblematic, as is revealed at the end of the story of Sayf al-Muluk, when it appears difficult to formalize his love with his *jinn* princess in legal matrimony (see Byrne 2016: 110, 116, 123; Van Leeuwen 2014).

The examples above show how in stories that are structured as journeys, the dominant element of mobility not only serves to integrate the story into space but also to integrate spaces into the story, as a device to steer the hero toward the plot, insert crossroads, ambiguous episodes, disorientation, meetings and separations, obstacles and passages, and so on. The sequence of spaces symbolizes the passage of time, as opposed to stagnancy and enclosure as temporal interruptions. Supernatural elements are used, first, to secure the correct outcome of the hero's peregrinations through demonic and magical interventions, but also to link his adventure to an overarching worldview, which is permeated by the overwhelming power of fate. Human power, even if personified by invincible heroes or exquisite princes, has to find accommodation with the world of the unseen, which they are chosen to explore through their exclusive properties. In the end, they have the blessing, not only of human but also of supernatural, sometimes even Divine, powers.

ENCHANTED PLACES

The romances referred to above are not fairy tales in the strict sense of the term, although they pertain to a world clearly associated with the imaginary function of fairy tales and include episodes that could well serve as self-contained fairy stories. There are examples of narratives in which the two generic types are more straightforwardly combined, such as stories in which the princes have to enter magical worlds to fulfill some specified tasks. A work that represents this quite popular type is *Les aventures des trois princes de Serendip* (The Adventures of the Three Princes of Serendip), which goes back on old Persian texts and was translated, reworked, and supplemented in French by Louis de Mailly in 1719.[8] Because of its hybrid character, the work epitomizes the amalgamation of oriental and European literatures, which occurred throughout the eighteenth century. These examples indicate that fairy stories can be linked to journeys and mobility, but they also show how in narrative worlds the forces of the supernatural can be connected to specific places and spatial structures. In these stories, magic and demonic interventions seem strange but natural, part of a self-contained narrative world in which visible and less visible realms converge (see Mailly 2011).

That in China this type of tale was not only popular but also of intellectual interest can be gleaned from the famous collection *Strange Tales from a Studio*, by Pu Song Ling (1640–1715), published in 1740 (see Figure 6.2). Taken from popular lore, most of the stories are brief accounts of dealings between humans and fox spirits, the creatures of Chinese demonology comparable to the Arabic *jinn*s and Persian *div*s or *peri*s. They usually appear in the shape of a beautiful young maiden, either hiding in the ruins of a Buddhist temple or walking by herself on the road. A nice example of the play with spatial elements connected with the supernatural is Pu Song Ling's story "The Celestial Palace," in which a student is seduced by an old lady to drink a strange intoxicating drink and

FIGURE 6.2: A nineteenth-century illustration of a story from *Strange Tales from a Chinese Studio* concerning a female ghost, dreamscapes, and resurrrection. Public domain.

awakes in a dark cave, which turns out to be the living space of an immortal girl. She leads him to the splendid chambers of the Celestial Palaces where he falls asleep in a beautiful room. When he awakes he is back in his own study. The story shows the interaction between levels of reality, which is steeped in mystery, taboos, sexuality, intermittent zones, unconsciousness, and illusion (see Pu Songling 1978: 37–42; 1993).

The general purport of these stories is twofold: they show the places where the supernatural world spills into the human world, such as dilapidated sanctuaries, family mansions, and imaginary villages, and the interzones in which encounters can take place, such as darkness, love/lust, dreams, visions, coincidences, and curses, magic, and spells. They also contain a clear moral dimension: the foxes interfere in human life with good or bad intentions, either to redress some injustice committed in the past or for revenge, the fulfillment of a curse, or merely for creating havoc in human lives. They show the general framework of Chinese cosmologies, in which endless categories of supernatural beings and forces join the human efforts to realize the ordinances of fate and the celestial emperor, manifested in the balance of Yin and Yang. A collection of tales similar to Pu Song Ling's is a work by Ji Yun (1724–1805) entitled "Brushed Notes from a Straw Barn Contemplating the Great in Small Things," which is particularly concerned with fox spirits in their diverse spatial surroundings (see Ji Yun 1983).

In the Persian/Arabic traditions, the central figure in fairy stories, or *khurafat*, is the *jinn*, the demon that is not of a semi-divine nature but rather belongs to one of the layers of created reality. *Jinn*s can be believers or unbelievers, good or bad, congenial or perfidious, malicious and refractory. Like foxes, they can transform themselves and possess magical powers. They usually abide in deserted places, ruined buildings, forests, deserts, and wells, but they also live under water, in bathhouses, and lavatories. Sometimes they can be summoned by specific magical objects. Typical intrigues involve young ladies who are abducted by spiteful or amorous *jinn*s and are held captive in enchanted castles or crypts. The hero has to find them, dissolve the talisman imprisoning the lady, and slay the *jinn*.[9] The intervention of *jinn*s in the human world can sometimes lead to enchanted "enclaves" in human society, as in the story of the "Three Ladies and the Porter" in *The Thousand and One Nights*, where Harun al-Rashid by coincidence enters a house that is secluded from its environment as the result of a curse by a *jinn*.[10] Another example of the regimentation of space through the intervention of *jinn*s is the motif of the forbidden room, which stages a protagonist in an enchanted castle who is allowed to open thirty-nine doors, but not the fortieth. Here, again, the encounter of a human hero with an enchanted place leads to a fairy tale-like plot and a clear moral message.[11]

As in non-Western literatures, in Europe, too, a long tradition of fairy tales and similar material existed that was given a new impetus through the popular collections of Charles Perrault and Marie-Catherine d'Aulnoy. The popularity of this type of literature endured throughout the eighteenth century, although attitudes toward it did not remain unchanged. In the beginning of the century it converged with the instant popularity of *The Thousand and One Nights* translated by Galland, which, although not strictly speaking a collection of fairy tales, provided a huge reservoir of models for tales of wonder of various kinds. It coalesced in the generic type of the "oriental tale" or "conte oriental," which became a structural element in European literature in the eighteenth century and beyond, and which provided inspiration for types of narrative alternatively labeled as "fantastic," "Gothic," or "romantic." Although these tales are perhaps not synonymous with fairy tales, they can be seen as an evolutionary continuation of the fairy tale in a form adapted to its changing environment (see Aravamudan 2012; Ballaster 2005; Dufrenoy 1946–75; Martino 1906).

Early examples of the hybrid amalgamation of the fairy tale and the oriental tale can be found in the work of the aforementioned Antoine Hamilton, showing the confluence of different tendencies. More mature forms, which clearly show the influence of *The Thousand and One Nights*, are represented by the novel *Le Sopha* (1742) by Crébillon fils, in which a young man is magically transformed into a sopha and tells tales of love and perfidity, and Denis Diderot's *Les Bijoux indiscrets* (1748). In the latter work a king and descendant of Shahriyar—the king of the framing story of *The Thousand and One Nights*—receives a ring that can force the "jewels"—code for genitalia—of ladies at the court to tell him about their exploits. Secretly sneaking into their rooms, the king is enabled by the ring to discover the true nature of women and the intrigues, scandals, and depravity taking place at his court, as a microcosm of French society. In this delightful novel we perceive the concurrence of familiar elements, such as the magical object, the telling of tales, the confined space, and the moral message retrieved from secrecy and hypocrisy (see Crébillon [1742] 1984; Diderot [1748] 1965).

Diderot's novel should be seen as a parody of existing literary genres, and not as an effort to encourage the generic type of the fairy tale. In general, writers of the eighteenth-century Enlightenment were critical of the fanciful emplotment and unbound imagination of fairy tales. This did not mean that they eschewed the fairy tale as a literary form; on the contrary, they intended to use the popular form of the tale to convey didactic and exemplary allegories. Voltaire wrote several oriental and non-oriental tales in this vein, which included enchanted spaces.[12] In English literature Francis Sheridan published the philosophical tale *The History of Nourjehad* (1767), in which the magical intrigues of a *jinn* are staged in the confined spaces of an oriental palace, to convey moral admonitions about the intricate relationship between power and morality (see Hawkesworth 1992; Sheridan 1992). A similar moral tale about power, greed, and the intervention of a genie, entitled "Almoran and Hamet" was published by John Hawkesworth in 1761. In Germany, the literary form of the fairy tale was practiced, among others, by Christoph Martin Wieland, who introduced *The Thousand and One Nights* as a source of inspiration in several short and longer texts. He translated and wrote a number of fairy tales, among them the story "Die eiserne Leuchter" ("The Iron Candlesticks"), which combined the motif of the magical object with an enchanted space and a moral lesson. It was inspired by the story of "Aladdin" in Galland's *Les Mille et une nuit* and contains elements that remained important motifs in European literature: the enchanted underground crypt and the Faustian complex of taboo, power, and fate. Similar motifs can be found in other German fairy tales (*Kunstmärchen*) and romantic novels, for example Ludwig Tieck's "Abdallah" (1792).[13]

In the stories of the enlightened authors, the combination of demons, magic, and supernatural forces with specific, often oriental, spaces was used not to present the enchanted world-vision as truthful but rather to construct emplotments that reveal and discuss moral issues in a didactic manner. Some of their contemporaries used similar narrative strategies not to disclose a rational worldview, but rather to reveal the darker side of human nature. Jacques Cazotte, for instance, adapted a collection of tales from *The Thousand and One Nights* to which he added some stories composed by himself, which are steeped in sorcery, black arts, and power abuse, to explore a demonology that pervades human reality primarily in its psychological depth. Its central space is the sorcerer's castle located somewhere in North Africa, from which the sorcerer plans his vicious schemes. His youthful captives can only be saved by breaking a talismanic spell (Cazotte [1788] 2012). As a master of black romance, Cazotte has a British counterpart in William Beckford, who wrote several parodies of *The Thousand and One Nights* in which magic and demons play a decisive role. His novel *Vathek* (1786) recounts how an Abbasid caliph sells his soul to a demon and in his unremitting lust for power enters the sublime landscape of a demonic inferno. This novel, with its Faustian and Aladdin motifs and its exuberant, sublime setting, is one of the great sources for the Gothic and romantic trends in literature.[14]

The stories discussed in this section include examples of the nexus between spaces and supernatural forces not so much as part of narrative trajectories but rather as disclosing the essences of moral and immoral attitudes. In Chinese, Arabic, and European tales, demons and magic are often related to specific spaces, or specific types of space, but they are also connected to psychological conditions and moral types. They intervene to represent—and thereby reveal—forms of immorality, lust, greed, power, and so on, thereby confirming the relationship of this type of narrative to the fairy tale, both in its moral purport and in its use of narrative spaces.

REAL SPACES AND THE IMAGINATION

The analysis above has concentrated mainly on the construction and use of narrative spaces and their relationship with supernatural forces to support narrative structures, plots, metaphoric meaning, and interpretation. What remains to be examined is how these constructions were employed to produce a form of referentiality. We have argued that narrative constructions of space are so basic for the human experience of reality that they are vital for manipulating the relationship between a text and its non-textual environment as perceived by the reader. It is of special relevance here, since the stories under discussion exploit potential aberrations in perceptions of reality, by the incursions of irregular, invisible, and supernatural forces. In this way a zone is created in which imaginary and real worlds overlap, not merely by fictionalization but by conscientiously evoking doubt about the nature of fictional and unfictional realities and their relationships (Berg 1991).

As has been remarked above, the experience of reality, and thereby of the epistemological and ontological nature of narratives, is related to cultures, places, and times. Moreover, from ancient times it is in all cases incorporated into or influenced by cosmological and philosophical visions of the world and humankind in religion. Religion designed an overall, coherent vision of the universe, including the divine essences and supernatural phenomena. It provided an eschatological and moral framework for humans' place in creation and their relationship with the realm of the invisible. And, importantly, it defined the standards for what was "true" and "real," not only in the sense of doctrines but also with regard to the human imagination. In the worldview dominated by religion, reality is ultimately derived from the Divine; the seen and the unseen are part of the same reality, which is explained by the presence of God and His communication with the human. Supernatural forces, angels, demons, magic powers are all just aspects of this cosmological unity and do not require ontological examination (Daston and Park 1998: 351, 354, 358, 361–2; Cameron 2010; Van Leeuwen 2015).

In Europe, this hegemonic discourse explaining the nature of the universe and the occurrence of (super)natural phenomena was severely shaken in the seventeenth and eighteenth centuries. The spreading of the Reformation, the encounter with other, Eastern, religions, and the progress of the natural sciences threatened the monopoly of the worldview propagated by the Catholic Church and opened the gates for new speculations about the nature of reality. To what extent could supernatural phenomena be detached from the religious explanations of reality and related to the domains of science and human rationality? This shift in approach did not automatically result in the marginalization of religion and the gradual substitution of religion by a materialist philosophy. On the contrary, it gave an impetus to the exploration of all kinds of religiosity and the supernatural, as is witnessed by the enormous increase in marvelous literature during the eighteenth century, and the flourishing of heterodox sects. Perhaps it is justified to say that in this period the spiritual heritage of Neoplatonism in Europe sought new forms of expression, fighting the strengthening of the Aristotelian worldview based on the natural sciences. In the Eastern traditions the Neoplatonist foundations remained relatively unscathed, although here too rationalist tendencies questioned the ontological nature of reality. At approximately the same time when the collections of fairy tales by Pu Song Ling and Yun Li appeared, other authors such as Feng Meng Long and Ling Mengchu deliberately avoided narrative material that would be conducive to what they considered to be superstition (see Mengchu 1998; Menglong 2008). This changing outlook explains the interest of eighteenth-century authors in nonreligious or semi-religious demonology and the ontological status of dreams, visions, and clairvoyance. It is here that strategies of referentiality become more sophisticated and relevant: how can the relationship between a fictional text and a contextual space be construed and defined?

As far as perceptions of space are concerned, the tension between religious and scientific worldviews can perhaps best be characterized as the rivalry between space seen as an abstraction permeated by the Divine, which obeys no systematic laws and has no homogeneity, and space as part of human observation, with its own reality subject to natural laws, which are geographically homogenous. In the Middle Ages, when the Orient was a distant Other and worldviews were not based on scientific rationality, it was unproblematic to stage magic, wonders, and miracles in the Orient, where anything might happen if God so wills. In fictional narratives of the eighteenth century the same incidents could be projected on the Orient, but not without considering the problem that this Orient ontologically obeyed the same natural laws as Europe. This, of course, created new possibilities for exploring relationships between the realms of the natural and the supernatural, including the exotic regions, which became less and less abstract.

It is perhaps in referentiality where we find the most important differences between spatial strategies in fairy tales, which only refer to generic, unspecified spaces (forests, caves, palaces), and the various kinds of marvelous tales in the eighteenth century, which aspired to a certain measure of realism. For instance, in oriental tales, which often retained their fairy-tale form, spatial environments are often elaborately described, based on "authentic" descriptions in *The Thousand and One Nights* or in travelers' accounts. Both in European and in non-European traditions stories coalesced around historical figures and geographical locations, not only to accentuate their realism but also to link the moral message of the story to cultural and political identities. Heroes such as Hamza, Yue Fei, and Harun al-Rashid are not merely strong magnets attracting narrative material; they are also the personification of moral virtues, which are connected to specific political territories and religious and cultural traditions. Alphonse van Worden, in Potocki's *Manuscrit trouvé à Saragosse*, has a well-defined, albeit double, identity that is tightly embedded in the region he traverses. In all these narratives, supernatural forces are linked to broader worldviews, which touch upon the essence of the traditions in which they occur, and by themselves serve as elements of referentiality.

An example of the way in which in the eighteenth century the Orient was transformed from an abstract, imagined space into a hybrid space that was at the same time real and imagined, is Wieland's philosophical novel *Der goldene Spiegel* (The Golden Mirror). This complex book, which follows the generic model of the mirror-for-princes genre, but which is pervaded by an allegorical and fairy-tale mode derived from *The Thousand and One Nights*, is presented as an authentic history of the Chinese kingdom of Scheschian. It features a descendant of Shahriyar, the king of *The Thousand and One Nights*, who, for his entertainment, is told episodes of the history of Scheschian by his concubine and his court philosopher. The story fits into two trends: the first trend in which the Orient becomes a real, existing, civilization that can provide examples for Europe in the domains of administration and wisdom; and the second trend in which the Orient is an imagined, fairy-tale-like space in which the struggle between Good and Evil is essentialized. It also conforms to Wieland's adage, that fairy tales should not be employed to strengthen superstition among the audience but rather to spread an enlightened, rational view of the world (Wieland [1772] 2008).

Strategies of referentiality can not only result in an enhanced sense of realism in the text but also in an accentuation of its fictionality. If a worldview is basically materialist, any supernatural intervention will automatically be relegated to the domain of fictionality, dispensing of its realist claims. A nice example of a text in which epistemological complexities of this kind are explored is Abbé de Bignon's *Abdalla, fils d'Hanif* (1712), which is presented as an authentic oriental text, in which a number of fairy tale-like stories are inserted, which include the appearance of *jinn*, magic, and supernatural worlds. Within the realist frame of the narrative, these stories are presented as true within the context of the Muslim cosmology. But then, of course, Islam is not considered to be a true faith, and even the Muslim protagonists doubt the veracity of the tales and condemn them as fanciful. Here we find an ingenious play with several levels of reality in which the status of the text and the tales is blurred by the opposition of epistemologies derived from religion and rationality. It is the oriental dimension that complicates matters, requiring the textual complexity to investigate the relationship between the real world, supernatural phenomena, and fictional texts. The procedures used in the novel are reminiscent of the layered structure of *The Thousand and One Nights*, which Abbé de Bignon certainly knew.[15]

The examples discussed above show how strategies of referentiality serve several aims. In most cases they are implemented to define a kind of cultural identification, a cultural territory that thereby claims its place in history. In many cases it is also used to evoke an existing counterworld, which is imbued with characteristics defining it as an "otherworld," but without its mythical implications. Often, the cultural spaces defined in this way are connected to historical figures, such as kings and knights, or to historical events, such as the crusades, or the wars between the Chinese emperors and the Mongols, or the Muslims against the Persians. In all cases, the texts are meant to inculcate specific essentialized values into the defined territories, thus serving as part of the moral, ideological basis for cultural and political identification in empires, kingdoms, and republics. These texts convey these values through space and time. In the eighteenth century they became entwined with the global realm of narratives, in which "otherworlds" were not always associated with negative countervalues. As in Wieland's *Der goldene Spiegel*, the setting of moral discussions in the "otherworld" of the Orient enabled him to detach them from the

European-Christian framework and thereby present the positive values not as particularly Christian or "oriental," but rather as universal values beneficial to all humankind.

It is remarkable that the European texts in which imagined and realistic visions of the Orient were combined, apparently to experiment with new epistemologies to incorporate civilizational boundaries, show a narrative complexity that seems to have been imposed by the aims of the author. The texts are presented as "authentic" oriental texts, in which clearly fictional, allegorical tales or fairy tales are inserted, in an effort to destabilize the interaction between European and oriental, and fictional and realistic dimensions of the text. This strategy can be partly explained by the influence of the translations of *The Thousand and One Nights*, with its layered structure of frame and embedded stories, but it is also a result of a change of perspective and of the perception of the Orient as a basically "real" cultural and social space. This increasing complexity in which multifaceted, fissured, visions of reality are translated into textual complexity, finds expression in Montesquieu's *Lettres persanes* (1712/54), which presents the authentic/fictional letters of two Persian noblemen relating their experiences in Europe and, in particular, France. The book provides a critical self-image seen from an outsider's perspective, in which the outsider becomes "real" and France an exotic "otherworld," and is supplemented with allegorical fairy tales (Montesquieu 1946).

CONCLUSION

In this chapter we have discussed a great variety of texts from different cultural backgrounds that have some basic properties in common: they explore the interaction between the realms of the natural and the supernatural as narrative reflections of cosmic-religious worldviews; they are all somehow connected to the repository of folkloric material within their respective traditions; and they employ similar strategies to use spatial structures in their stories as a device to support narrative composition and to complicate the fiction/realism and natural/supernatural nexus. In the eighteenth century, these types of marvelous literature continued to flourish, in spite of the rise of the realistic novel in the European and Chinese traditions, and the changing interpretative contexts. The material was gradually incorporated into broader generic frameworks, or into more programmatic literary trends, such as collections of marvelous anecdotes, oriental tales, and realist novels exploring the effects of supernatural forces. These trends, which coincided with the development of a scientifically explained worldview and the fragmentation of religious cosmologies, stimulated inquiries into the nature of reality and the unseen, and, simultaneously, between reality and fiction.

The diversity of the texts preclude straightforward comparisons or generalizing conclusions. As far as spatial strategies are concerned, however, we can discern several similarities that seem to transcend cultural boundaries. These can be summarized as follows, taking spatial types as categories:

1. Labyrinthine landscapes: in many stories the hero has to pass through landscapes that are composed to steer the trajectory of the hero toward his destiny. These landscapes reflect the successive phases of the narrative to create a balance between the progress of the hero and postponement of the final denouement. They also support the metaphorical/moral substructure of the narrative, which reflects the psychological state of the hero and the moral values that he represents or incorporates.
2. Confined spaces: forms of enclosure serve as a contrast to the mobility of heroes and the confirmation of hierarchical boundaries and differences. They can also serve as spaces where the supernatural forces of several kinds interfere with human reality, through demons, spells, and magic, etc. They represent fissures in the continuum of "real" space, allowing hidden forces to penetrate human lives and societies. They are often associated with moral weakness or social anomalies, which provoke the intervention of fate.
3. Otherworlds: these spaces can be defined as separate spatial domains within narrative space endowing the story with a (fictional) counterspace, which represents a world in which regular natural or social laws are unknown or suspended and which maintains a hierarchical relationship to the narrated human world. Otherworlds produce adventure, privileges, and confirmation of the moral strength and authority of the hero, accentuating his exceptional qualities.
4. "Real" spaces: the notion of "real" space refers to forms of referentiality within the three aforementioned categories used, on the one hand, to suggest a familiar spatial setting of the story and, on the other hand, to destabilize the reader's perception of reality. For instance, the Orient, an abstract Otherworld in medieval European romances, became an increasingly realistic spatial reference in the eighteenth century, complicating the relationship between fiction and reality as a derivative of spatial representations. Even in marvelous narratives, referential spaces endured as cultural-historical markers reinforcing the transmission of the moral/ideological heritage of societies.

Since, as we argued above, the awareness of a coherent spatiotemporal environment is crucial for the perception of reality, it follows that the manipulation of these environments in marvelous stories reflect the author's effort to problematize the hero's relationship with the reality in which he acts. Stories often begin with an event producing a disequilibrium in the spatiotemporal environment of the hero, which indicates a similar fragmentation of his mental or moral state. The story is subsequently required to describe his efforts to return to a state of equilibrium, which is symbolized by the restoration of spatiotemporal harmony. Narrative landscapes are therefore often connected to psychological and moral struggles, which are reflected in the spatial environment containing the trajectory of the hero.

In eighteenth-century Europe, when the hegemony of the Catholic cosmology and its concomitant homogeneity declined, new images were sought to define the relationship between the "real" and the "unseen" as mirrored in spatial elements. Demonic forces, magic, dreams, hallucinations, visions, and so on served as intermediary phenomena to impregnate the "real" space of human society with forms of the supernatural. This experience of mental complexity connected to spatial fragmentation evolved in the eighteenth century from a projection of mental states into an external landscape, to internal mental experiences relating to irregularities in the coherent spatial environment.

To conclude, our discussion of various types of fictional texts shows how fundamental visions of space are for any form of storytelling. It is no coincidence that many of the main literary works of humanity are shaped as journeys, nor that these journeys contain many unfamiliar and exotic experiences. And it is no coincidence that the relationship between texts and spatial representations raise discussions about the relationship between texts and reality and between fiction and the perception of reality. It is in the eighteenth century in particular that these issues became increasingly intricate, as new visions of spatial reality imposed themselves on the various literary traditions.

CHAPTER SEVEN

Socialization

Tales of Wonder as Slight Channels

RANIA HUNTINGTON

In an introduction to his English translation of Marie-Catherine d'Aulnoy's (c. 1650–1705) fairy tales, the translator James Planché (1796–1880) quotes Charles Dickens's judgment of the value of such stories, made only a few years earlier, with approval:

> It would be hard to estimate the amount of gentleness and mercy that have made its way among us through these slight channels. Forbearance, courtesy, consideration for the poor and aged, kind treatment of animals, the love of nature, abhorrence of tyranny and brute force—many such good things have been nourished in the child's heart through this powerful aid. It has greatly helped to keep us ever young by preserving in our worldly ways one slender track not overgrown with weeds, where we may walk with children, sharing their delights.
>
> (d'Aulnoy 1855: xvii)[1]

Dickens and Planché were looking back at the fairy-tale tradition that had formed over the course of the long eighteenth century in Europe. If we extend our scope to a more global range of narratives than they consider, would this still be the list of values that they nourish? What kind of track, slender or otherwise, did they provide, and was it a path where children and adults would walk together?

The concept of the fairy tale as it was codified in the nineteenth century in English, drawing on imported continental examples, has subsequently been applied globally and retroactively to narratives of different genres in their original contexts.² In this chapter I am considering relatively short narratives (not long enough to have chapter divisions, with the exception of long works with many short narratives within a shared frame story) that include transformations, non-human sapient beings (fairies, transforming animal spirits, *jinn*, talking animals, oni, etc.), and/or magic. This is a more capacious definition of "wonder tale" than that used by other authors and scholars, and it encompasses narratives that could be labeled as legends, ghost stories, anecdotes, or comic books.³ In their native genre terms, I am including Japanese *akahon* 赤本 ("red books," or illustrated popular fiction often aimed at children) and other verbal-visual narratives; Japanese *kaidan* 怪談 (narrative of the strange); Urdu/Persian *qissa* قصه; and Chinese *zhiguai* 志怪 (tales of the strange) as well as *conte*, fairy tale, and *märchen*. My definition of the long eighteenth century is a calendrical hybrid between Europe and East Asia, from the 1680s until approximately 1820, a golden age in print production of the wonder tale in both regions.⁴ I am considering stories that can be confidently dated to this period, which leads to a privileging of written, especially printed, material over oral tales.

The range of lessons conveyed by tales of wonder surpass Dickens's list of virtues. Beyond moral guidance, the wonder tale could support or undermine a religious vision of the cosmos, promise knowledge of the culture or even the language of different places, and more broadly provide a model of how one should or should not learn from stories.

LESSONS OF THE MANDARINS: FEIGNED, WOULD-BE, AND ACTUAL

In the pseudo-translation *Chinese Tales: Or, the Wonderful Adventures of the Mandarin Fum-Hoam* (1725) by Thomas-Simon Gueulette (1683–1766), the title character tells the newlywed empress of China the stories of all his previous incarnations, up to the present day. The empress is Gulchenraz, the princess of Georgia, until recently an exile traveling cross-dressed with her father, the king of Georgia, who lost his throne to a usurper; Fum-Hoam was instrumental in bringing down the usurper and restoring the throne to the king of Georgia. Fum-Hoam tells the princess tales not simply for her diversion, though they fascinate her. She had agreed to marry the emperor Tongluk, with whom she was in love and also indebted due to his role in the restitution of her father's throne, despite their difference in religions. Her new husband assures her that either Fum-Hoam's stories will persuade her to convert to Chinese religion, in which reincarnation is central (Buddhism is not named as such in the text), or that he will convert to Islam if the stories do not succeed in convincing her.⁵ Thus the stories ostensibly have the function of persuading the listener to adopt the religious belief they illustrate.

Over the following forty-six nights Fum-Hoam relates his experiences of a series of incarnations of both sexes and multiple species. He has been a flea, a dog, and a monkey; a shepherdess, an iman, a warrior, a king, and a queen, in places ranging from Southeast Asia to Greece. He has been both a sympathetic character and a villain, though the former more often than the latter. There are messages to be learned along the way: adultery is always discovered and usually punished, though sometimes treated with sympathy; villains never get away with their misdeeds, but some sympathetic figures die tragically as well.

Overall, the empress is impressed with the lessons of many lives. "The morality they [the events described] contain infinitely pleases me" (Guelette 1725: 2:223). Yet the main purpose of his narration has not been fulfilled, as her religious convictions are unshaken. But the night after the narration had brought him up to his present lifetime, the storyteller reveals himself: all along he has not been Fum-Hoam but Gulchenraz's long-lost brother in enchanted disguise. With this discovery we realize that the true purpose of the stories related had been to exploit the emperor's oath that he would convert if his wife had not been convinced by the storyteller's tales. Thus the conversion has worked in reverse: it is the emperor of China who must renounce belief in reincarnation. After a series of tales that often involved mistaken and concealed identities, the exposure of the narrator in the frame story is the ultimate twist.

The false Fum-Hoam is a telling alter ego for Gueulette, who made a shift from presenting himself as a translator to an author in several successive books with different geographical frames (see Raleigh 2017). If Fum-Hoam was justified in claiming stories from multiple sources as his own, then so was Gueulette. The compelling figure of the exotic female teller of tales from *The Arabian Nights*, Scheherazade, both captive and captivating, inspired Gueulette to other configurations of gender and power. In Scheherazade's stories, one of the most important messages is that demons, fishermen, princes, and princesses all have their own stories to tell to persuade or divert, and they narrate their tales in their own voices through the interpolated stories within the frame narrative dominated by the voice of Scheherazade. In the case of *Chinese Tales*, the conceit of reincarnation interestingly allows Gueulette to collapse one dimension of the story within a story, such that Gueulette makes all of these different, distinct narrators a single person (Figure 7.1). Moreover, just as Fum-Hoam is not actually teaching the sultana Gulchenraz about reincarnation, Gueulette is not actually proselytizing for Islam; rather, religion is essential to the exotic world he is creating for his European readers. Ideas about Asian beliefs are both entertaining and informative, but not edifying in any spiritual sense.

Half a world away, if an actual mandarin (meaning a Chinese man who had achieved government rank) in 1723 had the opportunity to read *Chinese Tales*, he would be appalled by the lack of explicit moral sequence in the series of incarnations. Only Fum-Hoam's first transition as related by Gueulette,

FIGURE 7.1: Frontispiece from the 1725 edition of *Chinese Tales: Or, the Wonderful Adventures of the Mandarin Fum-Hoam* (London, 1725). Public domain.

from Persian tyrant to a flea observing his former self's favorite concubine complaining about him to her new lover, has a causal link between one life and the next. Regardless of the degree of his personal skepticism or piety, the mandarin would be familiar with traditions of reincarnation narratives going back a millennium or more, and these tales tended to have two essential messages: though its workings were usually obscured by transformation and forgetting, in exceptional cases reincarnation could be confirmed; and deeds in former lives would be repaid in future ones, without fail. Narratives that connected two or three lives together were common, but a succession of dozens of unconnected lives as in Fum-Hoam's story sequence was not.

To allow the most celebrated Chinese collection of tales of wonder to represent a commonly shared story type, a case in point is *Strange Tales from a Chinese Studio* (c. 1670s–90s; first published 1766).⁶ Writing a few decades before Gueulette, Pu Songling 蒲松齡 (1640–1715) was not a mandarin himself, though he aspired earlier in his life to hold office. In his autobiographical introduction, he tells of a single previous incarnation, a sickly monk who appeared to his father in a dream at the moment of his son's (that is, Pu Songling's) birth. A mark on the monk's shoulder matches one on his own (Pu 1992: 1:1.3). He himself cannot recall this earlier life. The story of the dream connects him both to another life and to a great predecessor, Su Shi 蘇軾 (1073–1101), who had also been a monk in another life and whose fondness for the dubious and marginal genre of ghost stories did not prevent him from being viewed as the foremost literary man of his age (He Yuan 1983: 6.93; Huihong 1983).

Pu recounts his stories not in the mode of an oral storyteller but in that of a historian relating tales in dense allusive language, often capped with interpretative commentary. He writes two stories under the title "Three Lives." In this set Buddhist phrase, the number three—referring to the past, present, and future incarnations—stood in for the multitude of lives in the endless cycle (Figure 7.2).

In the first story of the two tales of this title from Pu's collection, Liu, who passed the exam in the same year as Pu's elder cousin, described his previous lives embodying first a morally flawed nobleman, then a horse, a dog, and finally, a snake. There were similar tales included in a Chinese collection a century earlier, *Kuaiyuan zhiyi* 獪園志異 (*Records of Wonder from the Garden of Cleverness*), but Pu brings sharper focus to the sensory experience of the animal incarnations and the range of moral choices available to them.⁷ The lessons are contained in several levels of the text: in the king of the underworld's judgments each time he dies; in Liu's warning to others to use thick saddlepads when riding, to ease the horse's suffering; and in Pu's own final comment: "Among those with hair and horns there are lords and nobles; the reason why it is so is that there were likely originally those with hair and horns among the lords and nobles" (2006: 98–101).⁸ Thus there are both specific and general messages to be learned from these experiences. Deeds of all living beings have consequences. Not only is the suffering of animals meaningful but also suffering inflicted on other beings could one day be your own. The place of individual souls in interspecies hierarchies is constantly shifting, to say nothing of human social hierarchies.

In addition to demonstrating retribution for individual sin, reincarnation stories often work through the love or resentment between two or more beings that lasts beyond the grave. In contrast, Fum-Hoam's series of incarnations has only his first-person perspective as the link between the various lives; he does not encounter other souls a second time. Pu's second story under the title "Three Lives," in an entirely different part of the collection, is a means of working through the great resentment an exam candidate unfairly passed over feels toward his examiner. They meet again as an official executing a suspected bandit, and

FIGURE 7.2: Illustration of a scene from "Three Lives" collected in *Strange Tales from a Chinese Studio* (1886 edition). Public domain.

two dogs that kill each other in a fight. Only when they become human father and son-in-law are they reconciled (Pu 1992: 2:10.1330–2). While the earlier "Three Lives" story was an occasion for reflection on the general need for moral cultivation, Pu's final comment on this story focuses on the rage and pain of men of his own class. One exam failure caused three lifetimes of resentment, and though he admires the ingenuity of the king of hell in resolving this particular case, he doubts that the grievances of all of the throngs of frustrated candidates could be addressed. The systems of justice of the other world are ultimately inadequate to address the systemic injustices of the human world.[9]

At the other end of the long eighteenth century, ranked in modern literary histories as a distant second to Pu Songling among authors of the strange tale, Ji Yun 紀昀 (1724–1805) would indisputably be called a mandarin. A graduate of the top levels of the civil service examination that Pu never reached, he served in the highest echelons of the bureaucracy, including as editor-in-chief for a vast imperial project assembling a compendium of all the books deemed worthy of record. His tales are shorter and less elaborate than those of Pu, with a closer link to casual oral storytelling, and instead of commentary separated from the main text in the persona of the historian, his own comments or dialogues with others about the meaning of stories are included directly in the text. Ji Yun does not talk about his previous incarnations, though later authors pass on the legend that he had been an ape spirit or a female fire spirit (1995: 3.524–5).

Ji Yun records an uncharacteristically long and detailed story told by a monk seen weeping beside a slaughter yard to the butcher and other passers-by. The monk could remember his two previous lives, the first as a butcher and the second as a pig. Most of his fellows beside him in the sty had also been humans in the past; they spoke to one another in the language of swine but could no longer talk with humans. He provides a vivid description of the discomfort of a pig's life up to the excruciating pain of slaughter. Now he weeps for the present agony of the pig, his own past agony, and the future agony of the man holding the knife. The tale is immediately efficacious: the butcher gives up his trade and becomes a vegetable vendor (Ji Yun 1982: 21.515–16).

The animal lives Gueulette's Fum-Hoam relates in detail are those in which animals have an opportunity to witness and engage in extraordinary human stories, as a pet dog or ape. The power of Ji's story, however, resides in living out an ordinary pig's life with the suffering it entails. Fum-Hoam focused on his individual path through his incarnations, but the monk in Ji's story is both a sufferer and a witness of a collective experience. From the Chinese perspective these transformations are not in themselves marvels, because there is nothing extraordinary about the commonplace cycle of karma. Only the ability to remember and narrate the experience is remarkable. Unlike Fum-Hoam's diverting but ultimately unconvincing tales, his story is powerful enough to change the listener.

Ji Yun includes two accounts of humans reappearing in animal form to pay a debt that have direct links to himself or his family. To say "I will repay you as a horse or dog" is a figure of speech expressing utmost gratitude that can be understood either as metaphor or, with reincarnation, as literal. Usually the one who repays is from the servant or peasant class already, and there is a parallel drawn between the condition of servant or peasant and that of a horse or dog. Ji Yun tells a personal story about a dog who accompanied on the long road back from his exile in Xinjiang. The night before he was given the dog as a gift, he dreamed of a deceased servant saying he would accompany Ji on the long journey. He accepts the dog as a reincarnation of a former servant but wonders why the dog was more loyal and honest than the servant had been (Ji Yun 1982: 5.96–7). Going back to an earlier generation, his grandfather unexpectedly has a dream of a deceased man who had owed him a large sum of money. Immediately after, a mule is born in the stable, so that everyone concludes the mule is the debtor reborn. Ji's grandfather himself was quite skeptical: "Many owe me debts—why would only this man have to repay in this way? And this man owed many people's debts—why would he only repay me?" Despite his grandfather's doubts, Ji seems to leave the question open, noting the evidence for reincarnation: whenever people called the late man's human name, the mule would look up angrily; and whenever they played the tunes the deceased had enjoyed, the mule would seem to listen intently (5.96–7). The Ji family's multigenerational experience shows that the conventions of matching a dream of a deceased human debtor with the appearance of an animal are shared by the community, even when the dreamer himself is a reluctant participant. In contrast with the first-person stories' emphasis on suffering, tales of reincarnation told in the third person delineate the network of interconnections between species and classes. As opposed to Gueulette's *Chinese Tales*, which presents European readers with an exotic phenomenon in exotic settings, reincarnation is taking place in a familiar physical and social environment, teaching quotidian morality.

Subsequent republications and translations of *Chinese Tales* place differing degrees and kind of emphasis on reincarnation and the religious traditions of the East. When the book is translated and circulated as an independent volume in English, the paratexts frame the collection as an opportunity to teach the reading public about the (misguided) beliefs of Buddhism and Islam. The earliest English edition, translator uncredited, adds a scholarly introduction explaining how "an opinion so little known, and so much detested in Europe, came to prevail among the Chinese" (Gueulette 1725: vi). In his dedication to a female patron, Mrs. Pultaney, in the 1740 edition, the English translator Reverend Thomas Stackhouse presents the book, saying that, "However diverting the work may be, I should not have expended so much time had I not perceived that its end and intent were to instruct as well as to please, and to recommend an excellent moral under the agreeable veil of allegory and fable" (Gueulette 1740: iv–v). Yet at the same time that he lauds the morals, he believes the text demonstrates the absurdity of two religious traditions—Buddhism and Islam—juxtaposed within. In some ways his attitude is similar to that of Gulchenraz within the story: the particular lessons are accepted but the general premise is questioned. With respect to gender dynamics, Stackhouse mirrors the situation within the story, as he plays the role of the long-lost brother disguised as a mandarin, and his patron that of the princess. His identity as a Christian clergyman adds an additional layer to the religious ventriloquism already present in Gueulette's *Chinese Tales*: just as the false mandarin pretended to advocate for Buddhism while actually demonstrating its absurdity and the superiority of Islam, Stackhouse presents the text to belie both. In the appendix to the same edition the editorial voice (presumably Stackhouse) quotes a facetious passage from Joseph Addison (1672–1719) in *The Spectator* in which a jilted lover writes a letter in the voice of a pet monkey, the lover's purported next incarnation (Gueulette 1740: 232–5). Whether as cultural curiosity or joke, the English translators and publishers judge framing reincarnation as their central task in presenting the collection.

When included in great forty-volume compendium of fairy tales and oriental tales, *Le Cabinet des fées* (1785–9), *Chinese Tales* is recognized as being of the same type as Antoine Galland's *Arabian Nights*, and more distantly the stories of Charles Perrault and Marie-Catherine d'Aulnoy. Reincarnation is not singled out for particular attention. For Ji and Pu, rebirth stories are a regular feature of the genre in which they work, and within the thematic range of the strange story not a particular specialty of either one of them. The one certainty Pu and Ji would recognize in Fum-Hoam is that it is the scholar who gets to retell everyone else's stories, human and inhuman, male and female, peasant and merchant. Yet they could not imagine recounting tales before an empress, and although both male and female voices were preserved or imagined in their collections, their imagined audience was their male peers, for Pu a relatively small and provincial circle, for Ji a national male elite.[10] This can be contrasted with the French and English renditions of "oriental" and fairy tales, intended for an elite readership of both women and men.

THE CLASSROOM AND THE NURSERY

As discussed above, some printings of *Chinese Tales* foreground learning about reincarnation as an idea present in other, what would have been understood as exotic, places, for a European readership. The closest that Fum-Hoam's reincarnations come to France is as a shepherdess in Greece. Although Fum-Hoam addresses his empress, apparently with no difficulty finding a common language between China (though Fum-Hoam's origins are more precisely assigned to Gannan, now Vietnam) and Georgia, Gueulette's footnotes address a reader unfamiliar with the geographical and cultural terms employed. The geography is real, although historically inexact. Chinese reincarnation stories almost all had the human lives contained within the borders of China, or at most featured a monk from India or Central Asia reborn in China. Pu Songling, Ji Yun, and Ueda Akinari 上田秋成 (1734–1809, the most renowned eighteenth-century Japanese author of the strange tale) have no need to footnote their place names, as the readership is already familiar with this mundane geography. The ways in which marvel is mapped is thus fundamentally different: is an unfamiliar place defined by the tale of marvel, or is the marvelous dimension of a known place revealed?

By including "Oriental Tales" alongside fairy tales by d'Aulnoy and Perrault, the *Le Cabinet des fées* seems, then, to contain two kinds of places, the unnamed culturally European kingdoms with in some cases a conceptual relationship to France or Spain, and those marked as an exotic elsewhere. In the tale "The Green Serpent" by d'Aulnoy, the presence of pagods, idols from Asian temples, as the enchanted servants in the title character's palace reveals the proximity between the two realms (Zipes 1991a: 97–8). Yet although the Orient borders directly on Fairyland, the kind of learning one can gain from these two types of tales is different within specific readerly contexts.

In his preface to *Tales of the East* (1812), which he labels as a selection of the best translations of oriental tales and their imitations by European writers, including three of Gueulette's collections, Henry Weber (1783–1816) allows that although there may be disagreement about their positive moral influence, "As conveying in general a true and striking picture of the manners and customs prevalent in some of the most interesting nations of the earth, the value of these tales has been less disputed" (1812: 1). Travelers' experience had confirmed the observations made in these stories. As we have seen above, figures such as Stackhouse saw some moral value in what became known as oriental tales, at the same time that these types of narratives were also understood as educating the public in the ways of the Asian, exotic other. Nevertheless, the tales remained extracurricular reading; boys would learn about the cultures of Greece and Rome in the classroom, the Orient in their leisure reading outside of it, confirming the latter as ultimately more entertaining than edifying and of secondary importance.

The qıssa (tale-length Urdu or Persian narrative) printed by Fort William College in Calcutta in the earliest years of the nineteenth century, Urdu or Hindi renderings of story collections in other languages intended for teaching British men Asian languages, moved tales into the colonial classroom. The story collections provided a range of different narrators speaking to kings. In *Bagh o Bahar*, known in the west as *Tales of the Four Dervishes*, four dervishes explain their misfortunes in love to a king in despair at his lack of an heir. In *Baital pachīsī* (or *Twenty-Five Tales of a Vetala*) a *vetala* or vampire tells stories to a king in a bargain to avoid being trapped. In *Siñhāsan battīsī* (*Thirty-Two Tales of the Throne*) a king unearths the throne of his illustrious forebear, and the statues of apsaras (celestial female singers and dancers) on the throne tell stories of that ancestor's greatness to persuade him he is not worthy to sit on it. (The latter two are based on much older Sanskrit texts.[11]) Those who had learned about other cultures from the *Arabian Nights*, perhaps in childhood, were now to learn new languages in narratives with similar generic features. Yet printing these versions as textbooks had the effect of codifying the languages being learned and bringing them into print, as well as stabilizing the texts themselves. The first printed Arabic text of *The Thousand and One Nights*, as opposed to the much older Arabic manuscripts, was actually produced at Fort William College.

What was the educational value of tales that were not introducing an exotic culture, and when and where did the view Dickens expresses in the quote that opens this chapter become mainstream? In Europe the second half of the eighteenth century saw the fairy tale move from primarily adult or mixed age settings to being packaged for children. Zipes credits Jeanne-Marie Leprince de Beaumont's version of "Beauty and the Beast" as a turning point (2000: 864); more on this below. A 1752 English translation of a selection of d'Aulnoy's tales states in the preface, "Although these ingenious tales are most immediately designed for the innocent Amusement of children, they may not perhaps be wholly unentertaining to those of a more advanced Age and riper Judgement" (d'Aulnoy 1752: iv). Children's supposed edification provides the excuse for adult pleasure in wonder, with nostalgia for an idealized childhood as part of the pleasure.

It is arguable that the earliest cases of wonder tales as printed children's literature in the world are from Japan, predating the long eighteenth century. This is proven most decisively by the incredible discovery of a particular child's book collection that a mourning father placed inside a statue of the Boddhisattva Jizō after his son had passed away in 1678. These were all illustrated picture books, with the boy's name written in them, some images colored in by his own hand. R. Keller Kimbrough argues that his collection is actually distinguished by the lack of moral messages and the celebration of violence (see Kimbrough 2015). Williams contends that over the course of the eighteenth century a canon of children's stories formed in Japan, many of which were later reclassified as fairy tales (2012: 74).[12] Part of what the books taught was for children to see themselves as readers and storytellers (95). On the first page of a red book relating the story of Momotarō 桃太郎 (Peach Boy), a group of boys are depicted settling down for a storytelling session. One of the boys declares, "Momotarō's fun."[13]

In his kindness to animals who then help him on his quest to battle against demons and reward his aged parents, Momotarō seems to illustrate many of the virtues Dickens listed, in particular consideration for the aged and the kind treatment of animals, but the illustration foregrounds pleasure instead.

In China the audience for tales of wonder remains mixed in age, with elementary literacy primers eschewing the morally suspect subject matter of the strange tale. Nevertheless Ji Yun records specific oral teaching contexts in which stories were retold: a patriarch recounts them to the boys and young men of the family, an old village woman to young wives, or a Confucian schoolmaster to his pupils. In some of these stories, adults make sense of children's experience of marvel, and turn it into instructive narrative or family history. One of Ji Yun's uncles relates a story about when he was a boy of ten or eleven. He glimpsed a beautiful woman in his father's locked study, but the mirror reveals her true shape, a fox. Dissatisfied, she breathes on the mirror, and the image within the mirror matches that on the outside. The boy runs away in terror. In adulthood Ji's father uses this story about Ji's uncle as a pedagogical tool to show how illusions, once they arise, cloud the originally clear mind (Ji 1982: 2.24–5). Ji includes a village woman's tale addressed to young wives that, in contrast, makes no use of metaphor: she is able to see ghosts, and her description of the sorrow of a ghost whose widow was preparing to remarry made the young wives of the village swear they would never do the same to their husbands (4.66–7). The narratives Ji shows in use are often single incidents rather than complete stories, and their claim to didactic value is that they are grounded in experience rather than fantasy.[14] Yet both literal and metaphorical applications of strange experience to daily life are shown as effective teaching tools; the latter is the prerogative of the male elite, the former is used by tellers of all backgrounds.

THE FALSE GRANDMOTHER AND THE GIRL IN THE WOODS: PERSPECTIVE AND FRAMING

Huang Zhijun 黃之雋 (1668–1748) wrote "The Tale of Old Woman Tiger," which closely resembles "Little Red Riding Hood" by Charles Perrault (1628–1703), as well as "Little Red Cap" by the Brothers Grimm. Each of these tales relates the experience of a young girl confronting a false grandmother turned predator.[15] The species of the intruder differs, a tiger in China rather than a wolf, as in the French and German versions. In the Chinese variant the girl—along with her brother—brings her grandmother dates rather than biscuits and butter (Perrault) or cake and wine (Brothers Grimm). In the Chinese case the tiger-grandmother is a specific grandmother: maternal rather than paternal. Because wives were expected to live with their husband's multigenerational family, the maternal grandmother thus belongs to the "outside" alien family rather than the one with whom a grandchild presumably lives. Closer to "Hansel and Gretel," the false grandmother asks which child is fatter, and when the brother answers that he is she asks that he sleep by her head and the girl by her feet. It is in the middle of the night when sleeping with the false grandmother that the girl notices her hairiness, and in this version she furthermore hears the sounds of her eating. The question dialogue echoes the one we know from Perrault and the Grimms: why are you hairy, what are you eating? The grandmother/tiger answers she is wearing a sheepskin and eating the dates they had brought her. Yet when the girl asks for one she is given a cold human finger (presumably her brother's). When the girl says she has to get up to go to the bathroom, the false grandmother doesn't want to let her go, ironically warning her that there are tigers outside. The girl offers to tie herself to a rope, and pull on it in case of emergency. This the false grandmother accepts.[16] When she goes outside, she recognizes the rope as intestines, and severs it to escape up a tree. She is rescued by a passerby and leaves her clothes in the tree as a decoy. When the false grandmother leads two tigers in their original forms to the tree and discovers the deception, the other tigers, finding no other meal forthcoming, eat her.

The Chinese variant opens with a general discussion of old female tigers in the mountains of Anhui assuming human form; the real grandmother never appears in the tale. Huang Zhijun is not a prominent writer of weird tales, and this story was not published until 1801, in a relatively obscure collection of tales by many authors, the *Guang Yu Chu xinzhi* 廣虞初新志 (*Expanded New Records of Yu Chu*). Like its more famous early eighteenth-century predecessor the *Yu Chu xinzhi*, this book includes biographies of exemplary figures, travelogues, and other miscellaneous texts as well as tales of marvel.[17] Extrapolating back from twentieth-century folklore collections, this tale was likely popular in the oral tradition. Unlike the case of "Little Red Riding Hood" in Europe, in China "The Tale of Old Woman Tiger" was not a story that attracted much attention from the scholarly compilers of strange tales.

Perrault's moral to the story targets young women who are warned to stay away from male seducers, symbolized by the wolf of the tale: "One sees here that young children, / Especially pretty girls, / Polite, well-taught, and pure as pearls, / Should stay on guard against all sorts of men ... Sweetest tongue has the sharpest tooth" (Zipes 2000: 747). In the Grimms' version Rotkäppchen speaks the message in her own mind, "Never again will you stray from the path by yourself and go into the forest when your mother has forbidden it." The stress is on the child's obedience rather than the enticing stranger. The compiler of the collection Huang Chengzeng 黃承增, however, comments that those who deceive others will end up destroying themselves, thus targeting the evildoer of the tale more than the heroine, even though he ends on a rhetorical question, "If one meets someone who is both a tiger and an old woman, can one not be cautious?" "Tiger" was a common metaphor for formidable women, so Huang's warning here is that when the metaphor turns literal, two categories already dangerous on their own become even more deadly. It does not seem to particularly address young girls. Though he comments in a more serious mode, Huang and all of his readers would find Perault's comments familiar in their combination of worldly application of the lessons of the story and tongue-in-cheek humor, because Pu Songling had made that mode of commentary a model for the genre.

Taken at face value, the tale teaches fear of strangers, even if they pretend to be kin. The road in the wilderness is a dangerous place, but so is the bed. However, Ter Haar argues that it actually encourages independence for girls, for survival demands cutting the rope that would bind them (2006: 84–5). In the Chinese case, the girl has gone a long way toward rescuing herself when she is saved by a kind stranger. Despite what generalizations about female agency in China and Europe might suggest, she is shown as more resourceful than Perrault's heroine who is ultimately devoured, or the Grimms' who is rescued entirely by an outside male force (see Zipes 2000: 744–50).

MARRIAGE AND THE BEAST

Internationally many of the protagonists of tales of marvel are older than Red Riding Hood, and many tales about a girl venturing out of her family home are, whether she knows it or not, about finding her way to a husband's house rather than a grandmother's. Behind that door too she faces the prospect of sharing a bed with a menacing, inhuman presence. The beast husband tale type was of great concern to d'Aulnoy and her peers in the salons (Warner 1996: 284–90). Its variations can be read as challenging or questioning the constraints of marriage for young women, or as training her to survive them. By some balance of submission and self-assertion, she will transform the beast into a husband, and herself into a wife.

Gabrielle de Villeneuve's (1685–1755) version of "Beauty and the Beast" (1740), a tale of over a hundred pages contained within an even longer novel, violates my restriction on short narrative.[18] Jeanne-Marie Leprince de Beaumont (1711–80) adapted the tale to a much shorter version in a reader intended for girls in 1756.[19] In its long descriptions of the amusements of the Beast's castle, the Villeneuve version provides a model of what an intelligent and exemplary girl would find entertaining: the library, pet monkeys, and birds, but also windows that gave her access to seeing anywhere in the world, allowing her to watch the latest Italian comedies and to see the fashionable Parisian garden of the Tuileries, but also the important events of the world, including "the last revolt of the Janizaries" (Villeneuve 1858: 258).

In both versions, Beauty's origins in a merchant family are conspicuous in a genre dominated by princesses. This class background allows for a plausible reversal that forces the family to face an ominous unknown future, moving to the countryside in straitened circumstances, before the encounter of Beauty's father with the beast. Class remains a much more important theme in Villeneuve, as after the beast has been transformed into a prince, his royal mother balks at having him wed a merchant's daughter. A benevolent fairy argues that virtue should matter more than class, but this argument is undermined by what she knows and soon reveals: Beauty is by birth the child of a fairy and a king, and the prince's cousin (Zipes 2000: 788).

Leprince de Beaumont's version places weight on the punishment of Beauty's jealous sisters, turned into statues until their hearts are reformed. In the dialogue that frames the story between the governess Mrs. Affable and the young girls she oversees, one of the listeners asks, "And were her two sisters always statues?" Mrs. Affable replies, "Yes, my dear, because their hearts were never changed."[20] In Villeneuve, although the sisters remain jealous of Beauty's good fortune, they attempt to conceal it, and everyone else politely decides to pretend their happiness for her is sincere (1858: 333). This suggests different didactic contexts: Villeneuve teaches adult women how to coexist in complex family relationships with siblings and in-laws, even if that entails feigning the emotions one should feel and accepting others' social performances, while Leprince de Beaumont frightens girls with the consequences of jealousy, living petrified while others enjoy a happy ending.

In both versions, Beauty must learn to overcome not only fear of the Beast's appearance but also her disappointment with his stupidity. The prince had been forbidden from revealing his intelligence at the same time as his shape was transformed. It is clear that Beauty's sacrifice would have been far less impressive if the Beast had been an engaging conversationalist (as are d'Aulnoy's beast husbands, the Ram and the Green Serpent). All that he has to offer is a good heart. Such tales communicate the idea that intimate contact with an alien body is not the only thing to be dreaded in marriage to a stranger; it is also the long hours with nothing to say to one another.

That the extraordinary story of Beauty and the Beast and the backstories from the senior generation of characters carry messages generalizable to all marriage is made clear at several points in the Villeneuve version. When Beauty's father urges her to accept the Beast's marriage proposal, he argues: "How many girls are compelled to marry rich brutes, much more brutish than the Beast" (Villeneuve 1858: 266). Beauty's father, however, came from Fortunate Island where everyone could marry as they chose, which allowed him to marry Beauty's mother, whom he imagined was a shepherdess, though in fact she was a fairy in disguise (302). The Prince, when propositioned by a fairy much older than he is, knows that marriage is happy when celebrated between those compatible in age and character (287). But the emphasis on free choice is undermined by the way that Beauty and the prince are arranged to be together in advance by their elders.

In Japan, the red book "The Rat Wedding" 鼠のよめ入り (c. 1737–47), and similar animal wedding tales such as "The Foxes' Wedding," offer another form of training a girl for marriage. This picture book pushes the limits of our definition of wonder tale. Anthropomorphized mice perform all the ritual stages of a wedding, from engagement to birth of a first child (but with sex alluded to only obliquely). There is not a narrative as such, only a progression through the pages of illustrations, with lines of dialogue from everyone involved, including bride, groom, their families, and their servants.[21] While "Beauty and the Beast" and its kin teach the abstract ideal of adaptation and learning to love an alien being and thereby transforming him, "The Rat Wedding" models the concrete details of what will happen throughout the marriage process, with the animal characters placing the events at a distance from the human readers and rendering them comic and endearing (Figure 7.3). The child can learn about the process of marriage, but those who already have been involved in weddings can knowingly laugh at the multiple voices in the text.

FIGURE 7.3: Bridal procession in the Rat's Wedding, from *Aka-hon Nezumi no yomeiri* (*Red Book: The Mouse's Wedding*) (Tsuruya, c. 1735–45). Public domain.

As Wendy Doniger points out, the tale of the beast groom and the beast bride address distinct fears and desires (2000: 122–8, 139). The encounter of the human man with the alien woman (ghost, fox, or other transformed animal or flower spirit) is a central topic for Pu Songling, as well as for all his later imitators. The reversed gender situation of a human woman and an alien lover is described in only a handful of stories, and regarded more as a psychiatric affliction, possession by an alien spirit that prevents a woman's participation in normal life, than an occasion for romance.[22] For human men paired with alien women, Pu crafts a mix of cautionary tales and sympathetic romances, from the perspective of the relatively ordinary heroes and with attention focused on the extraordinary women. Cautionary tales about deadly demon lovers are an old tradition by the time he writes, but it is in fashioning happy endings and enabling long-term domestic bliss for human–alien couples that he makes his indelible mark. His alien women do not demand that their lovers overcome aversion to their forms, for their animal forms or corpses appear briefly, if at all, but instead the men must overcome repulsion at their partners' origin. In China, consideration of the woman's perspective overcoming extraordinary and ordinary obstacles to achieve a harmonious marriage was largely in long forms, either the (presumably) male-authored talent and beauty romance novel *caizi jiaren xiaoshuo* 才子佳人小說, dramas with related plots, or the often female-authored *tanci* (plucking rhymes) 彈詞.

Two of Pu Songling's most popular stories for modern retellings overcome the grim consequences of the cautionary tale in opposite ways. In "The Painted Skin," a man named Wang begins an affair with a beauty he meets on the road who introduces herself as a concubine fleeing an abusive first wife. He continues trysting with her despite the objections of his wife, who argues her husband should no longer see his new lover not in terms of fidelity to her but rather due to the problems that could arise from involvement with a runaway concubine. He also ignores the warnings of a Daoist exorcist at the marketplace who sees the aura of a monster on him. Finally, peeking in from the window of a locked study, he sees a horrifying monster touching up a human skin with a small brush. Satisfied with its work, it shakes out the skin like a cape, puts it on, and resumes the shape of his beautiful lover. Wang's subsequent attempts at exorcism result in the monster tearing out his heart and swallowing it.

The Daoist exorcist succeeds in capturing the monster, but Wang's bereaved wife begs him to return her husband to life. He redirects her to a filthy, raving beggar on the marketplace, warning her she must do everything the beggar asks. The beggar humiliates her, finally asking her to swallow a large clot of his phlegm. She forces herself to do this, with no result, save a revolting sensation in the back of her throat. Seemingly defeated, she returns to prepare her husband's corpse for burial. While she bends over him, she coughs up the phlegm, which is now transformed into a human heart. It falls into her husband's chest, the rent flesh knitting over it, and he is revived.[23]

Pu Songling's "Historian of the Strange" comment laments the folly of the protagonist, who could recognize neither the monstrousness of his lover nor the loyalty of his wife, but extends it to all the people of the world. "If you covet other's beauty and catch them, then your wife will have to eat another's phlegm and think it sweet. The way of heaven favors repayment but those who are foolish and deluded do not wake up. How pitiful!"

Pu's final comment treats husband and wife as a single body in terms of retribution: his mistakes can only be atoned for with her humiliation. He is beguiled by beautiful surfaces, so she is forced to ignore repulsive surfaces. However, the message for her is that she has this capability: she can make whole what the demon playing on her husband's desires has torn asunder and accomplish what the male exorcist alone could not. The interlinear commentators feel wronged on her behalf, hoping that the heart she has replaced in her husband is better than the one he lost.

In "Nie Xiaoqian," a young man named Ning staying at a temple refuses the advances of a beautiful stranger, Nie Xiaoqian, who tempts him first with sex and then with money. Impressed, she tells him the truth, that she is a ghost forced to entrap travelers for an older and more powerful demon. She helps him to avoid the demon's next attack (with the aid of a traveling swordsman), and in turn asks that he take her bones and rebury them in his family graveyard.

When he complies with her request, she follows him home and attempts to ingratiate herself with his family, especially his mother. By diligently performing the duties of a daughter-in-law while chastely returning to her grave to sleep, she gradually wins her mother-in-law over, so that when Ning's wife dies of illness, Xiaoqian is accepted as his bride. Slowly she becomes able to eat human food. After a last attempt on their lives by the demon is thwarted, they live happily ever after, Ning, Nie, a concubine he takes later, and the sons born to both women.[24] As opposed to European variants of monstrous brides and grooms, whose social order is grounded in monogamous marriage practices, Pu's happy endings often reflect the structures of a polygamous society.

Pu's romances vary greatly in their details, but they can be distilled down to two sets of messages. For human men: the man of integrity and passion can be rewarded, even if he is (and perhaps in part because he is) foolish. Blind lust can have fatal consequences. When your lover reveals her inhuman origins, keep faith nonetheless. Maintain your vows to her and listen to her counsel. For the inhuman women: you must tell the truth about your origins rather than having someone else expose your secrets. Use all of your powers to aid not just your lover but his entire family; never despise the mundane domestic labor of a daughter-in-law serving her elders either. Embrace your co-wives and concubines with affection and grace, mindful of your respective places in the hierarchy. You must provide any needed sexual restraint, for the man will not. Such messages are clearly expressed in "Painted Skin," in which the threat of the demon lover is contained by a self-sacrificing wife; and in "Nie Xiaoqian," in which thanks to the man's self-control and the heroine's own will the would-be demon lover herself becomes the self-sacrificing wife.

Arakida Reijo 荒木田麗女 (1732–1806), the exceptional case of a female author of the Japanese strange tale, and Ueda Akinari present two different views of the erotic cautionary tale about a man's relationship with a snake spirit, drawing on both Japanese and Chinese sources. For Akinari, the serpent woman relentlessly pursues a fisherman's son who has desires beyond his station until she is finally imprisoned by a Buddhist exorcist. In Reijo's telling, it is the young nobleman who pursues and forces himself on the serpent woman, becoming her lover. She pursues him angrily only after his spying reveals her serpent form. Although she does not catch him, she is also not punished for her relationship with a human man. Fumiko Jōo argues this is typical of Reijo's treatment of the alien woman.[25] During the same time period in China, the same source material was developing in the direction of the serpent woman as a sympathetic heroine, but since that occurred in full-length plays, it is beyond my scope here.

D'Aulnoy's "The White Cat" offers a case in which the woman is the beast, although an attractive one. The title character overcomes the consequences of her parents' (both biological and adoptive) mistakes to make a marriage of her choosing. The final moral in verse gives the last word to criticism of her mother, who traded away her newborn to the fairies for forbidden fruit. The fairies in turn attempt to marry her off to a repulsive partner. "The White Cat" contains elements also found in the strange stories of Pu Songling, notably in the male character's passivity. We have seen how the husband of the "Painted Skin" draws his downfall on himself and contributes nothing to his own rescue. In "Nie Xiaoqian" Ning prevails through fortitude and faithfulness, but he also depends on the swordsman's powers. In another tale, "Lianxiang," the ability to accept his ghost and fox lover after understanding their true nature is enough to win the protagonist polygamous marital bliss with both, largely orchestrated by the two women.[26] In d'Aulnoy's tale, the prince is the one who enjoys the great luxuries and unique entertainments of an enchanted castle with an animal companion, whereas female characters enjoy such pleasures in d'Aulnoy's "The Ram" and "The Green Serpent," and later Villeneuve's "Beauty and the Beast." The White Cat provides all the means for her prince to satisfy his own father's unreasonable demands, and all that he needs to do is love and obey her despite her alien form. Living in a palace with illustrations from the author's earlier tales on the walls, the cat gets to be the narrator of her own story.[27] In both Asian and European traditions, a non-human origin may allow a woman more leeway in negotiating the terms of marriage, but gender is ultimately more constraining than species.

LEARNING (AND FAILING TO LEARN) FROM STORIES

As the decorations on the walls of the White Cat's palace suggest, in the literary tales of the eighteenth century there is self-conscious awareness verging on metafiction. The characters have read or heard stories and attempt to use them to interpret their own situations, or exploit other's knowledge about stories to their own ends. They do not always succeed. The heroine of "The Green Serpent" reads the story of Cupid and Psyche repeatedly, but it does not prevent her from making the same error as Psyche, breaking her husband's commandment not to gaze upon him and shining the lamp on him in the night (Zipes 1991a: 102–3).

Ji Yun mercilessly mocks the fan of Pu Songling's supernatural romances who thinks he can reenact the experiences of the characters. A man who thinks he will be married to a lovely fox bride is drafted to be merely an extra groomsman at the wedding party (Ji 1982: 15.303). Another avid reader who leaves a love letter at an abandoned tomb known to be inhabited by foxes is rewarded with a vixen who ruins him both sexually and financially (17.425).

Because of the greater sexual autonomy granted foxes and ghosts in the Chinese tale tradition, some of Ji's female informants and characters for their part try to claim those stories for themselves. Non-human identities allow women both to reject unwanted sexual advances and to indulge in sexuality, sometimes running away from an unwanted spouse or would-be rapist, other times engaging in a clandestine affair.[28] Male characters can be fooled by these deceptions, or complicit in them. Ji's sympathy depended on his judgment of sexual propriety. In one story attributed to an old woman who sold flowers, a residence in Beijing was close to an abandoned garden known to be haunted by foxes. A young wife who was having an affair with a neighboring youth, fearing the truth would come out, told her lover she was a fox from the garden. He was too overcome with lust to care. Yet later the actual foxes throw down tiles from the roof of the woman's house, denouncing this besmirching of their name and exposing the affair (Ji 1982: 2.25). In another story, the daughter of Ji Yun's brother's wet nurse, rushing alone to visit her sick mother at night, is followed by a threatening man. She dishevels her hair, sticks out her tongue, and ties a silk sash around her neck to disguise herself as a ghost that died of hanging. Her assailant faints in terror, and she runs away. Later she learns that he was suffering from mental illness because of haunting by a ghost (3.43). Through the aid of superhuman forces Ji Yun keeps moral control over these situations. The female characters are shown as exploiting general categories of possibly oral lore, in comparison with the men trying to reenact their favorite, particular written texts, especially Pu Songling's.

For all that we sometimes fail to learn or learn the wrong things, the final message of many of the stories with frames in both Asian and European traditions is that one should keep listening to and telling stories. In thirteenth-century collection *Bagh-o-bahar*, also known as *The Tale of the Four Dervishes*, the king who heard the stories told by the four dervishes marries each man to the princess he had hopelessly desired with help from the king of the *jinn*, while celebrating the birth of his long-awaited son. These matches cross geographical, class, and species lines.[29] In *The Arabian Nights,* Shahryar learns to trust and to love, and Scheherazade is able to survive and rule as queen. For her part, the Empress hearing Fum-Hoam's stories both converts her husband and regains her brother while the storyteller himself regains his true face, his family, and his kingdom.

Pu Songling or Ji Yun would have looked with approval on the list of virtues that Dickens ascribed to the tale of wonder: "forbearance, courtesy, consideration for the poor and aged, kind treatment of animals, the love of nature, abhorrence of tyranny and brute force." The fundamental value of reciprocity between beings across divisions of species or the living and the dead was essential to traditions of the strange tale they inherited.[30] However, neither would imagine children as the only or even the primary audience potentially transformed by wonder.

Wonder tales have their potential socializing power because of the fundamental strangeness of life and death; maturity and marriage; and relations with kin, strangers, and animals. The eighteenth century was a moment where in both Europe and Asia more different voices and different conceptions of the audience for the tales were being preserved in print, and the global flows of narrative created new formations of both knowledge and wonder.

CHAPTER EIGHT

Power

Gender, Class, and Politics in Ancien Régime Fairy and Oriental Tales

ANNE E. DUGGAN

When thinking about the representation of power as it relates to the cultural history of the fairy tale in the early modern period, several related questions come to mind: first, how does one attain power; second, how does power manifest itself; and third, what can one do with this power? Finally, what do these representations of power have to do with "real" power struggles in the period? Over the course of the long eighteenth century, such questions play out in different ways and are imbricated in both "vertical" power struggles based on social, gendered, and ontological hierarchies (i.e., between men and women, noble and commoner, adult and child, or fairy/genie and mortal) as well as "horizontal" power struggles among relative equals (i.e., between two kings or queens, two fairies, or two genies). The representation of such power struggles cannot be separated from the sociohistorical context in which the tales were written. Shifts in the types of tales that were popular in a particular period can be read as different ways of dealing with questions of gender, social, and political power. For instance, the ways in which power was represented in works by the French women fairy-tale writers of the 1690s maintain continuities and discontinuities with questions of power in the oriental tale, produced predominantly by male writers, which became popular in France and more generally in Europe with the early eighteenth-century translation and adaptation of *Les Mille et une nuits* (*The Thousand and One Nights*, 1704–17) by Antoine Galland.¹

This chapter will focus on tales penned in France—including Middle Eastern tales adapted into French—which became the center of tale production in Europe in the long eighteenth century. Fairy tales by Marie-Catherine d'Aulnoy ([1697] 1997, [1698] 1998), Charles Perrault (1695, 1697), and later Jeanne-Marie Leprince de Beaumont ([1757] 2011) were widely translated in England, often shortly after their initial publication in French, throughout the late seventeenth and eighteenth centuries.² European elites spoke French, meaning that they could read popular writers such as d'Aulnoy and Perrault in the original, and tales by French authors were widely available in England, German states, and Holland, among other countries. Beginning in 1704, when Galland began translating and adapting into French *The Thousand and One Nights*, based on a Syrian manuscript and oral tales told to him by the Syrian maronite Hanna Diyab, he launched a new wave of tale production, the "oriental tale." Following Galland's lead, François Pétis de La Croix translated and adapted two tale collections, *Histoire de la sultane de Perse et les visirs, contes turcs* (Story of the Sultana of Persia and the Vizirs; Turkish Tales, 1707) and *Les Mille et un jours, contes persans* (*Thousand and One Days, Persian Tales*, 1710–12), drawing from Turkish manuscripts of Turkish and Persian tale collections. These collections were followed by works questionably claiming the status of translation, for instance Jean-Paul Bignon's *Les Aventures d'Abdalla, fils d'Hanif* (*The Adventures of Abdalla, Son of Hanif*, 1712–14) and Thomas-Simon Gueulette's *Mille et un quart d'heures* (*Thousand and One Quarters of an Hour*, 1712), among many others. Both the fairy- and oriental-tale trends had a significant impact throughout Europe on the field of literary as well as oral tales.³

This shift in production from the fairy tale—which continued to be republished throughout the century—to the oriental tale represents different relationships between the creation, consumption, and meaning of tales in different moments of the long eighteenth century. With respect to fairy tales in the tradition of d'Aulnoy, we can understand the figure of the powerful fairy as being representative of the powerful female figures in the French literary scene and at court. This is made nowhere more clear than in Henriette-Julie de Murat's dedicatory epistle "To Modern Fairies" that introduces her collection of fairy tales, *Histoires sublimes et allégoriques* (Sublime and Allegorical Stories, 1699):

> The ancient fairies, your predecessors, pass for little more than fools [*badines*] next to you. Their activities were base and childish, amusing only to Servants and Nurses. They cared only to sweep the house well, put the pot on the fire, do the wash, rock and put the children to bed, milk cows, churn butter, and a thousand other low things of this nature .... They were almost always old, ugly, poorly dressed, and poorly housed; and, except for Melusine and

a few half-dozen like her, the rest were nothing but beggars. But as for you, Mesdames, you have taken a different road: You concern yourselves with only great things, the least of which are giving spirit to those who have none, beauty to the ugly, eloquence to the ignorant, riches to the poor, and clarity to the most obscure things. You are all beautiful, young, well formed, gallantly and richly dressed and housed, and you live in only the Courts of Kings or in magic Palaces.

(Murat 1699: 2–4; translated by Tucker and Siemens 2005: 129)

Far from the foolish, old, and lower-class fairies of ancient times, the 1690s fairy is young, courtly, elegant, powerful, and eloquent. All in all, the fairy was a figure for powerful women, including the elite women who hosted literary and philosophical salons, serving as arbiters of culture, and the women writers (many of whom were salon women) who dominated the fashion of fairy tales in the last decade of the seventeenth century, using their voices to criticize everything from arranged marriages and abuses of power to restrictive gender roles.

When Galland produced his *Thousand and One Nights*, the figure of Scheherazade represented a line of continuity with the powerful female voice of the 1690s, which would be challenged by later writers of oriental tales, most notably Pétis de La Croix and Denis Diderot. Whereas women writers dominated the fairy-tale wave of the 1690s, with d'Aulnoy taking the lead in the production of tales, male writers dominated the fashion of oriental tales. Perhaps what made the oriental tale so appealing was its ability to address and criticize issues related to political power at a time when Louis XIV's monarchy had increasingly become more authoritarian. Rebecca Johnson, Richard Maxwell, and Katie Trumpener argue that *The Thousand and One Nights* "pushed eighteenth-century novelists not only to reconsider the relationship of episode to overall narrative arc but also to explore the novel's large-scale formal and philosophical possibilities" (2007: 247). In particular, "the *Nights* dramatized the clash of moral codes and worldviews, offering contradictory perspectives on fate, agency, and the interactions between the human and the supernatural worlds. Enlightenment novelists interpreted these features of the *Nights* as an incitement to relativistic thinking" (248).[4] Such relativistic thinking was instrumental in challenging the traditional structures of power such as the monarchy and the church in the period of the Enlightenment. In the eighteenth century, the *Nights* in particular and the oriental tale in general would serve as a useful genre through which to explore questions of power within eighteenth-century French culture from the perspective of an outsider—as in the case of Montesiquieu's Persians who offer analysis of the court of Louis XIV—and by projecting French problems onto Eastern cultures—as in the case of Voltaire's Zadig, persecuted by a dysfunctional judicial system in ways reminiscent of Voltaire's own situation. Although I will not be discussing the question of Orientalism in detail, it is important at the outset to emphasize the problematic nature of eighteenth-century writers using the term "oriental tale" as an umbrella category for narratives that encompass many different national traditions and which frames Middle Eastern and Asian narratives, beliefs, and cultural practices in terms of exoticism and otherness. At the same time, in this period before the age of empire, in which the Ottoman Empire was a formidable global force, Orientalism, as Srinivas Aravamudan has argued, was of a more complex nature: "a transcultural, cosmopolitan, and Enlightenment-inflected Orientalism existed at least as an alternative strain before 'Saidian' [that is, instrumentalized] Orientalism came about" (2012: 3).[5]

Throughout the rest of this chapter, we will look at specific examples of how one attains power, how power manifests itself, to then focus on what one can do with power, taking into account the changing cultural context in which the fairy tale and oriental tale are embedded. As we will see, such questions intersect with gender, class, and political structures in important ways. While narratives issuing from both the fairy-tale and the oriental tale traditions address political despotism, the "masculinization" of the genre of the tale—taking the specific form of the oriental tale—slowly erodes away at the power of the female voice and female characters, at least within the domain of fiction.[6]

ATTAINMENT AND MANIFESTATION OF POWER

The attainment and manifestation of power interact in different ways, accommodating different situations, genders, social classes, and physical or political abilities in fairy and oriental tales. In many cases one attains power because one is born into a powerful political position or one is endowed with powers such as magic, beauty, or intelligence that allow one to either take power or avoid being oppressed by the powerful. Tales often begin with a king and queen who already exercise power, and that power is destabilized or weakened by various forces in the tale, with the ending bringing about a return to stability and usually a reestablishment of the family line. In the case of characters like fairies and genies, their very beings embody magical forces that can topple the most powerful humans. They can step into tales to support, destroy, elevate, or restore power to different characters, for both good and evil.

Ruth Bottigheimer's notion of "restoration" as opposed to "rise" tales is useful in thinking about the attainment (or restoration) of power in tales from this period.[7] In the case of tales by many of the women writers, whether we think of d'Aulnoy's Aimée from "L'Oranger et l'abeille" ("The Bee and the Orange Tree," 1697), who regains her noble identity after living on an island with ogres, or Gabrielle-Suzanne de Villeneuve's version of "Beauty and the Beast" (1740), in which her Beauty discovers she is indeed of royal and not commoner birth, characters born noble who lose their identity at one point in their story recover their social and political power by the end of the tale. That recovery can be effectuated through the power of their wit, beauty, virtue, or with the assistance of magic. In the case of "rise" tales, low-born characters are able to transcend their lot in life thanks to a magical helper, as in the case of the miller's youngest son in Perrault's "Le Chat botté" ("Puss in Boots"), who becomes a prince through marriage with the assistance of a magical cat; or Galland and Diyab's "Aladdin,"[8] a lazy and poor youth who, with the help of the magical lamp, becomes a prince through marriage to Princess Badroulbadour.

There are several ways in which characters can "take" power. In the case of "Puss in Boots," the title cat manages to claim possession of a fiefdom from an ogre he kills through a clever ruse and attribute the land to the miller's son, which legitimates the hero's ability to marry the princess. In d'Aulnoy's tale "Gracieuse and Percinet," the wealthy Grognon, referred to as the "so-called" duchess, has recourse to another method of conquering a territory and a place on the throne: she buys her way into the heart—or at least the castle—of the king, Gracieuse's father. The lower-ranking (and probably non-noble) stepmother uses her position to torture the high-born princess, Gracieuse.[9] In some ways the messages of these two tales contradict each other. We might read the ogre of Perrault's tale as a figure for a nobleman, whose territory is usurped by a commoner; the tale thus could be read as a projection of the desire of non-nobles to gain power over the traditional nobility in France. For her part, d'Aulnoy lamented the decline of the traditional French nobility from which she issued. Through the figure of Grognon, d'Aulnoy arguably criticizes the power of money—increasingly in the hands of the rising bourgeoisie in the period—to buy nobility and political power. In this restoration tale, the rightful balance of power is restored with the magical assistance of the fairy prince Percinet, and the usurper Grognon's power as a wealthy queen becomes useless when a fairy is able to magically slip past her guards and literally wring her neck (Figure 8.1). Depending on the ideology of the particular writer, a commoner taking power or a noble maintaining theirs can be justified or deemed problematic.

As has been the case throughout history, power can also be taken through warfare. Perhaps more than other fairy-tale writers, d'Aulnoy includes several examples of wars between monarchs in which the rightful ruler is restored with the help of a fairy or magical helpers, and that rightful ruler is often a woman. The evil and toad-like prince Furibond (whose name means "furious" or "enraged") seeks to conquer the Island of Tranquil Pleasure—ruled by a princess—but he is killed by the title character, "Le Prince Lutin" ("The Sprite Prince") Leandre, who protects the Amazonian queendom. In "La Bonne petite souris" ("The Good Little Mouse"), the evil king of the Kingdom of Tears wages war against the king of the Kingdom of Joy, taking over the latter, killing its king, and imprisoning the pregnant queen, whose daughter Joliette is eventually restored to her father's throne with the help of a fairy. In the case

FIGURE 8.1: The "so-called" Duchess Grognon seducing Gracieuse's father with her wealth, illustrated by Gustaf Tenggren, from *d'Aulnoy's Fairy Tales* (Philadelphia: David McKay, 1923). Public domain.

of the king from "Belle-Belle, ou le Chevalier Fortuné," he loses his capital city to the emperor Matapa and it is only with the assistance of the cross-dressed heroine and her magical helpers that his kingdom can be restored. With "The Sprite Prince," a matriarchal world is protected from destruction by a fairy prince, while "The Good Little Mouse" concludes with the princess taking her father's throne. Women play powerful roles in d'Aulnoy's tales, including saving a kingdom from invading forces, as in the case of "Belle-Belle, ou le chevalier Fortuné." This positioning of women hearkens back to the period of queen regents in France that punctuated the late sixteenth and seventeenth centuries, which included the regencies of Catherine de' Medici (1560–3), Marie de' Medici (1610–17), and Anne of Austria (1643–51). Powerful female figures abound in this period, which also saw women such as Louis XIV's cousin Anne Marie Louise d'Orléans, duchesse de Montpensier, and Anne Geneviève de Bourbon, duchesse de Longueville, actively engage in the civil war known as the Fronde, and who were themselves considered to be Amazons.[10] Including women among the power struggles between realms in fiction foregrounds as well the power real women wielded in this period.

Sometimes power is acquired by usurping another individual's identity. In d'Aulnoy's tale "L'Oiseau Bleu" ("The Blue Bird"), the princess Florine's evil stepmother wishes to marry her cruel and ugly daughter Truitonne—which comes from "truite" or "trout"—to King Charming so that she becomes queen.[11] But the king is in love with Florine. One night, King Charming comes to Florine's window in the tower where she was imprisoned to swear his eternal love, sealing it with a ring; however, he ends up giving his oath to Truitonne, for the evil stepmother had arranged to sit a disguised Truitonne at the window, in place of Florine. The next day, when King Charming realizes his mistake and refuses to marry Truitonne, he is persecuted by Truitonne's fairy godmother, Soussio. But in the end, love proves to be a force stronger than fairy magic, and Florine and King Charming are united.

A striking example of how taking another's identity can be a means to acquire power in different ways is the story of Dilnouaze and Mocbel from Pétis de La Croix's *Thousand and One Days*. As a young woman Dilnouaze used her beauty to enrich herself by taking multiple lovers, but when old age sets in, she seeks help from the female magician Bedra, who gives Dilnouaze and Mocbel each a magical ring that allows them to transform into any woman or man they wish. In one case, at Dilnouaze's initiative, the duo takes advantage of a kingdom in which the very young princess of Naïmans has acceded to the throne after the death of her father. Pretending to be her uncle Mouaffec believed to be dead, Mocbel makes a triumphant "return," claims the throne, forces the real princess to flee, and rules with Dilnouaze (pretending to be a foreign princess) as his queen. When they learn that the princess of Naïmans had married the king of Tibet and now wishes to take back her father's throne, Dilnouaze and Mocbel take on the identity of their rivals; however, in the end their ruse is unveiled and Dilnouaze is killed.

In often gendered ways, beauty and intelligence allow characters to attain certain levels of power. Exemplified in the story of Dilnouaze before she ages and must resort to the magical ring, beauty—a rather passive form of power— can allow usually female characters to exercise power over male characters. It can also—fortuitously or not—attract powerful suitors, which leads female characters to attain the throne. In the case of the aforementioned "The Blue Bird," despite the poor attire her stepmother forces her to wear, Florine is so beautiful that King Charming is nevertheless swept away by the princess. A more negative representation of the powerful effects of female beauty is found in the frame narrative of *Thousand and One Days*. The princess of Cashmire, Farrukhnaz, is so beautiful she (albeit passively) drives men mad. The narrator explains: "this princess was so beautiful and so striking that she inspired love in every man who dared look at her; but this love became deadly to them, for the majority of them lost their wits, or they fell into a languor that gradually ate away at them" (Pétis de La Croix [1710–12] 2011: 77).[12] Her beauty is so deadly that her father desperately wishes to marry her off to contain the effects of her fatal appearance, but she has developed a complete disdain for men and marriage. In the end, however, Farukhnaz overcomes her repulsion for men and agrees to wed the prince of Persia, Farrukschad, and all's well that ends well. Such a conclusion suggests that marriage can serve as a means to contain the power of women: married, Farukhnaz's beauty no longer poses a threat to the lives of men.

Intelligence is one of the most compelling forms of power in fairy and oriental tales. Intelligence can allow less powerful characters within gendered, social, and ontological hierarchies to overcome the ostensibly stronger character: women are able to overcome men, a commoner cat can overcome an aristocratic ogre, a mortal fisherman can overcome a supernatural genie. Starting with the frame narrative, *The Thousand and One Nights* provides numerous examples of how wit can subdue the most powerful and repressive forces. Betrayed by his wife the sultana with a slave, Shariar goes on a killing spree, marrying a young woman each day only to have her killed the next day to avoid ever being betrayed by a woman again. To stop further shedding of innocent blood, the heroine of *The Nights*, Scheherazade (Figure 8.2), wishes to marry Shariar, believing she can put an end to his violence, and we come to understand that this is due to her superior intelligence. Scheherazade is described as having

> a courage beyond her sex, infinite wit, with admirable wisdom. She was well-read and had such a prodigious memory that nothing escaped her from all of her readings. She had happily applied herself to the study of philosophy, medicine, history, and fine arts; she wrote verse better than the most celebrated poets of her time. Besides all of that, she was endowed with an excellent beauty, and a solid virtue crowned all of these beautiful qualities.
> (Galland [1704–17] 2004: 1:35)

While beauty and virtue close the description of Scheherazade, her intelligence is foregrounded to such a degree that later we are not surprised by the fact that through her storytelling skills—that is, through her intelligence—she is able to contain the violence of the sultan Shariar.

Intelligence overcoming brute force is a theme as well in "The Story of the Fisherman and the Genie," which in some respects reflects back on the frame narrative of *The Thousand and One Nights*. In the tale a fisherman frees a genie who has been imprisoned in a sealed vessel for hundreds of years, and the genie arbitrarily wishes to kill the fisherman for saving him. Seemingly in an impossible situation, the fisherman quickly devises a plan: he challenges the

FIGURE 8.2: Scheherazade, the heroine of *The Thousand and One Nights*, illustrated by Edmund Dulac in *Stories from the Arabian Nights*, retold by Laurence Housman (New York: George H. Doran, 1907).

genie's ability to climb into the vessel, refusing to believe it is possible until he sees the feat. After the genie manages to get back into the vessel, exclaiming "Hey, incredulous fisherman, can you see me in this vase? do you believe me now?" (Galland [1704–17] 2004: 1:70), the fisherman reseals it, saving his skin. As the narrator explains, "Necessity gives wit" (1:69), and this wit has the power to save a mortal from the whims of a powerful genie.

A similar ruse is used by Perrault's cat from "Puss in Boots." To take over the ogre's castle and gift it to his human companion, the master cat "took care to inform himself about who this Ogre was, and what he was able to do" (Perrault 1967: 160). When the cat arrives at the castle, he tells the ogre that he had heard that he was capable of transforming himself into all kinds of animals, and asks for a demonstration. The cat first asks the ogre if he can transform into a large animal, like a lion or an elephant, and the ogre takes the form of a lion. The cat then wonders if the ogre could transform himself into small animal, like a rat or a mouse, suggesting this would be impossible. Taking this as a challenge, the ogre transforms himself into a mouse, and, not surprisingly, the cat eats him up. As this tale suggests, knowledge is indeed power. In some respects, Perrault's tale allegorically represents the changes occurring in early modern French society. Whereas the power of the traditional feudal nobility resided in their military prowess, that of the rising bourgeoisie resides in knowledge: knowledge about the law, finance, and commerce. And it was this knowledge that allowed the bourgeoisie to raise their economic, social, and even political status over the course of the early modern period.[13]

THE EXERCISE OF POWER IN THE TALE

As we have seen, power can be attained by many means and manifest itself in a character in different ways, while the exercise of power can take negative and positive forms, depending upon one's ideological position and the nature of the power used. During the long eighteenth century, France saw the height of absolute monarchy under Louis XIV, and the latter part of his reign was viewed in a particularly negative light. Several of the women fairy-tale writers of the 1690s were interned or exiled by the monarchy. Forcibly married, d'Aulnoy conspired to have her husband falsely convicted of *lèse-majesté*—meaning any verbal or physical offense of the monarch—and was exiled; after being allowed to return to Paris, she was later confined to a convent due to her supposedly improper behavior.[14] Murat was exiled to Loches in 1702, possibly due to a pamphlet she wrote against the monarchy or due to, again, her supposedly inappropriate conduct.[15] Charlotte-Rose de Caumont de La Force also found herself marginalized from court. Juliette Cherbuliez explains: "A scandalous marriage and a trial that secured its dissolution compelled Louis XIV to send La Force first into exile at the château of Mme d'Arpajon and later to a convent where she remained for years" (2005: 206). At the same time that women fairy-tale writers drew from the earlier examples of queen regents and Amazonian noblewomen, they were writing at a time of political, gender, and religious oppression. As Domna Stanton and Rebecca Wilkin explain,

> Once of age, king Louis XIV (1660–1714) would succeed in eliminating the ideal of the *femme forte* [or "strong woman"], along with other perceived forms of subversion and deviance, in his efforts to establish an absolutistic state. Maïté Albistur and Daniel Armogathe, after Michel Foucault, coined the phrase "the great enclosing of women" (*le grand renfermement des femmes*) to describe the declining economic and professional status of women during Louis's reign.
>
> (2010: 5)

James R. Farr (1991) has also documented the increased scrutiny more generally in French society of women's social and sexual behavior, the surveillance of which increased during the second half of the seventeenth century, and which resulted in more severe punishments of transgressive behavior than earlier in the century.

While the women writers of fairy tales felt particularly targeted by the monarchy, other writers also criticized what they saw as the tyranny of Louis XIV, who revoked the Edict of Nantes in 1685, which had legalized the practice of Protestantism, and who, for many, unjustly supported the Ottoman attacks on Christian territories under the Hapsburg rule. A 1687 treatise, *La Cour de France turbanisée et les trahisons démasquées* (The Turbanized Court of France and Treachery Unmasked) accused the monarchy of allying itself to the Turks, chasing "God from his Temples, in order to make them into Mosques and to place Mohamed and his Coran there" (1687: 40). The author discusses the "insatiable ambition of France," which leads to scorn for the law, broken promises, and the exercise of tyranny, and he points to the problematic position of the monarchy, which "persecutes Huguenots in France" but does not "have any scruples about increasing the power of the Turks in order to destroy Christians" (40). As Michèle Longino observes, "*La France turbanisée* surfaced around 1686, just three years after the French conspicuously failed to come to the aid of the Habsburg stronghold of Vienna, as it was under siege from the Ottomans" (2002: 212).

Such demonstrations of power on the part of the monarchy could indeed feel arbitrary and thus despotic.[16] Men had much more sexual freedom than women and were not confined, for the most part, to convents or prisons or exiled for engaging in the kind of extramarital affairs for which our *conteuses* were punished. While Protestants were being persecuted in France, the king was supporting the Muslim Ottoman Empire over the Christian (both Catholic and Protestant) lands of the Hapsburgs, all for the glory of Louis XIV's reign. Fairy and oriental tales provide numerous examples of the exercise of arbitrary, despotic power, which reflect back in different ways on the sense of injustice that prevailed in France.

In tales by the *conteuses*, particularly d'Aulnoy and Louise d'Auneuil, the arbitrary exercise of power is often in the hands of bad fairies, who support negative characters and punish those who have a will of their own—usually with respect to questions about marriage—and that punishment often takes the form of being metamorphosed. For instance, in d'Aulnoy's tale "The Blue Bird," King Charming is transformed into a bird by the fairy Soussio because he refuses to marry her ugly goddaughter Truitonne. After turning him into a bird, Soussio tries to find another prince for Truitonne to marry, but they only ask for the beautiful Florine, whom Soussio has imprisoned in a tower. When so many princes refuse Truitonne's hand in marriage, Soussio comes up with a conspiracy theory based on the jewelry the imprisoned princess receives from her beloved blue bird: "She must secretly be corresponding with foreign countries. She is at the very least a criminal against the state"; the fairy then directly accuses her of "intrigues against the state" (d'Aulnoy [1697] 1997: 92, 93). Here d'Aulnoy uses political language to describe the persecution of the princess and the prince, which foregrounds the role of the state in monitoring marriage practices, and the power of the state to imprison those who disobey the authority of parents and guardians in such matters.[17] J. H. Shennan remarks that despite "glaring examples of arbitrary action" on the part of Louis XIV, "the use of royal *lettres de cachet*, which allowed the king to imprison subjects without reference to the courts, was generally employed not as a political weapon but on behalf of heads of families anxious to control their way-ward children" ([1986] 2005: 18). That being said, the fact remains that the state indeed backed the often arbitrary and self-interested nature of heads of families to exercise power over their charges.

Marking the latter part of the fairy-tale vogue that began in the 1690s, d'Auneuil produced *La Tyrannie des fées détruite* (The Tyranny of Fairies Destroyed) in 1702, which goes against the grain of many of the tales produced by writers such as d'Aulnoy. The introduction to the collection paints a rather grim picture of a society in which fairies tyrannize princesses and princes. It reads:

> The power of the fairies had come to such a high point of supremacy that even the great nobles of the courts feared displeasing them. This accursed brood, whose origin we do not know, had become so dreadful due to the evils they inflicted on those who dared to disobey them. Their fury was never satisfied except by transforming the most amiable people into the most horrible monsters, and if they did not give you a quick death, it was only to make you languish longer in a miserable condition.
>
> (d'Auneuil [1702] 1990: 24)

The frame narrative concerns the beautiful princess Philonice, abducted by the evil fairies who wish to marry her to the king of the monsters. Protected by the fairy Serpente from her nasty sisters, Philonice encounters several victims of the fairies' persecution. She sees two turtledoves, in reality a metamorphosed prince and princess who accidentally saw a fairy bathing, covered in turtledove feathers; the fairy changed them into two turtledoves so that they could not reveal her secret. Similarly, Philonice learns that several subjects of a prince had seen the fairies dancing in the moonlight; when the humans mocked them, the fairies turned them into statues. The first of four interpolated stories concerns the princess Cléonice, another victim of the fairies whose lover was turned into a dragon, and who reveals the prophecy that the tyranny of the fairies will be destroyed by a powerful princess. At the end of the frame narrative, the prophesied princess arrives, frees the metamorphosed characters, and condemns the evil fairies to serve, basically, to motor a hydraulic machine that feeds "enchanted gardens" (d'Auneuil [1702] 1990: 91; see Figure 8.3), a veiled reference to Louis XIV's Machine de Marly, which pumped water to the fountains of Versailles.[18]

As Anne Defrance remarks, "The political figure [the princess] appropriated the traditional magical power [of the fairies]. With respect to the fairies, the worst of them became slaves to the regime" (2002: 59). Given the reference to Louis XIV's Marly, which contemporary readers would have immediately recognized, the regime in question is that of the Sun King. Not surprisingly, Louis XIV sought to reduce the cultural authority of the women-run salons

FIGURE 8.3: The punished fairies from d'Auneuil's *La Tyrannie des fées détruite* (Amsterdam: Estienne Roger, 1710) toiling away to run the machine that feeds water into the enchanted gardens. Public domain.

through the proliferation of all-male state academies from the 1660s onward.[19] Within Parisian society, modern fairies were being marginalized by the regime, and this marginalization takes literary form not only in d'Auneuil but, as we will see, in the works of Jean de Préchac and the fashion of the oriental tale.

In some respects, the rise of the oriental tale appeared on the literary scene at a prime moment. Riding the tide of the 1690s fairy-tale vogue, the oriental tale appealed to the French reading public already well versed in the genre of the tale. At the same time, pamphlets circulated that accused Louis XIV of exercising power in the manner of an oriental despot, a problematic racist representation based on stereotypes about the sultans of the Ottoman Empire. The figure of Shariar, then, could serve as an allegorical figure for the Sun King, even if this was not Galland's intention. Influenced by Galland's *Thousand and One Nights*, Montesquieu published *Les Lettres Persanes* (*The Persian Letters*, 1721) six years after Louis XIV's death, in which the sultan Usbek demonstrates tyrannical powers over the women of his harem, much like Shariar does. Scholars such as Ruth Bernard Yeazell have remarked upon the "implicit parallels between Usbek's *sérail* [harem] and the court of Louis XIV" (2000: 66). And Roger Boesche argues that "Montesquieu's analysis of despotism [in the *Letters*] is partly an attack on the monarchies of Louis XIV and Louis XV" (1990: 746).[20] What makes Shariar despotic is his arbitrary exercise of power in the wake of the sultana's sexual betrayal. Whereas Shariar's brother Shahzenan, similarly betrayed by his wife and a house slave, kills only the guilty parties, Shariar murders dozens of innocent women. He kills arbitrarily, and it is precisely this arbitrary exercise of power that makes him despotic.

The genies of the *Nights* provide several examples of the arbitrary exercise of power. For instance, in "The Merchant and the Genie," a merchant throws the pit of a date on the ground, and suddenly a genie appears, accusing the merchant of killing his son, and threatening to kill him in revenge, in some ways hearkening back to the violence of the frame narrative. Taken aback, the merchant pleads with the genie that he had no intention of killing anyone upon tossing away the pit, but the genie shows no mercy. The merchant then asks for time to prepare his affairs and inform his family of his circumstances, which the genie allows. The tale ends happily when three old men each exchange a story for one-third of the merchant's life, which recalls Scheherazade exchanging stories for her own life and that of the women of the kingdom. "The Story of the Fisherman and the Genie" provides another striking example of arbitrary power. Sealed in a vessel by King Soloman, the genie swore that the person who would free him during the first century of his imprisonment would become rich; for his second century of confinement, he promised to open all of the earth's treasures to the person who freed him; the third century he would make his liberator a powerful monarch. Finally, when all hope was lost, the genie swore that he would "unmercifully" kill the person who freed him, leaving them only the choice of how they would die. In effect, there is no rhyme or reason as to why the fisherman should die and, as we saw above, it is thanks to the fisherman's intelligence that he is empowered to save his own life and overcome the genie's arbitrary exericse of power.

The oriental tale branched out into the philosophical tale, which includes texts such as Montesquieu's *Persian Letters* and Voltaire's *Zadig* (1747), among many others. Like the 1690s *conteuses* before him, Voltaire often found himself at odds with the monarchy. In 1717 he was imprisoned in the Bastille for having published satirical verses about the regent Philippe d'Orléans and in 1726 he negotiated his exile to England to avoid a second stint in the Bastille after an altercation with the chevalier de Rohan-Chabot; this would not be his last exile.[21] Through *Zadig*, Voltaire uses the genre of the oriental tale to criticize the arbitrary use of power to unjustly imprison or fine individuals, actions often upheld by irrational or corrupt principles. In the chapter "The Dog and the Horse," the queen's men search for her lost dog; Zadig provides a description of the dog, but assures them he did not see it. The same thing happens with the king's horse, which also goes missing. Because Zadig could describe the dog and the horse, he was arrested, even though he was not in possession of either. Judges were about to exile him when the dog and the horse return. Embarassed, the judges nevertheless subjected Zadig to a fine of 400 ounces of gold for having supposedly lied about not seeing the dog or the horse. After Zadig explained that he had divined the traits of the two animals based on their traces in the sand—which led some priests to demand that he be burned at the stake for witchcraft—Zadig was exonerated, and the king returned the fine. However, the men of the court retained 398 ounces of gold for the "costs of justice." By showing his hero first unjustly arrested and condemned to exile, then unjustly fined, and finally simply robbed, Voltaire foregrounds different levels of corruption and lack of transparency and accountability in what amounts to an illegitimate exercise of state power against Zadig.

Although fairy tales and oriental tales provide many examples of the despotic, arbitrary, and corrupt exercise of power, they also are filled will examples of good characters who use their powers to save others and reward kindness. In some cases, the reward serves to shape the behavior and values of readers, who are encouraged to be kind and to value more solid virtues over superficial ones such as beauty and wealth. For instance, in Perrault's "Les Fées" ("The Fairies"), a tale about kind and unkind girls, a fairy rewards the persecuted Cinderella-like character for her kindness by endowing her with the gift of emitting diamonds as she speaks, while her unkind stepsister is punished for her bad behavior by having to emit toads and snakes. In the case of d'Aulnoy's "Le Rameau d'or" ("The Golden Bough"), the Princess Trognon is ugly at birth, but when enchanted characters give her the choice of beauty or intelligence, she chooses intelligence; because of her wise choice, Trognon is rewarded with both, becoming the beautiful Princess Brillante.

At other times, certain characters endowed with the power of magic attempt to prevent forms of injustice. For instance, at Sleeping Beauty's baptismal scene, Perrault introduces a wicked old fairy, who is offended she hadn't been invited to the festivities even though she was believed to be dead. While the other fairies present grant the infant qualities like beauty, wit, and grace, the old fairy curses the child, explaining that she will prick her finger on a spinning wheel and die. Not having enough power to completely counter the curse, the last fairy to grant a gift is able to modify the curse of death to one hundred years of slumber. Similarly, in d'Aulnoy's "Gracieuse and Percinet," although the fairy prince Percinet is not able to outright save Gracieuse from the persecutions of her cruel stepmother Grognon, he can transform instruments of torture—the rods used to flog the princess—into feathers to avert harm to his true love. Such characters manage to at the very least curb, if they cannot eliminate, the forces of evil.

As we have already seen, *The Thousand and One Nights* represents storytelling as a power: Scheherazade has the power to prevent Shariar from killing women, and the three old men tell stories to prevent the genie from killing the merchant. In fact, two of the stories they tell concern women who save men from both women and men, an implicit message to Shariar that women don't only betray men but they can also protect and save them. In the first story, the narrator's barren wife transforms his son by a slavewoman into a calf, and his slavewoman into a cow, while he is away. Upon his return, the wife claims the slavewoman died and the son ran off. Later the narrator wishes to butcher the cow, but somehow feeling pity, he can't muster up the strength to kill it; when his wife scolds him for his weakness, the narrator has his farmhand take care of it. When it comes time to sacrifice the calf, the farmhand's daughter realizes the calf is the narrator's metamorphosed son, is able to transform him back into a human, and condemns the wife to the form of a doe. In the second story, a female genie constantly saves her husband from the evil schemes of his two brothers, eventually having to transform them into two dogs to prevent them from further trying to harm her husband. In these cases, characters with magical powers preserve the lives of the innocent.

The Thousand and One Days presents an interesting tale about misunderstanding the exercise of power. The female genie Cheheristany demands absolute obedience from her husband Ruzvanschad, the king of China; since he is mortal, he cannot comprehend the meaning of her actions but she insists that they all consist of good intentions. When she appears to throw their infant son into a fire, we later learn she was sending him to a salamander to educate him; when she has a dog carry off their infant daughter, we later learn that the dog is a fairy who will educate her; and when genies destroy all of her husband's provisions as he was preparing for war against the Mogols, we later learn this was only to save the army from the poison applied to the food by the king's minister Wely, who was conspiring with the

Mogols after being paid off by them. Finally, her genie army helps the Chinese overcome the invading Mogols, but because the king of China disobeyed Cheheristany she must leave him, a husbandly disobedience that recalls the medieval story of Melusine.[22]

As these examples make clear, characters exercise arbitrary power for many reasons, including jealousy, vengeance, and simply the desire to wield power over others. In d'Aulnoy's "The Blue Bird," personal envy of the heroine takes political form when, to eliminate the object of jealousy, the heroine is deemed a criminal of the state. Shariar's Bluebeard-like behavior in his serial killing of women is supported by the fact that he is king, and he can use the political apparatus to satisfy his personal desire for what basically becomes an irrational form of vengeance. For their part, the judges of *Zadig* try to pin a crime on the hero when there is none, and when all else fails, they still retain the power to unjustly bill the hero for their supposed services. In all of these cases, authors use the tales to reflect back on the political situation in France, where many felt the monarchy was exercising its powers in unjust ways. One wonders, then, if the fairies, genies, and other characters who are able to counter the forces of injustice, reward the virtuous, and save the innocent could be viewed as serving the purposes of wish-fulfillment in a pre-revolutionary society that hoped for a more just world.

THE POWER OF THE FEMALE VOICE

Over the course of the long eighteenth century, as noted above, the shift from the fairy tale to the oriental tale is accompanied by a shift in the power of the female voice. While in the 1690s women authors dominated the fairy-tale genre, giving voice to women's concerns and providing many models of empowered female characters, this voice dissipates as we move through the eighteenth-century tale tradition. Even before the tide of the oriental tale tradition, dominated by male authors, came into fruition, d'Auneuil's 1702 *Tyranny of Fairies Destroyed* and Préchac's earlier "Sans Parangon" ("The Peerless Prince," 1698) and "La Reine des fées" ("The Queen of the Fairies," 1698) stage the subjugation of (usually female) fairy powers to the (patriarchal) French monarchy. In these texts, the only good fairy is one who supports kings and queens, while bad fairies, as we saw in d'Auneuil's tale, are quite literally tethered to the machine of the state.

With respect to Préchac's tales, Defrance explains that "the devalorization of fairy power corresponds to the necessity to erect a monument to the glory of an absolute monarch whose genius claims to owe nothing except to himself" (2002: 62). This is particularly clear in "The Peerless Prince." As critics have noted, the tale is a "thinly veiled" history of Louis XIV's reign, which allegorically represents everything from Anne of Austria's inability to produce an heir for the first twenty-one years of her marriage to Louis XIII, to much later Louis

XIV building Versailles, a palace that exceeds in skill and beauty anything that the fairies could possibly build, to finally Louis XIV's pursuit of glory through war.²³ As Hall Bjørnstad argues, "royal reality supplants fairy illusion, the real palace surpasses the enchanted palace. True marvels are not found in fairy tales, but at Versailles" (2009: 172).

This supplanting of fairy powers by royal powers takes a slightly different form in Préchac's "Queen of the Fairies." In this case, the title character—a royal princess who becomes a fairy queen—punishes the rest of her sisters for their bad deeds toward humans by depriving them of their functions, only leaving them the freedom to do good for three hundred years to correct their bad behavior; if they are successful in their good deeds, they will recover their fairy functions. The idea of them losing their "function" is akin to the nobility losing their sociopolitical functions—offices at court, in the government, and positions in the army—and being exiled from court. It also arguably serves as a figure for Louis XIV's attempt to marginalize the salons with his acceleration in founding the state-sponsored cultural institutions that were the academies. Interestingly, the successful fairies attach themselves to the royal and Bourbon palaces of Fontainebleau, Chambord, Chantilly, Amboise, and Blois. As opposed to d'Auneuil, who punishes the fairies by integrating them into the Machine de Marly, here Préchac allows the fairies to rehabilitate themselves by serving as supports to the monarchy and Bourbon dynasty. Defrance succinctly summarizes the rationale of such literary strategies: "because the royal figure must be omnipotent and perfectly autonomous, certain authors believed it necessary to submit their fairies to him as a token of their own submission" (2002: 69). Whereas d'Aulnoy used her tales to criticize the monarchy, Préchac and d'Auneuil deployed theirs to celebrate it, staging the subjugation of the fairies—of female powers—to Louis XIV.

Just two years after d'Auneuil declared the end of the tyranny of fairies, Galland published his first volumes of *The Thousand and One Nights*, whose Scheherazade represents a continuity with the powerful female voice. But just as the powers of fairies were being questioned at this time, so was the power of the female voice. Following in the wake of Galland's translation and adaptation of *The Nights*, Pétis de La Croix published his *Story of the Sultana of Persia and the Forty Vizirs, Turkish Tales*, followed shortly thereafter by *Thousand and One Days, Persian Tales*, both of which were quickly translated into English, the *Turkish Tales* appearing in 1708, and both collections published together in 1714 as *The Persian and the Turkish Tales compleat*. Interestingly, both tale collections are presented as a sort of anti-*Thousand and One Nights*.²⁴

In *A Thousand and One Days*, whose title and structure Pétis very consciously modeled on *The Nights*, the princess Farrukhnaz plays the role of Schariar, mistrusting all men and being the bearer of a fatal beauty that drives men to their death; although deemed responsible for the downfall of numerous men, it must be said that Farrukhnaz possesses only a passive form of power—her beauty—as opposed to Shariar's active killing of women due to his political power as sultan. It is Farrukhnaz's nursemaid Sutlumemé who attempts, albeit unsuccessfully, to cure the princess of her hatred of men through stories about faithful lovers to restore order to the kingdom. Change only comes, however, with male trickery, thus foregrounding the powerlessness of the lower-class female storyteller. As Jean-François Perrin explains: "In the end, the tales by the nursemaid have no significant effect on the imagination of the princess; it will take a false priest sent by a prince in love with her ... for her to finally accept, thanks to certain manipulations of her imagination ... to realize she is in love and desires to be married" (2004: 47).

In *The Turkish Tales*, the figure of the sultan, unlike Schariar, is too trusting of his wife, the sultana Canzade, who tries to convince the sultan to kill his own son (and her stepson) after the latter rejects her semi-incestuous advances. The discourse of the male Scheherazade-like characters—the forty vizirs who try to convince the king not to kill his son—alternates with that of the evil sultana who wishes to see her stepson dead, in other words, who incites the sultan to violence. In the case of both texts, it is in the end the male storytellers or tricksters who work toward the reestablishment of what is ultimately a male sociopolitical order.[25] Whereas in the *Nights* Scheherazade tries to counter *male* violence toward women, the Scheherazade-like characters in the case of Pétis de La Croix's collections try to ebb the flow of *female* violence toward men.

Read together, *The Persian* and *The Turkish Tales* could be viewed as working in concert to morally legitimate male subjects, all the while questioning the agency of powerful women. The female narrative voice is either rendered impotent, as in the case of Sutlumemé, or it is depicted as suspicious or even nefarious, as in the case of the sultana Canzade. Powerful women in both collections are represented as threatening to the male body and to male sovereignty: princes are killed or threatened with death while the kings are rendered vulnerable due to the demands of their daughters or wives. Although Sutlumemé attempts, like Scheherazade, to subdue the main source of violence in the story, unlike Scheherazade, her attempts prove fruitless; only a man can overcome the source of female violence toward men. The case of the sultana Canzade proves even more problematic: whereas it is Princess Farrukhnaz's beauty and indifference that is fatal—a passive form of violence—it is Canzade's poisonous tongue that threatens Prince Nourgehan and ultimately the male lineage of the emperor of Persia, posing, in the final analysis, a political threat to the kingdom. In its status as a sort of response to *The Thousand and One Nights*, Perrin argues that "the *Thousand and One Days* questions ... the power of tales in general" (2004: 50).[26] We might add: it also questions the power wielded by women, whether that power reside in their beauty, their social positions, or their words. The female storyteller has been disempowered.

Such disempowerment of women takes new shape in Diderot's *Les Bijoux indiscrets* (*The Indiscreet Jewels*, 1748). Already from the birth of the sultan Mangogul, the oriental tale's hero, fairies are delegitimated. Whereas fairies from the 1690s often gave newborns various qualities and talents, the father of Mangogul, Erguebzed, "didn't gather the fairies around the cradle of his son, for he had remarked that most of the princes of his time whom these female intellects had educated, had been nothing but fools" (Diderot [1748] 1965: 29). We have come a long way from Murat's fairies, who give wit and eloquence to the worthy, or Galland's Scheherazade, endowed with "admirable wisdom" and a "prodigious memory." The pretext of Diderot's novel comes about when the sultan's favorite, Mirzoza, runs out of scandalous stories to tell him, and bored, Mangogul obtains a ring from the male genie Cucufa, which gives the sultan the power to make women's sex organs—referred to as "jewels"—speak. Given the favorite's name, one wonders if Diderot was familiar with Basile's *Tale of Tales*, whose heroine Zoza (recalling Mirzoza) incites the storytelling process and is the final storyteller of the collection, powerfully relating the truth that leads to the frame narrative's resolution. Mirzoza is clearly cast as a Scheherazade who has lost her power to entertain the sultan, and as such she anticipates Théophile Gautier's "Mille et deuxième nuit" ("Thousand and Second Night," 1842), in which Scheherazade, no longer able to invent more stories for Shariar, goes to the male author for a story she can relate to the sultan to avoid being killed. In the end, the figure of Mirzoza stages women's loss of storytelling powers.

Not only do women lose their storytelling power in the tale, as in the case of Mirzoza, but also their voices are further delegitimated. Mangogul wishes to learn the "adventures" of the women of court, but the only way to access this knowledge, according to Cucufa, is not through their mouths but through their "jewels," which he calls "the most honest part that is in them, and the best instructed in the things you wish to know" (Diderot [1748] 1965: 40). Later the question arises, "when the mouth and the jewel of a woman contradict each other, which one is to be believed?" and the answer, unsurprisingly within the logic of the tale, is the jewel, for, as Mangogul insists, "what reason would jewels have to disguise the truth?" (53). In effect, the sultan uses magical powers to extract the truth from his female subjects, a truth that will not come from their speech but forcibly from their sex. In line with earlier misogynistic traditions, Diderot's text suggest that most women are hardly faithful, at the same time that it sexualizes "exotic," oriental women through the jewels' narratives of their sexual exploits.

Drawing from the work of previous scholars, Madeleine Dobie reiterates the ways in which *The Indiscreet Jewels* serves as an allegory for the reign of Louis XV:

> Mangogul's use of the ring operates on one level as a thinly veiled allegory of Louis XV's use of police reports to garner information about the goings-on at his court. The king purportedly devoted his *petits levers* to hearing

the accounts of scandalous behavior gathered in the course of the previous evening by his chiefs of police. This practice of espionage may have served primarily as an amusement, but it certainly also fulfilled the king's will to exercise control over his subjects by learning their secrets, a technique that has been a feature of all authoritarian regimes ... Viewed in this light, Mangogul begins to look like an "Oriental despot": a figure for the absolutist tendencies and social and political corruption of the Bourbon monarchy.

(2001: 117)

As we saw in other fairy and oriental tales, authors use the imaginary space of the storyworld—whether that be fairyland or the Orient—to grapple with questions related to political power in France, and Diderot's oriental tale is no exception. However, even if we read Mangogul's despotic attempts to forcibly attain knowledge from the women at court in terms of a critique of Louis XV, the allegorical reading nevertheless fails to undo the delegitimation of the power of the female voice.[27] Even if Diderot is seeking to criticize Louis XV, the tale only victimizes the female characters, it is only the women who are subjected to acts of sexual aggression—a man forcibly using their sexual organs—which violates the integrity of their subjectivity. Moreover, the stories related by the jewels only make the female characters appear all the worse, revealing that they hide behind façades of virtue and prove to be, more often than not, unfaithful. Even if Mangogul rids himself of the ring after using it on Mirzoza—ostensibly to revive her when she is unconscious—the damage is done. Women have been revealed to be untrustworthy, their words deemed suspect, and it is the male genie who has the last word.

Beginning with Préchac and d'Auneuil, we witness the undoing of powerful female characters when fairies are painted in predominantly negative terms and slavishly subjugated to the apparatus of the state, whether by being quite literally attached to architectural monuments of the monarchy or to machines that support its glory. And while Galland's Scheherazade represents a continuity with the heroines of the 1690s *conteuses* in the power of her words, the oriental tales that grow out of the tradition of *The Thousand and One Nights* tend to turn Galland's frame narrative on its head. Pétis de La Croix casts female storytellers who lack power to transform through storytelling or whose storytelling skills are to be mistrusted. This disempowerment takes new shape in Diderot's Mirzoza, a Scheherazade-like figure whose pool of stories has dried up, which leads the sultan to use magical powers to force women to reveal their secrets through their sex organs. Even taking into account the allegorical meanings of *The Indiscreet Jewels*, the violation of women's agency and the delegitimations of their words is never quite undone.

Such shifts in the power of women's words as represented in fairy and oriental tales corresponds to shifts in French society. The women-led salons were being challenged by the monarchy, which sought to increase its hegemony over the French cultural and literary field through the proliferation of official and for the most part exclusively male academies. This gendered shift occurs just as, in the realm of the tale, the woman-dominated fairy tale gives way to the almost exclusively male-authored tradition of the oriental tale.[28] Within the general genre of the tale, women indeed lost their storytelling powers.

While fairy tales are often construed as being innocent, escapist, and sometimes frivolous narratives, this overview of power in the fairy and oriental tale in the long eighteenth century clearly foregrounds the ways in which tales indeed can be used to reflect on questions of political and social power. In a period in which direct criticisms of the monarchy could land someone in prison or force one into exile, authors could use tales to allegorically question what many felt was the arbitrary exercise of power. Through fairy tales, women authors could both represent the "real" empowered women who thrived before Louis XIV's monarchy peaked in authoritarianism, and take issue with and imagine alternatives to his patriarchal and absolutist regime. With the rise of the oriental tale, which relied on the racist stereotype of the oriental despot based primarily on early modern perceptions of the Ottoman Empire, authors used the figure of the sultan to criticize the authoritarian and repressive monarchies of Louis XIV and Louis XV.

With the exception of Préchac and d'Auneuil, authors of fairy and oriental tales predominantly used the genre to attack and not support absolute monarchy. However, a split occurs with the rise of the oriental tale when it comes to the question of gender and the social and political power of women. Already through the genre of the fairy tale, Préchac and d'Auneuil stage the decline of the fairies, that is, of powerful women, who are subjugated to the machine of the state, as if powerful women represent an antithesis to absolutism, which only foregrounds the patriarchal nature of the latter. Authors of oriental tales, in particularly Pétis de La Croix and Diderot, further implement the disempowerment of women and the female voice through various strategies of delegitimization. Scheherazade marks the last of the powerful women storytellers and "fairies" (as defined by Murat), to be supplanted by female characters whose storytelling powers are weak or weakened, as in the case of Sutlumemé or Mirzoza; or whose words are suspect, as in the case of Canzade as well as the mouths—vs. the "jewels"—of Diderot's female characters.

At a time of political and social repression, fairy and oriental tales not only provided a venue for criticism; they could also provide imaginary sites through which to imagine other possibilities. Through the genre of the tale, a commoner could become noble, a mortal could overcome a genie, a woman could outsmart her abuser through the use of wit and sometimes a bit of magic. The use of imaginary spaces allows one to imagine other, more just worlds, where arbitrary, patriarchal power can be overturned and defeated. Far from being simply a literature of diversion, the fairy and oriental tale are grounded in the social and political power dynamics of their time.

NOTES

Introduction

1. On the disempowerment of the female storyteller, see Chapter 8, this volume, "Power: Gender, Class, and Politics in *Ancien Régime* Fairy and Oriental Tales."
2. On the culturally different understandings of the marvelous, see Chapter 7, this volume, "Socialization: Tales of Wonder as Slight Channels."
3. On the importance of the Italian tradition on the French tale, see Chapter 2, this volume, "Adaptation: From Italy and France to Folk Traditions."
4. The data for Tables 0.1 and 0.2 draws from the work of Bottigheimer (2002b), Grenby (2006), Jones (2008), Lathey (2016), Palmer (1975), and Schacker (2018). As Palmer and Palmer have documented, d'Aulnoy's name became synonymous with the concept of "fairy tale" to the point where tales by other authors were attributed to her: "In 1785 when Clara Reeve looked back seven or eight decades recalled Mme d'Aulnoy as 'a famous composer of Fairy Tales' was correct in singling Mme d'Aulnoy out for special attention as an of *contes de fées*, but she did not know that twenty-eight of the tales which came into England under Mme d'Aulnoy's name were by four other French writers" (1974: 227).
5. Bottigheimer argues "the d'Aulnoy material was first marketed to economically and socially privileged buyers, later to merchant readers, and finally to artisanal and child readers. As the collection of tales moved downmarket in social and/or economic terms, its prose was altered to address the consumers its publishers sought" (2002b: 15n1). Jones also remarks on this shift in audience (2008: 242). Regarding adaptations of d'Aulnoy's tales in British pantomime productions, see Schacker (2018).
6. Regarding the popularity of *The Nights* in England, Duncan Macdonald notes that "this title was already so well known in 1709 that literary allusion could be made to it" (1932: 406).
7. Zipes reiterates this in *Grimm Legacies*, stating: "The group of young women in the Hassenpflug family ... spoke French at home and were clearly influenced by reading or hearing French fairy tales. They contributed over thirty stories [to the Grimms] and may have heared some from an elderly housekeeper by the name of Marie Müller. They generally spoke in a Hessian dialect and mixed German with French stories" (2015: 17).

8. On the type of works published and an overview of percentages of what was covered by two of the presses, see Martin (1978: 79). Upon consulting the *Bibliothèque bleue* databased through the ARTFL Project with the University of Chicago and "Le Patrimoine numérisé" (The Digital Patrimony) through the Troyes Champagne médiathèque, which is far from exhaustive, at least twelve of d'Aulnoy's tales were issued at least once in the eighteenth century, including: "Gracieuse et Percinet" (1738, 1754), "Le Prince Marcassin" (1745, 1762), "La Grenouille bienfaisante" (1765, 1788), "Le Prince Lutin" with "Fortuné" (1765), "Babiole" (1782), "Le Nain jaune" (1782), "Serpentin vert" (1782), "La Bonne petite souris" (1790), "Le Mouton" (1790), "La Princesse Belle-Etoie et le Prince Chéri" (1795), and "Le Rameau d'or" (1795). Between the two databases, we find only "Peau d'âne" by Perrault, two tales by Murat—"Le Parfait amour" (1765) and "Jeune et belle" (1754–65)—one by Lubert, "La Princesse Lionnette et le Prince coquerico" (1700), and two published together by La Force, "Tourbillon" and "Le Prince désiré" (1795).
9. With respect to German women's role in the development of the genre, Blackwell importantly remarks: "Between 1790 and 1810, Sophie Albrecht, Benedikte Nauvert, Caroline Auguste Fischer, Frederike Helene Unger, Karoline de la Motte-Fouqué, Johanna Eleonore von Wallenrodt ... all published fairy tales or fairy tale collections. All this publication preceded the appearance of the Grimms' two-volume collection in 1812/1815" (2001: 3).
10. On Tieck and other German writers' drawing from French and oriental tales, see Zipes (2006: 80).
11. On the role of Fielding and Leprince de Beaumont in the emergence of children's literature, see Chapter 3, this volume, "Gender and Sexuality: From the *conteuses* to the English Governess."
12. On the problematic representation of gender in Perrault's tales, see for instance Duggan (2008, 2019).
13. On Perrault limiting women's agency to the domestic sphere, see for instance Duggan (2008).
14. For example, in Leprince de Beaumont's discussion following the telling of "Beauty and the Beast," one of the girls compares the Beast to her father's Black lackey, positing the equivalency of blackness and ugliness.
15. See in this volume Chapter 4, "Humans and Non-Humans: Ambiguities of Agency and Personhood in Fairy Tales, 1650–1800"; Chapter 5, "Monsters and the Monstrous: Of Ogre Pyramids, Ruby-Eyed Dragons, and Gnomes with Crooked Spines"; and Chapter 6, "Space and Narrative Strategies in Eighteenth-Century Tales in East and West."
16. On the relation between French opera and fairy tale, see Duggan (2004). On the impact of the fairy tale on French, Italian, and Russian theater, opera, and ballet, see Chapter 1, this volume, "Forms of the Marvelous: The Eighteenth-Century *merveilleux*."

Chapter 1

1. For a thorough survey of the oriental tales, see Perrin (2004–5).
2. On the influence of theatrical works on magical subjects on Marie-Catherine d'Aulnoy and other French fairy-tale writers, see Duggan (2005: 201–39).
3. See Racine's preface to his *Iphigénie* in which the playwright claimed that the marvelous whatever might have "found some credence in the age of Euripides ... would have appeared to us as too absurd and incredible" (quoted in Garlington 1963: 485).

4. Carlo Goldoni's comedies were such an accurate representation of everyday Venetian life that the audience was convinced it was watching real events affecting real people during the performance. In his numerous formulation of his dramatic poetics, Goldoni continued to refer to the terms of neoclassical poetics (*bienséance, vraisemblance*, order, nature), clearly positioning himself in the context of French rationalist aesthetic thought.
5. For further information on English pantomime, cf. Schacker (2012). For an account of German fairy *singspiels*, see Buch (2004).
6. See Bahier-Porte (2007).
7. For the complete list of dramatic works based on Perrault's collection of the *contes de fées*, see the appendix to Poirson (2009: 310–15).
8. Cf. also Sermain (2013: 138–40).
9. Grétry's comic opera has largely inspired George Colman's pantomime *Blue Beard, or Female Curiosity!* (1798) that in its turn gave rise to the transposition of literary fairy tales, already well established in English chapbook form, into pantomimes, opera parodies, and orientalized melodramas on the British eighteenth-century stage. Cf. Hermansson (2009: 55–66).
10. The discussion of Gozzi's fairy play is adapted from Korneeva (2019: 91–114).
11. Over the next several years following the first performance of *L'Amore* by Antonio Sacco's *commedia dell'arte* troupe in the 1761 carnival season, Gozzi produced nine more theatrical fables: *La donna serpent* (The Serpent Woman), *Turandot*, *Il Corvo* (The Raven), *Il Re Cervo* (The Stag King), *L'uccellino belverde* (The Green Bird), *I Pitocchi Fortunati* (The Fortunate Beggars), *Il Mostro Turchino* (The Blue Monster), *La Zobeide*, and *Zeim, re de' geni* (Zeim, King of the Genies).
12. Recent scholarship has acknowledged that the play's main sources lie in the fairy-tale and *commedia* traditions. On folktales as a principal source of Gozzi's inspiration, see Fabrizi (1978). Fabrizi's analysis of the six Italian versions of *L'amore* underscores the divergence of Gozzi's play from the literary tradition of fairy tales stemming from Giambattista Basile's collection *Lo cunto de li cunti*, evident already in how Gozzi transforms the princess Zoza who never laughs from Basile's frame story into a male protagonist of his dramatic tale. In his 1989 study, Piermario Vescovo emphasizes, on the other hand, Gozzi's heavy reliance on the *commedia* tradition (Vescovo 1989).
13. It is useful to recall that *L'amore delle tre melarance* is the only one of Gozzi's plays that was published not as a fully scripted dramatic text, as was the case for his other nine fairy-tale dramas, but in the unusual form of a "reflexive analysis" (a term taken from the complete title of the play, *Analisi riflessiva della fiaba "L'Amore delle tre melarance"*): a dramatic outline with extensive authorial commentary on the comedy's content.
14. See "La prefazione al 'Fajel'," in Gozzi (2013: 189).
15. Catherine II (1786), *Fevei, opera comicheskaia, sostavlena iz slov skazki, pesnei russkikh i inykh sochinenii*. *Fevei* was staged at Saint Petersburg Stone Theatre on April 19, 1789, and presented for the court audience at the Hermitage Theatre a few days later. Catherine was not the sole author of the text, which was subtitled "compiled from the words of a fairy tale, Russian songs and other works," as the verses of the vocal numbers were largely composed by her private secretary Alexander Khrapovitskii or taken from the preexisting poetry. Vasilii Pashkevich's music was a mixture of folk songs, which Catherine's probably saw as a tribute to native Russian arts, and reminiscences of Italian comic opera.

16. This precursor to Leprince de Beaumont's version of "Beauty and the Beast" is embedded in Gabrielle-Suzanne Villeneuve's 1740 novel *La Jeune Américaine et les contes marins*, where it is also recounted by a governess for the entertainment and instruction of her pupil during the course of a sea voyage.
17. A rich vein of recent critical works on fairy tales has shown how many fairy-tale writers questioned the official order and the norms of femininity and marriage through their tales and proposed more liberatory models. While acknowledging that there are also some important limits to the *conte*'s ideological subversiveness, Seifert recognizes in the tales of women writers a rethinking of sexual desire and gender, which sometimes threw into question the very possibility of matrimonial bliss and the "happy ending" we expect from the genre; see in particular Seifert (1990).
18. Voltaire ([1767] 1877: 277). Translation is from the Introduction to *Candide and Other Stories* (2006: xliii).
19. Sade's relationship to the fairy-tale fiction has been explored by Rifelj (1990).
20. On the subversion of the moral tales and the rise and the popularity of the immoral tales, see Veysman (2009).
21. See Defrance (2002).

Chapter 2

1. On the leather binding of this edition, the title is "Fairy Tales." The edition is available at the Pierpont Morgan Library in New York.
2. The fairy tale as a literary genre is a name for a group of stories scattered in a broader category that Stith Thompson categorized in the subcategorization A: Ordinary Folktales, as "Tales of Magic." Until recently, scholars used to categorize the corpus of fairy tales from this literary vogue as divided between folktales and tales purely invented by the writers. The folktales are classified under a tale-type, by a number according to the main structure and motifs recurring. This number starts with ATU, which stands for Aarne, Thompson, and Uther, the folklorists who invented or completed this classification.
3. The pastoral novel was a fashionable literary genre in the sixteenth and seventeenth centuries and idealized the countryside life, focusing on the love of shepherds and shepherdesses. Famous examples are Torquato Tasso's *Aminta* (1573), Honoré D'Urfé's *L'Astrée* (1607–27), and Charles Sorel's satirical *Le Berger extravagant* (1627–8), all bestsellers in France at the time of their publication.
4. On Leprince de Beaumont as the first fairy-tale author targeting a children's audience, see Seifert (2004).
5. For more on French editions, see Bottigheimer (2005).
6. Nicolò Toppi's *Bibliotheca Napoletana* was printed for the first time by Bulifon in 1678. This ambitious book referred Neapolitan authors and their manuscript and printed works from the origins of Naples to the year of publication. Nicodemo took over Toppi's task on his death in 1681. The *Addizioni* date from 1683 and came from the printing press of Giacomo Raillard, Bulifon's colleague, another French installed in Naples (Magnanini 2007b: 81–5).
7. Straparola never integrated this sort of narrative into his tales, but instead he always opened the story with a precept in prose.
8. Benedetto Croce specifies that "peccerille" should not be taken literally: he gave the title of *Lo cunto of the cunti overo lo trattenemiento de' peccerille*, which did not mean that it was composed for children, as some and especially the Grimms

believed, taking literally the joke of the title. It was, on the contrary, composed for literate, expert, and experienced men, who knew how to understand and appreciate complicated and ingenious things (Croce 1982: xxxiv).
9. In Basile the sleeping princess gives birth to twins, one of whom suckles at her finger, removes the splinter that put her to sleep, and the heroine awakes.
10. "Donkey Skin" was recently analyzed by Catherine Velay-Valentin in relation to the French tradition, although she did not include the Italian sources that correspond to the tale-type in her analysis. For Perrault, see "L'orza" (II-6) by Basile and I-4 by Straparole, which correspond to the legend of "Donkey Skin"; "The Penta mano-mozza" (III-2) by Basile, which corresponds to that of "The Maiden without Hands." For L'Héritier, see Velay-Valentin's analysis of "The Soldier-girl" as a source of "Marmoisan," which does not establish the relationship between her tale and that of Basile (III-6). If Velay-Valentin was aware of these versions, she probably would not have repeated a historical aberration such as: "The sources of Charles Perrault, Mlle L'Héritier, Madame d'Aulnoy and other storytellers from the provincial aristocracy are the results of listening and collecting works from nannies and farmer storytellers. They allowed the court aristocracy to recognize themselves in these authors" (Velay-Valentin 1992: 32; my translation).
11. See my article (Trinquet 2007) "On the Literary Origins of Folkloric Fairy Tales"; and Barchilon's (2009) "Adaptation of Folktales and Motifs in Madame d'Aulnoy's Contes."
12. On the folklorization of literary tales, see Trinquet (2007: 37).
13. This is typical of not only Straparola but also Basile's stories, and of the entire tradition of early modern fairy tales. It is also how Basile's frame story is formed.
14. In the Grimm brothers' version, the stepmother turns the brother half-blind and the heroine half-deaf through witchcraft. Following an absurd dialogue between the three characters, the stepmother throws the heroine into the river through the car window as it drives over a bridge. The blindness of the brother explains the fact that he did not see the substitution and that he presents his stepsister to the king.

Chapter 3

1. Emphasizing the consistent treatment of gender in the interpolated tale and framing novel, Stedman (2005) discusses how d'Aulnoy encouraged her salon contemporaries "to view the literary fairy tale as a powerful new genre" capable not only of representing society but of participating in "changing the rules that governed it" (41).
2. For the titles of tales written by women in this period see Seifert and Stanton (2010: 311–13).
3. Marriages such as that of the King and Grognon have been read as representations of *mésalliance* (misalliance) between nobility and a financier class; see Hannon (1998: 52–4).
4. Published in L'Héritier's *Oeuvres meslées* (1695–8), this tale was long attributed to Perrault. Multiple editions of Perrault's works published in England, in both English and French, included the tale as his.
5. See Duggan (2001) for a discussion of d'Aulnoy's rejection of gendered mind/body, culture/nature dichotomies.
6. This deliberately truncated history refers only to fairy tales from the 1690s. Along with Perrault's "Donkey Skin" and "Sleeping Beauty," and L'Héritier's "Finette," d'Aulnoy refers to three of her own works. On framing and intertextuality in the works of the conteuses, see Harris (2001: esp. 31–3 and 40–3).

7. For an account of relationships between the late seventeenth-century French fairy tale and the earlier Italian works of Basile and Straparola, see Trinquet (2012).
8. See Duggan (2005: 198–207).
9. On the relationship of "Little Red Riding Hood" to the oral tradition, and to versions of the tale in which the little girl escapes the wolf, see Zipes (1993: 18–31) and Vaz da Silva (2016: 167–90).
10. Sharon P. Johnson has found "striking similarities" between Perrault's "normalizing voice of violence" and "entries of *rapt*, rape, and murder in contemporary legal manuals" describing how the manuals represent men as naturally aggressive and "women are blamed for the criminal behavior of their aggressors" (2003: 325). For a discussion of the exculpation of predatory male desire and the consequent abjectification of female characters in several of Perrault's works, see Duggan (2008).
11. Villeneuve included the tale in her *La jeune Américaine et les contes marins* ([1740] 2008). The most accessible version of the tale in English is in Zipes (1991a: 153–229).
12. The story was anthologized as "Beauty and the Beast, an entertaining moral tale from the French" in *The Polite Academy, or school of behaviour for young gentlemen and ladies*, 4th edn (London, 1762). This work was in its tenth edition by the end of the century.
13. For the argument that Leprince de Beaumont's *Magazine* enables unconventional gender identification, see Seifert (2004: 35–6).

Chapter 4

1. Defining the relation between the human and the non-human necessarily implies consideration of the relation between nature and culture. The binary oppositions nature vs. culture and human vs. non-human are of course closely—inextricably— linked, even if usefully understood as separate. As categories, "nature" and "culture" are broader and more general than "human" and "non-human," which focus on the actors within both nature and culture. Nature is the raw material humans use to produce culture. It is thus the realm of the non-human *and* the human. Culture is the human product that requires natural resources in addition to human effort.
2. This is a problematic distinction to be sure, especially when narratives from other cultures are considered (e.g., African animal "fables").
3. In his *Morphology of the Folktale* (1928), Vladimir Propp studied a corpus of one hundred Russian folktales to arrive at a set of structural laws involving seven "spheres of action" (villain, donor, helper, princess and father, dispatcher, hero, false hero) and thirty-one "functions" or narrative sequences, of which the most fundamental are "lack" and "liquidation of lack" (Propp 1968).
4. "Femme de courage masle & Guerrier" (Académie française 1694). Unless otherwise indicated, all translations are my own.
5. The word "jargon" in seventeenth-century France is defined as "Faulty and corrupted language of the people, of peasants, that is difficult to understand" (Furetière 1701).
6. On the intersection of d'Aulnoy's fairy tales and French colonial attitudes, see Lau (2016).
7. To the extent that the term "non-human" retains the centrality of the human as a point of reference, it is admittedly problematic if the critical impetus behind the human vs. non-human binary is to decenter the human and to resituate it within the full range of life forms and material objects on Earth. However, because it is widely accepted and because there is no other ready equivalent, I will use the term in this chapter, alongside others such as natural, material, animate, and inanimate.

8. I treat the case of non-human life forms that are the result of metamorphosis later in this chapter.
9. It is noteworthy that Propp's morphological scheme designates "departure" as a "connective" rather than a "function."
10. D'Aulnoy's treatment of nature also contrasts with Perrault's, particularly as a basis for gender difference. Anne Duggan has argued that, for Perrault, the natural ideal creates a passive, submissive femininity that contrasts sharply with the dominatrix of "civilized" femininity. His is a highly traditional and patriarchal conception whereby women are matter to which men must give form. For d'Aulnoy, by contrast, nature provides for the equality of the sexes and further for active and powerful women. Duggan also shows how d'Aulnoy anticipates Rousseau's tripartite distinction between "savage," "barbaric," and "civilized" man, with the "barbaric" being the self-conscious natural ideal. See Duggan (2001). In their treatment of nature, d'Aulnoy's fairy tales in particular display a sensitivity to the interconnections between nature and culture even as they anticipate evolving philosophical understandings of how the human is imbricated in and with the non-human.
11. See Sahlins (2017) on the transition from "humanimalism" (the tendency to blur distinctions between human and animal and to endow animals with anthropomorphic traits) to what he calls "Classical naturalism" (the clear distinction between categories of human and animal that devalorized both). On the early modern representation of animals, see also Fudge (2006).
12. One sees here that young children,
    Especially young girls,
    Beautiful, good looking, and nice,
    Are very wrong to listen to all manner of people,
    And that it's not a strange thing,
    If there are so many the wolf eats.
    I say the wolf, for all wolves
    Are not of the same sort;
    There are some of an affable disposition,
    Without clamor, without bile, without anger,
    Who, overly friendly, obliging and gentle,
    Follow young Maidens
    Right into their homes, right to their bedsides;
    But alas! Who doesn't know that these sweet-talking Wolves,
    Of all the Wolves are the most dangerous.
    (Perrault 2005: 202–3)
13. If the son of a Miller, with such speed,
    Wins the heart of a Princess,
    And gets her to look at him with expiring eyes
    It's that clothing, countenance, and youth
    To inspire tenderness,
    Are, for that, not always unimportant means.
    (Perrault 2005: 218)
14. On animal-human relations in this fairy tale, see Seifert (2011).
15. For other important theoretical work in this emerging field, see Bennett (2010), Braidotti (2019), Grosz (2017), and Latour (2004).
16. This tale, first published in 1710, does not appear in the Arab manuscript that is the basis for the first volumes of Galland's *Thousand and One Nights* but a version of it

was orally related to Galland by Diyab, and Galland then expanded upon the overall structure of the tale provided by Diyab.
17. My thanks to Anne Duggan for suggesting this insight.
18. Bronwyn Reddan has argued that tales by d'Aulnoy, L'Héritier, and Murat place limits on the agency of their heroines, yet their use of magical objects "opens up spaces for imagining different identities for women" (Reddan 2016: 205).

Chapter 5

1. The examples are discussed below.
2. Translations of text are mine throughout, unless otherwise indicated. When possible, I have used existing translations of the titles of tales.
3. "Tourbillon" was first published in 1698 in Charlotte-Rose de Caumont La Force's *Les Contes des contes,* par Mademoiselle de ***. All references to "La Force" are to Caumont la Force.
4. *Oeuvres badines* and *badinages* can be translated as light-hearted works, or works of banter, chit-chat, or jest.
5. See Brunet (1866) on imaginary imprints in France.
6. See Barthes (1971), Butor (2008), and Serres (1968, 1980).
7. The beast with clinking scales who offers fireworks is Gabrielle-Suzanne de Villeneuve's beast in her *La Belle et la Bête* (*Beauty and the Beast*, [1740] 2010: 87). The crystal palace with its lake of mercury is from d'Aulnoy's "La Grenouille Bienfaisante" (*Contes des fées*, 2004: 677). I used this scene previously in Hoffmann (2005, 2016: n17).
8. On marvel in fairy tales, theater, and opera, see Duggan (2005: 216–49), Norman (2001), and Robert (1982: 372–3).
9. Robert (1982) devoted attention to things in fairy tales. Historians including Daston and those who contributed to *Things that Talk* (2007), Walvin (2017), and many others have allowed even the tiniest things to speak in new ways, to tell broad tales of culture, history, and meaning.
10. For a developed study of monsters within the broad category of "wonders," see Daston and Park (1998).
11. References to Antoine Furetière's *Dictionnaire universel* are to the 1690 edition, unless otherwise indicated.
12. "Ces gens ont versé dans un bourbier, quand ils en sont sortis c'étoit des monstres, on ne les conoissoit plus …. Monstre, se dit aussi de ce qui est mal fait, mal ordonné. Ce bâtiment est fort massif, a bien coûté, mais c'est un monstre en architecture, il n'ay a aucune symmetrie. Ce livre est fort sçavant, mais il n'y a point d'ordre, c'est un monstre, on n'y connoît rien."
13. The word "ogramorphosis" is a tip of my hat to Butor (2008) and "textamorphose." Butor's work has long influenced mine.
14. See the discussion of Giambattista Basile's "Lo cunto dell'uerco" ("Tale of the Ogre") below.
15. Pourquoi fait-il s'émerveiller,
    Que la raison la mieux sensé,
    Lasse souvent de trop veiller,
    Par des contes d'Ogre et de Fée,
    Ingénieusement bercée,
    Prenne plaisir à sommeiller?

    Perrault, "A Madame la Marquise de L***"
    ("To Madame the Marquessa of L***") "Peau d'Ane" (1991: 57)

16. For a brief overview of ogres, see France ([1992] 2006), Geider (2016), and Huet (1908).
17. "L'ogre était six fois plus haut que sa femme ... il n'avait qu'un grand vilain oeil ... il avait dans sa main un panier couvert; il en tira quinze petits enfants qu'il avait volés par les chemins, et qu'il avala comme quinze oeufs frais" (d'Aulnoy 2004: 448).
18. The double lumps front and back are a fairy-tale staple during this period and are used for both men and women. Grognon, in d'Aulnoy's "Gracieuse et Percinet" is also "bossue devant et derrière, et boîteuse des deux côtés" ("humped front and back, and limping on both sides," d'Aulnoy 2004: 52).
19. On pagodas, see the discussion below.
20. On cannibalism in fairy tales, see Fay (2008). Her article includes sources.
21. Anna Maria Luisa's eighteenth-century collection at the Pitti Palace.
22. The salamanders are in d'Aulnoy, "Chatte Blanche" ("White Cat," 2004: 786) and the bats in her "La Princesse Printanière" (282). The white viper with flaming eyes is in Lintot's "Le Prince Sincer" ([1735] 2007a: 205).
23. The term "megafauna" is Groom's (2018).
24. The green mice and winged frogs are in d'Aulnoy's "L'Oiseau Bleu" ("The Blue Bird," 2004: 218, 196) and the chickens in "La Princesse Printanière" (281–2). The snails are in "La Princesse Coque-d'oeuf et le Prince Bonbon" ("The Princess Eggshell and the Prince Bonbon") attributed to Lubert.
25. "La 'modernité' de ces 'objets' fantastiques tient non à la 'creation' personnelle des écrivains mais à la liberté et la fantaisie avec lesquelles ils ont agencé et associé des figures et des motifs empruntés; de là la fécondité de ces 'monstres' poétiques" (Sempère 2009: 245).
26. On the history of the *jeu de bague chinois* at the Trianon, see Heitzmann (2009). Her article includes engravings and watercolors of both the Monceau and Trianon carousels.
27. For some of the sleighs still at Versailles in the Musée des Carosses, see Figoli (2010, 2011). The Museum of the Decorative Arts in Montreal has a sleigh, possibly German from 1720 to 1750, in the shape of a winged dragon, inv. 1949.50.Df.6. Giuseppe Arcimboldo's 1585 sketches for elaborate sleighs are in the Uffizi Galleries and available on a number of sites, including the Web Gallery of Art (n.d.). See, for example, the sketch for a sleigh with figures of sirens.
28. See, for example, the chests of drawers with dragons by Antoine-Robert Gaudreaus in the Wallace Collection (1735–40 and 1739).
29. While French dictionaries have relatively little to say on the topic of the origins of the fairies, the 1741 Chambers *Cyclopaedia* reported various notions: that fairies descend from either the Larvae, the Lamia, the Parques, or the nymphs of Greek and Roman mytholgy, that they are some form of intermediate beings not gods, angels, men, or devils, that they are of "oriental extraction," inventions of the Persians and the Arabs, or a form of future-telling witches.
30. *Magotine* could be translated as an ugly, deformed, grotesque woman or a little monkey. Furetière's definition of *magot* in the *Dictionnaire universel* shows the intertwinings of meanings in the root: "signifie aussi un gros singe" ("also signifies a big monkey"); "se dit figurément des hommes difformes, laids, comme sont les singes, des gens mal bâtis. On a marié cette fille à un vilain magot, à un gros magot" ("is said figuratively of men who are deformed, ugly, as monkeys are, people who are poorly formed. That girl was married to an ugly magot, to a big magot," 1690: vol. 2, s.v. "magot").

31. Johns provides the conversion: 1 arshin = 28 inches, or 71 centimeters (Johns 2004: 12n4).
32. On "Baba Yaga," see Forrester (2013), Johns (2004), Naroditskaya (2018: 84, 109).
33. On frog and toad tales in trial fictions and fairy tales, see also Hoffmann (2001).
34. Muyart de Vouglans (1780: 103), cited in Milner (1960: 1:22).
35. The bibliography of the witch trials is enormous. For broad approaches to European trials, see Bechtel (1997) and Ankarloo and Henningsen (2001). Bechtel includes references to works, bibliographies, and specialized catalogs.
36. The verb *"féer"* could be translated as "to enchant" but it then loses its ludic effect. I prefer "to fairy."
37. The animal examples are taken from the following tales: cats (d'Aulnoy, "La Chatte Blanche," "The White Cat"); deer (d'Aulnoy, "La Biche au bois," "The Hind in the Woods"); monkey and princes with snail helmets (d'Aulnoy, "Babiole"); whiting king and coutiers with fish heads (Lubert, "La Princesse Camion," "Princess Camion"); rooster (Lubert, "La Princesse Lionette," "Princess Lionette"); beasts (versions of *La Belle et la Bête* by Villeneuve [1740] and Jeanne-Marie Leprince de Beaumont [1757]), crayfish (Lintot, "Tendrebrun et Constance").
38. On the tale in the context of porcelain, see Jones (2013: 185–6, 190).
39. The original German version is listed in the Bibliography. Shawn C. Jarvis (1992) summarizes the tale in English. He does not translate the title.
40. For more analysis of this tale see Sempere 2017:2–1.
41. For the history of Ferry, see Bondeson 2004:189–216.
42. See Bondeson 2004: 120–40; Hoffmann 2013: 299–305.
43. For additional details, see Hoffmann 2005.
44. On female imagination see also Park and Daston 1981: 162, 221, 330, 339–43, 363; Huet 1993; Todd 1995; Bondeson 1997: 144–69; Hoffmann 1997a, b.
45. "Orientalism" in the eighteenth century is an enormous field with many more tales and critical works than could be mentioned here. For aspects of orientalism specific to fairy tales, readers are referred to the critical notes, introductions, and bibliographies in Pétis de La Croix ([1707] 2006).
46. "Ethnology," Centre National de Ressources Textuelles et Lexicales (2012).
47. The entry for "cheval marin" which fits the description of a hippopotamus, includes: "Il y a quelques uns qui le décrivent avec des griffes aux pieds" ("Some describe it as having clawed feet"). The entry for *licorne* begins: "Animal sauvage, selon certains naturalistes. La licorne se trouve seulement en Afrique" ("Wild animal, according to certain naturalists. The unicorn is found only in Africa," Furetière 1690: s.v. "cheval marin"). I thank Kaleb Hardy for bringing the entry on the unicorn to my attention.
48. Pierre Richelet's *Dictionnaire françois* (1680) defined *barbares* as "peuples sans police, ignorans, et qui vivent d'une maniere grossière." The 1690 edition of Furetière's *Dictionnaire universel* added details: "Estranger qui est d'un pays fort éloigné, sauvage, mal poli, cruel, et qui a des moeurs forts differents des nostres. Rome a été plusieurs fois pillée par les barbares, on n'est plus si sujet aux incursions des barbares, les sauvages de l'Amerique sont fort barbares" ("Foreigner who is from a country far away, savage, impolite, cruel, and who has habits/customs very different from ours. Rome was pillaged several times by barbarians, we are no longer subjected as often to incursions by barbarians, the savages of America are very barbarian," Furetière [1690] 1978: s.v. "barbares"). In the 1727 edition revised and expanded by Henri Basnage de Beauval and Jean-Baptiste Brutel de la Rivière, the

Iroquois were specified and moved up in the definition: "Sauvage; féroce; cruel; qui a des moeurs grossieres, incultes, et farouches. Les Iroquois sont de vrais barbares" ("Savage, ferocious, cruel, who has habits/customs that are unrefined, uneducated and fierce. The Iroquois are true barbarians," Furetière 1727: s.v. "barbares"). On the complex history and usage of the words *barbare, barbaresque, Barbarie, berbère,* and *Berberie,* see Turbet-Delof (1973).
49. Among the many works on chinoiserie, see the exhibition catalog *Cathay Invoked* (1966[?]) and the book edited by Alden Cavanaugh and Michael E. Yonan (2017). Nodding pagoda figurines, both eighteenth-century antiques and copies, can be easily found on the internet.
50. I wrote on luxury glass and fairy tales in Hoffmann (2016).
51. "Au-delà de l'agrément, de la curiosité, de toutes les émotions que nous donnent des récits, des contes et des légendes ... le but réel du voyage merveilleux est, nous sommes déjà en mesure de le comprendre, l'exploration plus totale de la réalité universelle" ("Beyond pleasure, curiosity, all the emotions that stories, tales and legends give us ... the real goal of the marvelous voyage is, we are already in a position to understand it, the more complete exploration of universal reality," Mabille 1962: 24; cited by Todorov [1970] 2013: 62).
52. The notion of hinges belongs to Barthes and his discussion of "play" in texts, in the senses of playing games, playing an instrument, and play in doors. See Barthes (1971: 231 [French]; 1977: 162 [English]).
53. "They are the forerunners of the *Cabinet des Fées,* that monstrous collection in which the voice of tradition grows fainter almost with each successive tale, and the style increasingly flatulent" (Briggs 1976: 91). I have quoted her previously (Hoffmann 2005).

Chapter 6

1. See for general discussions of the phenomenon of space, among many others: Casey (1998); Crang and Thrift (2000); Lefebvre (1996); Malpas (1999).
2. For uses of space as narrative strategies in fantastic literature, see Wünsch (1991).
3. See, for instance, Davison (2009); see also Van Leeuwen (2017).
4. For discussions about this in various traditions, see Bonebakker (1997: 56–77; 1992: 21–43); Gernet (1987); and Minnis, Scott, and Wallace (1988).
5. For the influence of *The Thousand and One Nights* on European literature in the eighteenth century, see, among others, Dufrenoy (1946–75); Martino (1906); and Marzolph and Van Leeuwen (2004).
6. About this story, see Marzolph and van Leeuwen (2004: 1:341–5).
7. The story was first published in Caylus's collection *Le pot-pourri* (1748), after a more garbled French version had been published in Pétis de La Croix's collection *Les Mille et un jours.*
8. Mailly translated the initial stories from a 1557 Italian version by Cristoforo Armeno; Armeno presents his collection of tales as having been brought back from the Orient by an adventurer, translated into Italian; see Aude Volpilhac's "Une belle infidèle endormie," in Mailly ([1719] 2011).
9. See, for instance, "Abu Muhammad hight Lazybones," in Marzolph and Van Leeuwen (2004: 1:71–3).
10. See "The Porter and the Three Ladies of Baghdad" in Marzolph and Van Leeuwen (2004: 1:324–6).

11. See especially the stories of "Janshah" and the story of the "Third Qalandar" in Marzolph and Van Leeuwen (2004: 1:238–41 and 1:340–1).
12. "Le Crocheteur Borgne" ("The One-Eyed Porter") contains motifs such as a rogue confronting a princess, fate, an admonishing formula, a magical ring, an enchanted palace, etc. "Le Blanc et le noir" ("The White and the Black") is an oriental love story after the fashion of the *Nights*. Other stories, too, exemplify Voltaire's orientalism, such as "Aventure indienne" ("Indian Adventure"), "Lettre d'un turc sur les fakirs et sur son ami Babec" ("Letter by a Turk about Fakirs and His Friend Babec"), and "La Princess de Babylone" ("The Princess of Babylon"). See Voltaire (1958).
13. See Wieland (1992): "Die eiserne Armleuchter" (469–84), "Adis und Dahy" (49–95), and "Die Greif vom Gebirge Kaf" (487–96). See also Grätz (1988) and Tieck (1792).
14. Beckford adapted some stories from the Wortley-Montague manuscript of *The Thousand and One Nights*, which was in his possession at the time. See Beckford (1948).
15. Bignon's novel *Les Aventures d'Abdalla, fils d'Hanif* was published in 1712–14 in two parts under the pseudonym Sandisson. The work was left incomplete; it was completed by Colson and published in 1775. See Bignon ([1712–14] 1773: 1: 1–99, 132–77). For a modern edition, see that of Raymonde Robert (Bignon [1712–14] 2006).

Chapter 7

1. See also Dickens (1853).
2. See, for example, the book series *Pantheon Fairy Tale and Folklore Library*, which includes both translations of written tale collections from different moments of history and collections of oral folklore. In both Chinese and Japanese "fairy tale" is translated as "children's story" 童話.
3. For definitions of wonder tale in the European context, see the introductions by Zipes (1991b) and Warner (1994).
4. For notes on periodization in Japan, see Shirane (2004: 19). For an example equating the High Qing (*c.* 1683–1839) in China to the long eighteenth century, see Mann (1997).
5. I believe Fum-Hoam's name is inspired by a romanization of *fenghuang* 鳳凰, the legendary bird of East Asia often inaccurately translated as "Phoenix." The *fenghuang* shares the phoenix's rarity, but there is no legend of rebirth from ashes. *Feng* is a commonly used character in men's names, but *Huang* is not as it describes the female bird in a pair, and from the Chinese perspective he is lacking a family name. Though culturally inaccurate the name is serendipitously apt, suggesting a magical being further transformed by translation.
6. I am following the dating arguments in Barr (1984).
7. See "Liu zhihui zi ji san shang shi" 劉指揮子記三生事 *Kuai yuan* 8.6a–7b and "Wan shilang san sheng lunhui" 萬侍郎三生輪迴, *Kuai yuan* 8.11a–13b in Qian (2014: 8.247–8 and 8.250–2).
8. For the Chinese, see Pu (1992: 1:1.72–4).
9. For more on the frustrations common to men of Pu's class, see Barr (1986).
10. There were elite women capable of reading their works, and some certainly did so, but they did not explicitly address this audience. For more on this, see Huntington (2010).

11. Referring to *Bagh-o-Bahar* (*Garden and Spring*, or *The Tale of the Four Devishes*, 1801); *Baital paccisi* (*Twenty-five Tales of the Vampire*, 1802); and *Sinhānsan battīsī* (*Thirty-two Tales of the Throne*, 1801). See Pritchett (1991: 10).
12. See Williams (2012: 74). For more examples with full images and plot descriptions, see Edo Picture Books and Japonisme (2018).
13. Reprinted in Williams (2012: 97).
14. For more on Ji Yun's didactic practice, see Chan (1998).
15. See extensive discussion and complete translation in Ter Haar (2006: 58–60 and *passim*); for another translation and a reprint of the Chinese text, see Huang Chi-chun et al. (1993).
16. As Ter Haar points out, this plot point is more similar to an oral versions from France ([1992] 2006: 83).
17. An undated, late nineteenth- or early twentieth-century edition of this book from the collection of the Keio library is available through the Hathi Digital trust. Huang Chengzeng 黄承增 preface 1803, *Guang yu chu xin zhi* 廣虞初新志 (Huang 1803).
18. For a translation, see Planché (1867: 225–329).
19. See a reprint of the tale in original context in the appendix of Hearne (1989: 189–203).
20. Reprinted in Hearne (1989: 203).
21. See complete translation and discussion in Williams (2012: 160–95).
22. See, for example, "Gu'er" 賈兒; "Wutong" 五通 Pu (1992: 1:1.125–9; 10:1417–25).
23. Pu (1992: 1:1.119–24). Translated (except for final comment) by Minford in Pu (2006: 126–32).
24. Pu (1992: 1:2.160–8). Translated by Minford in Pu (2006: 168–79).
25. See Jōo (2011: 156–69). For a translation of Akinari's "A Serpent's Lust," see Shirane (2004: 287–302).
26. Pu (1992: 1:2.220–32). Translated by Minford in Pu (2006: 211–28).
27. Translation by John Ashberry in Warner (1994: 19–64). See discussion in Harries (2001: 40–3).
28. Ji (1982: 13.310) is a case of a concubine saying she is a fox whose destined time with her husband has ended, while in truth her mother had sold her to a second master and she was using this as a means of escape. 2.29 is an example of a woman who falsely blamed her out-of-wedlock pregnancy on an animated tomb figure, only to have both lovers punished by the slandered god.
29. See "Tale of the Fourth Dervish" on Frances Pritchett's site (Pritchett n.d-a, n.d.-b).
30. See the discussion of the formative period of strange tales in Campany (1996: 365–94).

Chapter 8

1. While the term "oriental" tale is indeed problematic and cannot be separated from the history of Orientalism, it is commonly used to refer to this tale trend. However, it is important to acknowledge Edward Saïd's observation about the genre: "the very power and scope of Orientalism produced not only a fair amount of exact positive knowledge about the Orient but also a kind of second-order knowledge—lurking in such places as the 'Oriental' tale, the mythology of the mysterious East, notions of Asian inscrutability—with a life of its own, what V.G. Kiernan has aptly called 'Europe's collective day-dream of the Orient'" (1979: 52). Also, I will use *The Thousand and One Nights* instead of the more commonly used *Arabian Nights* in English to respect the original title and foreground the connections with Pétis de La Croix's *Thousand and One Days*.

2. D'Aulnoy published her first tale, "L'Ile de la Félicité" ("The Island of Felicity") in 1690; it was interpolated into her novel, *Histoire d'Hypolyte, comte de Duglas*; her two collections of tales appeared in 1697–8 and 1698. Perrault had published individual tales in the French literary magazine *Le Mercure Galant* in 1691, 1693, 1694, and 1696; his first collection of verse tales appeared in 1695 and his most famous work in 1697.
3. For more on the impact of the French and Franco-Middle Eastern tale tradition on European fairy tales, see the "Introduction," this volume.
4. I also quote Johnson, Maxwell, and Trumpener in Duggan (2020a) where I discuss in more detail the specific impact of *The Thousand and One Nights* on the eighteenth-century French literary field.
5. Aravamudan explains: "*Enlightenment Orientalism* is the term that I propose for this nebulous form of transcultural fiction that interrogated settled assumptions. Enlightenment Orientalism was very much an imaginative Orientalism, circulating images of the East that were nine parts invented and one part referential, but it would be anachronistic to deem these images ideological, as they did not tend principally toward domination of the East in any single register" (2012: 3).
6. This is not meant to suggest in any way that the oriental tale is somehow inherently more problematic when it comes to gender than the fairy tale. Pétis de La Croix definitely shaped the future of the oriental tale by fashioning his collections as anti-*Arabian Nights*, and the fact that the genre was dominated by French male writers also explains in part this tendency.
7. On rise and restoration tales, see Bottigheimer (1994, 2002a).
8. Critics have determined that Diyab orally recounted the tale of Aladdin to Galland, who then greatly embellished it. On the history of Diyab's role in "Aladdin," see for instance Marzolph (2018).
9. In the tale, the future stepmother is "called" (*appelée*) the duchess Grognon, which suggests she isn't actually a duchess.
10. Hubert Carrier notes that during the Fronde "Madame de Longueville, in particular, seems to have distinguished herself in a specifically military role" by presiding over the war council, recruiting troops, and organizing defenses (2003: 50). For her part, Montpensier ordered "the firing of the Bastille cannon fired against the royal army" (45).
11. "The Blue Bird" draws its inspiration from the frame narrative of Giambattista Basile's *Tale of Tales, or Entertainment for Little Ones* in which the slave Lucia usurps the place of Princess Zoza beside Prince Tadeo.
12. Unless otherwise indicated, all translations are mine.
13. In his *Les Bourgeois Gentilshommes: An Essay on the Definition of Elites in Renaissance France* (1977), George Huppert discusses at length the financial and legal strategies the bourgeoisie used to acquire noble lands. Much of their success was due to the nobility's ignorance of how interest works. See in particular chapter 5 on the *bourgeois conquérant*, or "bourgeois conqueror."
14. On d'Aulnoy's biography, see Jasmin (2012). Some of this information is also based on an unpublished conference paper by Volker Schröder (2019).
15. On Murat's biography, see Patard (2012).
16. Although French dictionairies don't include the notion of "arbitrary" in their defininitions of "despot" and "despotism" until later in the eighteenth century, Antoine Furetière's 1690 dictionary suggests as much when he states: "A *despotic*

government is one in which the Prince does anything he wants, without justifying it to anyone."
17. D'Aulnoy's tale "Le Mouton" ("The Ram") similarly concerns a prince who refuses to give his heart to the ugly fairy Ragotte; the fairy punishes his failure to reciprocate her love by transforming him into a ram.
18. On the relation between the tale and the Machine de Marly, see Olivier (2005).
19. The first two state academies were created in 1635 (Académie Française) and 1648 (Académie royale de peinture et de sculpture, the only academy to admit women). From 1661—the year Louis XIV began his direct rule—to 1671, six state academies were created. See Duggan (2005: 45–8).
20. On the connections between Shariar, Usbek, and Louis XIV, see also Duggan (2020a).
21. On his exiles to England, see Davidson (2010: 58–73); on his alternation with Rohan-Chabot (54–5); and on his confinement to the Bastille (51–7).
22. Melusine forbids her husband to look upon her on Saturdays, when she turns half-serpent; she provides him numerous sons and he becomes very powerful, but eventually violates the taboo, and Melusine must leave him.
23. See, for instance, Jones (2013: 54–6); Méchoulan (2006); Defrance (2002: 61–2); and Bjørnstad (2009).
24. For a longer discussion of the relationship between these texts by Galland and Pétis de La Croix, see Duggan (2020b).
25. Although the manuscript from which Pétis de La Croix drew for his translation and adaptation was incomplete, the 1886 English translation of G. W. Gibb is based on a complete, undated manuscript from Constantinople, where we find a conclusion to the frame narrative, a conclusion that fits within the logic of what we already see in Pétis's version.
26. Perrin rightly argues that Farrukhnaz is a more active listener than Schariar, resisting the seductive and transformative function of the tales. However, this is not presented as something positive: her resistance to the moral of the stories demonstrates her irrational hatred or fear of men.
27. Dobie similarly remarks: "it is far from clear that this problematization neutralizes the exposure of female identity that these narratives perform" (2001: 119).
28. A few women such as Marianne-Agnès Falques (or Fauques), Olympe de Gouges, and the Anglo-Irish author Frances Sheridan penned oriental tales, but male writers dominated the trend. Besides the authors already mentioned, other important male authors include: Thomas-Simon Gueulette, Antoine Hamilton, Crébillon fils, Anne-Claude de Caylus, and Jacques Cazotte.

REFERENCES

Académie française, ed. (1694), *Le Dictionnaire de l'Académie Françoise: dédié au Roy*, Paris: Veuve Coignard.
Aldrovandi, Ulisse (1642), *Monstrorum historia, cum paralipomenis historiae omnium animalium*, Bononiae: typ. N. Tebaldini.
Ankarloo, Bengt and Gustav Henningsen, eds. (2001), *Early-Modern European Witchcraft: Centres and Peripheries*, New York: Oxford University Press.
Aravamudan, Srinivas (2012), *Enlightened Orientalism: Resisting the Rise of the Novel*, Chicago: University of Chicago Press.
Astbury, Katherine (2000), *The Moral Tale in France and Germany, 1750–1789*, Oxford: Voltaire Foundation.
Aulnoy, Marie-Catherine d' ([1697] 1997), *Contes I*, intro. Jacques Barchilon, ed. Philippe Hourcade, Paris: Société des Textes Français Modernes.
Aulnoy, Marie-Catherine d' ([1698] 1998), *Contes II*, intro. Jacques Barchilon, ed. Philippe Hourcade, Paris: Société des Textes Français Modernes.
Aulnoy, Marie-Catherine d' (1752), *The Court of Queen Mab: Containing a Select Collection of the Best, Most Instructive, and Entertaining Tales of the Fairies*, London: M. Cooper.
Aulnoy, Marie-Catherine d' (1855), *The Fairy Tales of Countess D'Aulnoy*, trans. J. R. Planché, London: G. Routledge & co.
Aulnoy, Marie-Catherine d' (2004), *Contes des fées: suivis des Contes Nouveaux, ou, Les fées à la mode*, ed. Nadine Jasmin and Raymonde Robert, Bibliothèque des Génies et des Fées 1, Paris: Champion.
Auneuil, Louise de Bossigny d', comtesse ([1702] 1990), *La Tyrannie des fées détruite*, Paris: côté-femmes.
Auneuil, Louise de Boissigny d', comtesse ([1702] 2005), "La Princesse Léonice," in Raymonde Robert (ed.), *Contes/Mlle Lhéritier, Mlle Bernard, Mlle de La Force, Madame Durand, Madame d'Auneuil*, Bibliothèque des Génies et des Fées, 571–94, Paris: Honoré Champion.
Auneuil, Louise de Boissigny d', comtesse (1710), *La Tyrannie des Fées détruite: Nouveaux contes*, Amsterdam: Estienne Roger.
Autreau, Jacques (1737), *La magie de l'amour*, La Haye: Antoine Van Dole.

Bahier-Porte, Christelle (2007), "Le conte à la scène: Enquête sur une rencontre (XVIIe–XVIIIe siècles)," *Féeries*, 4: 1–20.
Ballaster, Ros (2005), *Fabulous Orients: Fictions of the East in England 1662–1785*, Oxford: Oxford University Press.
Barchilon, Jacques (2009), "Adaptation of Folktales and Motifs in Madame d'Aulnoy's *Contes*: A Brief Survey of Influence and Diffusion," *Marvels & Tales*, 23 (2): 353–64.
Barr, Allan (1984), "The Textual Transmission of Liaozhai zhiyi," *Harvard Journal of Asiatic Studies*, 44 (2): 515–62.
Barr, Allan (1986), "Pu Songling and the Qing Examination System," *Late Imperial China*, 7 (1): 87–111.
Barthes, Roland (1971), "De l'oeuvre au texte," *Revue d'esthétique*, 24 (3): 225–32.
Barthes, Roland (1977), *Image-Music-Text*, trans. Stephen Heath, New York: Hill and Wang.
Basile, Giambattista (1634–6), *Lo cunto deli cunti overo lo trattenemiento de' peccerille, De Gian Alessio Abbattutis*, 5 vols, Naples: Ottavio Beltrano.
Basile, Giambattista ([1634–6] 1976), *Lo cunto de li cunti: Overo a trattenemiento de peccerille*, ed. Mario Petrini, Rome: Gius. Laterza & Figli.
Basile, Giambattista ([1634–6] 2007), *Giambattista Basile's The Tale of Tales, or, Entertainment for Little Ones*, trans. Nancy L. Canepa, Detroit, MI: Wayne State University Press.
Basile, Giambattista (1932), *The Pentamerone of Giambattista Basile*, ed. and trans. N. M. Penzer, 2 vols, London: E. P. Dutton and Company.
Basile, Giambattista (1982), *Il Pentamerone, Ossia la Fiaba delle Fiabe*, ed. Benedetto Croce, 2 vols, Rome: Editori Laterza.
Basile, Giambattista (1986), *Lo cunto de li cunti*, ed. and trans. Michele Rak, Milan: Garzanti.
Basile, Giambattista (2016), *The Tale of Tales, or Entertainment for Little Ones*, trans. Nancy L. Canepa, Detroit, MI: Wayne State University Press.
Bechtel, Guy (1997), *La Sorcière et l'Occident: La destruction de la sorcellerie en Europe des origines aux grands bûchers*, Paris: Plon.
Beckford, William ([1782] 1993), *Histoire du prince Ahmed*, Paris: José Corti.
Beckford, William (1948), *Vathek et les épisodes*, Paris: Stock.
Beckford, William (1992), *Suite de contes arabes*, Paris: José Corti.
Bennett, Jane (2010), *Vibrant Matter: A Political Ecology of Things*, Durham, NC: Duke University Press.
Berg, Stephan (1991), *Schlimme Zeiten, böse Räume; Zeit- und Raumstrukturen in der phantastischen Literatur des 20*, Stuttgart: Jahrhunderts, J. B. Metzler.
Bernard, Catherine, ([1694] 2005), "Riquet à la Houppe," in Raymonde Robert (ed.), *Contes/Mlle Lhéritier, Mlle Bernard, Mlle de La Force, Madame Durand, Madame d'Auneuil*, Bibliothèque des Génies et des Fées, 287–92, Paris: Honoré Champion.
Bernard, Catherine (1697), *Inès de Cordoue, nouvelle espagnole*, Paris: Martin et George Jouvenel.
Bignon, Jean-Paul ([1712–14] 1773), *Les aventures d'Abdalla, fils d'Hanif*, Paris: J. B. G. Musier.
Bignon, Jean-Paul ([1712–14] 2006), *Les aventures d'Abdalla*, ed. Raymonde Robert, Bibliothèque des Génies et des Fées 8, Paris: Champion.
Bjørnstad, Hall (2009), "Le savoir d'un conte moins conte que les autres: Le 'Sans Parangon' de Préchac et les limites de l'absolutisme," *Féeries*, 6: 163–78.

Blackwell, Jeannine (2001), "The Historical Context of German Women's Fairy Tales," in Shawn Jarvis and Jeannine Blackwell (eds. and trans.), *The Queen's Mirror: Fairy Tales by German Women, 1780–1900*, 1–10, Lincoln: University of Nebraska Press.

Boccaccio, Giovanni ([1353] 1955), *Il Decameron*, Bari: Laterza i Figli.

Boesche, Roger (1990), "Fearing Monarchs and Merchants: Montesquieu's Two Theories of Despotism," *Western Political Quarterly*, 43 (4): 741–61.

Boguet, Henry (1602), *Discours exécrable des sorciers, ensemble leur procez, faits depuis deux ans en ça, en divers endroits de la France, avec une instruction pour un juge, en faict de sorcelerie*, Paris: Denis Binet.

Bollème, Geneviève (1971), *La Bibliothèque bleue: La littérature populaire en France du XVIe au XIXe siècle*, Paris: Julliard.

Bondeson, Jan (1997), *A Cabinet of Medical Curiosities*, New York: W. W. Norton.

Bondeson, Jan (2004), *The Two-Headed Boy and Other Medical Marvels*, Ithaca, NY: Cornell University Press.

Bonebakker, S. A. (1992), "Some Medieval Views on Fantastic Stories," *Quaderni di studi arabi*, 10: 21–43.

Bonebakker, S. A. (1997), "*Nihil obstat* in Storytelling?," in Richard C. Hovannisian and Georges Sabbagh (eds.), *The Thousand and One Nights in Arabic Literature and Society*, 56–77, Cambridge: Cambridge University Press.

Bottigheimer, Ruth (1994), "Straparola's *Piacevoli Notti*: Rags-to-Riches Fairy Tales as Urban Creations," *Merveilles et Contes*, 8 (2): 281–96.

Bottigheimer, Ruth (2000), "Fairy Tales," in Matthias Konzett (ed.), *Encyclopedia of German Literature*, 267–70, Chicago: Fitzroy Dearborn Publishers.

Bottigheimer, Ruth (2002a), *Fairy Godfather: Straparola, Venice and the Fairy Tale Tradition*, Philadelphia: University of Pennsylvania Press.

Bottigheimer, Ruth (2002b), "Misperceived Perceptions: Perrault's Fairy Tales and English Children's Literature," *Childrens's Literature*, 30: 1–18.

Bottigheimer, Ruth (2005), "France's First Fairy Tales: The Restoration and Rise Narratives of *Les facetieuses nuictz du Seigneur Francois Straparole*," *Marvels & Tales*, 19 (1): 17–31.

Braidotti, Rosi (2019), *Posthuman Knowledge*, Cambridge: Polity Press.

Bree, Linda (1996), *Sarah Fielding*, New York: Twayne Publishers.

Brémond, Claude (1973), *Logique du récit*, Paris: Seuil.

Briggs, Katharine (1976), *An Encylopedia of Fairies*, New York: Pantheon Books.

Brunet, Gustave (1866), *Imprimeurs imaginaires et libraires supposés: étude bibliographique, suivie de recherches sur quelques ouvrages imprimés avec des indications fictives de lieux ou avec des dates singulières*, Paris: Tross.

Buch, David J. (2004), "Die Zauberflöte, Masonic Opera, and Other Fairy Tales," *Acta musicologica*, 76 (2): 193–219.

Buch, David J. (2008), *Magic Flutes and Enchanted Forests: The Supernatural in Eighteenth-Century Musical Theatre*, Chicago: University of Chicago Press.

Butor, Michel (2008), *Matière de rêves: Oeuvres complètes de Michel Butor*, ed. Mireille Calle-Gruber, vol. 8, Paris: Editions de la différence.

Byrne, Aisling (2016), *Otherworlds; Fantasy and History in Medieval Literature*, Oxford: Oxford University Press.

Cai, Qian (1995), *General Yue Fei*, trans. T. L. Yang, Hong Kong: Joint Publishing Co.

Cameron, Euan (2010), *Enchanted Europe: Superstition, Reason and Religion, 1250–1750*, Oxford: Oxford University Press.

Campany, Robert Ford (1996), *Strange Writing: Anomaly Accounts in Early Medieval China*, Albany: State University of New York Press.
Campbell, Joseph (1973), *The Hero with the Thousand Faces*, Princeton, NJ: Princeton University Press.
Canepa, Nancy L., ed. (1997), *Out of the Woods: The Origins of the Literary Fairy Tale in Italy and France*, Detroit, MI: Wayne State University Press.
Canepa, Nancy L. (1999), *From Court to Forest: Giambattista Basile's* Lo cunto de li cunti *and the Birth of the Literary Fairy Tale*, Detroit: Wayne State University Press.
Canepa, Nancy L. (2003), "Entertainment for Little Ones"? Basile's *Lo cunto de li cunti* and the Childhood of the Literary Fairy Tale," *Marvels & Tales*, 17 (1): 37–54.
Caracciolo, Peter L. (1988), "Introduction: 'Such a store house of ingenious fiction and of splendid imagery,'" in Peter L. Caracciolo (ed.), *The Arabian Nights in English Literature*, 1–80, New York: St. Martin's Press.
Carmontelle, Louis Carrogis (1779), *Jardin de Monceau*, Paris: Delafosse.
Carrier, Hubert (2003), "Women's Political and Military Action During the Fronde," in Christine Fauré (ed.), *Political and Historical Encyclopedia of Women*, 34–55, New York: Routledge.
Carter, Angela ([1978] 1993), *The Sadeian Women: An Exercise in Cultural History*, London: Virago.
Casey, E. S. (1998), *The Fate of Place: A Philosophical History*, Berkeley: University of California Press.
Cathay Invoked: Chinoisierie, a Celestial Empire in the West (1966[?]), California Palace of the Legion of Honor, Catalog of an exhibition held June 10 to July 31, 1966 [San Francisco].
Catherine II (1786), *Fevei, opera comicheskaia, sostavlena iz slov skazki, pesnei russkikh i inykh sochinenii*, Saint Petersburg: Izd-vo Imperatorskoi Akademii Nauk.
Cavanaugh, Alden and Michael E. Yonan, eds. (2017), *The Cultural Aesthetics of Eighteenth-Century Porcelain*, New York: Routledge.
Caylus, Anne Claude de (1748), *Le pot-pourri*, Amsterdam.
Cazotte, Jacques ([1772] 1957), *Le Diable amoureux: Nouvelle espaganole*, Lausanne: Guilde du Livre.
Cazotte, Jacques ([1788] 2012), *La Suite des Mille et une nuits; contes arabes*, ed. Raymonde Robert, Paris: Honoré Champion.
Centre National de Ressources Textuelles et Lexicales (2012), "Ethnologie." Available online: https://www.cnrtl.fr/definition/ethnologie (accessed December 6, 2020).
Chambers, Ephraim (1741), *Cyclopaedia, or, A Universal Dictionary of Arts and Sciences*, 4th rev. edn., London: D. Midwinter.
Chan, Leo Tak-Hong (1998), *The Discourse on Foxes and Ghosts: Ji Yun and Eighteenth Century Literati Storytelling*, Honolulu: University of Hawaii Press.
Chartier, Roger (1987), *Lectures et lecteurs dans la France d'Ancien Régime*, Paris: Seuil.
Cherbuliez, Juliette (2005), *The Place of Exile: Leisure Literature and the Limits of Absolutism*, Lewisburg, PA: Bucknell University Press.
Colman, George (1798), *Blue Beard, or Female Curiosity! A Dramatick Romance*, London: Cadell & Davies.
Contes/Madame Levesque, Madame de Gomez, Madame de Dreuillet, Madame de Lintot, Madame Fagnan, Madame de Gomez, Madame le Marchand, Madame de Lassay, Mademoiselle Falques (2007), ed. Raymonde Robert, Bibliothèque des Génies et des Fées 13, Paris: Champion.

Cottino-Jones, Marga (2000), "Princesses, Kings, and the Fantastic: A Re-Vision of the Language of Representation in the Renaissance," *Italian Quarterly*, 37: 173–84.

La Cour de France turbanisée et les trahisons démasquées (1687), Cologne: Pierre Marteau.

Courtès, Noémie (2004), *L'Ecriture de l'enchantement: Magie et magiciens dans la littérature française du XVIIe siècle*, Paris: Honoré Champion.

Crang, Mike and Nigel Thrift, eds. (2000), *Thinking Space*, London: Routledge.

Crébillon, Claude Prosper Jolyot de ([1742] 1984), *Le sopha*, Paris: Desjonquères.

Crébillon, Claude Prosper Jolyot de (1743), *The Sofa*, trans. Eliza Haywood, and William Hatchett, London: John Nourse & Thomas Cooper.

Crébillon, Claude Prosper Jolyot de (2009), *Contes: Bibliothèque des Génies et des Fées 17. IV. Contes parodiques et licencieux (1730–1754)*, ed. Régine Jomand-Baudry, Véronique Costa, and Violaine Géraud, Paris: Champion.

Croce, Benedetto, ed. (1982), *Il Pentamerone, Ossia la Fiaba delle Fiabe*, Rome: Editori Laterza.

Daston, Lorraine, ed. (2007), *Things that Talk: Object Lessons from Art and Science*, Brooklyn, NY: Zone Books.

Daston, Lorraine and Katharine Park (1998), *Wonders and the Order of Nature 1150–1750*, New York: Zone Books.

Davidson, Ian (2010), *Voltaire: A Life*, New York: Pegasus.

Davison, Carol Margaret (2009), *Gothic Literature 1764–1824*, Cardiff: University of Wales Press.

Defrance, Anne (2002), "Le Conte de fées au risque de l'éloge politique: *La Tyrannie des fées détruite* (Mme d'Auneil) et autres contes de la première génération," in R. Jomand-Baudry and Jean-François Perrin (eds.), *Le conte merveilleux au XVIIIe siècle: une poétique expérimentale*, 55–73, Paris: Kimé.

Delarue, Paul and Marie-Louise Tenèze ([1953] 1997), *Le Conte populaire français: Catalogue raisonné des versions de France*, Paris: Maisonneuve & Larose.

Descola, Philippe (2005), *Par-delà nature et culture*, Paris: Gallimard.

Dickens, Charles (1853), "Frauds on the Fairies," in *Household Words*, vol. 8, October 1: 97.

Diderot, Denis ([1748] 1965), *Les Bijoux indiscrets*, in *Oeuvres*, Paris: Gallimard.

Diderot, Denis and Jean le Rond d'Alembert, eds. (1778), *Encyclopédie, ou dictionnaire raisonné des sciences, des arts et des métiers, etc.*, vol. 22, Geneva: Pellet.

Diderot, Denis and Jean le Rond d'Alembert, eds. (2017), *Encyclopédie, ou dictionnaire raisonné des sciences, des arts et des métiers, etc.*, Autumn 2017 edn., ed. Robert Morrissey and Glenn Roe, 17 vols of articles, plus 11 vols of plate legends, Chicago: University of Chicago, ARTFL Encyclopédie Project. Available online: http://encyclopedie.uchicago.edu/ (accessed December 16, 2020).

Dobie, Madeleine (2001), *Foreign Bodies: Gender, Language, and Culture in French Orientalism*, Stanford, CA: Stanford University Press.

Doniger, Wendy (2000), *The Bedtrick: Tales of Sex and Masquerade*, Chicago: University of Chicago Press.

Douglas, Aileen (2015), "Women, Enlightenment and the Literary Fairy Tale in English," *Journal for Eighteenth-Century Studies*, 38 (2): 181–94.

Dreuillet, La Présidente ([1735] 2007), "Le Phénix," in Raymonde Robert (ed.), *Contes/Madame Levesque, Madame de Gomez, Madame de Dreuillet, Madame de Lintot, et al.*, Bibliothèque des génies et des fées 13, 477–89, Paris: Honoré Champion.

Dufrenoy, Marie-Louise (1946–75), *L'Orient Romanesque en France (1704–1789)*, 3 vols, Montreal: Mouton; Amsterdam: Rodopi.
Duggan, Anne E. (2001), "Nature and Culture in the Fairy Tale of Marie-Catherine d'Aulnoy," *Marvels & Tales*, 15 (2): 149–67.
Duggan, Anne E. (2004), "Women and Absolutism in French Opera and Fairy Tale," *French Review*, 78 (2): 302–15.
Duggan, Anne E. (2005), *Salonnières, Furies, and Fairies: The Politics of Gender and Cultural Change in Absolutist France*, Newark: University of Delaware Press.
Duggan, Anne E. (2008), "Women Subdued: The Abjectification and Purification of Female Characters in Perrault's Tales," *Romanic Review*, 99 (3–4): 211–26.
Duggan, Anne E. (2019), "The *Querelle des femmes* and Nicolas Boileau's *Satire X*: Going beyond Perrault," *Early Modern French Studies*, 41 (2): 144–57.
Duggan, Anne E. (2020a), "*Métissage* and the Literary Field of the French Enlightenment: The Impact of Galland's Translation of *The Arabian Nights*," in Ibrahim Akel and William Granara (eds.), *The Thousand and One Nights: Sources and Transformations in Literature, Art, and Science*, 69–81, Leiden: Brill.
Duggan, Anne E. (2020b), "Regenrer Schéhérazade et Shariar: *Les Mille et un jours* et *Les Quarantes Vizirs* comme contre-discours," *Oeuvres & Critiques*, 45 (1): 31–45.
Durand, Catherine (1699), *La Comtesse de Mortane*, La Haye: Veuve de Claude Barbin.
Eco, Umberto (2007), *On Ugliness*, trans. Alastair McEwen, New York: Rizzoli.
Edo Picture Books and Japonisme (2018), "Bibliography." Available online: https://www.kodomo.go.jp/gallery/edoehon/bunbuku/index_e.html (accessed April 20, 2020).
Ellis, Erle C. (2018), *Anthropocene: A Very Short Introduction*, Oxford: Oxford University Press.
El-Zein, Amira (2017), *Islam, Arabs, and the Intelligent World of the Jinn*, Syracuse, NY: Syracuse University Press.
Fabrizi, Angelo (1978), "Carlo Gozzi e la tradizione popolare (a proposito de *L'amore delle tre melarance*)," *Italianistica*, 7 (2): 336–45.
Farr, James R. (1991), "The Pure and Disciplined Body: Hierarchy, Morality, and Symbolism in France During the Catholic Reformation," *Journal of Interdisciplinary History*, 21 (3): 391–414.
Fay, Caroline (2008), "Sleeping Beauty Must Die: The Plots of Perrault's 'La Belle au bois dormant,'" *Marvels & Tales*, 22 (2): 259–76.
Fielding, Sarah (1968), *The Governess; or Little Female Academy*, ed. Jill E. Grey, Oxford: Oxford University Press.
Figoli (2010), "Traineaux … jeux et oeuvres d'art, 2° partie," [Blog] attelage-patrimoine. Available online: http://www.attelage-patrimoine.com/article-traineaux-jeux-et-oeuvres-d-art-2-partie-43451680.html (accessed April 20, 2020).
Figoli (2011), "Musée des carosses de Versailles," [Blog] attelage-patrimoine. Available online: http://www.attelage-patrimoine.com/article-musee-des-carrosses-de-versailles-1-traineaux-84772722.html (accessed April 20, 2020).
Fish Wilner, Arlene (1995), "Education and Ideology in Sarah Fielding's *The Governess*," *Studies in Eighteenth-Century Culture*, 24: 307–27.
Forrester, Sibelan, Helena Goscilo, Martin Skoro, and Jack Zipes (2013), *Baba Yaga: The Wild Witch of the East in Russian Fairy Tales*, Jackson: University Press of Mississippi.
Fougeret de Monbron, Senneterre, Chevrier, La Morlière, Bret, Boissy, Gautier de Montdorge, Voisenon, Cahusac, Galli de Bibiena, Mme Fagnan, Baret et Anonymes

(2007), *Contes parodiques et licencieux (1730–1754)*, ed. Françoise Gevrey, vol. 4, Bibliothèque des Génies et des Fées 18, Paris: Champion.

Fox, Paul W. (1960), "Louis XIV and the Theories of Absolutism and Divine Right," *Canadian Journal of Economics and Political Science/Revue Canadienne d'Economique et de Science*, 26 (1): 128–42.

France, Peter ([1992] 2006), *Politeness and its Discontents: Problems in French Classical Culture*, Cambridge: Cambridge Univesity Press.

Fudge, Erica (2006), *Brutal Reasoning: Animals, Rationality, and Humanity in Early Modern England*, Ithaca, NY: Cornell University Press.

Fumaroli, Marc (1982), "Les Enchantements de l'éloquence: *Les Fées* de Charles Perrault ou de la littérature," in Marc Fumaroli (ed.), *Le Statut de la littérature: Mélanges offerts à Paul Bénichou*, 153–86, Geneva: Droz.

Furetière, Antoine (1690), *Dictionnaire universel, contenant generalement tous les mots françois, tant vieux que modernes, et les termes des sciences et des arts*, 3 vols, La Haye and Rotterdam: Chez Arnout & Reiner Leers.

Furetière, Antoine (1701), *Dictionnaire universel contenant generalement tous les mots françois tant vieux que modernes, et les termes des sciences et des arts*, ed. Henri Basnage de Beauval, 3 vols, La Haye: Arnout & Reiner Leers.

Furetière, Antoine (1727), *Dictionnaire universel contenant generalement tous les mots françois tant vieux que modernes, et les termes des sciences et des arts*, rev. edn., ed. Henri Basnage de Beauval and Jean-Baptiste Brutel de la Rivière, 4 vols, La Haye: Pierre Husson, Thomas Johnson, Jean Swart, Jean Van Duren, Charles le Vier, La Veuve Van Dole.

Galland, Antoine ([1704–17] 2004), *Les mille et une nuits: contes arabes*, ed. Jean-Paul Sermain and Aboubakr Chraïbi, 3 vols, Paris: GF-Flammarion.

Garlington, Aubrely S. (1963), "Le Merveilleux and the Operatic Reform in the 18th-Century French Opera," *Musical Quarterly*, 49 (4): 484–97.

Gaudreaus, Antoine-Robert (1735–40), "Chest of Drawers: Antoine-Robert Gaudreaus (1682–1746)," London, The Wallace Collection, Inventory F85. Available online: https://wallacelive.wallacecollection.org/eMP/eMuseumPlus?service=ExternalInterface&module=collection&objectId=63712&viewType=detailView (accessed April 20, 2020).

Gaudreaus, Antoine-Robert and Jacques Caffieri (1739), "Commode/Louis XV's Commode," London, The Wallace Collection, inventory F86. Available online: https://commons.wikimedia.org/wiki/File:The_Wallace_Collection_-_King_Louis_XV%27s_commode_for_Versailles_by_Gaudreaus.jpg (accessed December 4, 2020).

Geider, Thomas (2016), "Ogre, Ogress," in Anne E. Duggan, Donald Haase, and Helen J. Callow (eds.), *Folktales and Fairy Tales: Traditions and Texts from around the World*, vol. 3, 732–5, 2nd edn., 4 vols, Santa Barbara, CA: Greenwood.

Genlis, Stéphanie Félicité de ([1779] 2002), "La Belle et la Bête," in Sophie Allera and Denis Reynaud (eds.), *La Belle et la Bête: Quatre métamorphoses (1742–1779)*, 159–85, Saint-Etienne: Publications de l'Université de Saint-Étienne.

Gernet, Jacques (1987), *A History of Chinese Civilization*, ed. J. R. Foster, Cambridge: Cambridge University Press.

Gozzi, Carlo (1772), "Zeim, Re de' genj," in *Opere del Co: Carlo Gozzi*, vol. 3, 123–231, Venice: Colombani.

Gozzi, Carlo (1804), "La più lunga lettera di risposta che sia stata scritta inviata da Carlo Gozzi a un poeta teatrale italiano de' nostri giorni," in *Opere edite ed inedite del Co: Carlo Gozzi*, vol. 14, 3–168, Venice: Zanardi.

Gozzi, Carlo (2004), *L'amore delle tre melarance*, in Alberto Beniscelli (ed.), *Fiabe teatrali*, 3–38, Milan: Garzanti.
Gozzi, Carlo (2006), *Memorie inutili*, ed. Paolo Bosisio and Valentina Caravaglia, vol. 1, Milan: LED.
Gozzi, Carlo (2013), *Ragionamento ingenuo: Dai "preamboli" all "Appendice," Scritti di teoria teatrale*, ed. Anna Scannapieco, Venice: Marsilio.
Grätz, Manfred (1988), *Das märchen in der deutschen Aufklärung: Vom Feenmärchen zum Volksmärchen*, Stuttgart: J. B. Metzler.
Greenhough, Amy (2019), "New Materialism and Contemporary Fairy-Tale Fiction," in Andrew Teverson (ed.), *The Fairy Tale World*, 451–561, Abingdon: Routledge.
Grenby, M. O. (2006), "Tame Fairies Make Good Teachers: The Popularity of Early British Fairy Tales," *The Lion and the Unicorn*, 30: 1–24.
Grimm, Wilhelm and Jacob Grimm ([1812–58] 2015), *Kinder-und Hausmärchen*, Berlin: Verlag.
Groom, Angelica (2018), *Exotic Animals in the Art and Culture of the Medici Court*, Boston: Brill.
Grosz, Elizabeth (2017), *The Incorporeal: Ontology, Ethics, and the Limits of Materialism*, New York: Columbia University Press.
Grotzfeld, Heinz (2004), "Creativity, Random Selection, and *pia fraus*: Observations on Compilation and Transmission of the *Arabian Nights*," *Marvels & Tales*, 18 (2): 218–28.
Gueulette, Thomas-Simon ([1712] 1730), *Mille et un quart d'heures, contes tartares*, Paris: André Morin.
Gueulette, Thomas-Simon (1725), *Chinese Tales: Or, the Wonderful Adventures of the Mandarin Fum-Hoam*, London: Printed for J. Brotherton.
Gueullette, Thomas-Simon ([1733] 1783), *Les Mille et une heure, contes péruviens*, 2 vols, Lille.
Gueullette, Thomas-Simon (1740), *Chinese Tales: Or, the Wonderful Adventures of the Mandarin Fum-Hoam. Related by Himself to Divert the Sultana upon the Celebration of Her Nuptials*, trans. Thomas Stackhouse, London: printed for J. Osborn, at the Golden-Ball, in Pater-Noster Row.
Haase, Donald, ed. (2004), *Fairy Tales and Feminism: New Approaches*, Detroit, MI: Wayne State University Press.
Hamilton, Antoine (1813), *Contes d'Antoine Hamilton, avec la suite des Facardins et de Zeneydepar*, ed. M. de Levis, 2 vols, Paris: Renouard.
Hamilton, Antoine, Jean-Jacques Rousseau, Henri Pajon, Jacques Cazotte, Carl Gustav Tessin, Charles Duclos, and Denis Diderot (2008), *Contes*, ed. Anne Defrance and Jean-François Perrin, Bibliothèque des Génies et des Fées 16. IV. Contes parodiques et licencieux (1730–1754), Paris: Champion.
Hanley, Sarah (1989), "Engendering the State: Family Formation and State Building in Early Modern France," *French Historical Studies*, 16 (1): 4–27.
Hannon, Patricia (1998), *Fabulous Identities: Women's Fairy Tales in Seventeenth-Century France*, Amsterdam: Rodopi.
Harries, Elizabeth Wanning (2001), *Twice upon a Time: Women Writers and the History of the Fairy Tale*, Princeton, NJ: Princeton University Press.
Hawkesworth, John (1992), "Almoran and Hamet," in Robert L. Mack (ed.), *Oriental Tales*, 38–100, Oxford: Oxford University Press.
Hearne, Betsy (1989), *Beauty and the Beast: Visions and Revisions of an Old Tale*, Chicago: University of Chicago Press.

Heitzmann, Annick (2009), "Les Jeux de bague de Trianon," *Versalia: Revue de la Société des Amis de Versailles*, 12: 77–96.

Hennard Dutheil de la Rochère, Martine (2013), *Reading, Translating, Rewriting: Angela Carter's Translational Poetics*, Detroit, MI: Wayne State University Press.

Hermansson, Casie E. (2009), *Bluebeard: A Reader's Guide to the English Tradition*, Jackson: University Press of Mississippi.

He Yuan 何薳 (1983), *Chunzhu jiwen* 春渚紀聞, Beijing: Zhonghua shuju.

Hobson, Marian (1982), *The Object of Art: The Theory of Illusion in Eighteenth-Century France*, Cambridge: Cambridge University Press.

Hoffmann, Kathryn A. (1997a), "Matriarchal Desires and Labyrinths of the Marvelous: Fairy Tales by Ancien Régime Women," in Colette Winn and Donna Kuizenga (eds.), *Women Writers in Pre-Revolutionary France: Strategies of Emancipation*, 281–98, New York: Garland Press.

Hoffmann, Kathryn A. (1997b), "Monstrous Women, Monstrous Theorizing: Mothers, Physicians and *les esprits animaux*," *Papers on French Seventeenth-Century Literature*, 24 (47): 537–52.

Hoffmann, Kathryn A. (2001), "Flying Through Classicism's Night: The Witch in Myth and Religion," in Ronald Tobin (ed.), *Racine et/ou le classicisme*, 459–70, Tubingen: Papers on French Seventeenth-Century Literature/Biblio 17.

Hoffmann, Kathryn A. (2005), "Of Monkey Girls and a Hog-Faced Gentlewoman: Marvel in Fairy Tales, Fairgrounds, and Cabinets of Curiosities," *Marvels and Tales*, 19 (1): 67–85.

Hoffmann, Kathryn A. (2013), "Excursions to See 'Monsters': Odd Bodies and Itineraries of Knowledge in the Seventeenth Century," in Susan McClary (ed.), *Structures of Feeling in Seventeenth Century Cultural Expression*, 296–31, Toronto: University of Toronto Press.

Hoffmann, Kathryn A. (2016), "Perrault's 'Cendrillon' Among the Glass Tales: Crystal Fantasies and Glassworks in Seventeenth-Century France and Italy," in Martine Hennard Dutheil de la Rochère, Gillian Lathey, and Monika Wozniak (eds.), *Cinderella Across Cultures: New Directions and Interdisciplinary Perspectives*, 52–80, Detroit, MI: Wayne State University Press.

Huang Chengzeng 黄承增 (1803), *Guang yu chu xin zhi* 廣虞初新志, Shanghai: Saoye shanfang 掃葉山房.

Huang Chi-chun, Huang Chengzeng, Annette Specht, Günter Lotzen, and Jacques Barchilon (1993), "The Earliest Version of the Chinese Little Red Riding Hood," *Merveilles & Contes*, 7 (2): 513–27.

Huet, G. (1908), "Ogre dans le Conte du Graal de Chrétien de Troyes," *Romania*, 146: 301–5.

Huet, Marie-Hélène (1993), *Monstrous Imagination*, Cambridge, MA: Harvard Univerity Press.

Huihong 惠洪 (1983), *Lengzhai yehua* 冷齋夜話, Siku quanshu 四庫全書, vol. 863, Tapai [Taiwan]: Taiwan shang wu yinshu guan 台灣商務印書館.

Huntington, Rania (2010), "The View from the Tower of Crossing Sails: Ji Yun's Female Informants," *Nan nü*, 12: 30–64.

Huppert, George (1977), *Les Bourgeois Gentilshommes: An Essay on the Definition of Elites in Renaissance France*, Chicago: University of Chicago Press.

Hutchinson, Steven (1992), *Cervantine Journeys*, Madison: University of Wisconsin Press.

Iotti, Gianni (2009), "Voltaire as Story-teller," in Nicholas Cronk (ed.), *The Cambridge Companion to Voltaire*, 109–24, Cambridge: Cambridge University Press.

Jarvis, Shawn C. (1992), "The Vanished Woman of Great Influence: Benedikte Naubert's Legacy and German Women's Fairy Tales," in Katherine Goodman and Edith Josefine Waldstein (eds.), *In the Shadow of Olympus: German Women Writers around 1800*, 189–210, Albany: State University of New York Press.

Jarvis, Shawn C. (2016), "German Tales," in Anne E. Duggan and Donald Haase (eds.), *Folktales and Fairy Tales: Traditions and Texts from Around the World*, vol. 2, 406–13, Santa Barbara, CA: ABC-CLIO.

Jasmin, Nadine (2002), *Naissance du Conte Féminin: Mots et Merveilles, Les Contes de fées de Madame d'Aulnoy*, Paris: Honoré Champion.

Jasmin, Nadine (2012), "Marie-Catherine Le Jumel de Barneville, Baroness d'Aulnoy," in Sophie Raynard (ed.), *The Teller's Tale: Lives of the Classic Fairy Tale Writers*, 61–8, Albany: State University of New York Press.

Ji Yun 紀昀 (1982), *Yuewei caotang biji* 閱微草堂筆記, Shanghai: Shanghai guji.

Ji Yun (1983), *Pinselnotizen aus der Strohütte der Betrachtung des Grossen im Kleinen*, trans. Konrad Herrmann, Bremen: Schünemann.

Ji Yun (1995), Sun Zhizhong 孫致中, Wu Enyang 吳恩揚, Wang Peilin 王沛霖, and Han Jiaxiang 韓嘉祥, ed. *Ji Xiaolan wenji* 紀曉嵐文集, Shijiazhuang: Hebei renmin.

Johns, Andreas (2004), *Baba Yaga: The Ambiguous Mother and Witch of the Russian Folktale*, New York: Peter Lang.

Johnson, Rebecca Carol, Richard Maxwell, and Katie Trumpener (2007), "The *Arabian Nights*, Arab-European Literary Influence, and the Lineages of the Novel," *Modern Language Quarterly*, 68 (2): 243–79.

Johnson, Sharon P. (2003), "The Toleration and Erotization of Rape: Interpreting Charles Perrault's 'Le Petit Chaperon Rouge' within Seventeenth- and Eighteenth-Century French Jurisprudence," *Women's Studies*, 32 (3): 325–52.

Jones, Christine A. (2008), "Madame d'Aulnoy Charms the British," *Romanic Review*, 99 (3–4): 239–56.

Jones, Christine A. (2013), *Shapely Bodies: The Image of Porcelain in Eighteenth-Century France*, Newark: University of Delaware Press.

Jōo, Fumiko (2011), "The Peony Lantern and Fantastic Tales in Late Imperial China and Tokugawa Japan: Local History, Religion, and Gender," PhD dissertation, University of Chicago.

Kimbrough, R. Keller (2015), "Bloody Hell! Reading Boys' Books in Seventeenth-Century Japan," *Asian Ethnology*, 74 (1): 111–39.

Korneeva, Tatiana (2014), "Desire and Desirability in Villeneuve and Leprince de Beaumont's "Beauty and the Beast," *Marvels & Tales*, 28 (2): 233–51.

Korneeva, Tatiana (2019), *The Dramaturgy of the Spectator: Theatre and the Public Sphere (1600–1800)*, Toronto: University of Toronto Press.

Kostiukhin, Evgenii A., ed. (1988), *Prikliucheniia slavianskikh vitiazei*, Moscow: Sovremennik.

La Chaussée, Pierre-Claude Nivelle de ([1742] 2002), "Amour pour Amour," in Sophie Allera and Denis Reynaud (eds.), *La Belle et la Bête: Quatre métamorphoses (1742–1779)*, 17–83, Saint-Etienne: Publications de l'Université de Saint-Etienne.

La Force, Charlotte-Rose Caumont de (1698), *Les Contes des contes*, 2 vols, Paris: Simon Bernard.

La Force, Charlotte-Rose Caumont de (2005a), "Plus belle que fée," in Raymonde Robert (ed.), *Contes/Mlle Lhéritier, Mlle Bernard, Mlle de La Force, Madame Durand, Madame d'Auneuil*, Bibliothèque des Génies et des Fées 2, 309–29, Paris: Honoré Champion.

La Force, Charlotte-Rose Caumont de (2005b), "Tourbillon," in Raymonde Robert (ed.), *Contes/Mlle Lhéritier, Mlle Bernard, Mlle de La Force, Madame Durand, Madame d'Auneuil*, Bibliothèque des Génies et des Fées 2, 357–71, Paris: Honoré Champion.

Lakhnavi, Ghalib and Abdullah Bilgrami (2007), *The Adventures of Amir Hamza*, trans. Musharraf Ali Farooqi, New York: The Modern Library.

Lathey, Gillian (2016), "The Translator as Agent of Change: Robert Samber, Translator of Pornography, Medical Texts, and the First English Version of Perrault's 'Cendrillon' (1729)," in Martine Hennard Dutheil de la Rochère, Gillian Lathey, and Monika Wozniak (eds.), *Cinderella across Cultures: New Directions and Interdisciplinary Perspectives*, 81–94, Detroit, MI: Wayne State University Press.

Latour, Bruno (2004), *Politics of Nature: How to Bring the Sciences into Democracy*, Cambridge, MA: Harvard University Press.

Lau, Kimberly J. (2016), "Imperial Marvels: Race and the Colonial Imagination in the Fairy Tales of Madame d'Aulnoy," *Narrative Culture*, 3 (2): 141–79.

Lefebvre, Henri (1996), *The Production of Space*, trans. Donald Nicholson-Smith, Oxford: Blackwell.

Lemirre, Elizabeth, ed. (1994), *Le Cabinet des fées*, vol. 2, *Plus Belle que fée et autres contes*, Paris: Piquier.

Le Noble, Eustache ([1700] 1980), *Le Gage touché, histoires galantes et comiques*, Geneva: Slatkine Reprints.

Leprince de Beaumont, Jeanne-Marie (1756), *Magasin des enfans, ou Dialogues entre une sage gouvernante et plusieurs de ses élèves*, 4 vols, London: J. Haberkorn.

Leprince de Beaumont, Marie-Jeanne ([1756] 2008), "Magasin des enfants," in Elisa Biancardi (ed.), *La Jeune Américaine et les contes marins ("La Belle et la Bête"); Les Belles Solitaires; Magasin des enfants ("La Belle et la Bête")*, by Gabrielle-Suzanne Barbot Gallon Villeneuve and Marie-Jeanne Leprince de Beaumont, 959–1418, Paris: Champion.

Leprince de Beaumont, Jeanne-Marie ([1757] 2011), "La Belle et la Bête," in *La Belle et la Bête et autres contes*, Paris: Larousse.

Leprince de Beaumont, Jeanne-Marie (1767), *The Young Misses Magazine*, 2 vols, 2nd edn., London: Printed for J. Nourse, in the Strand, Bookseller in Ordinary to His Majesty.

Levesque, Louise Cavalier ([1722] 2007), "Le Prince des Aigues Marines," in Raymonde Robert (ed.), *Contes/madame Levesque, madame de Gomez, madame de Dreuillet, Madame de Lintot, et al.*, 25–56, Bibliothèque des génies et des fées 13, Paris: Honoré Champion.

Levesque, Madame, Madame de Gomez, Madame de Dreuillet, Madame Le Marchand, Madame de Lintot, Madame de Lassay, Madame Fagnan, and Mademoiselle Falques (2007), *Contes*, ed. Raymonde Robert, Bibliothèque des Génies et des Fées 13, Paris: Champion.

Levshin, Vasilii. A. (1780–3), *Russkie skazki* [Russian Fairy Tales], Moscow: V universitetskoĭ tip. u N. Novikova.

L'Héritier de Villandon, Marie-Jeanne (1696), *Œuvres Meslees*, Paris: Jean Guignard.

L'Héritier de Villandon, Marie-Jeanne (1705), *La tour ténébreuse et les jours lumineux: Contes Anglois, accompagnez d'historiettes, & tirez d'une ancienne Chronique composée par RICHARD, Surnommé COEUR DE LION, Roy d'Angleterre. Avec le Récit de diverses Avantures de ce Roy*, Amsterdam: Jacques des Bordes.

Lintot, Catherine de ([1735] 2007a), "Le Prince Sincer," in Raymonde Robert (ed.), *Contes/madame Levesque, madame de Gomez, madame de Dreuillet, Madame de Lintot, et al.*, 609–28, Bibliothèque des génies et des fées 13, Paris: Honoré Champion.
Lintot, Catherine de ([1735] 2007b), "Tendrebrun et Constance," in Raymonde Robert (ed.), *Contes/madame Levesque, madame de Gomez, madame de Dreuillet, Madame de Lintot, et al.*, 629–59, Bibliothèque des génies et des fées 13, Paris: Honoré Champion.
Longino, Michèle (2002), *Orientalism in French Classical Drama*, Cambridge: Cambridge University Press.
Lubert, Marie-Madeleine de ([1737–55] 2005), *Contes*, Bibliothèque des Génies et des Fées 14, Paris: Honoré Champion.
Lussan, Mademoiselle de ([1731–41] 2007), *Les Veillées de Thessalie*, ed. Nadine Decourt and Jean-Claude Decourt, Bibliothèque des Génies et des Fées 13, Paris: Champion.
Mabille, Pierre (1962), *Le Miroir du merveilleux*, Paris: Editions de Minuit.
Macdonald, Duncan B. (1932), "A Bibliographical and Literary Study of the First Appearance of the *Arabian Nights* in Europe," *Library Quarterly*, 2 (4): 387–420.
Magnanini, Suzanne (2007a), *Fairy-Tale Science: Monstrous Generation in the Tales of Straparola and Basile*, Toronto: University of Toronto Press.
Magnanini, Suzanne (2007b), "Postulated Routes from Naples to Paris: The Printer Antonio Bulifon and Giambattista Basile's Fairy Tales in Seventeenth-Century France," *Marvels & Tales*, 21 (1): 78–92.
Mailly, Louis de (1698), *Les Fées illustres, contes galans dédié aux dames*, Paris: Brunet.
Mailly, Louis de ([1719] 2011), *Les aventures des trois princes de Serendip*, ed. Aude Volpilhac, Dominique Goy-Blanquet, and Marie-Anne Paveau, Vincennes: Thierry Marchaisse.
Mainil, Jean (2001), *Madame d'Aulnoy et le rire des fées: Essais sur la subversion féerique et le merveilleux comique sous l'Ancien Régime*, Paris: Kimé.
Malpas, J. E. (1999), *Place and Experience: A Philosophical Topography*, Cambridge: Cambridge University Press.
Mann, Susan (1997), *Precious Records: Women in China's Long Eighteenth Century*, Stanford, CA: Stanford University Press.
Marivaux, Pierre de ([1720] 1993), *Arlequin poli par l'amour*, in Henri Coulet and Michel Gilot (eds.), *Théâtre complet*, vol. 1, 111–36, Paris: Gallimard.
Marivaux, Pierre de ([1727] 1993), *L'Ile de la raison*, in Henri Coulet and Michel Gilot (eds.), *Théâtre complet*, vol. 1, 513–74, Paris: Gallimard.
Marivaux, Pierre de ([1757] 1994), *Félicie*, in Henri Coulet and Michel Gilot (eds.), *Théâtre complet*, vol. 2, 663–81, Paris: Gallimard.
Marmontel, Jean-François (1821), "The Sylph-Husband," in *Moral Tales*, 365–92, London: F. C. & J. Rivington.
Marmontel, Jean-François (2002), "Zémire et Azore," in Sophie Allera and Denis Reynaud (eds.), *La Belle et la Bête: Quatre métamorphoses (1742–1779)*, 103–58, Saint-Etienne: Publications de l'Université de Saint-Étienne.
Martin, Henri-Jean (1978), "The *Bibliothèque bleue*: Literature for the Masses in the Ancien Régime," *Publishing History*, 3: 70–102.
Martino, Pierre (1906), *L'Orient dans la literature française au XVIIe et au XVIIIe siècle*, Paris: Hachette.

Marzolph, Ulrich (2018), "The Man Who Made the *Nights* Immortal: The Tales of the Syrian Maronite Storyteller Hanna Diyab," *Marvels & Tales*, 32 (1): 114–25.

Marzolph, Ulrich and Richard van Leeuwen, eds. (2004), *The Arabian Nights Encyclopedia*, 2 vols, Santa Barbara, CA: ABC-CLIO.

MasterArt (2020), "GG: Chinese Export Porcelain Famille Rose Ewer and Cover with Bird-Head Spout." Available online: https://www.masterart.com/artworks/13213/gg-chinese-export-porcelain-famille (accessed December 6, 2020).

Mayer, Charles-Joseph, ed. (1785–9), *Le Cabinet des fées, ou Collection choisie des contes de fées et autres contes merveilleux*, 41 vols, Geneva: Barde, Manget & Cie.

Méchoulan, Eric (2006), "Le pouvoir féerique," *Féeries*, 3: 43–57.

Melzer, Sara E. (2012), *Colonizer or Colonized the Hidden Stories of Early Modern French Culture*, Philadelphia: University of Pennsylvania Press.

Mengchu, Ling (1998), *Amazing Tales*, trans. Wen Jingen and Perry W. Ma, Beijing: Panda Books.

Menglong, Feng (2008), *The Sorcerer's Revolt*, trans. Nathan Sturman, n.l.: Silk Pagoda.

Mercier, Louis-Sébastien ([1783] 1994), "Poèmes lyriques," in Jean-Claude Bonnet (ed.), *Tableau de Paris*, vol. 2, 444–6, Paris: Mercure de France.

Merryman, Dick (1734), "Enchantment Demonstrated, in the Story of Jack Spriggins and the Enchanted Bean; giving a particular account of Jack's arrival at the castle of Giant Gogmagog; his rescuing ten thousand ladies and knights from being broiled for the giant's breakfast …," in *Round about our coal fire, or, Christmas entertainments*, 35–48, 4th edn., London: J. Roberts.

Milner, Max (1960), *Le Diable dans la littérature française, de Cazotte à Baudelaire, 1772–1861*, 2 vols, Paris: J. Corti.

Minnis, Alastair J., A. Brian Scott, and David Wallace, eds. (1988), *Medieval Literary Theory and Criticism: The Commentary Tradition*, Oxford: Clarendon Press.

Montesquieu, Charles de Secondat, baron de (1946), *Lettres persanes*, ed. Conzague Truc, Paris: Éditions Garnier.

Morlini, Girolamo ([1520] 1855), *Hieronymi Morlini Parthenopei novellae, fabulae, comoedia*, Lutetiae Parisiorum: Apud P. Jannet.

Mouhy, Charles de Fieux, chevalier de (1737), *Lamekis; ou, Les voyages extraordinaires d'un Egyptien dans la terre intérieure avec la découverte de l'île des sylphides*, Paris: Chez Poilly.

Murat, Henriette-Julie de Castelnau (1699), *Histoires sublimes et allégoriques: Dediees aux fées modernes*, Paris: Florentin and Pierre Delaulne.

Murat, Henriette-Julie de Castelnau (2006), *Contes*, ed. Geneviève Clermidy-Patard, Paris: Champion.

Muyart de Vouglans, Pierre François (1780), *Les Lois criminelles de France, dans leur ordre naturel*, Paris: Mérigot.

Naroditskaya, Irina (2018), *Bewitching Russian Opera: The Tsarina from State to Stage*, Oxford: Oxford University Press.

Naubert, Benedikte (1795), "Der Riesentanz," in *Velleda: Ein Zauberroman*, 125–34, Leipzig: Schäfer.

Navarre, Marguerite, Reine de ([1512, Ms] 1982), *Heptaméron*, Paris: Flammarion.

Nodot, François (1700), *Histoire de Mélusine, Princesse de Lusignan, et de ses fils*, Paris: la Veuve de Claude Barbin.

Norman, Buford (2001), *Touched by the Graces: The Libretti of Philippe Quinault in the Context of French Classicism*, Birmington, AL: Summa.

Olivier, Marc (2005), "Engineering Nostalgia: The Machine de Marly in Madame d'Auneuil's *La tyrannie des fées détruite,*" *Romance Notes*, 46 (1): 13–21.

O'Malley, Lurana Donnels (2006), *The Dramatic Works of Catherine the Great: Theatre and Politics in Eighteenth-Century Russia*, Aldershot: Ashgate.

Osterhammel, Jürgen (2013), *Die Entzauberung Asiens: Europa und die asiatischen Reiche im 18*, Munich: Jahrhundert, Beck.

Palmer, Melvin D. (1975), "Madame d'Aulnoy in England," *Comparative Literature*, 27 (3): 237–53.

Palmer, Nancy and Melvin D. Palmer (1974), "English Editions of French 'Contes de Fées' Attributed to Mme d'Aulnoy," *Studies in Bibliography*, 27: 227–32.

Paré, Ambroise ([1573] 1982), *On Monsters and Marvels*, trans. Janis L. Pallister, Chicago: University of Chicago Press.

Park, Katharine and Lorraine J. Daston (1981), "Unnatural Conceptions: The Study of Monsters in Sixteenth- and Seventeenth-Century France and England," *Past and Present*, 92: 20–54.

Patard, Geneviève (2012), "Henriette-Julie de Castelnau, Countesse de Murat," in Sophie Raynard (ed.), *The Teller's Tale: Lives of the Classic Fairy Tale Writers*, 81–7, Albany: State University of New York Press.

Perrault, Charles (1695), *Contes en vers*, Paris: Cogniard.

Perrault, Charles (1697), *Histoires ou contes du temps passé. Avec des moralités*, Paris: C. Barbin.

Perrault, Charles (1729), *Histories or Tales of Past Times with Morals*, London: printed for J. Pote and R. Montagu.

Perrault, Charles (1967), *Contes*, ed. Gilbert Rouger, Paris: Éditions Garnier Frères.

Perrault Charles (1991), *Contes*, Paris: Garnier.

Perrault, Charles (1999), *Contes*, ed. Jean-Pierre Collinet, intro. Nathalie Froloff, Paris: Gallimard.

Perrault, Charles (2005), *Perrault, Fénelon, Mailly, Préchac, Choisy et Anonymes: Contes merveilleux*, ed. Tony Gheeraert and Raymonde Robert, Paris: Champion.

Perrin, Jean-François (2004), "Les transformations du conte-cadre des *Mille et une Nuits* dans le conte orientalisant français du début du XVIIIe siècle," *Revue d'histoire littéraire de la France*, 104 (1): 45–58.

Perrin, Jean-François (2004–5), "L'invention d'un genre littéraire au XVIIIe siècle: Le conte oriental," *Féeries*, 2: 9–27.

Perrin, Jean-François (2008), "Introduction," in Antoine Hamilton, Jean-Jacques Rousseau, Henri Pajon, Jacques Cazotte, Carl Gustav Tessin, Charles Duclos, and Denis Diderot, *Contes*, ed. Anne Defrance and Jean-François Perrin, Bibliothèque des Génies et des Fées 16. IV. Contes parodiques et licencieux (1730–1754), Paris: Champion.

Pétis de La Croix, François ([1707] 2006), *Histoire de la sultane de Perse et des vizirs*, ed. Raymonde Robert, Bibliothèque des Génies et des Fées, Paris: Champion.

Pétis de La Croix, François ([1710] 2006), *Les Mille et un jours, contes persans*, ed. Pierre Brunel, Christelle Bahier-Porte, and Frédéric Mancier, Bibliothèque des Génies et des Fées 8, Paris: Champion.

Pétis de la Croix, François ([1710–12] 2011), *Mille et un jours, contes persans*, Champion: Paris.

Pétis de La Croix, François (1714), *The Persian and the Turkish Tales, Compleat. Translated formerly from those languages into French, by M. Petis de la Croix*, trans.

Dr. King and several other hands, London: Printed for W. Mcars at the Lamb, and J. Browne at the Black Swan.

Planché, J. R. (1867), *Fairy Tales by Perrault, de Villeneuve, de Caylus, de Lubert, de Beaumont, etc.*, London: George Routledge and Sons.

Poirson, Martial, ed. (2009), *Perrault en scène. Transpositions théâtrales de contes merveilleux, 1697–1800*, St. Gély du Fesc: Éditions Espaces 34.

Potocki, Jean ([1810] 2008), *Manuscrit trouvé à Saragosse*, ed. François Rosset and Dominique Triaire, Paris: Flammarion.

Préchac, Jean de ([1698] 1993), *Contes moins contes que les autres, précédés de L'Illustre Parisienne*, Paris: Société des Textes Français Modernes.

"Prince Perinet ou l'origine des Pagodes, Le" ([1730] 1988), in *Le Cabinet des fées*, vol. 2, *Plus Belle que Fée et autres contes*, 311–27, Arles: Philippe Piquet.

Pritchett, Frances (n.d.-a), *Bagh-o-bahar*. Available online: http://www.columbia.edu/itc/mealac/pritchett/00urdu/baghobahar/index.html (accessed April 20, 2020).

Pritchett, Frances (n.d.-b), "Tale of the Fourth Dervish." Available online: http://www.columbia.edu/itc/mealac/pritchett/00urdu/baghobahar/06_fourthdarvesh.html (accessed December 6, 2020).

Pritchett, Frances (1991), *The Romance Tradition in Urdu: Adventures from the Dastan of Amir Hamza*, New York: Columbia University Press.

Propp, Vladimir (1958), *Morphology of the Folktale*, ed. and intro. Svatava Pirokova-Jakoboson, trans. Laurence Scott, Bloomington: Research Center, Indiana University.

Propp, Vladimir (1968), *Morphology of the Folktale*, Austin: University of Texas Press.

Pu Songling 蒲松齡 (1978), *De beschilderde huid*; *Chinese spookverhalen*, trans. W. L. Idema, B. J. Mansveldt Beck, and N. H. van Straten, Amsterdam: Meulenhoff.

Pu Songling (1992), *Liaozhai zhiyi huijiao huizhu huiping ben* 聊齋誌異會校會注會評本, Zhang Youhe 張友鶴, Shanghai: Shanghai guji.

Pu Songling (1993), *Le studio des loisirs*, trans. Hélène Chatelain, Paris: Éditions Sand.

Pu Songling (2006), *Strange Tales from a Chinese Studio*, trans. John Minford, New York: Penguin Classics.

Qian Xiyan 錢希言 (2014), *Kuai yuan zhi yi* 獪園志異, Beijing: Wenwu chubanshe.

Raleigh, Tegan (2017), "The Thousand and First Author: Thomas-Simon Gueullette's Repeating Fictions," *Canadian Review of Comparative Literature*, December: 701–17.

Reddan, Bronwyn (2016), "Thinking Through Things: Magical Objects, Power, and Agency in French Fairy Tales," *Marvels & Tales*, 30 (2): 191–209.

Richelet, Pierre (1680), *Dictionnaire françois: contenant les mots et les choses, plusieurs nouvelles remarques sur la langue françoise*, Geneva: J.-H. Widerhold.

Rifelj, Carol de Dobay (1990), "Cendrillon and the Ogre: Women in Fairy Tales and Sade," *Romanic Review*, 81 (1): 11–24.

Robert, Raymonde (1982), *Le Conte de fées littéraire en France de la fin du XVIIe à la fin du XVIIIe siècle*, Nancy: Presses Universitaires de Nancy.

Ronzeaud, Pierre (1988), *Peuple et représentations sous le règne de Louis XIV: Les Représentations du peuple dans la littérature politique en France sous le règne de Louis XIV*, Aix-en-Provence: Université de Provence.

Sahlins, Peter (2012), "The Royal Menageries of Louis XIV and the Civilizing Process Revisited," *French Historical Studies*, 35 (2): 237–67.

Sahlins, Peter (2017), *1668: The Year of the Animal in France*, New York: Zone Books.

Saïd, Edward (1979), *Orientalism*, New York: Vintage Books.

Schacker, Jennifer (2012), "Fairy Gold. The Economics and Erotics of Fairy-Tale Pantomime," *Marvels & Tales*, 26 (2): 153–77.

Schacker, Jennifer (2018), *Staging Fairyland: Folklore, Children's Entertainment, and Nineteenth-Century Pantomime*, Detroit, MI: Wayne State University Press.

Schröder, Volker (2019), "Entre cour, salon, et couvent: la 'solitude' de Madame d'Aulnoy," Paper presented at NASSCFL 2019, Salt Lake City.

Segrais, Jean Regnault de and Anne Marie Louise de Montpensier ([1656] 1990), *Les Nouvelles Françaises, ou les divertissements de la princesse Aurélie*, ed. Roger Guichemerre, 2 vols, Paris: Société des Textes Français Modernes.

Seifert, Lewis C. (1990), "Female Empowerment and Its Limits: The *Conteuses*' Active Heroines," *Cahiers du Dix-Septième*, 4 (2): 17–34.

Seifert, Lewis C. (1996), *Fairy Tales, Sexuality, and Gender in France 1690–1715: Nostalgic Utopias*, Cambridge: Cambridge University Press.

Seifert, Lewis C. (2004), "Madame Le Prince de Beaumont and the Infantilization of the Fairy Tale," in Buford Norman (ed.), *The Child in French and Francophone Literature*, 25–39, French Literature Series 31, Amsterdam: Rodopi.

Seifert, Lewis C. (2011), "Animal-Human Hybridity in d'Aulnoy's 'Babiole' and 'Prince Wild Boar,'" *Marvels & Tales*, 25 (2): 244–60.

Seifert, Lewis C. (2015), "Queer Time in Charles Perrault's 'Sleeping Beauty,'" *Marvels & Tales*, 29 (1): 21–41.

Seifert, Lewis C. and Domna C. Stanton, eds. and trans. (2010), *Enchanted Eloquence: Fairy Tales by Seventeenth-Century French Women Writers*, Toronto: Iter.

Sempère, Emmanuelle (2009), *De la Merveille à l'inquiétude: le registre du fantastique dans la fiction*, Bordeaux: Presses Universitaires de Bordeaux.

Sempère, Emmanuelle (2017), "Le Merveilleux à l'épreuve des sens: une phénoménologie sous contraintes (fin xviie siècle–xviiie siècle)," *Féeries*, 14. https://doi.org/10.4000/feeries.1174.

Sercambi, Giovani ([*Il novelliere*, c. 1374 unfinished] 1889), *Novelle inedite tratte dal cpf/Trivulziano CXCIII*, Turin: Loescher.

Sermain, Jean-Paul (2005), *Le Conte de fées du classicisme aux Lumières*, Paris: Desjonquères.

Sermain, Jean-Paul (2013), *Marivaux et la mise en scène*, Paris: Desjonquères.

Serres, Michel (1968), *Hermès ou la communication*, Paris: Minuit.

Serres, Michel (1980), *Le Parasite*, Paris: Bernard Grasset.

Shackle, Christopher (2007), "The Story of Sayf al-Muluk in South Asia," *Journal of the Royal Asiatic Society*, 17 (2): 115–29.

Shennan, J. H. ([1986] 2005), *Louis XIV*, London: Routledge.

Sheridan, Elizabeth (1783), *The Fairy Ring, or Emeline, A Moral Tale*, London: W. Lane.

Sheridan, Francis (1992), "The History of Nourjehad," in Robert L. Mack (ed.), *Oriental Tales*, 117–29, Oxford: Oxford University Press.

Shippey, Tom (2006), "Rewriting the Core: Transformations of the Fairy Tale in Contemporary Writing," in Hilda Ellis Davidson and Anna Chaudhri (eds.), *A Companion to the Fairy Tale*, 253–74, Woodbridge: D. S. Brewer.

Shirane, Haruo (2004), *Early Modern Japanese Literature: An Anthology 1600–1900*, New York: Columbia University Press.

Sorel, Charles (1627–8), *Le Berger extravagant: Où, parmy des fantaisies Amoureuse on void les impertinences des Romans et de la Poësie*, Paris: T. Du Bray.

Stanton, Domna C. and Rebecca M. Wilkin (2010), "Introduction," in Gabrielle Suchon, *A Woman Who Defends All the Persons of Her Sex: Selected Philosophical and Moral Writings*, ed. and trans. Domna C. Stanton and Rebecca M. Wilkin, 1–54, Chicago: University of Chicago Press.
Stedman, Allison (2005), "'Histoire d'Hypolite, comte de Duglas' (1690): A Fairy-Tale Manifesto," *Marvels & Tales*, 19 (1): 32–53.
Straparola, Giovanni Francesco (1550–3), *Le Tredici Piacevolissime Notte*, Venice: Zanetto Zanetti.
Straparola, Giovanni Francesco ([1573] 1857), *Les Facetieuses nuits de Straparole, traduites par Jean Louveau et Pierre de Larivey*, 2 vols, Paris: P. Jannet.
Straparola, Giovanni Francesco (2015), *The Pleasant Nights*, trans. Suzanne Magnanini, Other Voice in Early Modern Europe, Toronto: Iter Academic Press; Tempe: Arizona Center for Medieval and Renaissance Studies.
Tasso, Torquato ([1573] 1826), *Aminta, favola boschereccia*, Paris: Froment.
Tatar, Maria (1992), *Off with Their Heads!: Fairy Tales and the Culture of Children*, Princeton, NJ: Princeton University Press.
Tatar, Maria (2004), *Secrets beyond the Door: The Story of Bluebeard and his Wives*, Princeton, NJ: Princeton University Press.
Tatar, Maria (2014), "Show and Tell: Sleeping Beauty as Verbal Icon and Seductive Story," *Marvels & Tales*, 28 (1): 142–58.
Ter Haar, Barend J. (2006), *Telling Stories: Witchcraft and Scapegoating in Chinese History*, Leiden: Brill.
Tessin, Carl Gustaf (1741), *Faunillane ou l'infante jaune, conte*, Badinopolis [Paris]: chez les frères Ponthommes, à l'enseigne du Roi d'Egypte.
Tieck, Ludwig (1792), "Abdallah," in *Schriften*, vol. 8, 3–76, Project Gutenberg. Available online: http://www.gutenberg.org/files/31074/31074-h/31074-h.htm (accessed April 20, 2020).
Todd, Dennis (1995), *Imagining Monsters: Miscreations of the Self in Eighteenth-Century England*, Chicago: University of Chicago Press.
Todorov, Tzvetan ([1970] 2013), *Introduction à la littérature fantastique*, Paris: Seuil.
Trinquet, Charlotte (2007), "On the Literary Origins of Folkloric Fairy Tales: A Comparison between Madame d'Aulnoy's 'Finette Cendron' and Frank Bourisaw's 'BelleFinette,'" *Marvels & Tales*, 21 (1): 34–49.
Trinquet, Charlotte (2012), *Le Conte de fées français (1690–1700): Traditions italiennes et origins aristocratiques*, Tübingen: Narr Verlag.
Tucker, Holly and Melanie R. Siemans, trans. (2005), "Perrault's Preface to *Griselda* and Murat's 'To Modern Fairies,'" *Marvels & Tales*, 19 (1): 125–30.
Turbet-Delof, Guy (1973), *L'Afrique barbaresque dans la littérature française aux XVIe et XVIIe siècles*, Geneva: Droz.
Urfé, Honoré d' (1607–27), *L'Astrée*, Paris: Toussaint et du Bray.
Van Leeuwen, Richard (2007), *The Thousand and One Nights, Space, Travel and Transformation*, London: Routledge.
Van Leeuwen, Richard (2014), "Love or Lust: Sexual Relationships between Humans and Jinns in the *Thousand and One Nights* and *The Djinn and the Nightingale's Eye*," in Adam Talib, Marlé Hammond, and Arie Schippers (eds.), *The Rude, the Bad and the Bawdy: Essays in Honour of Professor Geert Jan van Gelder*, 208–20, n.l.: Gibb Memorial Trust.
Van Leeuwen, Richard (2015), "Religion and Oriental Tales in the Eighteenth Century: the Emergence of the Fantastic Genre," in Aboubakr Chraïbi and Ilaria

Vitali (eds.), "Variations françaises sur les Mille et une nuits: quelles versions pour quelles effets?," special issue of *Francofonia*, 69: 35–56.

Van Leeuwen, Richard (2017), *Narratives of Kingship, 1300–1800*, Leiden: Brill.

Vaz da Silva (2016), "Charles Perrault and the Evolution of 'Little Red Riding Hood,'" *Marvels & Tales*, 30 (2): 167–90.

Velay-Valentin, Catherine (1992), *L'Histoire des contes*, Paris: Fayard.

Vescovo, Piermario (1989), "Lo specchio e la lente: Il ruolo dello spettatore (1760–62)," in Ilaria Crotti and Ricciarda Ricorda (eds.), *Gasparo Gozzi: Il lavoro di un intellettuale nel Settecento veneziano, Atti del convegno (Venezia-Pordenone 4–6 dicembre 1986)*, 383–412, Padua: Antenore.

Veysman, Nicolas (2007), "Le féerique moral dans les contes moraux de Marmontel," *Féeries*, 4: 213–34.

Veysman, Nicolas (2009), "Introduction. Le catin, la sorcière et le succube," in Nicolas Veysman (ed.), *Contes immoraux du XVIIIe siècle*, 29–64, Paris: Laffont.

Villeneuve, Gabrielle-Suzanne de ([1740] 2008), *La jeune Américaine ou les contes marins*, Paris: Champion.

Villeneuve, Gabrielle-Suzanne de ([1740] 2010), *La Belle et la Bête*, Paris: Gallimard.

Villeneuve, Gabrielle-Suzanne de (1745), *Les Belles solitaires*, Paris: P. Marteau.

Villeneuve, Gabrielle-Suzanne de (1858), "The Story of the Beauty and the Beast," in J. R. Planché (trans.), *Four and Twenty Tales: Selection from Those of Perrault, and Other Writers*, 225–325, London: Routledge.

Voisenon, Claude-Henri de Fusée, abbé de (1746), *Le Sultan Misapouf et la princesse Grisemine*, 2 vols, London: n.p.

Voltaire ([1759] 2000), "Candide," in *Candide and Related Textes*, trans. David Wootton, 1–83, Indianapolis, IN: Hackett.

Voltaire ([1767] 1877), "L'Ingenu," in Louis Moland (ed.), *Oeuvres completes*, vol. 21, 247–304, Paris: Garnier.

Voltaire (1958), *Romans et contes*, Paris: Garnier.

Voltaire (2006), *Candide and Other Stories*, New York: Oxford University Press.

Walvin, James (2017), *Slavery in Small Things: Slavery and Modern Cultural Habits*, Chichester: Wiley-Blackwell.

Warner, Marina (1994), *Wonder Tales: Six Stories of Enchantment*, London: Chatto & Windus.

Warner, Marina (1996), *From the Beast to the Blonde*, New York: Farrar, Straus, and Giroux.

Warner, Marina (2013), *Stranger Magic: Charmed States and the Arabian Nights*, Cambridge: Belknap Press of Harvard University Press.

Warner, Marina (2014), *Once upon a Time: A Short History of Fairy Tale*, Oxford: Oxford University Press.

Weber, Henry, ed. (1812), *Tales of the East*, Edinburgh: John Ballantyne and Company.

Web Gallery of Art (n.d.), "Welcome to the Gallery." Available online: https://www.wga.hu/ (accessed April 20, 2020).

Wieland, Christoph Martin ([1772] 2008), *Der goldene Spiegel oder die Könige von Scheschian*, Berlin: Sammlung Zenodot.

Wieland, Christoph Martin ([1780] 1964), *Oberon*, Munich: Wilhelm Goldman Verlag.

Wieland, Christopher Martin (1786), *Dschinnistan*, Winterthur: Heinrich Steiner and Company.

Wieland, Christoph Martin ([1786–9] 1992), *Dschinnistan oder auserlesene Feen- und Geistermärchen*, Zurich: Manesse Verlag.
Williams, Kristin (2012), "Visualizing the Child: Japanese Children's Literature in the Age of Woodblock Print, 1678–1888," PhD dissertation, Harvard University.
Wünsch, Marianne (1991), *Die fantastische Literatur der frühen Moderne*, Munich: Wilhelm Fink Verlag.
Yeazell, Ruth Bernard (2000), *Harems of the Mind: Passages of Western Art and Literature*, New Haven, CT: Yale University Press.
Zipes, Jack, ed. and trans. (1991a), *Beauties, Beasts and Enchantment: Classic French Fairy Tales*, New York: Meridian.
Zipes, Jack, ed. (1991b), *Spells of Enchantment: the Wondrous Fairy Tales of Western Culture*, New York: Viking.
Zipes, Jack, ed. (1993), *The Trials and Tribulations of Little Red Riding Hood*, 2nd edn., New York: Routledge.
Zipes, Jack, ed. (2000), *The Great Fairy Tale Tradition*, New York: Norton.
Zipes, Jack (2002), *The Brothers Grimm: From Enchanted Forests to the Modern World*, New York: Palgrave Macmillan.
Zipes, Jack (2006), *Why Fairy Tales Stick: The Evolution and Relevance of a Genre*, New York: Routledge.
Zipes, Jack, ed. and trans. (2009), *Beauties, Beasts, and Enchantment: Classic French Fairy Tales*, Maidstone: Crescent Moon.
Zipes, Jack (2012), *The Irresistible Fairy Tale: The Cultural and Social History of a Genre*, Princeton, NJ: Princeton University Press.
Zipes, Jack (2015), *Grimm Legacies: The Magic Spell of the Grimms' Folk and Fairy Tales*, Princeton, NJ: Princeton University Press.
Zuerner, Adrienne E. (1997), "Reflections on the Monarchy in d'Aulnoy's *Belle-Belle ou le chevalier Fortuné*," in Nancy L. Canepa (eds.), *Out of the Woods: The Origins of the Literary Fairy Tale in Italy and France*, 194–220, Detroit, MI: Wayne State University Press.

CONTRIBUTORS

Aileen Douglas teaches in the School of English, Trinity College Dublin. She specializes in eighteenth-century writing, with a particular interest in women's writing, Irish writing, and print culture. Lately, she has published essays on Maria Edgeworth, and on early eighteenth-century Irish women poets. Her most recent book *Work in Hand: Script, Print and Writing 1690–1840* (2017) is an exploration of the vitality of script in the age of print.

Anne E. Duggan is Professor of French Studies at Wayne State University. She is author of *Salonnières, Furies, and Fairies: The Politics of Gender and Cultural Change in Absolutist France* (2005), *Queer Enchantments: Gender, Sexuality and Class in the Fairy-Tale Cinema of Jacques Demy* (2013; translated as *Enchantements désenchantés: les contes queer de Jacques Demy* [2015]), coeditor of *Folktales and Fairy Tales: Traditions and Texts from Around the World* (2016, with Donald Haase and Helen J. Callow), and coeditor of *Marvels & Tales: Journal of Fairy-Tale Studies*.

Kathryn A. Hoffmann is Professor of French at the University of Hawai'i. Her publications on the early modern period include *Society of Pleasures: Interdisciplinary Readings in Pleasure and Power during the Reign of Louis XIV* (1997, Scaglione Prize recipient) and more than two dozen essays on fairy tales, the history of medicine, museums, and material culture in France and Italy. Her latest essay "The Consumer Courtier: The Material Culture of *Honnêteté*" appeared in 2020 in *Biblio 17*.

Rania Huntington is a scholar of late imperial Chinese literature at the University of Wisconsin, Madison. Her research interests focus on narrative and drama, particularly the literature of the supernatural. Representative publications include *Alien Kind: Foxes and Late Imperial Chinese Narrative* (2003) and *Ink and Tears: Memory, Mourning, and Writing in the Yu Family* (2018).

Tatiana Korneeva is an Assistant Professor in Comparative Literature and Theater Studies at Ca' Foscari University of Venice and Freie Universität Berlin. She is the author of *The Dramaturgy of the Spectator: Italian Theatre and the Public Sphere (1600–1800)* (2019) and editor of *Il tappeto rovesciato: La presenza del corpo negli epistolari e nel teatro dal XV al XIX* (2019) and *Le voci arcane: Palcoscenici del potere nel teatro e nell'opera* (2018). She has published widely on early modern theater, opera, and performing arts.

Lewis C. Seifert is Professor of French Studies at Brown University. His research centers on early modern French literature and culture; folk- and fairy-tale studies; gender and sexuality studies; and environmental humanities. He is the author of *Fairy Tales, Gender, and Sexuality in France, 1690–1715: Nostalgic Utopias* (1996) and *Manning the Margins: Masculinity and Writing in Seventeenth-Century France* (2009). He is currently working on a study of tricksters in oral and literary traditions of the Francophone Atlantic world.

Charlotte Trinquet du Lys is a researcher. She focuses on the evolution and adaptation of European fairy tales and their impact on the societies for which they were produced. She specializes in early modernity, French women writers of fairy tales, and the transfer of popular culture from France to the American colonies. Her monograph, *Le conte de fées français (1690–1700): Traditions italiennes et origines aristocratiques* (2012), explains the importance of Italian sources in the institutionalization of French fairy tales and their transmission into European folklore. She is in the process of coediting an English translation of French fairy tales featuring strong heroines written by early modern women.

Richard van Leeuwen is Senior Lecturer in Islamic Studies with the Department of Religious Studies of the University of Amsterdam. He has a PhD from the University of Amsterdam (1992). His research fields are Islam, Middle Eastern history, Arabic literature, and the Hajj. His publications include *The Arabian Nights Encyclopedia* (2004); *The Thousand and One Nights: Space, Travel and Transformation* (2007); *Narratives of Kingship in Eurasian Empires 1300–1800* (2017); and *The Thousand and One Nights and Twentieth-Century Fiction* (2018).

INDEX

Notes: Fairy tales to receive multiple references or general treatment are indexed by title as well as at the authors' names.
Page numbers in *italic* refer to illustrations.
n = endnote; *t* =table.

Aarne-Thompson-Uther (ATU) Tale Type Index 38, 49, 50, 52, 196*n*2
adaptation 37–60
    French, of Italian originals 51–60
Addison, Joseph 156–7
Africa, as source of wonders 124–5
ageism 123
akahon (Japanese genre) *see* "red books"
Akinari, Ueda 158, 166
"Aladdin" (tale/theme) 1, 141–2, 175, 206*n*8
Aldrovandi, Ulisse, *Monstrorum Historia* 121, 122
Alexander I of Russia 26
"Ali Baba" (tale/theme) 1, 89
Amadis de Gaulle 134
Andersen, Hans Christian 1
animals 83–4, 93–6, 199*n*11
    anthropomorphic treatments 94–6, 163
    as companions/interlocutors 56–9, 94–6
    humans masquerading as 168
    masquerading as human *see* "Little Red Riding Hood"
    as narrators 95
    transformations into/from *see* metamorphosis; reincarnation
Anne of Austria, Queen 176, 187
Anthropocene era 84, 102
anthropocentrism 86, 91
apples, magical properties 44, 101, 118–19
The Arabian Nights see The Thousand and One Nights
Aravamudan, Srinivas 174, 206*n*5
Arcimboldo, Giuseppe 201*n*27
Ariès, Philippe 127
Ariosto, Ludovico 42
Armeno, Cristoforo 203*n*8
artifacts, magical 99–102, 140, 175, 177
Auneuil, Louise de Bossigny, comtesse *see* d'Auneuil
Autreau, Jacques, *La magie de l'amour* 39

Baba Yaga (legendary figure) 118, *119*
Bacon, Francis 85
Bagh o Bahar (Tales of the Four Dervishes) 158, 168
Baital pachīsī (Twenty-Five Tales of a Vetala) 158
Barthes, Roland 105, 203*n*52
Basile, Giambattista 2, 11–12, 14, 37, 38–9, 107, 197*n*13
    "Caglusio" 44, 48–9, 95–6
    Lo cunto de li cunti (The Tale of Tales) 23, 45–50, 190, 195*n*12, 206*n*11
    "Lo cunto dell'uerco" 108

"Le doie pizzelle" ("The Two Cakes")
    48, 50–1, 52, 54, 56–8
"Lo Gnorante" 49
"The Golden Root" 112
"La Polece" 49
"Sapia Liccarda" 48
"La serva d'aglie" 48
"Le sette cotennuzze" 48
"Sole, Luna e Talia" 47, 49, 74,
    197n9
"Le tre Fate" ("The Three Fairies")
    50–1, 52, 54
concluding verse proverbs 48, 54
influence on French storytellers 42, 45,
    46–7, 50
narrative structures 50–1
stylistic/narrative differences from later
    adapters 47–8, 52, 54
"Beauty and the Beast" (tale/theme) 1,
    28–9, 162–7
operatic adaptations 18–21
Oriental versions 163–7
prefigurings 69
reversed gender roles 166–7
treatment of social class 162–3
Beauval, Henri Basnage de 107–8
Beckford, William 132, 134–5, 204n14
    "Histoire du Prince Ahmed" 135
    Vathek 12, 142
Bernard, Catherine 38
    "Riquet à la houpe" 69, 110
Bernard, Claude 60
Bertuch, Friedrich Justin, Blaue Bibliothek
    aller Nationen 10
Bierling, Friedrich Immanuel, Cabinet der
    Feen 10
Bignon, Jean-Paul, Abbé, Aventures
    d'Abdalla fils d'Hanif 40, 145, 172,
    204n15
Bjørnstad, Hall 188
Blackwell, Jeannine 10
"Bluebeard" (tale/theme) 1, 100
    operatic adaptations 18, 22–3
Boccaccio, Giovanni 40, 42
    Decameron 12–13, 43
Boesche, Roger 184
Boguet, Henri, Discours execrable des
    sorciers 118
Boileau, Nicolas 17

Bollème, Geneviève 49
Bossuet, Jacques-Bénigne 46
Bottigheimer, Ruth B. 6, 13, 43–4, 174,
    193n5
Bree, Linda 79
Brémond, Claude 50
Buch, David 16–17
Bulifon, Antoine 45–6, 196n6
Butor, Michel 105

Callot, Jacques 116
    Cripple in a Hood 117
    Hunchback with a Cane 116
Canepa, Nancy 45
Caracciolo, Peter 7
Carrier, Hubert 206n10
Carter, Angela 1, 34
Catherine de' Medici, Queen 176
Catherine II of Russia 'The Great' 25–7
    Fevei 26–7, 195n15
    Gorebogatyr' Kosometovich 26
    Khrabroi i smeloi vitiaz' Akhrideich' ili
        Ivan Tsarevich 26
    Novogorodskii bogatyr' Boeslaevich 26
Caumont la Force, Charlotte-Rose de see
    la Force
Caylus, Anne-Claude de 203n7, 207n28
Cazotte, Jacques 132, 142, 207n28
    Le Diable amoureux 12, 121
    Mille et une fadaises: Contes à dormir
        debout 40–1
Charles IX of France 42
Chartres, duc de 115
Chaucer, Geoffrey 40
Cherbuliez, Juliette 180
Chiari, Pietro 23, 24
Chinese literature 133, 134, 138–40, 143,
    150, 159–61, 164–6
    debates on value of the fanciful 131
    moral content of reincarnation stories
        151–6
"Cinderella" (tale/theme) 1
    operatic adaptations 18
class (social)
    of protagonists 44, 162–3, 174
    of writers/readers 78, 81, 82
Colbert, Jean-Baptiste 45–6
Colman, George, Blue Beard, or Female
    Curiosity! 195n9

INDEX

commedia dell'arte 16–17
contes des fées, coinage of term 37, 62, 71
Copernicus, Nicolaus 85
Cottino-Jones, Marga 42
La Cour de France turbanisée et les trahisons démasquées (anon.) 181
Courtès, Noémie 127
Crane, Walter 55, 90
Crébillon, Claude-Prosper Joliot de (Crébillon fils) 132, 134, 207*n*28
  L'Ecumoire, ou Tanzaï et Néadarné 40–1
  Le Sopha, conte moral 30, 41, 141
Croce, Benedetto 45, 196–7*n*8

Daston, Lorraine 127, 200*n*9
d'Aulnoy, Marie-Catherine 2, 3–7, 11–13, 14, 15, 38, 43, 45, 157, 172, 194*n*8
  "Babiole" 66–7, 113, 115, 123, 202*n*37
  "La Belle aux cheveux d'or" 63–4
  "Belle Belle ou le Chevalier Fortuné" 49, 64, 64–5, 81, 94–5, 175–6
  "La Biche aux bois" 52, 54–5, 55, 59, 97, 113, 122, 124, 202*n*37
  "La Bonne petit souris" 175–6
  "La Chatte blanche" 47, 59, 70, 111, 113, 115, 118, 123, 167, 201*n*20, 202*n*37
  Contes des fées 62, 71
  Contes nouveaux ou les fées à la mode 62
  "Finette Cendron" 108–9
  "Gracieuse et Percinet" 63–4, 175, 176, 186
  "La Grenouille Bienfaisante" 113, 200*n*7
  Histoire d'Hypolite, Comte de Duglas 61, 206*n*2
  "Le Mouton" 92–3, 93, 163, 167, 207*n*17
  "Le Nain jaune" 112, 113, 115
  "L'Oiseau bleu" 55, 66, 67, 68, 81, 177, 181–2, 187, 201*n*24, 206*n*11
  "L'Oranger et l'abeille" 68–9, 109, 174
  "Le Prince Lutin" 175–6
  "Le Prince Marcassin" 97–9, 98
  "La Princesse Belle-Etoile et le Prince Chéri" 44, 118–19
  "La Princesse Carpillon" 87, 88, 112
  "La Princesse Printanière" 87, 117, 201*n*22, 201*n*24
  "La Princesse Rosette" 52, 54, 56–9
  "Serpentin vert" 67, 69, 81, 110, 111, 112, 125, 158, 163, 167
  anti-patriarchal stance 63–4, 82
  biographical background/exile 180, 206*n*14
  characters' social status 44
  English translations/adaptations 4–5t, 6, 13, 41, 78, 79, 149, 159, 193*nn*4–5
  German translations/adaptations 10, 41
  "L'Ile de la Félicité" 206*n*2
  impact on popular culture 140
  operatic adaptations 22–3
  social/political satire 175, 181–2
  treatment of gender 61–9, 71, 81, 82, 199*n*10
  treatment of nature 199*n*10
  treatment of source material 49
d'Auneuil, Louise de Bossigny, comtesse 38, 123, 191, 192
  "La Princesse Léonice" 120
  La Tyrannie des fées détruite 182–3, *183*, 187
Davis, Mary 123
Defrance, Anne 183
Delarue, Paul 44, 49, 55, 56, 59
Descartes, René 13, 85, 94–5, 96
Descola, Philippe 85
Dickens, Charles 149, 150, 159, 168
Diderot, Denis 2, 12, 17, 20, 132
  Les Bijoux indiscrets 30, 141, 173, 190–1, 192
Disney, Walt/Disney Studios 1
Diyab, Hanna 40, 101, 172, 175, 199–200*n*16, 206*n*8
Dobie, Madeleine 190–1, 207*n*27
Doniger, Wendy 164
Donoghue, Emma 1
d'Orneval, Jacques-Philippe 21–2
dragons 111–15
  defined 111
  as draught animals 112–14
  physical descriptions 111–12, *112*
  sculptures/merry-go-rounds 114–15, *115*
  variant forms 112–14
Dreuillet, Elisabeth 39
Dulac, Edmond *75,135,179*

Durand, Catherine 38
  "Le Prodige d'Amour" 22
d'Urfé, Honoré, *L'Astrée* 91–2, 196*n*3
dwarves 115–17
  descriptions of deformities 115–16, 116, 117, 201*n*17
  real-life exploitation 122

Eco, Umberto 127
Edgeworth, Maria 3
eighteenth century, break with older literary traditions 131
elevation tales 43–4
Encyclopédie
  condemnation of fairy tales 126
  entries concerning monsters/ogres 106–7, 108, 121–2
England, development of fairy tales in 78–81
Enlightenment
  attitudes to fairy tales 16, 126, 127, 141
  trends in storytelling 22–3, 34–5, 131–2, 206*n*5
Épernon, duchess of 46–7
erotic fiction 30, 41, 141
exoticism 13, 15, 30, 104, 134–5
  and the monstrous 123–6, 127
  see also oriental tales

fairies
  explications of role/background 69–71, 172–3
  malignant/monstrous 87, 117, 181–3, 186
  origins 201*n*29
  representations within tales 86–7, 173
fairy tales
  "canon" 1
  coinage of term 11–14, 37, 62, 71
  core values/attributes 149–50
  educational function 11, 12–13, 157–60, 167–9
  Enlightenment objections to 126, 127
  reading public 11–14
Falques, Marianne-Agnès Pillement 39, 207*n*28
  Contes du sérail 123
"False Bride" tale type 38, 50–1, 54–60
  folklore versions 56–60

Farr, James R. 181
Favart, Charles-Simon, *La fée Urgèle* 18
Feenmärchen für Kinder (anonymous publication) 10
féer (verbal form) 119–20
féeries 17–23
Fénelon, François de Salignac de La Mothe- 38
Feng Meng Long 143
Ferry, Nicholas 122
Fielding, Sarah 12–13, 14, 41, 62, 81
  The Governess 11, 78–9
  "The Princess Hebe" 79
forest(s), as actors 89, 91
Formey, Johann Heinrich Samuel 121–2
Fort William College, Calcutta 158
foxes, in Chinese tales/mythology 138–9, 167–8
France, as center of fairy tale production 2–3
  English translations 8–9*t*
  folklore versions of tales 56–60
  Italian influences 41–50
  sanitization of violent/sexual material 47, 56
Frederick the Great of Prussia 114–15
"The Frog Prince" (tale/theme) 1
Fumaroli, Marc 60
Furetière, Antoine, *Dictionnaire universel* 106, 107–8, 119–20, 121, 124, 201*n*30, 202–3*nn*47–48, 206–7*n*16
Fuzelier, Louis 21–2

Galileo Galilei 85
Galland, Antoine 2, 7, 15, 37, 38, 40–1, 100–1, 132, 140, 157, 172, 173, 178, 184, 188, 191, 199–200*n*16, 206*n*8
  see also The Thousand and One Nights
Gascony, folklore versions of tales 56–60
Gautier, Théophile 12, 41
  "Mille et deuxième nuit" 190
gender/sexuality 61–82
  and chastity 65–6, 82
  effeminacy 123
  fears of female imagination 123
  and female autonomy 63–6, 69–71, 79, 82, 168, 173, 175–6
  and metamorphosis 62–3, 66–9
  and power 173, 176–8, 187–92

re-establishment of male supremacy 187–92
reversal of traditional roles 166–7
women disguised as men 64–5
of writers 1, 173, 192, 206n6
Genlis, Stéphanie Félicité, comtesse de 13, 27
Théâtre à l'usage des jeunes personnes 21
Germany
assumption of French tradition 7–10
women writers 194n9
Giambologna (Jean de Boulogne) 110
giants 110
Gibb, G. W. 207n25
Gilbert, John 64
Gluck, Christoph Willibald 17
Goldoni, Carlo 17, 23, 24, 195n4
Gomez, Madeleine-Angélique de 39
Gonzales family 123
Gouges, Olympe de 207n28
governess, as narrator 12–13, 78–9, 162
Gozzi, Carlo 23–5
L'Amore delle tre melarance 23–5, 195nn12–13
Greenhough, Amy 99
Grenby, M. O. 6
Grétry, André
Raoul Barbe-bleue 22–3, 195n9
Zémire et Azor 18–21, 19
Grimm, Jacob/Wilhelm 1, 7, 41, 196–7n8
"Frau Holle" 59
"Das kleine Rotkäppchen" ("Little Red Cap") 160, 161
"Schneewittchen" ("Snow White") 44
"Die weisse und die schwarze Brau" 55, 58, 59, 197n14
influence in France 59–60
Groom, Angelica 127
Gryffyth, Margaret 122
Guang Yu Chu xinzhi (Expanded New Records of Yu Chu) 161
Gueullette, Thomas-Simon 158, 207n28
Chinese Tales or the Wonderful Adventures of the Mandarine Fun-Hoam 7, 150–2, 152, 155, 156–7, 168, 204n5
Les Mille et une heures: Contes Péruviens 124

Les Mille et une quart d'heures 172
English translations 156–7
Gustav III of Sweden 26

Hamilton, Antoine 40–1, 134, 141, 158
"Le Bélier" 40
"Hansel and Gretel" (tale/theme) 160
happy endings, and patriarchal ideology 62, 82, 196n17
Harries, Elizabeth Wanning 71
Hatchett, William 41
Hawkesworth, John, "Almoran and Hamet" 141
Haywood, Eliza 41
Heitzmann, Annick 201n26
Hoffmann, E. T. A. 12, 41
"horns" (skin growths), real people displaying 122–3
Huang Chengzeng 161
Huang Zhijun, "The Tale of Old Woman Tiger" 160–1
Huguenots 7, 181
Huppert, George 206n13
hypertrichosis (excessive hair growth) 123

inanimate objects
as active agents 89–90, 99–102
transformations into 120, 125, 141
Iotti, Gianni 31
Islamic literature 134
debates on value of the fanciful 131
Italy, as origin of tales 41–50

"Jack Spriggins and the Enchanted Bean" (anon.) 110
Japanese literature 150, 159, 163
Jarvis, Shawn C. 10
Ji Yun 154–6, 157, 158, 159–60, 167–8, 205n28
"Brushed Notes from a Straw Barn Contemplating the Great in Small Things" 140
biographical background 154–5
moral tales of reincarnation 155–6
jinn, figure in Persian/Arabic traditions 140
Johnson, Rebecca 173
Johnson, Sharon P. 198n10

Jomand-Baudry, Regime 41
Jones, Christine 3
Jōo, Fumiko 166
Jung, Carl Gustav 130

kaidan (Japanese genre) 150
Kew Gardens 114
Khrapovitskii, Alexander 195*n*15
Kimbrough, R. Keller 159
"Kind and Unkind Girls" tale type 38, 50–1, 52–4, 59–60
Kuaiyuan zhiyi (Records of Wonder from the Garden of Cleverness) (anon.) 153

La Chaussée, Pierre-Claude Nivelle de, *Amour pour amour* 18
la Force, Charlotte-Rose de Caumont de 11–12, 41, 43, 180
  "Persinette" 46, 48
  "Plus belle que fée" 113
  "Tourbillon" 200*n*3
  characters' social status 44
Lane, William 6
Larivey, Pierre de 42
Lassay, Julie de Guenani, Marquise de 39
Le Marchand, Françoise 39
Le Noble, Eustache 38
Leibniz, Gottfried Wilhelm 31
Leprince de Beaumont, Jeanne-Marie 2, 12–13, 14, 27–9, 62, 79–81, 172
  "La Belle et la Bête" ("Beauty and the Beast") 1, 11, 18, 28–9, 39, 41, 69, 80–1, 91, 97, 159, 162–3, 194*n*16, 202*n*37
  Magasin des enfants, ou Dialogues d'une sage gouvernante avec ses élèves de la première distinction 27–8, 29, 39, 79–80
Lesage, Alain-René, et al, *Arlequin roi des ogres ou Les Bottes de sept lieues* 21–2
Levesque, Louise Cavalier 39
  "Le Prince des Aigues Marines" 115–16, 125
Levshin, Vasilii A., "The Tale of the Noble Zoleshanin" 118
L'Héritier de Villandon, Jeanne-Marie 11–12, 15, 50, 82

Italian sources 48
  "L'adroite princesse" 48, 65–6, 71
  "Les Enchantements de l'éloquence ou les effets de la douceur" 44, 46–7, 48, 52–4
  "Marmoisan" 48, 49, 65
  Oeuvres meslées 197*n*4
  "Ricdin-Ricdon" 38, 48, 90
  treatment of source material 52–4
Ling Menchu 143
Lintot, Catherine de 39
  "Le Prince Sincer" 112, 116, 120, 201*n*22
  "Tendrebrun et Constance" 110, 113, 122, 123, 202*n*37
"The Little Mermaid" (tale/theme) 1
"Little Red Riding Hood" (tale/theme) 1, 73–4, 83–4, 90, 90
  as allegory of sexual predation 74, 95, 161, 198*n*10
  Oriental versions 160–1
"Little Thumbling" *see* "Tom Thumb"
Longino, Michèle 181
Longueville, Anne Geneviève de Bourbon, duchesse de 176–7, 206*n*10
Louis XIII of France 187
Louis XIV of France 30, 45–6
  absolutist rule/rhetoric 12, 63, 65, 173, 180, 182
  censorship/exile of writers 43, 48, 180
  creation of all-male academies 183–4, 191–2, 207*n*19
  female relatives 44, 71, 176–7
  religious policy 7, 181
  satirical/allegorical commentaries 181–4, 187–8, 192, 207*n*20
Louis XV of France 41, 190–1, 192
Louveau, Jean 42
Lowe, Elizabeth 123
Lubert, Marie-Madeleine de
  "Blancherose" 109, 119
  "Etoilette" 110, 123, 124–5
  "Peau d'Ours" 109
  "Le Prince glacé" 120
  "Princesse Belle-Etoile" 112
  "La Princesse Camion" 120, 202*n*37
  "La Princesse Coque-d'oeuf et le Prince Bonbon" (attrib.) 109–10, 115, 201*n*24

"La Princesse Couleur de Rose et le
  Prince Celadon" 113, 120
"La Princesse Lyonette et le Prince
  Coquerico" 112, 122, 202*n*37
"Tecserion" 111, 113
Lully, Jean-Baptiste 14, 16
Lussan, Marguerite de, *Les veillées de
  Thessalie* 39

Mabille, Pierre 125, 203*n*51
Mabillon, Jean 45–6
Macdonald, Duncan 7, 193*n*6
Magliabechi, Antonio 45–6
Magnanini, Suzanne 45–6
Mailly, Louis, chevalier de 38, 203*n*8
  *Les aventures des trois princes de
    Serendip* 138
  "Blanche-Belle" 52, 54, 56
  "Le Prince Perinet ou l'origine des
    pagodes" 125
Mainers, Margarethe 123
Marie-Antoinette, Queen 115
Marie de' Medici, Queen 176
Marivaux, Pierre de
  Arlequin poli par l'amour 22
  Félicie 22
  L'Ile de la raison 22
Marmontel, Jean-François
  Contes moraux 32
  "Le Mari Sylphe" 32
  Zémire et Azor 18–21, *19*
maternal imagination, bodily deformities
  attributed to 123
Maxwell, Richard 173
Mayer, Charles-Joseph (ed.), *Le Cabinet
  des fées* 39, 41, 50, 60, 127, 157–8
Melusine (legendary character) 187, 207*n*22
Mercier, Louis-Sébastien 18
Mérimée, Prosper 41
metafiction 167
metamorphosis/es 54–5, 58–9, 96–9, 120–1
  serial 121
  social/gendered implications 62–3,
    66–9, 81
  temporary 120
  see also reincarnation
Milner, Max 127
Monceau, park of *114*, 115
monsters/monstrosities 103–27

"anatomical monstrous" 121–3, 121–4
civilized behavior/lifestyles 103–4, 110,
  120
deformed humans seen as 106, 121–6
"ethnological monstrous" 123–6
evolving attitudes to 126–7
outwardly human appearance 88
range of appearances 103
range of milieux 104–5
real-life counterparts 121–6
sculptural depictions 110, *111*
seventeenth/eighteenth-century
  definitions 106–7, 202–3*nn*47–48
studies 127
see also dragons; giants; ogres
Montesquieu, Charles-Louis de Secondat,
  Baron de 12
  Lettres persanes 30, 146, 173, 184
Montpensier, Anne Marie Louise
  d'Orléans, duchesse de 43, 176–7,
  206*n*10
Morlini, Girolamo, *Fabulae/Novellae* 42
Mouhy, Charles de Fieux, chevalier de,
  Lamekis 113–14
Murat, Henriette-Julie de Castelnau,
  comtesse de 2, 15, 37, 38, 42, 43,
  47, 65, 82, 180
  Histoires sublimes et allégoriques 69–70
  "The Island of Magnificence" 92
  "Jeune et belle" 92
  "To Modern Fairies" (dedicatory
    epistle) 69–71, 172–3, 192
  characters' social status 44

nature, human relationships with 84–5,
  91–3, 130–1, 198*n*1, 199*n*10
see also animals
Naubert, Benedikte 10, 41
  "Der Riesentanz" 120
Navarre, Marguerite de, *Heptaméron* 43
Neoplatonism 143
Nicodemo, Liodardo 45–6
Nicolai I of Russia 26
Nodot, François 38
non-human characters 83–102, 198*n*7
  humanoid 87–9
  supernatural 87–8
  see also animals; fairies; monsters; ogres
nurse(s), as storytellers 46–7

ogres 74–6, 107–10, 179–80
   definitions 87–8, 107–8
   outwardly human appearance 88
   physical descriptions 88, 108–10
   (relatively) civilized behaviour 87–8
   sculptural depictions 110, *111*
O'Malley, Lurana 26
Once Upon a Time (TV, 2011–18) 1
opera 14, 16, 17–23
   opera-*skazka* 26–7
   see also féeries
oriental tales/Orientalism 30, 40–1, 132–3, 134–7, 144–6, 157–60, 205*n*1, 206*n*5
   amalgamation with fairy tales 140–1
   contrasted with medieval attitudes 144
   didactic/cautionary adaptations 141–2
   displacement of fairy tale 171–2, 173–4
   English translations 7, 8–9*t*
   representations of power 171–2
   studies 202*n*45
   see also The Thousand and One Nights
Orléans, Élisabeth-Charlotte d' 71–2
Orléans, Philippe II, duc d' 185
Orsini, Francesco, Prince 110
Otherworld(s) 136–8, 147, 191
   Orient as 144, 145–6
Ovid (P. Ovidius Naso), *Metamorphoses* 96

Palmer, Melvin 6
Palmera, Oliva de 134
Pantheon Fairy Tale and Folklore Library (ed. various) 204*n*2
pantomime 193*n*5, 195*n*9
Paré, Ambroise, *Des Monstres et prodiges* 106, 121
Park, Katherine 127
Pashkevich, Vasilii 195*n*15
pastoral novels 196*n*3
Paulmy, marquis de 60
Perrault, Charles 1, 10, 11–12, 14, 15, 18, 31, 38, 46, 82, 157, 172, 206*n*2
   "La Barbe-bleue" ("Blue Beard") 18, 71, 76–7, 76–8, 100
   "La Belle au bois dormant" ("Sleeping Beauty") 44, 47, 49, 74–6, *75*, 79, 88, 110, 186
   "Cendrillon" ("Cinderella") 18, 76, 79

"Le Chat botté" ("Puss in Boots") 18, 48–9, 71, 72, 95–6, 175, 179–80, 199*n*13
"Les Fées" 44, 49, 52–4, *53*, 60, 73, 185
Histoires et contes du temps passé (Contes de ma Mere l'oye) 3–6, 62, 70, 72
"Le Petit Chaperon rouge" ("Little Red Riding Hood") 71, 73–4, 83–4, 95, 160, 161, 199*n*12
"Peau d'Âne" ("Donkeyskin") 43, 44, 107, 197*n*10
"Le Petit poucet" ("Little Thumbling/Tom Thumb") 18, 71, 72–3, 88, 89, 100, 108
"Le Rameau d'or" ("The Golden Bough") 185
"Riquet à la houpe" 22, 69
dedication of *Contes* 71–2, 74, 200*n*15
English translations 5–6*t*, 7, 78
impact on popular culture 140
operatic adaptations 18, 22–3
treatment of female characters/gender 33–4, 71–8, 198*n*10, 199*n*10
treatment of source material 47, 48–9, 52–4
Perrin, Jean-François 189, 207*n*26
Persian/Arabic literature 140, 150, 158
Pétis de la Croix, François 2, 173, 191, 192, 206*n*6
   Histoire de la sultane de Perse et les visirs, contes turcs 7, 40, 124, 172, 188
   Les Mille et un jours, contes persans 7, 40, 110, 124, 172, 177, 186–7, 188–9, 207*nn*25–6
Philips, Ambrose 7
philosophical tales 30, 185
picture books *see* "red books"
Planché, James 149
Potocki, Jan, *Manuscrit trouvé à Saragosse* 12, 136, 144
power, representations of 171–92
   attainment/restoration 174–7
   beauty as power 177–8
   exercise of 180–7
   and gender 173, 176–8, 187–92
   intelligence as power 178–80, 184–5

seizure by force of arms 175–6
seizure by usurpation 177
Préchac, Jean de 38, 191, 192
"La Reine des fées" 187, 188
"Sans Parangon" 187–8
"Le Prince Perinet ou l'origine des pagodes" (anon.) 120
Propp, Vladimir 87, 107, 198*n*3
Pu Song Ling 138–40, 143, 151–4, 157, 158, 164–5, 167, 168
autobiographical detail 153
"The Celestial Palace" 138–9
"Nie Xiaoqian" 165–6, 167
"The Painted Skin" 165, 166, 167
Strange Tales from a Studio 138–40, *139,* 152–3
"Three Lives" 153–4, *154*
Pultaney, Mrs 156
"Puss in Boots" (tale/theme) 43–4, 48–9, 77
development of cat's character 95–6
intelligence as power 175, 179–80
operatic adaptations 18

qissa (Urdu/Persian genre) 150, 158
Quinault, Philippe 14, 17

Racine, Jean 17
Iphigénie 194*n*3
Radcliffe, Ann 3
Raillard, Gaicomo 196*n*6
Rameau, Jean-Philippe 16
"Rapunzel" (tale/theme) 1
"The Rat Wedding" (Japanese picture book) 163, *164*
recognition scenes 44, 58–9
"red books" (*akahon,* Japanese genre) 150, 159, 163
Reddan, Bronwyn 200*n*18
referentiality, strategies of 144–6, 147
Reijo, Arakida 166
reincarnation 150–7
Chinese *vs.* Western treatments of 152–4
restoration tales 43–4, 174–5
Rigaud, Benoist 42
Robert, Raymonde 43, 70, 200*n*9
Rogier, François 42–3
Rohan-Chabot, chevalier de 185

romances, medieval 133–4
continuing popularity/influence 134–7
Rouille, Guillaume 42
Rousseau, Jean-Jacques 17, 199*n*10
"La Reine fantastique" 30

Sade, Donatien Alphonse François, marquis de 33–4
Les Crimes de l'amour 34
Justine 33–4
Sahlins, Peter 127, 199*n*11
Saïd, Edward 205*n*1
Samber, Robert 7, 78
Sayf al-Muluk and Princess Badi'at al-Jamal (anon.) 136–7, 203*n*7
Schacker, Jennifer 3
scientific advances/discoveries 85
relationship with development of fairy tale 85–6
Sedaine, Michel-Jean, *Raoul Barbe-bleue* 22–3
Segrais, Jean de, and Anne Marie Louise de Montpensier, *Nouvelles Françaises* 43
Ségur, Sophie Rostopchine, comtesse de 13
Seifert, Lewis C. 29, 76, 196*n*17
Sempère, Emanuelle 127
Sercambi, Giovanni 40
Novellino 42
Serres, Michel 105
Shennan, J. H. 182
Sheridan, Elizabeth 79, 81
Sheridan, Frances 207*n*28
The History of Nourjehad 141
Siñhāsan battīsī (Thirty-Two Tales of the Throne) 158
"Sleeping Beauty" (tale/theme) 1, 47, 74–6
"Snow White" (tale/theme) 1, 44
society/socialization 149–69
educative/cautionary tales 157–60, 167–9
moral tales 151–7
treatment of social class 162–3
treatments of marriage 163–7
Sorel, Charles, *Le Berger extravagant* 196*n*3

Soriano, Marc 49, 60
space, treatments of 129–48
  confined 147
  enchanted places 138–42, 147
  labyrinthine 147
  and narrative strategies 133–8, 147
  real places 142–6, 147–8, 157–8
Stackhouse, Thomas, Rev. 156–7, 158
Stanton, Domna 180
Stedman, Allison 197*n1*
Straparola, Giovanni Francesco 12–13, 14, 37, 38–9, 196*n7*
  "Biancabella" 51–2, 54, 56
  "Constantino" 43–4, 48–9, 95–6
  "Costanzo-Costanza" 48, 49
  "The Doll That Bites" 44
  "Donkey Skin" 43
  Piacevoli Notti (Facetious Nights) 42–5
  influence on French storytellers 42, 44–5, 50
  sources 42
  stylistic differences from later adapters 47–8
Su Shi 153

Tasso, Torquato 42
  Aminta 196*n3*
Tatar, Maria 72
Tenggren, Gustaf 176
Ter Haar, Barend J. 161, 205*n15*
Tessin, Carl Gustf, *Faunillane ou l'Infante jaune* 110, 112, 120, 121
Thackeray Ritchie, Anne 3
Thompson, Stith 196*n2*
The Thousand and One Nights 37, 40–1, 89, 100–1, 124, 157, *179,* 199–200*n16*
  "The Fisherman and the Genie" 178–9, 184–5
  "The Merchant and the Genie" 184
  "Prince Ahmed and the Fairy Pari-Banou" 101–2
  "Qamar al-Zaman and Budur" 134
  "The Three Ladies and the Porter" 140
  adaptations/parodies 141–2, 144–6
  Arabic texts 158
  English editions 7, *135,* 193*n6*
  framework narrative 177–8
  gender-reversed reworkings 188–9, 190, 206*n6*
  influence in 18th-century Europe 2, 7, 15, 132, 134–5, 140, 141, 144, 146, 151, 173, 184
  treatments of power/marital relations 168, 177–8, 184–5, 186, 187
  see also Galland, Antoine
Tieck, Ludwig 10
  "Abdallah" 141
Todorov, Tzvetan 126
"Tom Thumb" (tale/theme) 77, 88, 100
  character of hero 72–3
  operatic adaptations 18
Tonson, Jacob 7
Toppi, Nicolò, *Bibliotheca Napoletana* 196*n6*
Tressan, comte de 60
Trouvillou, François 122
Trumpener, Katie 173

Urslerin, Barbara 123

Velay-Valentin, Catherine 197*n10*
Versailles 115, 183, 187–8
Veysman, Nicolas 32
Vienna, siege of (1683) 181
Villeneuve, Gabrielle-Suzanne de 28
  La Belle et la Bête 80, 81, 120, 162, 167, 174–5, 200*n7,* 202*n37*
  Les Belles solitaires 39
  La jeune Américaine ou les contes marins 39, 196*n16,* 198*n11*
Voisenon, Claude-Henri de Fusée, abbé de 134
Voltaire (François-Marie Arouet) 12, 207*n21*
  "Aventure indienne" 204*n12*
  "Le Blanc et le noir" 204*n12*
  Candide 30–1
  "Le Crocheteur Borgne" 30, 204*n12*
  L'Ingénu 30, 31
  "Lettre d'un turc sur les fakirs et sur son ami Babec" 204*n12*
  Micromégas 30
  "La Princess de Babylone" 204*n12*
  Zadig 173, 185, 187
  condemnation of fairy tales 126

Vouglans, Pierre-François Muyart de 119
Voyez, François-Robert, le jeune *19*

Walvin, James 200*n9*
Warner, Marina 99, 100
Wieland, Christoph Martin 132
  Dschinnistan 10, *11*
  "Die eiserne Leuchter" 141
  Der goldene Spiegel 144–6
  Oberon 134
Wilkin, Rebecca 180
Williams, Kristin 159
Willingham, Bill 1
witches, representations/(real-life) trials 118–19, 202*n35*

women, in society
  fictional(ized) representations *see* gender; power
  political power/influence 176–7, 206*n10*
  subjugation 180–1, 183–4, 187–8, 191–2
Wortley-Montagu, Lady Mary 134–5, 204*n14*

Yeazell, Ruth Bernard 184
Yun Li 143

zhiguai (Chinese genre) 150
Zipes, Jack 7, 10, 29, 62, 72, 159, 193*n7*
Zuerner, Adrienne E. 65